Group Creativity

Group Creativity

Innovation Through Collaboration

Edited by Paul B. Paulus and Bernard A. Nijstad

OXFORD
UNIVERSITY PRESS

2003

OXFORD
UNIVERSITY PRESS

Oxford   New York
Auckland   Bangkok   Buenos Aires   Cape Town   Chennai
Dar es Salaam   Delhi   Hong Kong   Istanbul   Karachi   Kolkata
Kuala Lumpur   Madrid   Melbourne   Mexico City   Mumbai   Nairobi
São Paulo   Shanghai   Taipei   Tokyo   Toronto

Published by Oxford University Press, Inc.
198 Madison Avenue, New York, New York 10016

www.oup.com

Oxford is a registered trademark of Oxford University Press

Library of Congress Cataloging-in-Publication Data
Group creativity: innovation through collaboration / edited by Paul B. Paulus and Bernard A. Nijstad.
p. cm.
Includes bibliographical references and index.
ISBN-13 978-0-19-514730-8
1. Creative thinking—Social aspects.   2. Creation (Literary,
artistic, etc.)—Social aspects.   3. Group problem solving.   I. Paulus,
Paul B.   II. Nijstad, Bernard Arjan, 1971–
BF408 .G696 2003
302.3'4—dc21   2002151032

9 8 7 6 5 4 3 2

Printed in the United States of America
on acid-free paper

To our parents,

Paul, Alice, Jan, and Hilly,

who have provided

the foundation and support

for our lives as creative scholars

Preface

Creativity, or the generation of novel ideas, especially ones that are useful, is essential for our survival as a species. Therefore, it is not surprising that we celebrate and revere those who make creative contributions in such areas as science, technology, and commerce. Indeed, *Time* magazine has chosen Albert Einstein as Man of the 20th Century because "with just pen and paper, he peeked farther behind Nature's curtain than anyone had since Newton" (see http://affiliate.timeincmags.com/time/time100/).

Although creativity may often involve solitary efforts, as in the case of Einstein, much creativity involves the combination of contributions from two or more individuals. For example, the double helix structure of DNA may not have been discovered by either Crick or Watson had they worked in isolation; the Manhattan Project surely would have failed if Robert Oppenheimer had not had a number of very competent coworkers; and the Walt Disney Studios may not have been so successful without the input of many creative artists.

Until recently, creative collaboration was essentially ignored in the creativity literature. However, in the past 10 years there has been a blossoming of theory and research on the subject. This volume brings together some of the latest work by scholars from a variety of fields and disciplines. We hope that the broad range of perspectives represented will contribute to the integration of the field of group creativity and stimulate additional research.

This volume is designed for students, practitioners, scholars, and laypersons interested in creativity from the perspective of psychology, sociology, or business. The chapters are written in a nontechnical fashion to make them accessible to a broad range of readers. Each chapter can be read separately, but when clear links to other chapters exist, the authors have made an effort to point them out. Further, the authors have tried to describe the practical implications of their work, sometimes leading to clear advice on how group creativity can be stimulated.

One impetus for this volume was a conference on group creativity sponsored by the National Science Foundation and the University of Texas at Arlington, which brought together the top scholars on group creativity for an exchange of perspectives and findings in April 2000. We appreciate the support of these institutions. We further acknowledge the assistance of Karen Twohey in the editing of the final manuscript. Finally, it should be noted that we not only share the same academic interests, but also the same background. We both grew up in the small town of Ermelo in the Netherlands, a place that continues to rejuvenate our spirits and creative energy.

Contents

Contributors

Linda Argote
Graduate School of Industrial
    Administration
Carnegie Mellon University
Schenley Park
Pittsburgh, PA 15213-3890

Caroline A. Bartel
Department of Management
Stern School of Business
New York University
44 West 4th Street
New York, NY 10012

Zachary Birchmeier
Department of Psychology
Miami University
Oxford, OH 45056

Vincent R. Brown
Department of Psychology
135 Hofstra University
Hempstead, NY 11549

Hoon-Seok Choi
Management and Organizations
    Department
Kellogg School of Management
Northwestern University
2001 Sheridan Road
Evanston, IL 60208-2001

Mihaly Csikszentmihalyi
Quality of Life Research Center
Claremont Graduate University
1021 N. Dartmouth Avenue
Claremont, CA 91711

Alan R. Dennis
Accounting and Information Systems
    Department
Kelley School of Business
Indiana University
Bloomington, IN 47405

Michael Diehl
Department of Psychology
University of Tübingen
Friedrichstraße 21
72072 Tübingen
Germany

Beth A. Hennessey
Department of Psychology
Wellesley College
Wellesley, MA 02481

Charles Hooker
Quality of Life Research Center
Claremont Graduate University
1021 N. Dartmouth Avenue
Claremont, CA 91711

Aimée A. Kane
Graduate School of Industrial
    Administration
Carnegie Mellon University
Schenley Park
Pittsburgh, PA 15213-3890

Terri R. Kurtzberg
Department of Management
Stern School of Business
New York University
44 West 4th Street
New York, NY 10012

John M. Levine
Department of Psychology
University of Pittsburgh
516 LRDC Bldg.
Pittsburgh, PA 15260

Frances J. Milliken
Department of Management
Stern School of Business
New York University
44 West 4th Street
New York, NY 10012

Richard L. Moreland
3103 Sennott Square
Department of Psychology
University of Pittsburgh
Pittsburgh, PA 15260

Jeanne Nakamura
Quality of Life Research Center
Claremont Graduate University
1021 N. Dartmouth Avenue
Claremont, CA 91711

Charlan Jeanne Nemeth
Department of Psychology
University of California, Berkeley
Berkeley, CA 94720-1650

Brendan Nemeth-Brown
Department of Psychology
University of California, Berkeley
Berkeley, CA 94720-1650

Bernard A. Nijstad
Department of Psychology
University of Amsterdam
Roetersstraat 15
1018 WB Amsterdam
The Netherlands

Paul B. Paulus
Department of Psychology
University of Texas at Arlington
Box 19528
Arlington, TX 76019

Dean Keith Simonton
Department of Psychology
One Shields Avenue
University of California, Davis
Davis, CA 95616–8686

Steven M. Smith
Department of Psychology
Texas A&M University
College Station, TX 77843-4235

Garold Stasser
Department of Psychology
Miami University
Oxford, OH 45056

Wolfgang Stroebe
Department of Psychology
University of Utrecht
Heidelberglaan 1
3584 CS Utrecht
The Netherlands

Michael A. West
Aston Business School
Birmingham
B4 7ET
United Kingdom

Mike L. Williams
Accounting and Information Systems
    Department
Kelley School of Business
Indiana University
Bloomington IN 47405

Group Creativity

1

Paul B. Paulus and Bernard A. Nijstad

Group Creativity

An Introduction

One constant in this world is change. There is continual change in governments, cultures, economies, technology, the arts, and fields of knowledge. What is the source of this continual change? It could be argued that the basis for much change comes down to the stimulating effects of new ideas. Someone may have a new idea about how to run a country or a company, artists may develop new types of music (Weisberg, 1999), and scientists may develop new techniques or knowledge that may have profound impact on society (Gruber & Wallace, 1999). This type of creativity has sometimes been called "big C" creativity (Gardner, 1993). There is also a lot of creativity in everyday life as people try to solve problems at work and at home or on the road in between ("little c" creativity). Of course, many novel ideas may not be successful or impactful. Creativity is therefore often defined as the development of original ideas that are useful or influential (Mayer, 1999). With the information explosion and growing necessity of specialization, the development of innovations will increasingly require group interaction at some stage of the process. Most organizations and much of the scientific process now rely on the work of teams with diverse skills and knowledge.

Most research and writing on creativity has focused on individual creativity, the "lone genius," with little recognition of the social and group factors that influence the creative process. Research on creativity has sought to understand the factors responsible for creative people and activities. Personality, developmental experiences, culture, motivation, and cognitive skills are just a few of the factors that appear to underlie creative behavior (Mumford & Gustafson,

1988; Sternberg & Lubart, 1999). The review by Mumford and Gustafson does not include a discussion of group processes. Literature searches in the mid-1990s revealed few if any citations of group creativity. Books on creativity or genius also made little if any mention of the issue, and then often noted group factors in a negative way. Isolation and individual reflection were often cited as key factors in creative accomplishments (Ochse, 1990; Simonton, 1988). There was some early work on group creativity in educational settings by Torrance (1972), highlighting the importance of group composition. Osborn (1963) promoted group brainstorming as a useful approach for enhancing group creativity. A recent handbook on creativity does mention group brainstorming but does not include "groups" or "group creativity" as terms in the subject index (Sternberg, 1999).

The lack of attention to group factors in the creativity field is consistent with much evidence in the literature that groups may inhibit intellectual activity or optimal performance. Groups may feel pressure to achieve premature consensus, leading to suboptimal and noncreative solutions (Janis, 1982). Group contexts can lower accountability and individual motivation to perform at a high level (Karau & Williams, 1983). Groups that share information tend to focus on common rather than unique ideas (Stasser, 1999). However, even in this literature there is a glimmer of hope. Research on minority influence in group contexts has discovered that exposure to minority points of view can increase creative thinking in other domains (Nemeth, 1992).

The main proponents of group creativity have been associated with innovation in organizations. Osborn (1963) began in the 1940s to promote group brainstorming as a useful technique for generation of novel ideas. Stein (1974) discussed group factors in his volume on stimulating creativity, and group processes were given a central role in the theory of organizational creativity by Woodman, Sawyer, and Griffin (1993). The greatest enthusiasm for group creativity can be found among those who promote teamwork (Agrell & Gustafson, 1996; Bennis & Biederman, 1997; Kayser, 1994; West, 2002) and collaborative learning (Johnson & Johnson, 1998). Although work teams and collaborative learning have become popular fixtures in organizational and educational contexts, the research basis for the efficacy of work teams and collaborative learning is still somewhat weak (Paulus, 2000; Paulus & Paulus, 1997).

In recent years, there has been increasing acknowledgment of the importance of social and contextual factors in creativity. Amabile (1983, 1996) noted the role of a variety of social factors such as mentoring, modeling, family influences, and social reward contexts. She and her colleagues developed a model of creativity that emphasized the central role of intrinsic motivation and the impact of organizational contexts on this type of motivation (Amabile, Conti, Coon, Lazenby, & Herron, 1996). Csikszentmihalyi (1999) has promoted a systems perspective that includes the interactive effects of personal background, society, and culture. Kasof (1995) highlighted the social factors important in the evaluation of creativity. An edited volume by Purser and Montuori (1999) focused on various aspects of social creativity in organizations. Several books on highly creative individuals have recognized the importance of social factors such as mentoring and support from family and colleagues in creative achievement (Gardner, 1993; John-Steiner, 2000).

Even though there has been increasing awareness of the importance of social, cultural, contextual, and organizational factors in creativity, there has thus far been much less systematic focus on the group processes related to creativity. This is a serious deficit because increasingly, creative achievements require the collaboration of groups or teams (Dunbar, 1997; Kanigal, 1993; Snyder, 1989; West, 2002). Fortunately, recently there have been a number of significant contributions relevant to an understanding of group creativity. We have brought these together in one volume to focus attention on this developing literature and its implication for theory and application.

We have drawn contributions from a broad range of perspectives. The literature relevant to an understanding of group creativity has evolved along a number of different lines in different areas of study and disciplines. Researchers come from the diverse traditions of cognition, groups, creativity, information systems, and organizational psychology. Creativity and cognitive researchers have examined the role of social and cognitive influences on the creative process. Organizational researchers have examined team innovation, organizational learning, and knowledge transfer. Group researchers have studied group brainstorming, and information systems scholars have examined brainstorming by means of computers. Other group scholars have examined the role of minority influence on creativity and information exchange in groups. These areas have developed largely in isolation and with little integration of the various findings and concepts. In addition, the scholars working on this topic have taken rather distinct methodological and theoretical approaches. Much of the research on groups and cognitive creativity is done in laboratory settings and focuses on detailed analyses of social and cognitive processes in the short term. Creativity researchers often examine the broader context of creative achievement, such as careers of highly creative people or several years of work in research teams. Researchers in organizational settings have examined innovative activities in groups and teams and their impact on organizational learning and innovation. Information systems scholars have examined idea exchange and decision processes using computer networks. It is hoped that by bringing together the contributions from these different fields we will facilitate integration of the various findings and theoretical models into a general framework of group creativity.

The chapters in this volume are organized into two sections. The first section deals with group processes in creative groups and the second with the impact of various contextual or environmental factors on the creative group process. The research discussed focuses primarily on task or work groups, but it is presumed that the same types of processes can occur in other types of groups, such as informal social groups and therapy groups.

Group Process and Creativity

The first section highlights the various processes that can inhibit or facilitate creativity in groups. Some of these processes are primarily cognitive in that they deal with the processing of information. Others are more social in nature, reflecting the influence of group members on motivation level, capability, and normative behavior.

An important component of the group creative process is the sharing of ideas. Although shared ideas can be very stimulating, Smith (Chapter 2) highlights the fact that exposure to others' ideas can actually limit one's ability to think divergently. That is, it may be difficult to think of novel ideas when previously expressed ideas are very salient. Smith provides a theoretical analysis of this dilemma and suggests ways to overcome such mental blocks or ruts. One obvious way for groups to overcome the tendency toward uniformity in thinking is to ensure that the group has members with diverse expertise and backgrounds. Milliken, Bartel, and Kurtzberg (Chapter 3) present a comprehensive perspective on the role of diversity in group creativity that provides some support for the positive effects of diversity. Yet, they note that diversity can have negative effects on both emotional reactions and cognitive processes. Differences among group members can be sources of conflict and frustration in the early formative phases of group interaction, and this can carry over to subsequent operational and performance phases. Although differences in expertise among group members can be beneficial for the creative process, the authors suggest that this may occur only under conditions where the group process is carefully managed. Nemeth and Nemeth-Brown (Chapter 4) focus on the dissent that is likely to occur in groups where there are differences of opinion. Although such dissent may lead to negative feelings among group members, there is some evidence that the dissent experience in groups can increase the subsequent tendencies toward creative or divergent thinking. Nemeth and Nemeth-Brown have demonstrated that such effects occur only if the dissent experienced is genuine and not based on someone's playing the role of devil's advocate.

For diversity to have positive effects on creativity it is necessary that group members share their diverse perspectives. Ironically, members tend to focus on ideas or knowledge that they have in common rather than unique information. This, of course, greatly limits the potential benefits of cognitive diversity in groups. Stasser and Birchmeier (Chapter 5) discuss the basis for this bias toward shared information and ways that it can be overcome.

One of the early proponents of group creativity was Alex Osborn (1963). He promoted group brainstorming, a process of exchanging a large number of ideas in a nonevaluative setting. Osborn believed that the unfettered exchange of ideas would stimulate additional novel ideas among group members. Therefore, he believed that group idea exchange would be a very effective means of enhancing creativity. Unfortunately, experimental research did not support this perspective and demonstrated that group brainstorming was typically less effective than solitary or individual brainstorming (Diehl & Stroebe, 1987). The remaining three chapters in the first section deal with different aspects of this somewhat puzzling dilemma. Paulus and Brown (Chapter 6) review the various social and cognitive factors that affect the generation of ideas in groups. They focus on ways that one can marshal the social and cognitive processes to demonstrate that group ideation can in fact exceed individual ideation in both the quantity and the quality of ideas produced. Nijstad, Diehl, and Stroebe (Chapter 7) analyze in some detail the various processes that can inhibit or facilitate the performance of idea-generating groups. They demonstrate that sharing of ideas can easily interfere with the creative flow of ideas or lead to fixation on a limited range of ideas. However, they also present a perspective on ways that groups can benefit from the cognitive stimulation inherent in the group exchange process. They present a model of the brainstorming process that presumes that idea generation involves a search of associative memory. This model is used to explain interference and stimulation effects in group ideation, in addition to predicting emotional reactions to the idea exchange process.

One problem with conventional group ideation is that only one person can share his or her ideas at a time. So, even though group exchange may be stimulating, group members are limited in their ability to express ideas that are being stimulated. One way to overcome this is to use techniques such as group writing and exchange of ideas by means of computers. In this way, group members can express ideas while monitoring the ideas expressed by others. Dennis and Williams (Chapter 8) discuss the literature on computer brainstorming and the evidence that with this technology larger groups lead to an enhanced generation of novel ideas. It appears that the increased development and utilization of computer-based means of exchanging ideas will help groups and teams to overcome some of the limitations of group interaction and to more fully tap their creative potential.

Group Creativity in Context

Although there has been a long history of viewing creativity from an individualist perspective, a number of scholars have recently emphasized the important role of social factors in creativity (Amabile, 1996; Hennessey, 1995). It is now recognized that family experiences, classroom climate, corporate cultures, and national cultures can influence creativity. In Part II of this volume, Hennessey (Chapter 9) evaluates this social perspective of creativity from the vantage point of the intrinsic motivation theory of creativity. It appears that conditions that limit feelings of autonomy limit the extent to which individuals are motivated for creativity. External pressures or rewards or a controlling environment are typically associated with low levels of intrinsic motivation. Yet Hennessey provides evidence that under some conditions, external incentives can have positive effects on creativity. She suggests that we need to consider carefully individual differences, culture, and the interpersonal context in understanding how to enhance both intrinsic and extrinsic motivation for creative behavior.

Without change of membership, groups may become rather "stale" and may have little motivation or ability to innovate. New members may provide not only new perspectives but also renewed motivation to develop innovative approaches. Levine, Choi, and Moreland (Chapter 10) analyze the way newcomers can increase innovation in groups and review the various factors that influence this process. Certain newcomer characteristics and tactics are likely to enhance their impact. Moreover, certain groups or teams are more susceptible than others to newcomer influence.

Although newcomers can be an important source of innovation, in many contexts newcomers themselves can benefit greatly by affiliating with certain groups to develop their creative skills. This perspective is highlighted by Hooker, Nakamura, and Csikszentmihalyi (Chapter 11). They analyze the mentoring process in a space science laboratory. Although much of the mentoring in this lab was informal and not very explicit, those who "graduated" from the lab tended to have successful careers because of what they learned in the lab and the social capital (status and power) derived from association with a renowned laboratory. In other words, scientific groups offer not only a direct means for learning and creativity, but they may also indirectly support continued creativity through the connections they provide.

Creativity involves the generation of novel ideas. However, unless one can persuade others to adopt or "buy" one's ideas, their impact will be limited. Eminent creators must have the ability to develop novel ideas and promote them (Simonton, 1997). This is often labeled the innovation process. West (Chapter 12) emphasizes the important role teamwork plays in the implementation of innovations. This can be a rather difficult process because there may be great resistance to new ways of doing things in organizations. West discusses characteristics of the team and organization that influence the innovation process. He also highlights team and leadership processes that are likely to facilitate the development of innovations in organizations.

Teamwork represents a major source of innovation in organizations. However, the innovation process in organizations also involves a range of direct and indirect learning experiences. Of particular interest in understanding the group creative process is the extent to which organizations can learn from the experience of other organizations; that is, to what extent will organizations adopt techniques for innovations developed by other organizations to increase their own effectiveness? Often, there is some resistance to taking over ideas from others; organizations may take pride in developing their own procedures and innovations. However, there may be great savings in adopting innovations from other organizations. Argote and Kane (Chapter 13) discuss the various factors that influence learning from direct and indirect experience in organizations. This experience can involve interactions with other members, tools, or tasks. The content, timing, and diversity of these experiences appear to be important. Direct experience with members and indirect experience with tools and tasks appear to be most optimal. Argote and Kane suggest that with the appropriate mix of direct and indirect experiences, organizations can demonstrate high levels of learning and innovation.

In the last chapter of this section, Simonton (Chapter 14) takes us from a focus on the creativity of individuals, groups, and organizations to the creativity of nations. This is, of course, quite a jump. However, his analysis of the factors that lead cultures, nations, and civilizations to be creative reflects many of the processes covered in some form in the prior chapters. Open exchange of ideas, support for intellectual inquiry, and the influx of immigrants with new perspectives are just some of the characteristics related to creative civilizations. These certainly are consistent with the conclusions of many of the prior chapters about conditions important for group creativity.

In the final chapter of the volume (chapter 15) we draw some conclusions from the contributed chapters. We discuss four common themes that run through the various chapters: group diversity and creative potential, obstacles to the realization of creative potential, group climate, and group environment. We integrate these common themes in a "combination of contributions" framework, and derive directions for future research from this framework and discuss its practical implications.

The chapters in this volume thus present a broad range of empirical and theoretical approaches. Some of the research emphasizes controlled laboratory studies; other researchers emphasize field studies, archival data, or qualitative observations. Some theoretical models deal with intrapsychic processes, some deal with group-level processes, and some focus on broader, system-level processes. This volume is not designed to be the last word on group creativity. In fact, it might be considered the first word, as it is the first volume to be published on this topic. We hope that this volume will lead to a broader recognition of the importance of group processes in creativity, stimulate further thinking and research on group creativity, provide a basis for further theoretical development, and provide useful information for practitioners concerned with optimizing creativity in work groups and organizations.

References

Agrell, A., & Gustafson, R. (1996). Innovation and creativity in work groups. In M. West (Ed.), *Handbook of work group psychology* (pp. 317–344). Chichester, UK: Wiley.

Amabile, T. M. (1983). *Social psychology of creativity.* New York: Springer-Verlag.

Amabile, T. M. (1996). *Creativity in context.* Boulder, CO: Westview Press.

Amabile, T. M., Conti, R., Coon, H., Lazenby, J., & Herron, M. (1996). Assessing the work environment for creativity. *Academy of Management Journal, 39,* 1154–1184.

Bennis, W., & Biederman, P. W. (1997). *Organizing genius: The secrets of creative collaboration.* Reading, MA: Addison Wesley.

Csikszentmihalyi, M. (1999). Implications of a systems perspective for the study of creativity. In R. J. Sternberg (Ed.), *Handbook of creativity* (pp. 313–335). New York: Cambridge University Press.

Diehl, M., & Stroebe, W. (1987). Productivity loss in brainstorming groups: Toward the solution of a riddle. *Journal of Personality and Social Psychology, 53,* 497–509.

Dunbar, K. (1997). How scientists think: On-line creativity and conceptual change in science. In T. B. Ward, S. M. Smith, & J. Vaid (Eds.), *Creative thought: An investigation of conceptual structures and processes* (pp. 461–493). Washington, DC: American Psychological Association.

Gardner, H. (1993). Seven creators of the modern era. In J. Brockman (Ed.), *Creativity* (pp. 28–47). New York: Simon & Schuster.

Gruber, H. E., & Wallace, D. B. (1999). The case study method and evolving systems approach for understanding unique creative people at work. In R. J. Sternberg (Ed.), *Handbook of creativity* (pp. 93–115). New York: Cambridge University Press.

Hennessey, B. A. (1995). Social, environmental, and developmental issues and creativity. *Educational Psychology Review, 7,* 163–183.

Janis, I. (1982). *Groupthink* (2nd ed). Boston: Houghton Mifflin.

John-Steiner, V. (2000). *Creative collaboration.* New York: Oxford University Press.

Johnson, D. W., & Johnson, R. T. (1998). Cooperative learning and social interdependence theory. In R. S. Tindale, L. Heath, J. Edwards, E. J. Posovac, F. B. Bryant, Y. Suarez-Balcazar, E. Henderson-King, & J. Myers (Eds.), *Theory and research on small groups* (pp. 9–35). New York: Plenum.

Kanigal, R. (1993). *Apprentice to genius: The making of a scientific dynasty.* Baltimore: Johns Hopkins University Press.

Karau, S. J., & Williams, K. D. (1993). Social loafing: A meta-analytic review and theoretical integration. *Journal of Personality and Social Psychology, 65,* 681–706.

Kasof, J. (1995). Explaining creativity: The attributional perspective. *Creativity Research Journal, 8,* 311–366.

Kayser, T. A. (1994). *Building team power: How to unleash the collaborative genius of work teams.* New York: Irwin.

Mayer, R. E. (1999). Fifty years of creativity research. In R. J. Sternberg (Ed.), *Handbook of creativity* (pp. 449–460). New York: Cambridge University Press.

Mumford, M. D., & Gustafson, S. G. (1988). Creativity syndrome: Integration, application, and innovation. *Psychological Bulletin, 103,* 27–43.

Nemeth, C. J. (1992). Minority dissent as a stimulant to group performance. In S. Worchel, W. Wood, & J. A. Simpson (Eds.), *Group process and productivity* (pp. 95–111). Newburg Park, CA: Sage.

Ochse, R. (1990). *Before the gates of excellence: The determinants of creative genius.* New York: Cambridge University Press.

Osborn, A. F. (1963). *Applied imagination* (2nd ed.). New York: Scribner.

Paulus, P. B. (2000). Groups, teams and creativity: The creative potential of idea generating groups. *Applied Psychology: An International Review, 49,* 237–262.

Paulus, P. B., & Paulus, L. E. (1997). Implications of research on group brainstorming in gifted education. *Roeper Review, 19,* 225–229.

Purser, R. E., & Montuori, A. (Eds.). (1999). *Social creativity in organizations.* Cresskill, NJ: Hampton.

Simonton, D. K. (1988). *Scientific genius: A psychology of science.* New York: Cambridge University Press.

Simonton, D. K. (1997). Creative productivity: A predictive and explanatory model of career trajectories and landmarks. *Psychological Review, 104,* 66–89.

Snyder, S. H. (1989). *Brainstorming: The science and politics of opiate research*. Cambridge, MA: Harvard University Press.

Stasser, G. (1999). The uncertain role of unshared information in collective choice. In L. Thompson, J. Levine, & D. Messick (Eds.), *Shared knowledge in organizations* (pp. 49–69). Mahwah, NJ: Erlbaum.

Stein, M. (1974). *Stimulating creativity* (Vol. 1). New York: Academic Press.

Sternberg, R. J. (Ed.). (1999). *Handbook of creativity*. New York: Cambridge University Press.

Sternberg, R. J., & Lubart, T. I. (1999). The concept of creativity: Prospects and paradigms. In R. J. Sternberg (Ed.), *Handbook of creativity* (pp. 3–15). New York: Cambridge University Press.

Torrance, E. P. (1972). Group dynamics and creative functioning. In C. W. Taylor (Ed.), *Climate for creativity* (pp. 75–96). New York: Pergamon Press.

Weisberg, R. W. (1999). Creativity and knowledge: A challenge to theories. In R. J. Sternberg (Ed.), *Handbook of creativity* (pp. 226–250). New York: Cambridge University Press.

West, M. A. (2002). Sparkling fountains or stagnant ponds: An integrative model of creativity and innovation implementation in work groups. *Applied Psychology: An International Review, 51*, 355–387.

Woodman, R. W., Sawyer, J. E., & Griffin, R. W. (1993). Toward a theory of organizational creativity. *Academy of Management Review, 18*, 293–321.

I

*Group Process
and Creativity*

2

████ *Steven M. Smith*

The Constraining Effects of Initial Ideas

████

What is the best source of creative ideas? The wisdom of proverbs advises us that if we are to see farther than others, we must "stand on the shoulders of giants." This means that we should use the prior knowledge that has been provided by our predecessors, because in solving problems there is no need to "reinvent the wheel." On the other hand, a different proverb advises us not to get "stuck in a rut," meaning that using prior knowledge to solve problems can lead us to the same old tired ideas and blocked thinking that stymied progress on those problems in the past. How are we to choose between these apparently contradictory sources of wisdom? One way to address this question is through empirical studies of creative thinking and problem solving, a method called the creative cognition approach (Smith, Ward, & Finke, 1995). In the present chapter, I review a number of such empirical studies that examine the potentially constraining effects of prior knowledge, studies motivated by the creative cognition approach.

Creative thinking can be classified in many ways; one such classification is paradigmatic versus revolutionary thinking. Paradigmatic creative thinking generates new ideas in small, incremental steps; revolutionary creative thinking opens bold new vistas and perspectives. Whereas most creative thinking is paradigmatic in nature, there are occasional flashes of insight that constitute revolutionary advances in creative thinking. While acknowledging the importance of incremental paradigmatic creativity, the present chapter focuses on the rarer form of creative cognition, that which leads to revolutionary ideas. The case is made, with supporting empirical evidence, that prior experience can sometimes block or impede cognitive operations in memory, problem solving, and creative thinking and that similar cognitive processes are involved in all three domains. Such constraints can have profound effects on the creative ideas generated not only in individuals but in groups of people as well.

Fixation: Blocks to Cognitive Operations

The term *fixation*, in the present context, refers to something that blocks or impedes the successful completion of various types of cognitive operations, such as those involved in remembering, solving problems, and generating creative ideas (e.g., Dodds & Smith, 1999; Smith, 1994b, 1995b; Smith & Blankenship, 1989, 1991; Smith & Vela, 1991). For example, fixation can obstruct memory retrieval of well-learned names or words, such as the names of famous celebri ties or politicians. The same fixating forces can likewise block solutions to puzzles or math problems, such as Luchins and Luchins's (1972) famous water jar problems or common anagrams. The ways that fixation can cause such blocks can also limit the directions taken in creative idea generation in such tasks as divergent thinking and brainstorming.

Although fixation can take many forms, there are a few general patterns in which it can occur: typical thinking, implicit assumptions, and recent experience. Typical thinking refers to taking the same approach to a problem that is usually taken for that class of problems and is essentially the same as paradigmatic thinking. Whereas typical thinking is usually effective for a class of problems, there are some problems for which typical approaches are inappropriate and can lead to dead ends in the problem-solving process (Smith, 1995a). Implicit assumptions are those that one automatically makes in the problem-solving process, without any awareness that such assumptions have been made. When implicit assumptions are incorrect or unfounded, they impede cognitive operations, and, even more insidiously, they do so invisibly, making them difficult to ferret out and reject. Recent experience often prepares us for events by teaching us to adopt mental sets, specific operations that are repetitiously carried out to solve each problem in a series of similar problems. For example, suppose you were calculating a long series of math problems, with each problem involving the same sequence of operations. It would be to your advantage in such a situation to automatize the sequence of operations so that the calculations would no longer require attentional resources. Whenever one's cognitive operations are reproductions of prior experiences, a mental set can guide one unerringly through the well-practiced operations. Although such mental sets usually work to our advantage because they free up our limited attentional resources, there are times when a problem cannot be solved with a recent approach; then, one can become fixated. The research presented in the present chapter focuses on blocks and constraints that are caused by the recent use of knowledge, but the same patterns and conclusions can be drawn from cases in which blocks occur due to other causes, such as typical thinking and implicit assumptions. In all three cases, prior knowledge is inappropriately reapplied, resulting in a less-than-optimal outcome.

A classic example of the way recent experience can cause fixation is the extensive work done by Luchins and Luchins (e.g., 1959, 1972), whose demonstrations of *Einstellung*, or mental set, show clearly the way that initial experiences can lead to a mechanization of thought in problem solving. In these demonstrations, subjects are given a series of mathematical puzzles, all of the same format, called water jar problems. The task in these problems is to measure out a specific volume of water using only three jars, each with a specifically defined capacity. Some examples are shown in Table 2.1.

Subjects typically discover early in the series of problems that the same algorithm, B – A – 2C, will produce the desired volume, and they usually reapply the same formula to problem after problem, offering the same solution to all 10 problems. Having recently used the algorithm, subjects mechanistically use the same knowledge throughout the entire sequence. The useful algorithm constrains thinking, however, on problems such as number 9, where a much simpler alternative (A – C) is equally effective. The recently used algorithm becomes a downright block on problem 10, in which the algorithm fails altogether, even though a simpler solution (A – C) is at hand. Thus, recent experiences can constrain and block successful thinking.

Experimental Evidence of Memory Blocks

Since memory was first experimentally studied, attention has focused on various aspects of phenomena related to forgetting. One aspect of forgetting is memory blocking, that is, the temporary obstruction of knowledge or memories from consciousness. Critically important components of memory blocks include the sought-for material's being encoded in memory, temporarily blocked

Table 2.1. Luchins' Water Jar Demonstration

	Jar A	Jar B	Jar C	Desired Volume	Algorithm
1	8	35	3	21	B – A – 2C
2	7	17	2	6	
3	20	57	8	21	
4	6	18	1	10	
5	5	32	4	19	
6	21	127	4	98	
7	15	90	4	67	
8	20	59	4	31	
9	14	36	8	6	
10	28	76	3	25	

from consciousness, and recoverable in its essentially original form. Although mysterious mechanisms have been imagined, such as repression, that might banish undesirable traumatic memories from consciousness, no such exotic explanations are necessary for the existence of blocks. The only mechanism necessary for blocks to occur is simple response competition: the dominance of unwanted responses over desired ones (see Figure 2.1).

In response competition, a stimulus is associated with multiple responses, including the sought-for response, known as the target response. For the purposes of the present chapter, the stimulus could be a memory prompt (e.g., What is the capital of Australia?), a problem to solve (e.g., What one word can be made with the letters NEW DOOR?), or a prompt for creative idea generation (e.g., What uses can be made of a 2-liter plastic bottle?). In each case, the stimulus has a certain probability of evoking the desired target response, as well as probabilities of evoking any blockers, or competing responses. When target responses are less dominant, the probability of finding correct targets decreases. Examples of factors that decrease the probability of evoking target responses by strengthening competing blockers are increased frequency or recency of occurrence of blockers.

Blocking in Memory Retrieval

A commonly experienced phenomenon in memory failures is the tip-of-the-tongue (TOT) state. The TOT refers to cases in which one is momentarily unable to think of a word or name, yet the target seems to be known and it feels as if the target is going to pop into mind at any moment. Thus, the TOT is defined in terms of both metacognitive components (it feels known and retrieval feels imminent) and memory components (successful retrieval initially fails, yet later it succeeds). Whereas memory is demonstrated by performance on such tasks as recall and recognition, metacognition refers to an awareness of one's own thought processes, such as a feeling that one has adequately learned some material. The present focus is on the memorial aspects of the

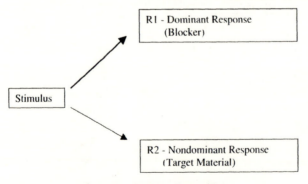

Figure 2.1. *Response Competition*

TOT state, particularly cases in which memory retrieval of a target word or name is blocked by persistent retrieval of competing blockers. For example, if the incorrect response "Sydney" continued coming to mind in the course of trying to remember the name of Australia's capital (Canberra), the competing blocker might be hindering memory retrieval of the target response, thereby evoking a TOT state.

TOT states have been studied experimentally using a variety of laboratory methods (e.g., Schwartz & Smith, 1997; Schwartz, Travis, Castro, & Smith, 2000; Smith, 1994a; Smith, Balfour, & Brown, 1994; Smith, Brown, & Balfour, 1991). Although not all TOT states constitute memory blocks, there is some evidence that competing blockers that are introduced to subjects can increase the incidence of TOT states (Smith, 1994a). For example (Smith, 1994a), when subjects first examined a set of blocker words that were semantically related to memory targets (e.g., hearth), they were less able to recall the targets of definitions (e.g., The facing around and over a fireplace—answer: MANTEL), and they were more likely to experience TOT states. Although the memory targets were usually well-known to the experimental subjects, the recent experience of seeing semantically related words served to block the already existing memories. Other examples of definitions, targets, and blockers are shown in Table 2.2.

The memory-blocking effects reported by Smith (1994a) and other memory blocks, as will be demonstrated, need not be caused by conscious retrieval of blockers from memory. Rather, retrieval of such blockers is unconscious and automatic and based on a type of memory often referred to as implicit memory. Whereas explicit memory refers to remembering that is accompanied by a deliberate attempt and an awareness of remembering, implicit memory is unintentional, swift, and involuntary. Thus, when prompted with the definition "The facing around and over a fireplace," a subject might implicitly retrieve the blocker *hearth*, which could, in turn, block retrieval of the correct target, *mantel*.

Table 2.2. Targets, Blockers, and Definitions for Smith's (1994a) TOT Study

Target	Blocker	Definition
ALLOY	*compound*	A mixture of metals, one of quality with a poorer one.
BALSA	*oak*	An extremely light and strong wood used in modeling.
HYPOCHONDRIAC	*pretender*	One who is healthy but thinks he or she has diseases.
HYPOCRITE	*imposter*	A person who does not practice what he or she preaches.
INCUBATE	*heat*	To keep eggs warm until they hatch.
MANTEL	*hearth*	The facing around and over a fireplace.
OPAQUE	*diffraction*	Impenetrable by light.
PASTEURIZE	*scald*	To heat milk below its boiling point to kill bacteria.
PEDIATRICIAN	*cardiologist*	Expert in children's diseases.
PERJURY	*subterfuge*	False testimony under oath.

Although memory blocks can be caused by a number of mechanisms, the present chapter focuses on two such devices: negative priming and retrieval bias. These theoretical mechanisms are implicated not only in memory research, but also in blocks to problem solving and creative idea generation.

Negative priming refers to implicit memory retrieval of blockers that one cannot successfully oppose or reject with conscious cognitive efforts. The term priming has been used a number of ways in the memory and cognition literature; typically, it refers to facilitation in using a word or concept as a result of recent use of the same word or a similar word. For example, priming on a word fragment completion task is found when subjects first see words such as TE-QUILA and later are asked to complete word fragments such as TE_UI_A. Priming is generally considered an implicit memory phenomenon, and it can be found even in brain-damaged patients who are unable to explicitly remember recent events. Negative priming (Smith & Tindell, 1997) can be found in certain cases in which subjects are exposed to words that are orthographically similar to correct responses on an implicit memory task. For example, subjects who are primed with the word ANALOGY have great difficulty completing the word fragment A_L_ _GY (solution: ALLERGY). Other examples from Smith and Tindell are shown in Table 2.3.

Smith and Tindell (1997) showed that subjects who had seen the negative priming blockers were greatly impaired when they tried to complete the orthographically similar word fragments. Furthermore, when subjects were given explicit warnings to avoid thinking about the negative primes, they still could not avoid or overcome this implicit memory-blocking effect. That is, the negative primes were implicitly and involuntarily retrieved when subjects saw the related word fragments, and they were unable to put those blockers out of mind to think of the correct answers. This same pattern of involuntary memory retrieval of inappropriate responses coupled with an inability to banish such re-

Table 2.3. Targets, Negative Priming Materials (Smith & Tindell, 1997)

Target	Negative Prime	Fragment
BAGGAGE	BRIGADE	B _ G _ A _ E
CATALOG	COTTAGE	C _ T A _ _ G
COUNTRY	CLUSTER	C _ U _ T R _
DIGNITY	DENSITY	D _ _ N I T Y
FAILURE	FIXTURE	F _ I _ U R E
HISTORY	HOLSTER	H _ S T _ R _
TANGENT	TONIGHT	T _ N G _ _ T
TRAGEDY	TRILOGY	T R _ G _ _ Y

sponses from conscious consideration is seen in experiments on blocking in problem solving and creative idea generation.

Biased Retrieval Set

A second memory mechanism that is very useful for explaining blocking effects is retrieval bias. If one thinks of memory as a big bag of information, each piece called a memory, then retrieval can be thought of as drawing a sample of these memories from the bag. Of course, retrieval must be conceived as sampling with replacement, because remembering something does not wipe it out of memory. In fact, when a memory is sampled, or retrieved, its retrieval strength increases, at least temporarily. That is, retrieving a memory increases the subsequent likelihood of retrieving that memory again. Increasing the likelihood of retrieving one memory necessarily decreases the chance of retrieving other memories. When memories are sampled, a subset of the memories, those that are initially retrieved, begin to take on such a large portion of the available retrieval strength that additional efforts to retrieve new memories fail. Such a situation is called a biased retrieval set, because one is biased to retrieve only a subset of the available memories, thereby rendering the other available memories at least temporarily inaccessible. The temporarily inaccessible memories can be said to be blocked from consciousness because of the biased retrieval set.

An example of retrieval bias in a memory task can be seen when words from a long list are remembered in a free recall task. What is "free" about free recall is that one may recall the items in any order. As each word on the free recall list is retrieved, it temporarily increases the chance of retrieving the same word again, to the exclusion of as yet unrecalled words. A biased retrieval set builds up for the already retrieved words, blocking recall of other list words that were memorized. This effect is referred to as output interference (e.g., Smith & Vela, 1991) and has been used to describe the self-limiting nature of recall (Roediger, 1978). It is also possible to induce output interference by providing the subject with a subset of the words from the memorized words just as the recall test is beginning (e.g., Rundus, 1973); the nonprovided words will be blocked from memory. This blocking technique is called part-list or part-set cuing inhibition. Part-set cuing inhibition has important implications for idea-generation procedures, such as brainstorming, particularly if one thinks of the ideas expressed by others in one's group, causing the buildup of a biased retrieval set and thereby blocking other, potentially useful ideas from consciousness.

The theory that a biased retrieval set can inhibit or interfere with memory retrieval, and which predicts and explains similar effects in problem solving and creative idea generation, has been used to explain related effects in brainstorming groups. In the course of a brainstorming session, the fluency of idea production declines over time (Diehl & Stroebe, 1991). Nijstad (2000) has explained this decline in terms of the same retrieval bias theory. A major advantage of this theoretical approach to idea production in brainstorming is that the theory predicts that certain remedies, such as time delays and context shifts, should be effective at reducing some production deficits in brainstorming groups.

Blocking in Problem Solving

The same sorts of blocking effects and the same theoretical mechanisms found in memory research are also found in problem-solving research. Just as negative primes seen prior to word fragments hindered solutions to the word fragments, so too do blocker words hinder solutions to problems.

One example of this blocking effect in problem solving was demonstrated by Smith and Blankenship (1989), who showed fixation effects in solving rebus problems, a special type of picture word problem. In a rebus problem, the configuration of letters and words shown in the problem depicts a common phrase. For example, the rebus "you just me" is solved with the common phrase, "just between you and me," because the word *just* is between the words *you* and *me*. Smith and Blankenship tested for fixation effects by including some misleading "clues" designed to draw attention to incorrect solutions. Figure 2.2 shows some rebus problems with blockers and correct solutions. For example, the blocker DESTROY is intended to lead to retrieval of the incorrect phrase *search and destroy*, diverting retrieval from the correct answer, *search high and low*.

Smith and Blankenship (1989) found that the presence of blockers impeded solutions of corresponding rebus problems. Furthermore, the blocking effect was weakened over time, consistent with restructuring theory. That is, with increasing time between attempts, subjects were more likely to forget the original fixated approach that led to a block and were more able to think of the correct solutions to the rebuses.

Another example of a blocking effect in problem solving was reported by Smith and Blankenship (1991) using Remote Associate Test (RAT) problems, which are sometimes used in tests of creativity. Each RAT problem consists of three words (e.g., APPLE, FAMILY, HOUSE), and the solution is a single word that makes a compound word or phrase with each of the three test words (e.g., *tree*: APPLE-*tree*, FAMILY-*tree*, and *tree*-HOUSE). In the fixation condition of Smith

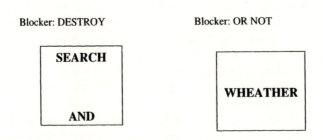

Solution: *Search high and low*   Solution: *An ill spell of weather*

Figure 2.2. *Rebuses, Solutions, and Blockers (Smith & Blankenship, 1989)*

and Blankenship's study, subjects first saw blocker words (e.g., black) and later saw RAT problems (e.g., CAT, SLEEP, BOARD). Subjects were unable to avoid or escape the deleterious effect of the blocker word (see Table 2.4 for some examples).

Just as in Smith and Tindell's (1997) study of implicit memory blocks, the Smith and Blankenship (1991) problem-solving study shows involuntary retrieval of incorrect blockers and an inability to escape or avoid the blocking effect. Thus, the same theoretical mechanisms at work in memory paradigms can be used to explain fixation and blocking in problem solving.

Fixation and Conformity in Creative Idea Generation

The artificial means of introducing blockers in the memory and problem-solving experiments described so far have a natural counterpart when it comes to creative idea generation: the effects of examples. In the course of creative idea generation, we are often given examples to help us get started, to exemplify the types of solutions that are desired, and to provide ideas for creative combinations. In brainstorming groups, in particular, example ideas are constantly generated by others in one's brainstorming team. Might such examples serve as blockers in creative idea generation?

This question was addressed by Smith, Ward, and Schumacher (1993), who experimentally examined the constraining effects of examples on creative idea generation. Whereas most laboratory tasks in cognitive psychological research are closed in the sense that they quantify accurate and inaccurate responses, these authors wanted to examine the more open-ended task of creative idea generation: the production of multiple nonveridical responses from a very large set of possibilities. In one task, they asked subjects to invent new toys they had never seen before; in another, subjects were asked to draw and describe new life forms

Table 2.4. *Remote Associate Test Problems and Blockers*

Remote Associate Test Problems			Solutions	Blockers
SHIP	SUIT	PARKING	space	jump
SALAD	HEAD	GOOSE	egg	lettuce
ELECTRIC	HIGH	EASY	chair	wire
BED	DUSTER	WEIGHT	feather	room
APPLE	HOUSE	FAMILY	tree	green
CAT	SLEEP	BOARD	walk	black
WATER	SKATE	CUBE	ice	sugar
DECK	RECORDER	SCOTCH	tape	flight
HOT	CATCHER	LICENSE	dog	plate
ARM	COAL	STOP	pit	rest
STORM	WHITE	BALL	snow	cloud
TOP	SHOE	CAR	box	horn

that might evolve on a planet similar to Earth. Prior to the creative generation task, half of the subjects saw three examples of ideas that were attributed to fictitious previous subjects. Although the three examples were different from each other, each contained three critical features in common. In the case of the creature generation task, all three of the fanciful, crudely drawn creatures had four legs, two antennae, and a tail; in the toy generation task, all three examples were electronic, involved a high degree of physical activity, and used a ball. Subjects in the Fixation Group saw all three examples just prior to the generation task, whereas the Control Group subjects saw no examples.

Smith et al. (1993) found that the Fixation and Control Group subjects generated the same number of ideas, on average, but the Fixation Group's ideas were far more likely than those in the Control Group to incorporate the three exemplified features in their own generated ideas. Smith et al. referred to this as a conformity effect, the tendency of generated creative ideas to include features seen in the examples. The conformity effect occurred in their experiments for the generation of toys and for the generation of creatures, and it even occurred when subjects were asked to generate ideas as different from the examples as possible. That is, subjects were unable to reject the examples when they tried to imagine novel ideas. This inability to reject inappropriate (blocker) ideas resembles the involuntary detrimental effects of priming inappropriate words in implicit memory (Smith & Tindell, 1997). In both cases, recent exposure to inappropriate responses is involuntarily retrieved and cannot be deliberately rejected, thereby continuing to hinder retrieval of more appropriate responses (see Figure 2.3).

A more realistic and applied version of such conformity effects in creative idea generation was reported by Jansson and Smith (1991), who observed and described a phenomenon called design fixation in engineering design students and professional design engineers. Some aspects of the conceptual design process closely resemble the creative idea generation paradigms used by Smith et al. (1993) in that a rough description of the design needs are described, and the designer must generate multiple ideas that address the general guidelines that are given. Jansson and Smith gave engineering design students open-ended design tasks, asking them to design a bicycle rack, a measuring cup for the blind, or an inexpensive spill-proof coffee cup. In each experiment, half of the students (the Design Fixation Group) first saw a sample design, and the other half (the Control Group) saw no example. In all experiments, students generated equal numbers of design ideas, regardless of their experimental treatment group assignments. However, in all experiments, the designs of students in the Fixation Group were far more likely than those in the Control Group to incorporate features of the examples in their design ideas. This design fixation effect occurred even when the features of the example were negative features. For example, in Experiment 2, the sample measuring cup for the blind needed an overflow device but had none (see Figure 2.4), yet students who saw that example were likely to omit the overflow device. In Experiment 3, negative fea-

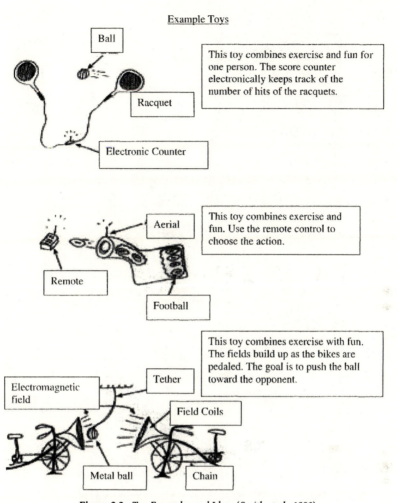

Example Toys

Ball

Racquet

Electronic Counter

This toy combines exercise and fun for one person. The score counter electronically keeps track of the number of hits of the racquets.

Aerial

Remote

Football

This toy combines exercise and fun. Use the remote control to choose the action.

Electromagnetic field

Tether

Field Coils

Metal ball

Chain

This toy combines exercise with fun. The fields build up as the bikes are pedaled. The goal is to push the ball toward the opponent.

Figure 2.3. *Toy Examples and Ideas (Smith et al., 1993)*

tures of the sample spill-proof coffee cup (mouthpieces and leaky straws) were explicitly pointed out and forbidden (Figure 2.5); nonetheless, designs of students who had seen the sample could not avoid incorporating those features in their conceptual designs, even if they had been explicitly warned not to use straws or mouthpieces. Not only was design fixation measured in Experiment 4, but measures of creative thinking, fluency, flexibility, originality, and practicality were also calculated for the designs. These measures indicated that the designs of the Fixation Group were less creative than those of the Control Group. Finally, Experiment 5 showed design fixation effects in professional engineering designers, underscoring the ubiquity and importance of the design fixation effect.

Toy from Fixation Group

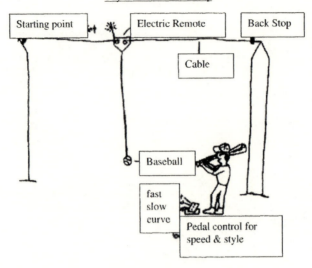

Toy from Control Group

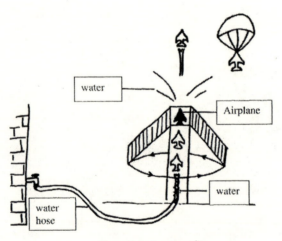

Figure 2.3. (*continued*)

Remedies

The conclusion of these creative idea generation experiments is that recently encountered ideas can sometimes block or constrain the creativity of subsequently generated ideas. It should be noted, however, that this conclusion is merely one aspect of a larger principle: that implicit assumptions can block creative idea generation. The memory experiments, in particular, indicate that the effects of the examples are in fact implicit, and that the implicitly retrieved ex-

Figure 2.4. *Example Measuring Cup for the Blind (Jansson & Smith, 1991)*

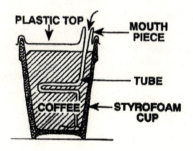

Figure 2.5. *Example Spill-Proof Coffee Cup (Jansson & Smith, 1991)*

amples cannot be voluntarily rejected to make way for more appropriate responses. Of course, implicitly retrieved ideas can arise from sources other than recent experience; they can also come from perceptual characteristics of stimuli or from long-term knowledge. In all cases, one of the most insidious aspects of blocks is that they are implicit and that they therefore are difficult to detect and identify. It is not always necessary, however, to detect and identify sources of blocks; what is more important is to escape or avoid the effects of the blocking assumptions.

In creative idea generation, the initial step is the critical one, because it can occur in a context that invites limiting assumptions, or it can occur more profitably in a novel context that is less likely to encourage such blocking constraints. When recently encountered examples are the source of constraining effects, an approach to avoiding or escaping such blocks is to take a break from the task and try to approach the problem with a fresh context. The effects of breaks and fresh contexts are usually referred to as incubation effects. Incubation is a mysterious and counterintuitive phenomenon because it is not time spent working on a problem that helps, but rather time *away* from the problem that is the key. Furthermore, the reason incubation helps one escape fixation is not always obvious. Although incubation effects are often attributed to unconscious autonomous processes, there is no evidence that such unconscious processes benefit incubation (Smith, Sifonis, & Tindell, 1998). The more likely cause is that an initially thwarted attempt can avoid fixation if a break and a novel context lead one to a different initial step in idea generation, one that is less likely to lead to previously encountered dead-end lines of thinking. Incubation effects have been shown to help people overcome initial impasses in memory (e.g., Smith & Choi, 2001; Smith & Vela, 1991), in problem solving (e.g., Smith & Blankenship, 1989, 1991), and in creative idea generation (e.g., Smith, 1995b).

No remedies for fixation, including incubation breaks and context shifting, are sure-fire methods, but it is logical to infer other solutions for fixation. One plausible notion is to make use of the perspectives of other individuals, such as members of a brainstorming group. Limiting assumptions that are implicit or invisible to one person might seem more apparent or obvious to other group members. Thus, having varied perspectives and backgrounds among brainstorming group members might help overcome fixation, both by identifying and breaking unsuccessful or limiting mental sets and by providing new approaches to problems. How to compose a brainstorming group to make optimal use of multiple perspectives and how to encourage the use of multiple knowledge bases and perspectives in the group should be important goals for successful brainstorming groups.

Implications for Brainstorming Groups

The patterns of cognition described for situations involving memory retrieval, problem solving, and creative idea generation have direct implications for brainstorming. In brainstorming groups, each participant generates ideas in the presence of others, the intention being to promote novel combinations of divergent ideas. An emphasis is placed on the number and imaginativeness of ideas. Thus, it is important to attend to the ideas generated by other participants in one's group. The benefits of attending to others' ideas, however, may not come without a cost, and that cost may be the breadth or flexibility of ideas generated. Memory retrieval can be biased or blocked by involuntary retrieval of other memories, problem solving can be fixated when inappropriate material is involuntarily retrieved, and creative idea generation can be constrained by implicit retrieval of examples. Therefore, it seems likely that seeing or hearing the ideas of others in one's group would likewise constrain idea generation in group participants. Such would not be the case in individual brainstorming, where one's ideas would not be involuntarily constrained from hearing and seeing ideas generated by other participants. Of course, individual brainstorming, unlike group brainstorming, may not benefit from exposure to the different knowledge and perspectives of others in one's group. One solution to the problem is to combine the individual and group methods, having individuals alternately generating ideas alone and as members of a group. Generating ideas when one is alone might make an individual's range of ideas broader because the ideas might suffer less output interference from the expressed ideas of other group members. This greater range of ideas can be explored from multiple perspectives by the group, and the broad range of knowledge bases that different group members generate can provide the foundation for more novel combinations of ideas.

As a final note, it is worth acknowledging that one should not always, or even usually, reject prior knowledge. The ideas of others, especially one's predecessors, are essential in most discoveries. To imply otherwise would be foolish. The purpose of the present chapter is to point out that there are sometimes situations in which the use of prior ideas can unnecessarily constrain the scope of ideas that one can generate.

Note

The present chapter was supported in part by NSF Grant DMI-0115447 to Steven M. Smith and Jami Shah.

References

Diehl, M., & Stroebe, W. (1991). Productivity loss in idea-generating groups: Tracking down the blocking effect. *Journal of Personality & Social Psychology, 61,* 392–403.

Dodds, R. A., & Smith, S. M. (1999). Fixation. In M. A. Runco & S. R. Pritzker (Eds.), *Encyclopedia of creativity* (pp. 725–728). San Diego, CA: Academic Press.

Jansson, D. G., & Smith, S. M. (1991). Design fixation. *Design Studies, 12*, 3–11.

Luchins, A. S., & Luchins, E. H. (1959). *Rigidity of behavior: A variational approach to the effect of Einstellung.* Oxford: Oxford University Press.

Luchins, A. S., & Luchins, E. H. (1972). *Wertheimer's seminars revisited: Problems in perception: I.* Oxford: State University of New York Press.

Nijstad, B. A. (2000). *How the group affects the mind: Effects of communication in idea generating groups.* Unpublished doctoral dissertation, University of Utrecht.

Roediger, H. L., III (1978). Recall as a self-limiting process. *Memory & Cognition, 6*, 54–63.

Rundus, D. (1973). Negative effects of using list items as recall cues. *Journal of Verbal Learning & Verbal Behavior, 12*, 43–50.

Schwartz, B. L., & Smith, S. M. (1997). The retrieval of related information influences tip-of-the-tongue states. *Journal of Memory & Language, 36*, 68–86.

Schwartz, B., Travis, D., Castro, A., & Smith, S. (2000). The phenomenology of real and illusory tip-of-the-tongue states. *Memory and Cognition, 28*, 18–27.

Smith, S. M. (1994a). Frustrated feelings of imminence: On the tip-of-the-tongue. In J. Metcalfe & A. Shimamura (Eds.), *Metacognition: Knowing about knowing* (pp. 27–45). Cambridge, MA: MIT Press.

Smith, S. M. (1994b). Getting into and out of mental ruts: A theory of fixation, incubation, and insight. In R. Sternberg & J. Davidson (Eds.), *The nature of insight* (pp. 121–149). Cambridge, MA: MIT Press.

Smith, S. M. (1995a). Creative cognition: Demystifying creativity. In C. N. Hedley, P. Antonacci, & M. Rabinowitz (Eds.), *The mind at work in the classroom: Literacy and thinking* (pp. 31–46). Hillsdale, NJ: Erlbaum.

Smith, S. M. (1995b). Fixation, incubation, and insight in memory, problem solving, and creativity. In S. M. Smith, T. B. Ward, & R. A. Finke (Eds.), *The creative cognition approach* (pp. 135–155). Cambridge, MA: MIT Press.

Smith, S. M., Balfour, S. P., & Brown, J. M. (1994). Effects of practice on TOT states. *Memory, 2*, 47–53.

Smith, S. M., & Blankenship, S. E. (1989). Incubation effects. *Bulletin of the Psychonomic Society, 27*, 311–314.

Smith, S. M., & Blankenship, S. E. (1991). Incubation and the persistence of fixation in problem solving. *American Journal of Psychology, 104*, 61–87.

Smith, S. M., Brown, J. M., & Balfour, S. P. (1991). TOTimals: A controlled experimental method for observing tip-of-the-tongue states. *Bulletin of the Psychonomic Society, 29*(5), 445–447.

Smith, S. M., & Choi, H. (2001, August). *Incubation in memory, problem solving, and idea generation: Autonomous unconscious processing vs. contextually influenced restructuring.* Paper presented at the third International Conference on Memory, Valencia, Spain.

Smith, S. M., Sifonis, C. M., & Tindell, D. R. (1998). Hints do not evoke solutions via passive spreading activation. *Proceedings of the twentieth annual meeting of the Cognitive Science Society.* Somerville, MD: Cascadilla Press.

Smith, S. M., & Tindell, D. R. (1997). Memory blocks in word fragment completion caused by involuntary retrieval of orthographically similar primes. *Journal of Experimental Psychology: Learning, Memory and Cognition, 23*, 355–370.

Smith, S. M., & Vela, E. (1991). Incubated reminiscence effects. *Memory & Cognition, 19*, 168–176.

Smith, S. M., Ward, T. B., & Finke, R. A. (1995). Cognitive processes in creative contexts. In S. M. Smith, T. B. Ward, & R. A. Finke (Eds.), *The creative cognition approach* (pp. 1–7). Cambridge, MA: MIT Press.

Smith, S. M., Ward, T. B., & Schumacher, J. S. (1993). Constraining effects of examples in a creative generation task. *Memory & Cognition, 21,* 837–845.

Ward, T. B., Smith, S. M., & Finke, R. A. (1999). Creative cognition. In R. Sternberg (Ed.), *Handbook of creativity* (pp. 189–212). New York, NY: Cambridge University Press.

Ward, T. B., Smith, S. M. & Vaid, J. (1997). Conceptual structures and processes in creative thought. In T. B. Ward, S. M. Smith, & J. Vaid (Eds.), *Creative thought: An investigation of conceptual structures and processes* (pp. 1–27). Washington, DC: American Psychological Association Books.

Widner, R. L. Jr., Smith, S. M., & Graziano, W. (1996). Effects of demand characteristics on feeling-of-knowing and tip-of-the-tongue reports. *American Journal of Psychology, 109,* 525–538.

Ziegler, R., Diehl, M., and Zijlstra, G. (2000). Idea production in nominal and virtual groups: Does computer-mediated communication improve group brainstorming? *Group Processes & Intergroup Relations, 3,* 141–158.

3

■■■■■ *Frances J. Milliken, Caroline A. Bartel, and Terri R. Kurtzberg*

Diversity and Creativity in Work Groups

A Dynamic Perspective on the Affective and Cognitive Processes That Link Diversity and Performance

■■■■

Tina approached her morning meeting with a good deal of apprehension. The meeting was the kickoff of a new project to which she had been assigned. The team had been asked to figure out a creative way to increase the market share of a new product line. One reason for Tina's apprehension was that the team was made up of people she had never met before, many of whom were senior to her. Another reason was that the members came from all different parts of her organization. The organization she worked for had historically been one characterized by departmental turf fighting, and she worried that the members of this group would perpetuate this turf-protecting attitude. She was also uncertain about what she would be able to contribute. Walking into the room, she was relieved to see that there was one other woman in the group. However, Tina's discomfort with the group remained. Indeed, it seemed as if the members who were speaking up were speaking different languages. The group seemed in danger of splitting into factions, each supporting movement in a different direction. She was amazed at how chaotic the process felt and how much conflict there seemed to be. She felt very uncomfortable about speaking up and noticed that there were others who said very little. After several meetings, though, she began to become interested in some of the ideas the group was talking about. She was particularly grateful when a more senior member of the team spoke out forcefully one day and emphasized the importance of the group's pulling together, as this could be a very important project for the organization. He also made a point of encouraging everyone, including Tina, to offer opinions. Tina gradually grew more comfortable with the way the group argued and began to feel that the group's differences and arguments about ideas might actually be beneficial to the team. Over time, she became more willing to participate and came to actually value her membership in the group, which became quite famous in the organization for its remarkable creativity in marketing.

The idea that diversity can promote creative and innovative outcomes in groups is widely accepted (Austin, 1997; Bantel & Jackson, 1989; McLeod, Lobel, & Cox, 1996). Nonetheless, as our opening story illustrates, the experience of being in a group with members who have different backgrounds and perspectives can often be difficult. Recent research has shown that groups with members who differ from each other on one or more salient characteristics may experience higher levels of conflict (Jehn, Chadwick, & Thatcher, 1997) and lower levels of cohesiveness (Jackson et al., 1991). "Diversity, thus, appears to be a double-edged sword, increasing the opportunity for creativity as well as the likelihood that group members will be dissatisfied and fail to identify with the group" (Milliken & Martins, 1996, p. 403).

Understanding the myriad ways in which diversity might affect a work group's interaction processes and its outcomes constitutes an intriguing puzzle that researchers have only begun to explore. In this chapter we attempt to develop a dynamic model of how a work group's actual creativity may be affected by its composition and by how its early interactions unfold as members develop ways of working together to perform their assigned tasks.

The chapter is organized into five sections. First, we present our perspective on our focal outcome: creativity in work groups. We then discuss different forms of diversity relevant to creativity. In the third section, we begin to develop our conceptual model of how diversity might affect a work group's early functioning; our focus here is on how diversity may influence members' affective reactions to one another as well as the cognitive processes they use. In the fourth section, we attempt to show how these early interactions combine with variables, such as performance feedback and a group's self-monitoring activities, to affect a work group's subsequent interactions and its creative performance. Accordingly, our discussion targets work groups in organizational settings that have fairly stable membership, or at least have a core set of members who remain with a group for multiple phases of its work life. We conclude with a discussion of the implications of our dynamic process model for future research on work group creativity.

Creativity in Work Groups

The vast majority of creativity researchers view creativity as both a process and an outcome (Ancona & Caldwell, 1993; Argote, Insko, Yovetich, & Romero, 1995; Dougherty & Hardy, 1996; Kessler & Chakrabarti, 1996; Mehr & Shaver, 1996; Stumpf, 1995) and take the perspective that an end is not well understood if one cannot understand the process that created it. Thus, researchers have sought to define creativity as an outcome and to understand the practices and methods that reliably predict creative outcomes (Pollick & Kumar, 1997; Ruscio, Whitney, & Amabile, 1998; Wallgren, 1998) at both the individual and group level (Bindeman, 1998; Patel & Ramachandrachar, 1971).

As an outcome, researchers have historically defined creativity in terms of several features; of primary importance are fluency, flexibility, and originality of thought (Guilford, 1950; Torrance, 1969). Fluency refers to the number of ideas presented to address a given situation or problem; flexibility reflects the number of different conceptual categories represented in a given set of ideas or the number of ideological shifts in thinking; and originality indicates the novelty or rarity of each idea (Kurtzberg, 1998; Vosberg, 1998). More recently, organizational theorists have asserted that creative outcomes should also be defined in terms of usefulness (Amabile, 1996), reflecting the practicality of a given set of ideas. In keeping with this literature, we view fluency, flexibility, originality, and usefulness as defining qualities of the creativity of a group's product or outcome.

When characterizing the process of creative thinking, creativity researchers often focus on the idea that creative processes require both divergent and convergent thinking. Consistent with this body of research, we focus our attention on understanding the creative processes, including both divergent and convergent thinking processes, that may allow for the sustained development of creative outcomes by work groups.

Though we may not traditionally describe the cognitive activities in which work groups engage as direct attempts toward creative ends, many of the mechanisms by which groups exchange ideas to generate decisions or products can be conceived of as requiring creative processes (Hinsz, Tindale, & Vollrath, 1997). The need for divergent thinking can be seen in terms of the need to take different perspectives and to generate alternative solutions when faced with a problem-solving or decision-making task, whereas the need for convergent thinking can be seen in a group's need to evaluate alternatives and choose one to use or to recommend. We describe these creative processes in more detail below.

Idea Generation through Divergent Thinking

Research on creativity has long recognized the need for divergent thinking for successful creative outcomes (e.g., Guilford, 1950; Torrance, 1969). Divergent thinking is manifested in a number of different ways in work groups, including the number of perspectives and alternatives offered and the degree to which members share uniquely held information.

Though it is possible for one person to take multiple perspectives on a problem or task, a wider range of perspectives is more likely when several members approach an issue or problem from different angles or backgrounds. Research on minority influence processes has also demonstrated that, compared to groups in which members share an identical perspective, products generated in groups with at least two perspectives represented are more original (Van Dyne & Saavedra,

1996), more complex (Gruenfeld, 1995), and more innovative (De Dreu &West, 2001; Nemeth, 1986) and may be of higher quality (Nemeth, Brown, & Rogers, 2001). Work groups can generate multiple perspectives spontaneously in their discussions or use some formal structure to do so, such as a devil's advocate role (Katzenstein, 1996; Valacich & Schwenk, 1995) or a decision support system such as Group Decision Support Systems (Lam & Schaubroeck, 2000; Sosik, Kahai, & Avolio, 1999). Research (Nemeth, Brown, et al., 2001; Nemeth, Connell, Rogers, & Brown, 2001), however, suggests that "authentic dissent" is much more successful at generating the cognitive engagement and high-quality solutions that are essential to achieving a creative outcome.

A second way that divergent thinking promotes creative cognition is in the degree to which a work group considers multiple alternatives before committing to any one decision or course of action (Hackman, 1987, 1990). We see this as especially critical when performance is contingent on producing creative decisions, plans, or products. Creativity theorists agree that this type of divergent thinking, often manifest in brainstorming activities, is a critical step in any creative process (Paulus & Yang, 2000; Thorn, 1987).

Yet another manifestation of a work group's capacity for divergent thinking is the degree to which members are willing to share unique information. Because work groups tend to stress uniformity in members' thoughts, feelings, and behavior (McGrath, 1984), they tend to focus more on information they have in common than on information that is unique to each member (Stasser & Titus, 1985; Stasser, Vaughan, & Stewart, 2000). However, sharing unique information is essential to a creative process. Notably, the more information that is available in a work group, the more likely it is that some element will provide a novel approach to a particular problem or task. The sharing of unique information may also enable members to successfully recombine old ideas and apply them to the current task, thereby creating something new (Hargadon & Sutton, 1997).

Idea Evaluation and Implementation through Convergent Thinking

A creative process, however, necessitates that work groups engage not only in divergent thinking, but also in convergent thinking (Moneta, 1994; Torrance, 1969). Whereas divergent thinking promotes the generation and sharing of as many different ideas and options as possible, convergent thinking allows groups to select among the available options and to put these ideas into practice (West, 2000). For work groups in organizational settings, convergent thinking is aimed at uncovering the most practical or feasible idea(s) from a set of options. Through convergent thinking, work groups funnel down a set of ideas or opportunities into a manageable decision from which to proceed to implementation. As researchers and business professionals remind us, implementation is crucial; ideas must be not only novel but practical as well.

Instinctively, people feel that working in a group has an advantage over working individually on many creative tasks (Homma, Tajima, & Hayashi, 1995;

Paulus, Larey, & Ortega, 1995). However, research with laboratory groups has consistently shown that on brainstorming tasks, interacting groups actually underperform groups of noninteracting individuals (e.g., Gallupe, Bastianutti, & Cooper, 1991; Mullen, Johnson, & Salas, 1991). There are many reasons given for why interacting groups fail to do as well as groups of noninteracting individuals, including evaluation apprehension, production blocking, and social loafing (Paulus, 2000). Despite these findings, we believe that interacting work groups in organizational settings may be able to achieve high-quality creative outcomes. This claim is motivated by two main differences between laboratory groups and work groups. First, work groups tend to interact for longer periods than laboratory groups, providing time for members to alter their processes and overcome potential obstacles to interaction. Although groups tend to quickly settle into habitual modes of interaction (Bettenhausen & Murnighan, 1985; Gersick, 1988; McGrath & Rotchford, 1983), it is possible for them to identify and change dysfunctional patterns of behavior (Gersick & Hackman, 1990). Second, work groups are more likely to work on tasks that require the ability to critically evaluate and implement ideas. Despite biases in group decision making (Kerr, MacCoun, & Kramer, 1996; Moorhead, Neck, & West, 1998), research has shown that groups generally outperform individuals on idea evaluation (McGrath, 1984; Rowatt, Nesselroade, Beggan, & Allison, 1997; Sutton & Hargadon, 1996). Work groups therefore may be in a strong position to engage in convergent thinking—a key creative cognitive process related to creativity.

Having described our perspective on creative processes and outcomes, we now turn to defining the forms of membership diversity that can affect such creativity in work groups.

Types of Diversity in Work Groups

The word diversity simply means variety. To say a work group is diverse is to say that it consists of members who differ from each other with respect to one or more features. Members of work groups can differ with respect to race, ethnic background, gender, average organizational tenure, or cognitive background variables (e.g., average education received, type of educational background, or type of functional background), cognitive styles (e.g., problem-solving orientations), cultural values (individualism vs. collectivism), personality profiles (e.g., low-anxiety vs. high-anxiety individuals), or myriad other variables. Some organizational researchers (e.g., Milliken & Martins, 1996; Williams & O'Reilly, 1998) have argued that there are similarities in group members' reactions to diversity whether that diversity is related to racial differences or to differences in other variables such as educational background. For example, diversity or heterogeneity in the composition of a group may tend to have a negative effect on members' initial degree of satisfaction with their group. This is because the differences among members, to the extent that they are salient sources of perceived difference, may cause members to not identify as strongly with the group as they might with a group of similar others (Milliken & Martins, 1996). However, although there may be some commonalities in members' reactions to the differences among them, some differences may matter more than others.

In this chapter we separate diversity into two categories of differences: differences in readily detectable attributes (e.g., differences in race, ethnic background, language, gender, age) and differences in unobservable or underlying attributes, such as differences in education, socioeconomic background, or values (Jackson, 1992; Jackson, May, & Whitney, 1995; Maznevski, 1994; Milliken & Martins, 1996; Pelled, 1996). Before explaining why we make this distinction between detectable and unobservable differences, we need to point out that there may be important contextual determinants of what differences are salient to people. In other words, not all detectable differences matter. Differences in eye color, hair color, and height, for example, are generally not salient sources of perceived difference among people, at least not in Western Europe and the United States. The same argument applies to unobservable differences. In some organizations, differences in functional backgrounds may elicit considerably more of a sense of difference than they would in other organizational contexts. It seems likely that the homogeneity or heterogeneity of the context as well as the specific values of the culture may be important in determining what differences people perceive as significant.

For the purposes of this chapter, we distinguish between readily detectable and unobservable forms of diversity because we believe that, all else being equal, the detectability of differences may matter in at least two ways. First, when a group is diverse on detectable variables that are salient to members, the simple act of observation of such differences may create a barrier to developing a shared group identity. Notably, a high degree of detectable diversity may fragment a work group, leading members to gravitate toward others they perceive as similar and drawing them away from those perceived as different (Byrne, 1971). The extent to which this is likely to happen depends on a number of factors, including the characteristics of the context (i.e., the organizational culture, the amount of diversity in the broader context, the existence of a superordinate goal), the configuration of the group, and members' prior experiences. A second reason for distinguishing between detectable and unobservable forms of diversity is that a work group may use detectable forms of diversity to make sense of its experiences, such as when members hold conflicting perspectives on issues or exhibit extensive conflict. When there are observable differences among group members, differences in perspectives that coincide with those observable differences may get attributed to the obvious differences. This could have a potentially negative outcome if "fault lines" (subgroups that differ from each other on more than one variable) subsequently develop in the group (Lau & Murnighan, 1998).

It is also important to note that the degree of heterogeneity in a group may not have a linear relationship to performance. The proportion of a group's members who belong to the various categories may affect the probability of in-group and out-group dynamics developing within the group. Thus, groups with identifiable subgroups may actually have more negative outcomes than groups that are truly pluralistic (Milliken, Wiesenfeld, Martins, Salgado, & Dunn-Jensen, 2001). Furthermore, a single individual who is different from others may not have sufficient power to sway opinions in a very large group. Thus, it may be necessary to have more than one individual who articulates a different position for that position to be heard effectively (Kitayama & Burnstein, 1994).

In the sections that follow, we outline some ideas about how different forms of diversity may affect the early life of a work group. In discussing diversity in underlying or invisible attributes, we focus particular attention on cognitive or information-related diversity (Jehn, Northcraft, & Neale, 1999). We focus on cognitive diversity because it is the form of invisible diversity most likely to have an effect on the creativity of a group's processes and outcomes. We argue that detectable forms of diversity act more immediately than unobservable forms of diversity (e.g., cognitive diversity) on a work group's process, primarily through the team's affective reactions; thus, we focus on these effects prior to examining the effects of unobservable differences. We also suggest some possible moderating conditions that influence the relationships between diversity and a work group's affective and cognitive processes.

▬
Diversity and the Phases of Group Work

We adopt the conceptualization of a group's life course developed by Arrow, McGrath, and Berdahl (2000), focusing on two phases that are conceptually distinct but have blurry temporal boundaries: the formative phase (here called Time 1) and the operations phase (here called Time 2). In the formative phase, members become organized into an initial network of relations that distinguish the group as a bounded social entity. As a group works actively toward its task goals, members elaborate, enact, monitor, and modify the patterns of interactions established during formation. This set of activities encompasses most of a work group's existence. At the start of a group's life, the group's composition is an important initial condition that can have enduring effects on its affective and cognitive processes. We describe these influences in detail below. Figure 3.1 summarizes our specific predictions on how the homogeneity or heterogeneity in a work group's composition shapes its affective and cognitive processes in the formative and operations phases of its development.

In discussing the effects of diversity, we start by describing the likely effects of detectable differences on group members' affective reactions to their group. We then discuss the effects of unobservable differences on members' affective reactions. Next, we look at the likely effects of diversity on a group's cognitive processes. We begin our discussion with members' likely affective reactions to diversity because we believe these early emotional reactions are likely to shape the cognitive capacity of the group.

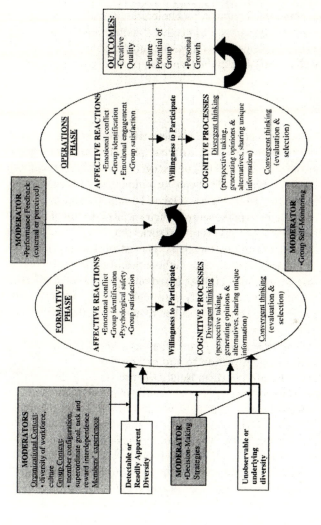

Figure 3.1. *Effects of Detectable and Undetectable Diversity on Work Group Processes Over Time*

The Early Effects of Diversity in a Work Group's Life

The Initial Effects of Diversity on Work Groups' Affective Reactions

We use the term *affective reactions* broadly to refer to several emotion-laden processes and "emergent states" (Marks, Mathieu, & Zaccaro, 2001) that we believe occur early in the life of a group. We focus particular attention on group identification, emotional conflict, psychological safety, and group satisfaction. Although there are other possible affective reactions that may be important in the life of a group, we believe that these four are likely to play a critical role in a work group's life, especially in the formative phase of its development.

Detectable Diversity

We begin our discussion of the effect of detectable differences on a work group's initial affective reactions by exploring the impact of these differences on group identification. When a work group comes together for the first time, social identity (Tajfel & Turner, 1986) and self-categorization theory (Turner, Hogg, Oakes, Reicher, & Wetherell, 1987; Turner, Oakes, Haslam, & McGarty, 1994) claim that members will aim to make sense of their social environment by construing themselves and others in terms of abstract social categories that account for similarities and differences among members. The categories may include ascribed social categories based on race, sex, or ethnicity and those reflecting formal and informal social groups, such as those based on organizational, professional, or departmental memberships. Readily detectable cues indicating specific social categories are likely to be especially salient to members and, therefore, to figure prominently in self-categorization.

When individuals are attuned to differences among group members, they may feel greater social attraction to and exhibit favoritism toward members perceived as similar and, in turn, isolate themselves from those perceived as different. Such fragmentation within the group may lead to implicit intragroup rivalries and negative stereotypes and distrust of out-group members, which blocks members from identifying with the work group as a whole (Brewer, 1979, 1995; Hogg & Abrams, 1988). Thus, work groups that are diverse with respect to gender, race, or ethnicity may have a lower level of initial group identification than work groups that are more homogeneous in their makeup. The likelihood that diversity will be associated with lower identification depends on the configuration of the group, the experience of its members in dealing with people of different backgrounds, and certain key aspects of the group and organizational context.

In addition, social identity theory suggests that intragroup distinctions may lead members to favor ideas and opinions offered by similar others and to reject or discount the ideas and opinions of those who are different, potentially leading to conflict in groups. Further, individuals may also have more difficulty understanding the expectations, intentions, or points of view of members whom they perceive as different (Cox, 1993; Larkey, 1996; Martins, Milliken, Wiesenfeld, & Salgado, 2001). This lack of understanding, coupled with differences of opinion and possible subgroup identification, can create conflict. Conflict arises in interdependent situations when members possess partially incompatible interests (Jehn, 1995) or when one or more members of a group are perceived as interfering with the ability of others to attain their goals (Katz & Kahn, 1978). Jehn has argued that there are two types of conflict that can occur in groups: emotional conflict and task conflict. Emotional conflict refers to disagreements related to members' personal preferences or members' interpersonal interactions (Jehn, 1995). Thus, work groups composed of members who possess considerable visible differences (e.g., race or gender) may experience higher levels of emotional conflict than more homogeneous work groups (Jehn et al., 1999).

The presence of readily detectable differences may also impact the degree of safety that members feel within the group context. According to Edmondson (1999), psychological safety stems from mutual respect and interpersonal trust among group members and reflects a sense of confidence that the group will not embarrass, reject, or punish someone for speaking up. Somewhat similar to the construct of cohesiveness that has been used extensively in the literature on groups (Hackman, 1992), group psychological safety, Edmondson argues, differs from cohesiveness in two important ways: (1) it does not reflect a generalized feeling of positive affect for the group as cohesiveness often does, and (2) it encourages risk taking and speaking out, whereas cohesion can reduce willingness to disagree (i.e., groupthink). We argue that group composition may partially determine the initial level of psychological safety that is perceived to exist in a group. When there are detectable forms of difference among members, the perceived existence of subgroups can lead to low levels of trust and identification within the group as a whole and produce a climate in which members do not feel safe discussing differences of opinion openly.

These early interaction difficulties are likely to impact how members feel about their membership in the group. An important outcome of member interactions at all phases of group development is the degree to which the group experience contributes to the personal well-being of members (Hackman, 1987). Some work groups operate in ways that frustrate rather than satisfy members' personal needs and interests. The initial interactions of work groups with detectable forms of difference among members may promote low levels of satisfaction with the group experience, in part, because of the potentially higher levels of conflict these groups may experience as well as the lower levels of psychological safety and identification with the group as a whole.

In sum, we see the potential for groups with high levels of observable or readily apparent differences among their members to experience initially lower levels of group identification, psychological safety, and group satisfaction than more homogeneous groups. They may also experience more misunderstandings and conflict than more homogeneous groups. The probability of these effects is likely to vary, however, as a function of a number of variables, including the configuration of the group, the characteristics of the group, organizational context, and members' range of past experiences. Further, as we will argue in a later section of the chapter, we believe that early interaction difficulties can be ameliorated by careful attention to the management of a group's interaction processes.

Cognitive Diversity

Work group members can also differ from each other in ways that are not immediately apparent. These include differences related to members' knowledge bases and perspectives resulting from their work experience, educational background, and training. We refer to differences in terms of what group members know or how they think about problems as cognitive diversity. Although cognitive diversity is less apparent to members in their initial interactions than visible diversity, these differences surface as the group's work gets underway. Within a short period of time, members usually become aware of the degree to which others hold similar or contrasting views about their task.

We expect that detectable differences and cognitive differences operate on a work group's initial affective reactions in similar ways, although the effects may not be of the same magnitude. When members are aware that other members are thinking differently about an issue, it is not always obvious to them what factors underlie these differences in perspective. Thus, when differences are more cognitive in nature, members may be confused about the reasons for their differences and may be more likely to make attributions to individuals rather than to observable differences among people. The group may become segmented, however, as members are drawn to others who hold their perspective for a given problem or task, thus weakening the probability that members identify strongly with the group as a whole. Moreover, when members draw boundaries within their group, the development of trust is delayed or blocked. Thus, members may feel less safe discussing differences of opinion or perspective. Finally, when a work group's formation phase primarily revolves around attention to differences among members and is characterized by difficult interactions among members, the group as a whole is likely to perceive the group experience as more frustrating than satisfying.

Early in the life of a group, we believe, readily detectable differences are likely to have a larger effect than cognitive differences on a group's affective reactions. One reason this is likely to be true is that, all else being equal, readily apparent differences are more likely to be salient and, thus, more likely to result in members categorizing themselves into one or another subgroup as opposed to identifying with the group as a whole. In general, the initial effects of cognitive diversity on a work group's affective reactions may be smaller in magnitude and less reliable than the effects of observable or readily apparent forms of diversity because of this salience. However, as we discuss later in the chapter, if not properly managed, these cognitive differences may create significant interaction difficulties later in the life of a work group.

Moderators of the Link between Diversity and Members'
Affective Reactions to the Group

As depicted in Figure 3.1, we believe that the perception of a superordinate goal is an important moderator of the relationship between diversity and a work group's affective reactions. A long-standing principle in the literature on groups is that a superordinate goal can bring together people from diverse social groups to shape the dynamics and outcomes of their interaction (Deutsch, 1973; Sherif, Harvey, White, Hood, & Sherif, 1961). Thus, the negative effects of both observable and cognitive diversity on a work group's initial affective reactions may be attenuated when members perceive that they are working toward a common goal.

The structure of a work group's task and reward system is a key factor promoting perceptions of a superordinate goal (Tjosvold, 1986). With respect to task design, Tjosvold (1988) showed that creating a common task requiring collective action among members can induce a cooperative orientation, promoting resource and information exchanges as well as openness to each other's ideas. Moreover, Wageman (1995) found that a group task requiring high task interdependence makes salient a collective sense of responsibility, increasing the need for collaboration and mutual adjustments among members.

Although the degree of task interdependence in a work group is partly determined by the design of the task (Goodman, 1986), it is also a function of the way members choose to plan, coordinate, and execute their activities (Saavedra, Earley, & Van Dyne, 1993). In work groups performing creative tasks, negative reactions associated with member differences may operate to reduce members' degree of experienced task interdependence and, thus, obscure perceptions that members share a superordinate goal. In these situations, a work group's reward system may become especially important in creating perceptions of a superordinate goal. Reward interdependence reflects the degree to which group members believe that their personal benefits and costs depend on successful goal attainment by other members (Deutsch, 1973; Kelley & Thibaut, 1978). Some research has argued that reward interdependence induces felt responsibility for both one's own and other members' work (van der Vegt, Emans, & van de Vliert, 1998), creating conditions of a *common fate* (Kramer, 1993). Wageman (1995) concluded that reward interdependence affects members' motivation to perform, leading to greater task-related effort. Thus, we argue that work groups that have high reward interdependence are likely to perceive that members share a superordinate goal, which should diminish the effects of visible forms of diversity on their initial affective reactions.

Other variables that are not directly under the group's control that could affect how members react to diversity include the diversity of the organizational and societal context (Martins et al., 2003; Williams & O'Reilly, 1998), the degree to which the culture of the organization communicates a value on diversity, the configuration of the group (i.e., whether the group subdivides into obvious subgroups based on observable or underlying differences), and the degree to which group members have prior experience dealing with people who are different from them.

The Initial Effects of Diversity on Work Groups' Cognitive Processes

When work groups come together they usually begin task work immediately (Hackman, Brousseau, & Weiss, 1976; Weingart, 1992), even as they are assembling a network of relations among members. For work groups charged with the task of producing some creative output, much of their task work is cognitive. We now turn our attention from the work group's initial affective reactions and toward the effects of detectable and cognitive forms of diversity on its cognitive processes. After considering the direct effects of diversity on a group's cognitive processes, we consider how a team's affective reactions might influence these processes as well.

Detectable Diversity

When readily apparent differences are associated with meaningful and useful differences in members' perspective on a task, those differences ought to enhance a work group's creative processes. The logic is that these differences are likely to increase the range of perspectives brought to bear on the task, the number of alternatives considered, and the probability that individual members will have unique information to share, all of which are key manifestations of the divergent thinking required for creativity. Watson, Kumar, and Michaelsen (1993), for example, found that group diversity in nationality or ethnic background was associated with a greater variety of perspectives and alternatives being generated by the group. Interestingly, however, McLeod and Lobel (1992) found that groups that were heterogeneous with respect to ethnic background did not always produce a greater number of ideas, but they did produce higher quality ideas in a brainstorming task. This finding points to the possibility that differences in members' perspectives may help the team to evaluate the utility of specific ideas, a key element of convergent thinking.

Cognitive Diversity

Organizational researchers have suggested that cognitive diversity in the composition of a group may enhance task-related or cognitive performance, especially on tasks requiring creativity (Austin, 1997; Bantel & Jackson, 1989; McLeod, Lobel, & Cox, 1996). One reason is that high levels of cognitive diversity increase the potential range of perspectives and opinions members bring to the task (Stasser, 1992). This, in turn, increases the potential for differences of opinion about how the task should be accomplished (so-called task conflict). Task conflict is thought to both encourage and legitimize the consideration of multiple alternatives (Jehn et al., 1997; Jehn et al., 1999). In addition to airing differences in perspective, task conflict or disagreements in opinion can serve to encourage each individual to give more careful thought and attention to his or her own viewpoint (Gruenfeld, 1995). All of these findings point to the likelihood that cognitive diversity in the composition of a group will be positively related to divergent thinking.

It is important to note, however, that high levels of any kind of disagreement, even task-focused, can spill over into more emotion-based reactions (Jehn, 1997) and escalate from substantive issues to personal attacks (Thomas, 1992). Task conflict, when it exists in moderation, can help promote both a broadening of thought and a closer examination of the opinions and perspectives presented, but it can also create problems if these differences of opinion come to be seen as blocking the group's progress or as associated with personal agendas.

Moderating Effect of Decision-Making Strategies

Work groups often use structured decision-making strategies to increase both the breadth and depth of information brought to a given problem or task. Common strategies include using a combination of divergent thinking tasks such as brainstorming or brainwriting (Osborn, 1953; Paulus, Larey, & Dzindolet, 2001; Paulus & Yang, 2000) with convergent thinking tasks such as criteria-based evaluation of alternatives (Keeney & Raiffa, 1976; Torrance, 1978). Techniques such as these may be able to bolster cognitive activities indicative of a creative process by forcing the consideration of many alternatives before systematically deciding on any one decision or course of action. When a work group's composition is diverse in terms of observable or cognitive differences, the use of structured decision-making strategies can thus bring forth the multitude of perspectives, ideas, and opinions that members may hold.

Relationships between Affective Reactions and Cognitive Processes during the Formative Stages of a Group's Life

Having defined important affective and cognitive variables that set the foundation for the possibility of creative processes in diverse work groups, we now focus on the dynamic interplay among some of these factors during the formative phase of work group life. A considerable body of research has shown that affect can have a large impact on memory, judgment, and decision making (see Fiske & Taylor, 1991; Forgas, 1992). Accordingly, work group members' affective reactions may have important implications for how groups approach their tasks (Hinsz et al., 1997).

Group Identification

Group identification reflects the cognitive and emotional connection that members feel toward their work group as a whole (Tajfel, 1978). Social identity theory asserts that a shared group membership accentuates attitudinal, emotional, and behavioral similarities between the self and in-group members. A perceived sense of similarity to others in a group is likely to be associated with greater social attraction, greater in-group cooperation, and higher levels of trust (Brewer & Kramer, 1986; Kramer, 1991, 1993). Thus, members who identify strongly will tend to engage in behaviors that support the group and may be more willing to contribute to the group's products. This means that members who identify strongly with their group will be more likely to actively contribute their knowledge, ideas, and opinions with the goal of promoting the group's performance. In contrast, in work groups where group identification is low, the motivation to see the group excel may also be low, thereby reducing the likelihood that members reveal their perspectives and ideas regarding the task.

Psychological Safety

In work groups where members perceive that voicing ideas or opinions is not safe, concerns about potential embarrassment, rejection, or punishment from other members are considerable. In these situations, perceptions of threat are likely to induce negative moods that direct members' attention and motivation toward self-protection (Turner & Horvitz, 2001). As a result, members may withdraw or distance themselves from the group, submit or yield to other members' wishes, and generally feel disinterested or apathetic about the group and its task. Work groups with low psychological safety are therefore unlikely to use cognitive processes that tap the wealth of knowledge and ideas that members bring to the group.

In contrast, members of work groups with substantial psychological safety are more likely to engage actively in the group, to offer contrasting or alternative viewpoints, and to feel positively about the group and its task. These claims are consistent with Osborn's (1953) early work on imaginative thinking, which stressed the importance of "deferred judgment" in helping to foster a comfortable environment in which individuals can generate a broad range of ideas. More recently, Edmondson (1999) found that psychological safety affects the ways that work group members acquire, share, and combine knowledge, with higher degrees of psychological safety leading members to speak up and test assumptions about issues under discussion. Madjar, Oldham, and Pratt (2001) also reported that bosses viewed their employees as more creative when these employees reported feeling a high level of support from their coworkers. It is possible that workplace support affects creativity by encouraging employees to voice and act on a wide range of ideas and opinions relevant to the task.

Emotional Conflict and Group Satisfaction

Many, if not most, affective states are aroused by interpersonal events (Parkinson, 1997), and recent research has shown that social interactions can lead work group members to experience shared moods (Bartel & Saavedra, 2000). We suspect that a negative mood is likely to develop in work groups with high levels of emotional conflict and low levels of group satisfaction. Negative moods tend to trigger vigilant, analytic, and effortful cognitive strategies (Forgas, 1992). Work groups experiencing negative mood may therefore overexamine situations to the point where details obfuscate the nature of the problem or situation, may amass inordinate amounts of information, or may employ rigid and slow analytic strategies. Such processing strategies are not conducive to divergent thinking and thus idea generation. Indeed, Carnevale and Probst (1998) showed that even the suggestion of conflict, without its actual occurrence, leads to narrow and rigid thinking and reduced creativity.

In contrast, a positive mood may enhance a work group's creative processes due to its influence on both participation and information seeking. Positive moods, such as enthusiasm and excitement, are associated with action readiness and an open orientation that leads to exploration, information gathering, and social interaction directed at attaining important goals (Frijda, 1986; Green & Sedikides, 1999). In addition to enhanced participation, positive mood may also allow members greater scope to engage in unusual, unorthodox, and creative thinking (Isen, Daubman, & Nowicki, 1987). Positive mood increases access to a broad range of procedural, semantic, and episodic knowledge that provides a basis for stimulus elaboration (Schwarz & Bless, 1991). In other words, the application of different types of knowledge to new situations increases members' capacity to integrate diverse information, elaborate unusual and creative associations, and generate new concepts (Forgas, 1992). Consequently, positive mood associated with low emotional conflict and high group satisfaction may bolster a work group's creative cognitive processes.

The Mediating Role of Willingness to Contribute

Initial levels of work groups' affective reactions are important conditions that influence a group's creative processes, mainly due to their impact on members' willingness to contribute to the group. Widespread participation can expose differences among members, both explicitly (through actual statements or assertions made by members themselves) and implicitly (through inferences members make about others). When members are inclined to share their ideas, opinions, and perspectives rather than self-censor them, a work group's creative potential is enhanced. Thus, willingness to contribute may be an important mediating variable that gives potency to work groups' affective reactions and shapes their subsequent cognitive processes.

Diversity in the Operations Phase of a Work Group's Life

Following the formative phase, work groups enter into the operations phase, in which they elaborate initial patterns of relations and activities based on feedback about group functioning and performance (Arrow et al., 2000). Most of a group's life is spent in this phase as it works actively toward its goals. Group members' initial patterns of thoughts, feelings, and behaviors have a strong propensity to persist in subsequent group interactions, even when the conditions present during group formation change considerably. Kelly (1988) and Kelly and McGrath (1985) use the term "entrainment" to describe how members synchronize their behavior to fit one another, establishing rhythms or patterns of activity that persist within a group despite changes in the surrounding context. For example, work groups tend to quickly establish expectations about goals and desired outcomes (Bettenhausen & Murnighan, 1985), patterns of task and social interaction (Gersick, 1988), and habitual work routines (Gersick & Hackman, 1990). As a group begins to work toward its task goals, members elaborate and enact the patterns of interaction established during this formative period (Arrow et al., 2000).

Therefore, the degrees of emotional conflict, group identification, and group satisfaction that were present during group formation are likely to carry over as a work group moves into its operations phase. The same effect is expected for a group's creative cognitive processes, with initial patterns of activity carrying over into subsequent task interactions. Despite this carryover phenomenon, we argue that a work group's affective reactions and creative cognitive processes can be transformed in the operations phase based on feedback the group gets about its initial performance progress and on its own self-monitoring activities. Figure 3.1 summarizes these proposed relationships. In this section, we discuss variables that may moderate the Time 1–Time 2 relationships, but first we discuss the nature of the expected relationship between affective and cognitive processes during a work group's operations phase.

The Relationship between Affective Reactions and Cognitive Processes during the Operations Stage of a Group's Life

We see several affective reactions as critical to a work group's continued use of creative cognitive processes in its second phase of life as well as to its overall performance. In addition to the constructs of emotional conflict, identification, and satisfaction discussed in earlier sections, we focus here on the construct of emotional engagement.

We believe that when a work group experiences a high level of psychological safety in its formative phase, this translates into feelings of emotional engagement with the group during its operations phase. As previously discussed, psychological safety is indicative of mutual respect and interpersonal trust among group members, which encourages high levels of member participation. A strong sense of psychological safety that endures through a work group's formative phase is likely to heighten members' interest in both task and group, as members perceive the group setting as a secure and welcoming venue for sharing their ideas. Thus, over time, initial levels of psychological safety may be experienced subsequently as a generalized feeling reflecting members' emotional investment in the group and thus their interest in engaging with members and in the task.

Our notion of emotional engagement is consistent with Fredrickson's (1998) discussion of interest and Amabile's (1996) notion of intrinsic motivation as a positive emotional state that arises in social settings perceived as safe and supportive and as bringing novelty, change, and a sense of possibility. According to Izard (1977), when people are interested in a topic, they are more likely to explore and investigate it with an eye toward becoming involved and gaining more knowledge about it. Thus, emotional engagement is indicative of members' openness to new ideas, actions, and events. High levels of emotional engagement are likely to motivate active participation in a work group, with members contributing their own knowledge, ideas, and opinion and being open to those offered by other members. In this way, emotional engagement can enhance a work group's ability to use creative cognitive processes as members become active and interested participants.

Effects of Group Self-Monitoring on Affective Reactions and Cognitive Processes

Work groups' affective reactions and cognitive processes in the operations phase are determined not only by the patterns set in the formative stage, but also by the manner in which groups choose to manage these processes over time. Arrow et al. (2000) note that, in the course of their interactions, work groups respond to past, present, and anticipated future changes or events in their work context by altering their structure, goals, or behavior. We suggest that work groups that engage in self-monitoring activities are in a strong position to achieve this type of directed adaptation. At the individual level, Carver and Scheier (1998) have noted that self-monitoring does not imply a prolonged or penetrating self-examination but, rather, selective attention to and processing of information that is relevant to some aspect of the self. In task settings, a heightened self-focus often results in greater task focus as individuals process information related to their goal progress or performance. We suggest that the notion of self-monitoring at the group level thus reflects an increased sensitivity to and interest in information related to group processes and outcomes. Group self-monitoring therefore implies several activities, including discussions of how to stay on or move toward a path that will achieve desired goals, monitoring whether group activities are having intended effects, and developing procedures for changing a course of action that closes the gap between the group's current state and its desired state. In this way, group self-monitoring is similar to West's (1996) concept of reflexivity, defined as the degree to which a group reflects on its objectives, strategies, and processes, as well as its embedding organizational context, and adapts its work accordingly. We see group self-monitoring as critical in work groups with diverse membership because it may alleviate or resolve difficulties that members experienced while working together during the early phases. This idea is consistent with Gersick and Hackman's (1990) findings that work groups can break dysfunctional habitual routines when they reflect on and evaluate how they perform their tasks. Similarly, group self-monitoring can also increase members' awareness of the potential value of their differences.

Group self-monitoring is more critical in the operations phase of a group's life for two reasons. An obvious first reason is that a work group is unable to reflect on its goals and evaluate how and why it has approached these goals in particular ways until the group has completed an initial period of task activity. A second reason is that work groups generally do not reexamine their own behavior to determine whether they could be operating better (Hackman & Morris, 1975) until they reach a milestone, natural breakpoint, or other transition point in their development (Gersick & Hackman, 1990). These situations generally involve a temporary lull or suspension of task work, creating opportunities for groups to reflect on their processes, though not all groups will choose to do so. Over time, engaging in self-monitoring activities can become a regular part of a group's life, essentially functioning as a norm that guides members' interactions and informs its performance strategies.

Group self-monitoring can potentially affect the degree to which initial patterns of affect and cognition in a work group persist in its operations phase. In his work on learning and problem solving among professionals, Schon (1983) noted that emotions as well as thoughts can serve as the focus of reflective processes. The objective is for individuals to get a feel for a situation and to understand the dynamics of the situation that triggered it. At the group level, self-monitoring activities can increase a work group's understanding of the possible sources of its affective experiences. When initial affective reactions are positive, work groups are unlikely to delve too deeply into feelings that do not seem to pose a salient threat to member relations or group functioning. Nonetheless, even a minimal level of group self-monitoring can have beneficial effects when it reaffirms the positive feelings that members derive from their group. This, in turn, increases the likelihood that such feelings will continue in the next phase of the group's life.

In contrast, work groups with highly unpleasant affective reactions in their formative phase may benefit from examining their group dynamics to develop possible ideas as to why such feelings exist. In fact, unpleasant affective reactions are a possible trigger for group self-monitoring. Negative moods can act as a signal that a current situation is problematic and that corrective action is needed (Frijda, 1986). Accordingly, such reactions may focus attention on and stimulate effort aimed at understanding and alleviating perceived problems and thus repairing the unpleasant mood (Saavedra & Earley, 1991). In this way, group self-monitoring can help members to reconsider their feelings and their stereotypes or attributions about other members. We propose that such activities should reduce the likelihood that unpleasant affective reactions persist with the same intensity in a work group's operations phase.

The same reasoning applies to work groups' creative cognitive processes, with group self-monitoring activities increasing a group's understanding of its cognitive approach to the task or problem at hand. Work groups in organizational settings usually have some knowledge of the processes needed to develop creative outcomes and may attempt to enact performance strategies that achieve such outcomes. A high level of group self-monitoring activity means that members actively assess these strategies, reflecting on the way the group has framed a problem or task and attempting to uncover the unspoken norms that regulate how and why it takes a particular approach to the work. For work groups that used creative cognitive processes extensively in their formative phase, group self-monitoring may affirm what is working well in the group as well as reveal areas where the group can strengthen its processes. For groups that made less use of creative cognitive processes, group self-monitoring may make members increasingly aware of the diversity that exists in the group and prompt them to devise ways of leveraging this variety as part of their group process.

In sum, group self-monitoring may moderate the relationship between Time 1 (formative phase) and Time 2 (operations phase) affective reactions and creative cognitive processes. Groups with generally positive affective reactions at Time 1 are more likely to experience a continuation of these positive reactions if they reflect on the causes of their successful interactions and try to replicate them (i.e., engage in self-monitoring behavior). In contrast, groups that experience negative affect at Time 1 are less likely to have that experience replicated in the operations phase if they reflect on the causes of their unsuccessful interactions. We believe the same logic applies to the quality of the cognitive processes being used. Self-monitoring can reinforce positive processes and help correct suboptimal processes.

The Impact of Performance Feedback on Affective Reactions and Cognitive Processes

Throughout a work group's life, members can receive feedback regarding their overall performance or progress toward achieving certain objectives from many sources, including managers and other people inside the organization as well as external constituencies (e.g., customers, suppliers, competitors, and shareholders). Feedback to which work groups are exposed can potentially shape their affective reactions and creative cognitive processes as they move into the second phase of development.

Affective Reactions

Positive feedback signaling that a group has performed well or is making good progress toward its goals may enhance members' affective reactions to the group. Members may come to identify more strongly with their work group when performance feedback indicates that others (nonmembers) perceive the group as successful, because individuals generally are motivated to belong to social groups that hold high social status or possess socially desirable features (Hogg & Abrams, 1988). Positive performance feedback also makes members more agreeable to subsequent interactions with the group (Hackman, 1987; McGrath, 1984), possibly by generating further interest or emotional engagement in the group's work. Overall, the experience of working in an effective group is highly satisfying, especially after receiving positive performance feedback (Mohrman, Cohen, & Mohrman, 1995).

Performance feedback may be especially advantageous to diverse work groups when members attribute their positive performance to specific differences among members. As members spend time together, they become more aware of the knowledge, skills, and points of view that each member brings to the group. Jung and Sosik (1999), however, reasoned that in contrast to more detectable forms of diversity (e.g., ethnicity), members' evaluation and perception of nondetectable or cognitive differences tend to be reinforced after successful enactment of a task. Performance-related feedback can motivate members to focus explicitly on aspects of the group and its members to develop an account for their performance level. Jung and Sosik found that performance feedback was positively associated with members' subsequent perceptions of their group's heterogeneity. We suggest that performance feedback can also influence the valence that a group associates with its perceived diversity. Members are likely to attribute positive performance feedback to aspects of the group itself rather than to external factors (Jones & Nisbett, 1972), possibly leading members to focus on or become aware of the unique qualities they each bring to the group. Work groups that develop the perception that differences among members contributed to their good performance are likely to experience more positive affective reactions in subsequent interactions than work groups that see member diversity as less influential.

Moderating Role of Group Self-Monitoring

A key issue for a work group is its ability to recover from a poor start or from initially negative feedback. We believe that a work group's ability to engage in self-monitoring is a key factor that increases its capacity to recover from early negative feedback. Feedback indicative of failure often promotes commitment to prior routines and strategies (Gersick & Hackman, 1990; Staw, Sandelands, & Dutton, 1981) unless a group makes a concerted effort to evaluate the appropriateness of its performance processes. Work groups that make a point to ask themselves "Why did we perform poorly?" are much more likely to discover means of improving their process than groups that do not ask themselves this question and do not make any obvious changes in their behavior. Thus, we see group self-monitoring as having a powerful influence on how negative performance feedback impacts a group's creative processes.

Implications for Group Performance

We conceptualize group performance as a multidimensional construct, consisting of several criteria as described by Hackman (1987, 1990). These include the quality of the group's products, members' ability to work together interdependently in the future, and members' satisfaction with the group experience. Although these criteria each describe an important facet of performance, we recognize that the actual output produced will be the primary focus for work groups performing tasks in organizational contexts.

The first performance criterion is the degree to which a group's output meets or exceeds the standards of those who will receive, review, or use that output. Work groups that are striving for creative outcomes will most likely be judged on the degree of fluency, flexibility, novelty, or usefulness of the final product (Woodman, Sawyer, & Griffin, 1993). The use of creative cognitive processes increases the breadth of information sharing (divergent thinking) that allows for a more complete analysis of possible alternatives (Crabbe, 1990; Torrance, 1979). Such processes also increase the depth of information processing, whereby work groups evaluate their different perspectives and alternatives and move toward convergence to develop a product that meets their performance standards (Crabbe, 1990; Torrance, 1979). The more a work group uses creative cognitive processes in its operations phase, therefore, the more likely it is to have higher quality creative outcomes.

The second criterion is the degree to which the process of generating the work enhances the capability of members to work together interdependently in the future. Work groups characterized by healthy and productive processes become highly skilled at coordination and collaboration, making them increasingly capable over time (Hackman, 1990). In contrast, work groups that experience destructive task and social dynamics often find it impossible to work together again. For example, when mutual antagonism and emotional conflict among members is intense or when members fail to generate interest in the group and its task, the group has diminished social and emotional resources to engage in further work together. Toward the end of a group's work, therefore, affective reactions will likely influence members' willingness to work together again.

Finally, work group performance is viewed in terms of the degree to which the group experience satisfies rather than frustrates members' needs, thus adding to their growth and personal well-being. On one hand, work groups that experience highly positive affective reactions (low emotional conflict and high group identification, group satisfaction, and emotional engagement) are likely to satisfy members' social needs (Hackman, 1992). On the other hand, the use of creative cognitive processes could contribute to members' professional needs by increasing their knowledge of a particular work-related problem or issue or their general understanding of the multiple perspectives held by members from different departments and hierarchical levels in the organization. Thus, the more positive a work group's affective reactions and the greater its use of creative cognitive processes, the more likely that members will perceive that their personal needs and interests were satisfied.

—

Discussion and Implications

In this chapter, we have sought to describe the manner in which diversity in the composition of a work group might affect the creativity of the group's processes and outcomes. We have sought to do this using a multistage model of group functioning (Arrow et al., 2000; Marks et al., 2001), thereby focusing on the effects of diversity in work group composition on the functioning of the group over time. One of the purposes of taking such a dynamic perspective is to offer a way of thinking about diversity that might begin to resolve some of the apparently conflicting predictions about the effects of diversity on a group's functioning. For example, the argument that diverse groups ought to outperform homogeneous groups or noninteracting individuals on creative tasks is based on the assumption that these diverse groups have a greater range of skills and resources from which to draw. However, the presence of such a range of skills and abilities does not guarantee their effective utilization. For example, in its early interactions, a group may experience negative affective reactions because of their diversity. These negative affective reactions to the group may make members less willing to contribute their ideas and knowledge to the group. Thus, we believe that the adoption of a multistage model of group functioning is useful because it highlights that the manner in which diversity plays out in the early stages of a group's life is likely to have a major impact on the group's processes and performance at later stages.

The idea that the manner in which diversity plays out initially in a group has potential repercussions over its lifetime suggests that interventions geared to helping members through the very early stages of their life together may be critical for diverse work groups. In the initial stages of group design, managers who assemble work groups that possess (either intentionally or unintentionally) high levels of readily detectable differences among members need to give careful consideration to other group design factors (e.g., a superordinate goal and reward interdependence) that could help counteract negative affective reactions associated with such diversity. Although we have argued that readily detectable differences may pose more severe management challenges than unobservable differences, all heterogeneous groups may need help in understanding how their differences may be a source of competitive advantage rather than a potential obstacle. Managers may need to explicitly tell groups that they have been composed in a particular way to maximize the probability that they will be able to come up with a creative or innovative solution to a problem. That is, managers could help identify the talents, skills, or expertise that members bring to the group as a function of their different backgrounds. Hackman (1990) argued that discussions of members' task-relevant knowledge and skills during group formation improves a work group's capacity to develop appropriate task strategies and an effective division of labor. However, work groups tend not to engage in such discussions spontaneously and thus could benefit from managerial intervention.

Groups may also need help in establishing the processes they will need to effectively manage their diversity. One process that we believe may have a positive effect on the evolution of diverse teams is group self-monitoring or reflexivity (West, 2001). Work groups that create self-monitoring norms may be able to learn from negative experiences and turn difficult interactions into positive outcomes. Groups may be able to learn how to become high self-monitors, but the timing of such learning is critical. Early on, managers could instruct members to create artificial transition points for themselves, stopping once every two or three meetings, for example, to ask themselves how things are going and whether they want to change the way they are going about their tasks. Making such behaviors a regular part of group interactions could prove beneficial later should problems or nonroutine events arise. Indeed, Waller (1999) recently showed that the timing of adaptive responses in work groups is critical to achieving high performance levels. When a novel event is encountered, work groups often cannot strategize overtly and must make quick decisions about what actions to take. We suggest that those work groups that have a system in place for assessing dimensions of the task and group are in a strong position to adjust their behavior quickly to produce high-quality, creative outcomes.

Similarly, group members who come to understand the value that diversity plays in their group's cognitive processes are likely to experience more positive affective reactions to their group during the later stages of the group's life. In fact, differences that were initially seen as problematic may become a source of distinctiveness and pride. Thus, training in what is known about the advantages and disadvantages of composing a diverse group to perform a task might be helpful. The danger, of course, is that by explaining the potential negative effects of diversity, one might create a self-fulfilling prophecy rather than help group members to understand themselves better.

The model of the effects of diversity that we present clearly points to the close connection between what group members feel (their affective reactions) and how the group performs (the cognitive reactions). Groups can short-circuit the very processes that are essential to creativity if they end up feeling bad about each other. Members can withhold contributions because they do not feel safe in the group or worse, feel angry with their fellow group members. Further, as Kurtzberg (2002) finds, when group members do not feel positively about their group, they are likely to rate their performance poorly. This could, in turn, reduce their commitment to the group and to its performance outcomes. Focusing attention on the processes that link emotion and cognition seems likely to be an especially fruitful area for research on the effects of diversity on group functioning.

Note

We thank Paul Paulus and Bernard Nijstad for their helpful comments and advice.

References

Amabile, T. M. (1996). *Creativity in context.* Boulder, CO: Westview.
Ancona, D. G., & Caldwell, D. F. (1993). Demography and design: Predictors of new product team performance. *Organization Science, 3*, 321–341.

Argote, L., Insko, C. A., Yovetich, N., & Romero, A. A. (1995). Group learning curves: The effects of turnover and task complexity on group performance. *Journal of Applied Social Psychology, 25,* 512–529.

Arrow, H., McGrath, J. E., & Berdahl, J. L. (2000). *Small groups as complex systems: Formation, coordination, development, and adaptation.* Thousand Oaks, CA: Sage.

Austin, J. R. (1997). A cognitive framework for understanding demographic influences in groups. *International Journal of Organizational Analysis, 5,* 342–359.

Bantel, K. A., & Jackson, S. E. (1989). Top management and innovations in banking: Does the composition of the top team make a difference? *Strategic Management Journal, 10,* 107–124.

Bartel, C. A., & Saavedra, R. (2000). The collective construction of work group moods. *Administrative Science Quarterly, 45,*197–231.

Bettenhausen, K., & Murnighan, J. K. (1985). The emergence of norms in competitive groups. *Administrative Science Quarterly, 30,* 350–372.

Bindeman, S. (1998). Echoes of silence: A phenomenological study of the creative process. *Creativity Research Journal, 11,* 69–77.

Brewer, M. B. (1979). In-group bias in the minimal intergroup situation: A cognitive-motivational analysis. *Psychological Bulletin, 86,* 307–324.

Brewer, M. B. (1995). Managing diversity: The role of social identities. In S. E. Jackson & M. N. Ruderman (Eds.), *Diversity in work teams: Research paradigms for a changing workplace* (pp. 47–68). Washington, DC: American Psychological Association.

Brewer, M. B., & Kramer, R. M. (1986). Choice behaviors in social dilemmas: Effects of social identity, group size, and decision framing. *Journal of Personality and Social Psychology, 50,* 543–549.

Byrne, D. (1971). *The attraction paradigm.* New York: Academic Press.

Carnevale, P. J., & Probst, T. M. (1998). Social values and social conflict in creative problem solving and categorization. *Journal of Personality and Social Psychology, 74,* 1300–1309.

Carver, C. S., & Scheier, M. F. (1998). *On the self-regulation of behavior.* Cambridge, UK: Cambridge University Press.

Cox, T. (1993). *Cultural diversity in organizations.* San Francisco: Berrett-Kohler.

Crabbe, A. (1990). *The coach's guide to future problem solving.* Aberdeen, NC: Future Problem Solving Program.

De Dreu, C. K. W., & West, M. A. (2001). Minority dissent and team innovation: The importance of participation in decision making. *Journal of Applied Psychology, 86,* 1191–1201.

Deutsch, M. (1973). *The resolution of conflict.* New Haven: Yale University Press.

Dougherty, D., & Hardy, C. (1996). Sustained product innovation in large, mature organizations: Overcoming innovation-to-organization problems. *Academy of Management Journal, 39,* 1120–1153.

Edmondson, A. (1999). Psychological safety and learning behavior in work teams. *Administrative Science Quarterly, 44,* 350–383.

Fiske, S. T., & Taylor, S. E. (1991). *Social cognition* (2nd ed.). New York: McGraw Hill.

Forgas, J. P. (1992). Affect in social judgments and decisions: A multiprocess model. *Advances in Experimental Social Psychology, 25,* 227–275.

Fredrickson, B. L. (1998). What good are positive emotions? *Review of General Psychology, 2,* 300–319.

Frijda, N. H. (1986). *The emotions.* Cambridge, UK: Cambridge University Press.

Gallupe, R. B., Bastianutti, L. M., & Cooper, W. H. (1991). Unblocking brainstorming. *Journal of Applied Psychology, 76,* 137–142.

Gersick, C. J. (1988). Time and transition in work teams: Towards a new model of group development. *Academy of Management Journal, 31,* 9–41.

Gersick, C. J. G., & Hackman, J. R. (1990). Habitual routines in task-performing groups. *Organizational Behavior and Human Decision Processes, 47,* 65–97.

Goodman, P. S. (1986). Impact of task and technology on group performance. In P. S. Goodman (Ed.), *Designing effective work groups* (pp. 120–167). San Francisco: Jossey-Bass.

Green, J. D., & Sedikides, C. (1999). Affect and self-focused attention revisited: The role of affect orientation. *Personality and Social Psychology Bulletin, 25,* 104–119.

Gruenfeld, D. H. (1995). Status, ideology, and integrative complexity on the U.S. Supreme Court: Rethinking the politics of political decision making. *Journal of Personality and Social Psychology, 68,* 5–20.

Guilford, J. P. (1950). Creativity. *American Psychologist, 5,* 444–454.

Hackman, J. R. (1987). The design of work teams. In J. W. Lorsch (Ed.), *Handbook of organizational behavior* (pp. 315–342). Englewood Cliffs, NJ: Prentice-Hall.

Hackman, J. R. (Ed.) (1990). *Groups that work (and those that don't).* San Francisco: Jossey-Bass.

Hackman, J. R. (1992). Group influences on individuals in organizations. In M. D. Dunnette & L. M. Hough (Eds.), *Handbook of industrial and organizational psychology* (2nd ed., pp. 199–267). Palo Alto, CA: Consulting Psychologists Press.

Hackman, J. R., Brousseau, K. R., & Weiss, J. A. (1976). The interaction of task design and group performance strategies in determining group effectiveness. *Organizational Behavior and Human Performance, 16,* 350–365.

Hackman, J. R., & Morris, C. G. (1975). Group tasks, group interaction processes, and group performance effectiveness: A review and proposed integration. In L. Berkowitz (Ed.), *Advances in experimental social psychology* (Vol. 8, pp. 45–99). New York: Academic Press.

Hargadon, A., & Sutton, R. I. (1997). Technology brokering and innovation in a product development firm. *Administrative Science Quarterly, 42,* 716–749.

Hinsz, V. B., Tindale, R. S., & Vollrath, D. A. (1997). The emerging conceptualization of groups as information processes. *Psychological Bulletin, 121,* 43–64.

Hogg, M. A., & Abrams, D. (1988). *Social identifications: A social psychology of intergroup relations and group processes.* London: Routledge.

Homma, M., Tajima, K., & Hayashi, M. (1995). The effects of misperception of performance in brainstorming groups. *Japanese Journal of Experimental Social Psychology, 34,* 221–231.

Isen, A. M., Daubman, K. A., & Nowicki, G. P. (1987). Positive affect facilitates creative problem solving. *Journal of Personality and Social Psychology, 52,* 1122–1131.

Izard, C. E. (1977). *Human emotions.* New York: Plenum Press.

Jackson, S. E. (1992). Consequences of group composition for the interpersonal dynamics of strategic issue processing. In J. Dutton, A. Huff, & P. Shrivastava (Eds.), *Advances in strategic management* (Vol. 8, pp. 345–382). Greenwich, CT: JAI Press.

Jackson, S. E., Brett, J. F., Sessa, V. I., Cooper, D. M., Julin, J. A. & Peyronnin, K. (1991). Some differences make a difference: Individual dissimilarity and group heterogeneity as correlates of recruitment, promotions, and turnover. *Journal of Applied Psychology, 76,* 675–689.

Jackson, S. E., May, K. E., & Whitney, K. (1995). Understanding the dynamics of diversity in decision making teams. In R. A. Guzzo & E. Salas (Eds.), *Team effectiveness and decision making in organizations* (pp. 204–226). San Francisco: Jossey-Bass.

Jehn, K. A. (1995). A multimethod examination of the benefits and detriments of intragroup conflict. *Administrative Science Quarterly, 40,* 256–282.

Jehn, K. A., Chadwick, C., & Thatcher, S. M. (1997). To agree or not to agree: The effects of value congruence, individual demographic dissimilarity, and conflict on workgroup outcomes. *International Journal of Conflict Management, 8,* 287–305.

Jehn, K. A., Northcraft, G. B., & Neale, M. A. (1999). Why differences make a difference: A field study of diversity, conflict, and performance in workgroups. *Administrative Science Quarterly, 44,* 741–763.

Jones, E. E., & Nisbett, R. E. (1972). The actor and the observer: Divergent perspectives of the causes of behavior. In E. E. Jones (Ed.), *Attribution: Perceiving the causes of behavior* (pp. 79–94). Morristown, NJ: General Learning Press.

Jung, D. I., & Sosik, J. J. (1999). Effects of group characteristics on work group performance: A longitudinal investigation. *Group Dynamics: Theory, Research, and Practice, 3,* 279–290.

Katz, D., & Kahn, R. L. (1978). *The social psychology of organizations* (2nd ed.). New York: Wiley.

Katzenstein, G. (1996). The debate on structured debate: Toward a unified theory. *Organizational Behavior and Human Decision Processes, 66,* 316–332.

Keeney, R. L., & Raiffa, H. (1976). *Decisions with multiple objectives: Preferences and value tradeoffs.* New York: Wiley.

Kelley, H. H., & Thibaut, A. (1978). *Interpersonal relations.* New York: Wiley.

Kelly, J. R. (1988). Entrainment in individual and group behavior. In J. E. McGrath (Ed.), *The social psychology of time: New perspectives* (pp. 89–110). Newbury Park, CA: Sage.

Kelly, J. R., & McGrath, J. E. (1985). Effects of time limits and task types on task performance and interaction of four-person groups. *Journal of Personality and Social Psychology, 49,* 395–407.

Kerr, N. L., MacCoun, R. J., & Kramer, G. P. (1996). When are N heads better (or worse) than one? Biased judgment in individuals versus groups. In E. H. Witte (Ed.), *Understanding group behavior, Vol. 1: Consensual action by small groups* (pp. 105–136). Hillsdale, NJ: Erlbaum.

Kessler, E. H., & Chakrabarti, A. K. (1996). Innovation speed: A conceptual model of context, antecedents, and outcomes. *Academy of Management Review, 21,* 1143–1191.

Kitayama, S., & Burnstein, E. (1994). Social influence, persuasion, and group decision making. In T. C. Brock & S. Shavitt (Eds.), *The psychology of persuasion* (pp. 175–193). Needham Heights, MA: Allyn & Bacon.

Kramer, R. M. (1991). Intergroup relations and organizational dilemmas: The role of categorization processes. In L. L. Cummings & B. M. Staw (Eds.), *Research in organizational behavior* (Vol. 13, pp. 191–228). Greenwich, CT: JAI Press.

Kramer, R. M. (1993). Cooperation and organizational identification. In J. K. Murnighan (Ed.), *Social psychology in organizations: Advances in theory and research* (pp. 244–268). Englewood Cliffs, NJ: Prentice-Hall.

Kurtzberg, T. R. (1998). Creative thinking, cognitive aptitude, and integrative joint gain: A study of negotiator creativity. *Creativity Research Journal, 11*, 283–293.

Kurtzberg, T. R. (2002). *Cognitive diversity and subjective versus objective creativity: Being creative and feeling creative.* Working paper, Rutgers University.

Lam, S. S. K., & Schaubroeck, J. (2000). Improving group decisions by better pooling information: A comparative advantage of group decision support systems. *Journal of Applied Psychology, 85*, 565–573.

Larkey, L. K. (1996). Toward a theory of communicative interactions in culturally diverse work groups. *Academy of Management Review, 21*, 463–491.

Lau, D. C., & Murnighan, J. K. (1998). Demographic diversity and faultlines: The compositional dynamics of organizational groups. *Academy of Management Review, 23*, 325–340.

Madjar, N., Oldham, G., & Pratt, M. G. (2002). There's no place like home? The contributions of work and non-work creativity support to employees' creative performance. *Academy of Management Journal, 45*, 757–767.

Marks, M. A., Mathieu, J. E., & Zaccaro, S. J. (2001). A temporally based framework and taxonomy of team processes. *Academy of Management Review, 26*, 356–376.

Martins, L., Milliken, F. J., Wiesenfeld, B., & Salgado, S. (2003). Racioethnic diversity and group members' experiences: The role of the racioethnic diversity of the organizational context. *Group & Organization Management, 28*, 1–32.

Maznevski, M. L. (1994). Understanding our differences: Performance in decision making groups with diverse members. *Human Relations, 47*, 531–552.

McGrath, J. E. (1984). *Groups: Interaction and performance.* Englewood Cliffs, NJ: Prentice-Hall.

McGrath, J. E., & Rotchford, N. L. (1983). Time and behavior in organizations. In L. L. Cummings & B. M. Staw (Eds.), *Research in Organizational Behavior* (Vol. 5, pp. 57–101). Greenwich, CT: JAI Press.

McLeod, P. L. & Lobel, S. A. (1992). The effects of ethnic diversity on idea generation in small groups. *Academy of Management Best Paper Proceedings*, 227–231.

McLeod, P. L., Lobel, S. A., & Cox, T. H. (1996). Ethnic diversity and creativity in small groups. *Small Group Research, 27*, 248–264.

Mehr, D. G., & Shaver, P. R. (1996). Goal structures in creative motivation. *Journal of Creative Behavior, 30*, 77–104.

Milliken, F. J., & Martins, L. (1996). Searching for common threads: Understanding the multiple effects of diversity in organizational groups. *Academy of Management Review, 21*, 402–433.

Milliken, F. J., Wiesenfeld, B. M., Martins, L. L., Salgado, S. R., & Dunn-Jensen, L. (2001). *Rethinking diversity and its effects: Using configurations to examine the effects of racioethnic and value diversity on group functioning.* Paper presented at the annual meeting of the Academy of Management, Washington, DC.

Mohrman, S. A., Cohen, S. G., & Mohrman, A. M., Jr. (1995). *Designing team-based organizations: New forms of knowledge work.* San Francisco: Jossey-Bass.

Moneta, G. B. (1994). A model of scientists' creative potential: The matching of cognitive structures and domain structure. *Philosophical Psychology, 6*, 23–37.

Moorhead, G., Neck, C. P., & West, M. S. (1998). The tendency toward defective decision making within self-managing teams: The relevance of groupthink for the 21st century. *Organizational Behavior and Human Decision Processes, 73,* 327–351.

Mullen, B., Johnson, C., & Salas, E. (1991). Productivity loss in brainstorming groups: A meta-analytic integration. *Basic and Applied Social Psychology, 12,* 3–23.

Nemeth, C. J. (1986). Differential contributions of majority and minority influence. *Psychological Review, 93,* 23–32.

Nemeth, C. J., Brown, K. S., & Rogers, J. (2001) Devil's advocate versus authentic dissent: Stimulating quantity and quality. *European Journal of Social Psychology, 31,* 1–13.

Nemeth, C. J., Connell, J. B., Rogers, J. D. & Brown, K. S. (2001). Improving decision making by means of dissent. *Journal of Applied Social Psychology, 31,* 48–58.

Osborn, A. F. (1953). *Applied imagination.* New York: Scribner.

Parkinson, B. (1997). Untangling the appraisal-emotion connection. *Personality and Social Psychology Review, 1,* 62–79.

Patel, A. S., & Ramachandrachar, K. (1971). Creativity: Its meaning and measurement. *Education and Psychology Review, 11,* 16–26.

Paulus, P. B. (2000). Groups, teams, and creativity: The creative potential of idea-generating groups. *Applied Psychology: An International Review, 49,* 237–262.

Paulus, P. B., Larey, T. S., & Dzindolet, M. T. (2001). Creativity in groups and teams. In M. E. Turner (Ed.), *Groups at work: Theory and research* (pp. 319–338). Mahwah, NJ: Erlbaum.

Paulus, P. B., Larey, T. S., & Ortega, A. H. (1995). Performance and perceptions of brainstormers in an organizational setting. *Basic and Applied Social Psychology, 17,* 249–265.

Paulus, P. B., & Yang, H. C. (2000). Idea generation in groups: A basis for creativity in organizations. *Organizational Behavior and Human Decision Processes, 82,* 76–87.

Pelled, L. (1996). Demographic diversity, conflict, and work group outcomes. *Organization Science, 78,* 615–631.

Pollick, M. F., & Kumar, V. K. (1997). Creativity styles of supervising managers. *Journal of Creative Behavior, 31,* 260–270.

Rowatt, W. C., Nesselroade, K. P., Beggan, J. K., & Allison, S. T. (1997). Perceptions of brainstorming in groups: The quality over quantity hypothesis. *Journal of Creative Behavior, 31,* 131–150.

Ruscio, J., Whitney, D. & Amabile, T. M. (1998). Looking inside the fishbowl of creativity: Verbal and behavioral predictors of creative performance. *Creativity Research Journal, 11,* 243–263.

Saavedra, R., & Earley, P. C. (1991). Choice of task and goal under conditions of general and specific affective inducement. *Motivation and Emotion, 15,* 45–65.

Saavedra, R., Earley, P. C., & Van Dyne. L. (1993). Complex interdependence in task-performing groups. *Journal of Applied Psychology, 78,* 61–72.

Sapp, D. D. (1992). The point of creative frustration and the creative process: A new look at an old model. *Journal of Creative Behavior, 26,* 21–28.

Schon, D. A. (1983). *The reflective practitioner: How professionals think in action.* New York: Basic Books.

Schwarz, N., & Bless, H. (1991). Happy and mindless, but sad and smart? The impact of affective states on analytical reasoning. In J. P. Forgas (Ed.), *Emotion and social judgments* (pp. 55–71). Oxford: Pergamon Press.

Sherif, M., Harvey, O. J., White, B. J., Hood, W. E., & Sherif, C. W. (1961). *Intergroup conflict and cooperation: The robber's cave experiment*. Norman: University of Oklahoma Book Exchange.

Sosik, J. J., Kahai, S. S., & Avolio, B. J. (1999). Leadership style, anonymity, and creativity in group decision support systems: The mediating role of optimal flow. *Journal of Creative Behavior, 33*, 227–256.

Stasser, G. (1992). Information salience and the discovery of hidden profiles by decision-making groups: A "thought experiment." *Organizational Behavior and Human Decision Processes, 52*, 156–181.

Stasser, G., & Titus, W. (1985). Pooling of unshared information in group decision making: Biased information sampling during discussion. *Journal of Personality and Social Psychology, 48*, 1467–1478.

Stasser, G., Vaughan, S. I., & Stewart, D. D. (2000). Pooling unshared information: The benefits of knowing how access to information is distributed among group members. *Organizational Behavior and Human Decision Processes, 82*, 102–116.

Staw, B. M., Sandelands, L. E., & Dutton, J. E. (1981). Threat-rigidity effects in organizational behavior: A multilevel analysis. *Administrative Science Quarterly, 26*, 501–524.

Stumpf, H. (1995). Scientific creativity: A short overview. *Educational Psychology Review, 7*, 225–241.

Sutton, R. I., & Hargadon, A. (1996). Brainstorming groups in context: Effectiveness in a product design firm. *Administrative Science Quarterly, 41*, 685–718.

Tajfel, H. (1978). The psychological structure of intergroup relations. In H. Tajfel (Ed.), *Differentiation between social groups: Studies in the social psychology of intergroup relations* (pp. 27–100). London: Academic Press.

Tajfel, H., & Turner, J. C. (1986). The social identity theory of intergroup behavior. In S. Worchel and W. G. Austin (Eds.), *Psychology of intergroup relations* (pp. 7–24). Chicago: Nelson-Hall.

Thomas, K. W. (1992). Conflict and negotiation processes in organizations. In M. Dunette & L. Hough (Eds.), *Handbook of industrial and organizational psychology* (pp. 651–718). Palo Alto, CA: Consulting Psychologists Press.

Thorn, D. (1987). Problem solving for innovation in industry. *Journal of Creative Behavior, 21*, 93–107.

Tjosvold, D. (1986). Dynamics of interdependence in organizations. *Human Relations, 39*, 517–540.

Tjosvold, D. (1988). Cooperative and competitive interdependence: Collaborations between departments to serve customers. *Group and Organization Studies, 13*, 274–289.

Torrance, E. P. (1969). *Creativity*. San Rafael, CA: Dimensions Publishing.

Torrance, E. P. (1978). Giftedness in solving future problems. *Journal of Creative Behavior, 12*, 75–86.

Torrance, E. P. (1979). *The search for satori and creativity*. Buffalo, NY: Creative Education Foundation.

Turner, J. C., Hogg, M. A., Oakes, P. J., Reicher, S. D., & Wetherell, M. S. (1987). *Rediscovering the social group: A self-categorization theory*. Oxford: Blackwell.

Turner, J. C., & Horvitz, T. (2001). The dilemma of threat: Group effectiveness and ineffectiveness under adversity. In M. E. Turner (Ed.), *Groups at work: Theory and research* (pp. 445–470). Mahwah, NJ: Erlbaum.

Turner, J. C., Oakes, P. J., Haslam, S. A., & McGarty, C. (1994). Self and collective: Cognition and social context. *Personality and Social Psychology Bulletin, 20,* 454–463.

Valacich, J. S., & Schwenk, C. (1995). Devil's advocate and dialectical inquiry effects on face-to-face and computer mediated group decision making. *Organizational Behavior and Human Decision Processes, 63,* 158–173.

van der Vegt, G., Emans, B., & van de Vliert, E. (1998). Motivating effects of task and outcome interdependence in work teams. *Group and Organization Management, 23,* 124–143.

Van Dyne, L., & Saavedra, R. (1996). A naturalistic minority influence experiment: Effects on divergent thinking, conflict and originality in work-groups. *British Journal of Social Psychology, 35,* 151–167.

Vosberg, S. K. (1998). Mood and the quantity and quality of ideas. *Creativity Research Journal, 11,* 315–331.

Wageman, R. (1995). Interdependence and group effectiveness. *Administrative Science Quarterly, 40,* 145–180.

Waller, M. J. (1999). The timing of adaptive group responses to nonroutine events. *Academy of Management Journal, 42,* 127–137.

Wallgren, M. K. (1998). Reported practices of creative problem solving facilitators. *Journal of Creative Behavior, 32,* 134–148.

Watson, W. E., Kumar, K., & Michaelsen, L. K. (1993). Cultural diversity's impact on interaction process and performance: Comparing homogeneous and diverse task groups. *Academy of Management Journal, 36,* 590–602.

Weingart, L. R. (1992). Impact of group goals, task component complexity, effort, and planning on group performance. *Journal of Applied Psychology, 77,* 682–693.

West, M. A. (1996). Reflexivity and work group effectiveness: A conceptual integration. In M. A. West (Ed.), *Handbook of work group psychology* (pp. 555–579). Chichester, UK: Wiley.

West, M. A. (2000). Reflexivity, revolution, and innovation in work teams. *Advances in Interdisciplinary Studies of Work Teams, 5,* 1–29.

West, M. A. (2002). Sparkling fountains or stagnant ponds. An integrative model of creativity and innovation implementation in work groups. *Applied Psychology: An International Review, 51,* 355–389.

Williams, K., & O'Reilly, C. (1998). Demography and diversity in organizations: A review of 40 years of research. *Research in Organizational Behavior, 20,* 77–140.

Woodman, R. W., Sawyer, J. E., & Griffin, R. W. (1993). Toward a theory of organizational creativity. *Academy of Management Review, 18,* 293–321.

4

Charlan Jeanne Nemeth and Brendan Nemeth-Brown

Better than Individuals?
The Potential Benefits of Dissent
and Diversity for Group Creativity

Groups are notoriously fallible when it comes to decision making and productivity (Hinsz, 1990; McGrath, 1984; Shepperd, 1993). Rather than profit from the resources that are available from each individual, groups often make poor decisions, some resulting in "fiascoes" (Janis, 1982). When it comes to creativity, the available literature repeatedly demonstrates that groups rarely achieve the level of the sum of the individuals (McGrath, 1984). The question, of course, is why groups are so suboptimal in performance. Is it the nature of groups to "dumb down" individual judgment, or is it the result of a particular set of processes that often occur in groups? Several researchers have argued the latter (e.g., Hackman & Morris, 1975) and have pointed to the importance of group strategies, member efforts, and the level and distribution of task-relevant skills. Others, reviewed below, focus on the influence processes that occur within groups and their importance for the quality of decision making and performance.

Much research documents that one of the culprits for poor group decision making is the desire for consensus. This desire leads to premature closure, such as that evidenced by research on groupthink. It leads to agreement with majority views, right or wrong, and it leads to extremism on issues where there is fundamental agreement. Attempts to raise the level of group creativity and decision making often focus on eliminating some of the hindrances or obstacles. The goal is to raise the level of group functioning to that of the sum of the individuals that compose the group. We argue, however, that groups can actually perform better than the sum of their individuals, and we emphasize the role of dissent. Dissent, as we document, can liberate individuals from conformity pressures and, more important, can stimulate thought that considers more information and more options and culminates in better decision making and productivity. The conflict generated by dissent, however, is not without costs, and we attempt to find ways to profit from dissent while maintaining unity and morale.

The Strain for Consensus: Groupthink

Part of the reason for the suboptimal performance of groups is that people strongly desire consensus, even straining for consensus, as argued by Janis (1982), under the rubric of groupthink. This popular and catchy term was applied to Janis's analysis of foreign policy decisions that were truly disastrous. The Bay of Pigs invasion is one such example. In 1961 President John Kennedy and his advisors tried to overthrow Fidel Castro with an invasion of Cuba by 1,400 CIA-trained Cuban exiles. The result was that nearly all were captured or killed, the United States was humiliated, and Cuba aligned itself even closer with the USSR. By all accounts, this was a truly poor decision.

In analyzing such fiascoes, Janis (1982) theorized that failure was not due to the stupidity of the participants. After all, in the Bay of Pigs decision, the group was composed of individuals such as Arthur Schlesinger (a noted Harvard historian), Robert McNamara (Secretary of Defense and former President of the Ford Motor Co.), Dean Rusk (Secretary of State and former head of the Rockefeller Foundation), and McGeorge Bundy (Dean of Harvard Letters and Science). Rather, he argued that groupthink arises from a situation marked by homogeneity of its members, strong and directed leadership, group isolation, and high cohesion. When people are similar, close-knit, isolated from contrary views, and have a strong leader who expresses a clear preference, groups strain to find a consensus around the preferred position.

Some by-products of such a tendency are that individuals are reluctant to voice dissent, to examine the negative aspects of the preferred position, to seriously consider alternatives, and to systematically develop contingency plans. The reluctance to voice dissent, even when such thoughts are contemplated, arises not only from self-censorship but also from pressures to conformity. People are made to feel that dissent is an obstacle to achieving a goal and a sign of disloyalty. One should "get on board" (see, generally, Janis, 1982; Esser & Lindoerfer, 1989; Moorhead, Ference, & Neck, 1991).

Such a description is not unlike that demonstrated by cults. There, too, cohesion, strong and directed leadership, and isolation are characteristics of such groups that achieve loyalty and adherence to positions—even those that result in members' suicide. Members fear the expression of dissent and the group quickly and consistently punishes its expression (Conway & Siegelman, 1979; Ornstein, 1991).

The Strain for Consensus: Majority Influence and Silence

Such reluctance to voice dissent and the strong pressure for consensus, perhaps exacerbated in the situations described above, are relatively common phenomena and can perhaps be understood in the context of experimental studies of conformity. In those studies, an individual is faced with a majority of others who offer a judgment differing from that of the individual. Literally hundreds of studies have documented that consensus is often achieved on the position taken by the majority. People often agree with the majority, even when they are wrong (Allen & Levine, 1969; Kiesler & Kiesler, 1969).

This is illustrated in the classic study on conformity by Asch (1956), in which people simply judged which of three lines was equal in length to a standard. Alone, people judged the stimuli correctly; it was an easy and relatively unambiguous task. When faced with a majority who agreed on a different (and erroneous) judgment, many individuals abdicated the information from their own senses and agreed with the incorrect majority. On average, 35% of the responses were in agreement with the erroneous majority, and nearly everyone agreed with the incorrect majority at least once. In naturalistic studies, the power of the majority is even more apparent. In a study by Kalven and Zeisel (1966) on decision making by actual juries, the vast majority of verdicts could be predicted by the initial ballot. The position favored by a majority of 7 to 11 jurors was the final verdict nearly 90% of the time. So why does the majority "win" even when they are wrong?

The reluctance to remain independent, to say what one "sees," appears to occur for two reasons. First, faced with a unanimous majority that differs from one's own judgment, one often assumes that the majority must be correct; error must lie with the minority position. Second, people fear the rejection and ridicule they believe will ensue from maintaining a minority position (Deutsch & Gerard, 1955). They often state that they fear "sticking out like a sore thumb" or being ridiculed. Such concerns are also voiced in organizations. For example, Ryan and Oestreich (1991) interviewed 260 employees from 22 different organizations. More than 70% expressed fear about speaking up—at least when it came to problems at work. Their stated reasons, much like the subjects in the experimental studies, were that negative repercussions were likely to ensue and that voicing their concerns would make little, if any, difference.

Although one might wish that such fears were ill-founded, the available evidence suggests that people *are* punished for dissent. In experimental studies, people who maintain a minority position are targets of communication aimed at changing their minds. If unsuccessful, they are rejected and disliked (Nemeth & Wachtler, 1983; Schachter, 1951). Thus, we see that there is a good basis for concern over the voicing of a dissenting minority opinion. This becomes exacerbated when one considers dissenting with one's superior. Some researchers (Summerfield, 1990) estimate that at least 7 out of 10 people in American business remain silent when their opinions are at odds with their superiors. Even when they know better, they permit their boss to make mistakes.

Such fears of rejection and reluctance to voice dissent are evident even in the groupthink examples given above. Following the Bay of Pigs Cabinet-level decision, Schlesinger (1972) bitterly reproached himself for "having kept so silent during those crucial decisions" but still felt that "a course of objection would have accomplished little save to gain me a name as a nuisance" (quoted in Janis, 1982, p. 39). Thus, one sees that individuals at even the highest level of power are reluctant to be in a minority.

The fact that people share such views exacerbates the problem. In organizational settings, for example, there is considerable evidence of a shared perception that expressing dissent is either futile or dangerous This has been termed "organizational silence" (Morrison & Milliken, 2000) and is an illustration of a more general phenomenon: that shared beliefs extremize individual judgments and concerns. This adds to the individual's tendency to remain silent about problems or issues encountered at work.

The Strain for Consensus: Polarization

The notion that shared beliefs exacerbate perceptions and behaviors is well documented in the social psychological literature under the term *polarization*. Even without the drama of a directed leader or crisis, as found in the groupthink work, there is considerable evidence that discussion among like-minded people can extremize their views and enhance their confidence in those views (Fraser, 1971; Moscovici & Zavalloni, 1969). The general phenomenon is as follows.

When individuals favor a particular side of the issue but differ in their specific judgments, discussion often leads to consensus, but the consensus position is more extreme than the average of the individual judgments. Further, the individuals themselves become more extreme and more confident in their position. Thus, if the individuals are essentially risky in a given situation, the group decision (and their own subsequent individual judgments) will be more risky after group deliberation. If they start out cautious, the decision and individual judgments will be more cautious. If they are anti-American, they will become more anti-American; if they are pro–de Gaulle, they become more so; if they believe a person is guilty of a crime, they become more convinced after discussion with like-minded people. The phenomenon is powerful and pervasive over many situations (see, generally, Moscovici & Doise, 1974; Myers & Bishop, 1970).

The elements that appear to create polarization are (1) a normative quality to the issue such that people favor a given pole or direction; (2) differences among group members in their specific judgments; and (3) discussion among these group members. Under such circumstances, the findings are consistent and replicable across a broad range of judgments. The group and, subsequently, the individuals become more extreme in the direction of the desired pole (Isenberg, 1986; Moscovici & Doise, 1974; Myers & Lamm, 1976).

Such a phenomenon helps to explain why homogeneity of members coupled with high levels of interaction and intolerance of dissent are successful in maintaining and even exacerbating the beliefs held in corporate culture or cults (C. O'Reilly, 1989; C. O'Reilly & Chatman, 1996). In these settings, interactions with insiders who hold similar beliefs are encouraged and, in some cases, required. This, coupled with an intolerance of dissent, leads to more extreme views and more confidence in those views.

The Problem with Majorities

Majority Influence—Whether to Truth or to Error

As demonstrated above, majority influence is strong and pervasive, even on issues that are factual and where there is a clear correct answer. Ordinarily, the majority position and reality coincide, which is one reason we assume—perhaps all too readily—that truth must lie with the majority judgment. Such persuasive power is not only evident in face-to-face groups, such as those in the experiments or in natural juries, but is widely used as a technique to induce desired behavior.

The ploy that "everyone is doing it" or that "everyone desires it" is a favorite technique of many advertisers and even public service messages. Rhoads and Cialdini (2002) point out the pervasiveness of such tactics, which range from information that a product is the "largest selling" or "fastest growing" to the "salting" of tip jars with dollar bills to give the impression that previous customers tipped with paper money rather than coins. Street musicians and panhandlers apparently know this technique as well. However, it can also backfire. As Rhoads and Cialdini point out, the high incidence of suicide and drug use sends the message that many people are participating in these undesirable behaviors and may unintentionally influence others to mimic them.

The real difficulty with majority views, especially when they are unanimous, is that people move to the majority position whether it is right or wrong (Nemeth & Wachtler, 1983). Thus, the power of the majority, which has even been termed "the tyranny of the majority" (Mill, 1859/1979), is so strong that it induces agreement often without reflection or consideration of the issue. In Janis's (1982) work, for example, the strain for consensus produced defective decision-making processes, among which were an incomplete survey of alternatives and objectives, poor information search, lack of scrutiny of the preferred alternative, and a failure to work out contingency plans. In those decision-making groups and in experimental studies, people are reluctant to voice dissent even if they recognize problems or consider alternatives. Perhaps more important, they are even less able to think about or consider alternatives.

Majorities Induce Convergent Thinking

Although adoption of a majority position that is incorrect is an undesirable outcome, there is a more subtle and possibly insidious aspect of majority views. Faced with a unanimous majority, people think from the perspective of the majority to the exclusion of other considerations. In other words, when one is faced with a majority of individuals who agree with each other on a position that differs from one's own, one not only doubts one's own position and feels pressure to agree with the majority, but, in a kind of tunnel vision, one thinks about the issue almost solely from the perspective of the majority (Nemeth, 1986).

The tendency to focus on the issue almost solely from the perspective of the majority arises, in part, from the stress of being in the minority. Individuals faced with a disagreeing majority report a great deal of stress (Nemeth & Wachtler, 1983). Stress has been found to affect attention: there is a concentration on the focal and not on peripheral stimuli, and there is a narrowing of the range of alternatives considered (Easterbrook, 1959). However, majorities do not induce just any kind of focus; they stimulate a focus that takes the majority perspective. The reason for this appears to lie in the fact that people try to understand why the majority takes its position and, further, they are motivated to find that perspective acceptable because that will permit agreement (Nemeth, 1995).

As a demonstration of this phenomenon, a study by Nemeth and Kwan (1987) gave individuals in groups of four a series of 5-letter strings (e.g., tMARe) and asked them to name the first 3-letter word they noticed. Under short exposures, all individuals named the word in capital letters from left to right (*mar* in the example). After 5 such letter strings, they were given feedback on the judgments of the four individuals. In the majority condition, they were led to believe that 3 of the 4 individuals first noticed the word formed by the backward sequencing of the capital letters (e.g., *ram*). Thus, they each believed that the other three individuals in their group agreed on a position different from their own and that this position was achieved by a backward sequencing of the capital letters. This was consistent over the 5-letter strings. Subsequently, they were given a new series of letter strings and were asked to name *all* the words they could form from the letters. They were given 15 seconds for each letter string. A control group was given no feedback on the responses of the individuals.

Comparing the majority condition and the control, there were no significant differences in the number of words they were able to find. However, the way they found the words differed considerably. People in the majority condition used the perspective of the majority to the detriment of other strategies. Consider the ways in which words can be formed: (1) one can use the letters from left to right (forward sequencing; in the example "tMARe," such words might be *tar, mar,* and *are*); (2) one can use the letters from right to left, as did the majority (backward sequencing; *rat, ram* and *eat*); (3) one can form words using the letters in some combination of forward and backward sequencing (mixed sequencing; *mat, art, ear* or *tear*). Compared to the control, those in the majority condition found more words using the backward sequencing of letters and fewer words using the forward or mixed sequencing. In other words, they adopted the perspective of the majority to the exclusion of other considerations.

Such a tendency for majorities to stimulate thinking that focuses on the majority perspective is evident in other studies as well. In an embedded figures task (Nemeth & Wachtler, 1983), for example, individuals were asked to name which of 6 comparison figures contained an embedded figure. When a majority made its selection, people adopted that position; they were not able to see the embedded figure not named by the majority.

Convergent Thought Can Be Adaptive

In general, convergent thinking is maladaptive in that alternatives are not fully considered; however, there can be positive aspects of such cognitive processes. In more naturalistic settings, for example, convergent thinking from the majority perspective may lead to a clear following of norms and agreement with goals (C. O'Reilly 1989). It is likely to result in efficiency and in the attainment of the agreed-upon goals (Collins & Porras, 1994). Further, such focus may aid groups in evaluating alternative perspectives and eliminating poor alternatives (Larey & Paulus, 1999).

One can see the operation of such advantages in an experimental study (Nemeth, Mosier, & Chiles, 1992). Whereas performance on most tasks is enhanced by a consideration of alternatives or multiple perspectives, this study used a task where convergent thinking is adaptive. This was done partly to demonstrate the generality of the phenomenon and partly to show that the consequences for performance of convergent thought depends on the requirements of the situation.

The experiment utilized the Stroop task (Stroop, 1935), one of the few tasks where convergent thought can be adaptive. Here, the ability to focus from one perspective while ignoring alternatives is advantageous, provided the focus is on the appropriate dimension. In this task, individuals are shown a series of color words (e.g., black, blue, green, red). However, the words are printed in an ink of a different color. For example, the word *green* might appear in red ink; the word *yellow* might appear in blue ink. The task is to read as quickly and accurately as possible the ink color (red and blue in the examples). The difficulty is that one tends to say the color word (*green* and yellow in the examples). In such a task, convergent thinking is adaptive provided one can focus on ink color; performance is improved if one can concentrate on the color of ink and ignore the color word. Conversely, concentration on the color word to the exclusion of the ink color is maladaptive.

In this study, individuals in groups of 4 were shown a slide on which were printed two color words. One was printed in an ink that was consistent with the word (e.g., the word *red* printed in red ink); the second was printed in an ink that was inconsistent with its word (e.g., the word *yellow* printed in green ink). Under short exposures, the first color noticed by all individuals was red. Feedback, however, indicated that 3 of the 4 individuals first noticed a different color. In one condition, this was the color word (*yellow* in the example). In a second condition, this was the ink color (green in the example). Subsequently, they were tested on the Stroop task. Individuals tried to read the color of ink as quickly and accurately as possible. As theorized, performance was greatly improved when individuals were exposed to a majority who concentrated on the ink color in the first session. Performance was greatly diminished when they were exposed to a majority who concentrated on the color word in the first session. In other words, they took the perspective of the majority in both cases. When that perspective was appropriate, performance was enhanced; when inappropriate, performance was diminished.

Consensus and Creativity

Convergent thought may have a place in efficiency, but it is unlikely to aid the generation of creative ideas (Hackman, 1990; Nemeth, 1997). Creativity generally requires novelty, a uniqueness or unusualness to the idea, plus appropriateness to solving a given problem (Amabile, 1983; Barron, 1968).[1] Thus, there is originality and a product: a solution.

Minimally, creativity, at least at the level of idea generation, tends to include flexibility, a term more identified with divergent than convergent thought (Guilford, 1950). Flexibility involves thinking in different conceptual categories. As an illustration, people who generate ideas for uses of a brick might come up with building a home, building a road, and building a factory. These are three different ideas but all represent a given conceptual category. This is evidence of relatively convergent thinking. Someone else might mention building a house, using the brick as a missile, and using it as a doorstop. Again there are three ideas but they represent different categories of thought. This is illustrative of divergent thinking.

As one tries to understand why groups are less creative than the sum of their individuals, the same considerations of cohesion, fear of dissent, and convergent thinking appear to be relevant. Hackman and Morris (1975), for example, argue that an important reason groups fail to outperform individuals is their premature movement to consensus, with dissenting opinions being suppressed or dismissed. In studies of brainstorming, there is ample evidence that interacting groups produce about half as many ideas as do the same number of individuals acting alone (Diehl & Stroebe, 1991; Larey & Paulus, 1999). One of the reasons for such lowered creativity appears to be a fear of evaluation. People worry that others will judge them negatively.

In a study by Camacho and Paulus (1995), such fear of evaluation was studied as an individual difference variable. Groups were composed either of individuals who were highly concerned about how others perceive and evaluate them or who had very low concern about such perceptions and evaluations. The researchers found that, for individual performance, the two types of individuals did not differ. As a group, however, those highly concerned about evaluation performed much more poorly than did those with low concern. The suggestion is that such concern leads to "social or cognitive inhibition," which would be one reason for low creativity in groups.

Reduced creativity in groups is also a by-product of the desire for consensus. The desire for consensus is not just operative in premature closure or movement to the majority; even the discussion is altered. Substantial evidence exists that individuals in groups tend to share and discuss ideas that they already have in common (Larey & Paulus, 1999; Stewart & Stasser, 1995;). The noncommon ideas are less likely to find expression and, thus, do not provide a basis for consideration of alternative or new ideas (for other lines of reasoning, see Nijstad, Diehl, & Stroebe, this volume; Paulus & Brown, this volume).

Still another reason for reduced creativity in groups is the convergent thinking stimulated by majorities. There is evidence, for example, that majorities stimulate less novel or original thinking. In one such study, Nemeth and Kwan (1985) showed individuals a series of blue slides and asked them to name the color they saw as well as indicate the perceived brightness. In one condition, they were exposed to a majority who agreed that the stimuli were all "green." In the control condition, they were not exposed to any judgments of others. Subsequent to this situation, they gave word associations to the words *blue* and *green* (7 associations to each word). Compared to a control group, those exposed to a unanimous (but erroneous) majority gave quite different associations.

Associations to a given word can be scaled in terms of their likelihood. In other words, a large percentage of people will respond to the word *blue* with "sky" and will respond to *green* with the association "grass." These are very common associations in that there is a high probability of their occurrence. Less common are associations to *blue* such as "jazz" and "jeans." The probability of a given association can be found in tables such as that produced by Keppel and Postman (1970). In the Nemeth and Kwan (1985) study, those exposed to a majority who called blue slides green, gave more conventional associations than did the control group. Whereas the first association in both conditions tends to be fairly conventional, the control group becomes more original from the second through the seventh association. By contrast, those in the majority condition remained conventional in their associations. The difference between the two conditions is highly significant and supports the notion that majority judgments can reduce the likelihood of creativity or novelty of response.

Value of Dissent

Given the problems associated with homogeneity, consensus, and majority views for both the quality of group decision making and creative idea generation, the question arises as to how one can counteract such processes and improve the divergence and creativity of ideas. One important antidote appears to be dissent. It is a liberator of thought and, perhaps more important, a stimulus to divergent and creative thought.

Dissent as Liberator

In the early studies of conformity, the majority consisted of a relatively large number of individuals who were unanimous. Subsequent research showed that one needed only three or four individuals in the majority to induce conformity; conformity increased as the majority rose to three or four individuals, after which, number made little difference. Thus, if you were going to conform, you would do so when faced with as few as three individuals in the majority. Raising the majority to 15 would not raise the amount of conformity (Asch, 1955, 1956). More important was whether the majority was unanimous. When unanimous, the majority wielded considerable power.

If a nonmajority individual had an ally in the group, however, conformity was drastically reduced (Asch, 1956). With an ally (a person who agreed with the subject and with the truth), conformity dropped to less than 10%, even if there were 15 in the majority. Such a finding may not appear surprising, especially in light of the fact that the ally's agreement might have raised the individual's confidence in the position and in himself or herself. Further, the ally's position is correct and corroborates the information from one's own senses. Perhaps not so self-evident are the findings that a dissenter, even one who disagrees with both the subject and the majority, also leads to a substantial reduction in conformity. Thus, we have a very interesting finding: dissent, even when it is wrong, serves to liberate the individual from a tendency to conform. In those studies, the individual was able to utilize the information from his or her own senses, ignore the erroneous but unanimous majority, and make accurate judgments (Allen & Levine, 1969).

To make the point even stronger, we now have evidence that exposure to a dissenter (one who persists in a position differing from a unanimous majority) can enhance independence even in subsequent settings. In one study, Nemeth and Chiles (1988) exposed individuals to dissent or to no dissent in a group asked to make judgments of color. Either everyone judged blue slides to be "blue" or there was one individual who consistently called the slides "green." Subsequent to this setting, subjects found themselves in a situation where they were now in the minority. A unanimous majority (three other people) consistently judged a series of red slides as "orange." The slides were not ambiguous; when alone, people were clear that the slides were red. Those exposed to no prior dissent conformed overwhelmingly: when faced with a majority who called the red slides "orange," over 70% of the responses were "orange." Simple exposure to dissent in a prior setting, however, liberated these individuals; they now called the red slides "red." In fact, the reduction in conformity was so dramatic that it was essentially zero.

Dissent as Stimulator of Divergent Thought

Perhaps one of the most important contributions of dissent is its ability to stimulate thinking about the issue from multiple perspectives (Nemeth, 1986). Further, the research offers special promise in that the contributions made by dissenting viewpoints appear to occur regardless of whether or not the dissenter is correct.

There are now a substantial number of studies, using very different paradigms and settings and conducted in different countries, that underscore this basic theoretical premise (De Dreu & De Vries, 1993; Nemeth, 1986; Volpato, Maass, Mucchi-Faina, & Vitti, 1990): minorities stimulate divergent thought, a consideration of the issue from multiple perspectives. This is manifested in the search for information, the use of strategies, thoughts about the issue, detection of novel solutions, and creativity of solutions (Nemeth, 1995). Some studies have shown that minority dissent, even when wrong, stimulates a search for information. Importantly, people search for information on all sides of the issue (Nemeth & Rogers, 1996).

Minority dissent stimulates the use of more strategies in the service of performance. Thus, in the Nemeth and Kwan (1987) study reported above with letter strings, majorities stimulated the use of the majority strategy (backward sequencing of letters). When a minority (of one in a group of four) repeatedly used the backward sequencing of letters, it stimulated the use of all strategies. Compared to a control group and the majority condition, those exposed to the minority position found more words overall on the anagram test. Further, they found the words using forward, backward, and mixed sequencing of letters.

Other studies demonstrate that minority dissent, because it stimulates a reappraisal of the situation and consideration of more aspects of the situation, serves the detection of solutions. In the embedded figure study outlined above, a differing position espoused by a minority of individuals stimulated a search of the full stimulus array and, in the process, led to detection of novel solutions that otherwise would have gone undetected (Nemeth & Wachtler, 1983). Such a finding that minorities stimulate the detection of more solutions can also be found in group decision-making settings, experimental or natural. There is evidence that minorities stimulate more thought about the issue and thought directed at more alternatives (De Dreu & De Vries, 1993; Martin & Noyes, 1996; Nemeth, Connell, Rogers, & Brown, 2001). Groups make better decisions (Van Dyne & Saavedra, 1996) when a minority view is consistently maintained.

Dissent as Stimulator of Creative Thought and Solutions

There is even evidence of greater creativity in response to minority dissent. To illustrate, the study by Nemeth and Kwan (1987) reported above showed how majorities can stimulate more conventional thinking. People exposed to a disagreeing majority had less original word associations than did a control group.

However, that study had another condition, one in which the disagreement came from a minority, a single individual. In that condition, a minority judged blue slides to be "green." When the dissent came from a minority, the associations to the words *blue* and *green* were highly original.

Compared to the control, those exposed to a minority judgment gave significantly more original associations, those with a low statistical probability. Thus, this study demonstrated two quite different phenomena. Compared to the control (no exposure to disagreement), majorities stimulated more conventional thought (less original associations) and minorities stimulated more original thought. Faced with disagreement from a majority about what is blue or green, people have highly conventional associations to these words; for example, their response to *blue* might be "sky." Faced with disagreement from a minority about what is blue or green, their associations are much more original or statistically infrequent; for example, their response to *blue* might be "jazz." Further evidence of the same kind of phenomenon comes from a study by De Dreu and De Vries (1993), who found that individuals generated more original word associations when confronted with a minority perspective.

Other studies show that minority dissent can stimulate creative solutions to problems. For example, Nemeth, Rogers, and Brown (2001) used a simulated work setting to investigate solutions to a problem with vacation scheduling. In the discussion, individuals in groups were either exposed or not to a dissenting opinion. Subsequent to the interaction, they were asked to come up with as many good solutions as they could to the general problem. Those exposed to minority dissent came up with more, and more creative solutions than did individuals in a control group (no dissent). Such findings are corroborated by studies of group decision making in both educational and organizational settings (Van Dyne & Saavedra, 1996; Volpato et al., 1990). In fact, the evidence from a study on existing organizations by De Dreu and West (2001) shows that dissent increases innovation in work teams but primarily when individuals participate in decision making. Thus, dissent can increase not only creative idea generation but also the implementation of creative ideas via the mechanism of high participation in decision making.

Gaining Perspective

The Role of Diversity

Apart from the stimulating properties of dissent, many researchers have argued that one way to raise the number of perspectives is to have a diverse workforce. The research, however, is complex. Diversity may raise the level of creativity in groups, but there are also a number of studies indicating little benefit in terms of creativity (Bantel & Jackson, 1989; Jackson, May, & Whitney, 1995; Williams & O'Reilly, 1998). The general pattern is that team task-related diversity is related to higher-quality team decision making (Gruenfeld, 1995; Jackson, 1992).

From the perspective of this chapter, diversity may be similar but is not identical to dissent. First, the fact that there exists some form of demographic diversity (e.g., ethnicity, gender, race) does not necessarily imply a difference in perspective that is applicable to the task at hand. One has only to look at Cabinet-level appointments to see that one can have varieties in gender and race but still achieve homogeneity of perspective.

Second, even if a differing perspective is held, it is not necessarily expressed (Janis, 1982; Morrison & Milliken, 2000; Nemeth, 1997). Most people are afraid to voice dissent or to raise questions about the status quo (Lawler, 1992; Pfeffer, 1994). This lack of voice can be one reason diversity, or at least diverse views, are not considered and, thus, available resources are not utilized. Third, even if a differing view is held and expressed, it is not necessarily maintained over time. A boundary condition for the substantial research showing the stimulating value of minority views for creative thought and solutions is that the minority view must be maintained over time (Nemeth, 1995; Nemeth, Mayseless, Sherman, & Brown, 1990). Thus, diversity can be a prelude to dissent but is not the same as dissent.

It should also be pointed out that diverse groups may not contain a majority versus a minority opinion. In fact, there may be multiple minorities; each individual may hold a differing position, making everyone a minority. This situation is quite different from one where two competing "truths" are argued, one held by a majority and the other by a minority of individuals. Some recent evidence (Brodbeck, Kerschreiter, Mojzisch, Frey, & Schulz-Hardt, 2002) suggests that when each person prefers a different alternative, consideration of unshared information and likelihood of discovering a superior solution are improved. There is also evidence that diversity enhances the quality of decision making when it gives rise to debate and disagreement (Simons, Pelled, & Smith, 1999). In keeping with the premises of this chapter, we argue that conflict among competing positions may be essential for raising the quality of decision making and creative solutions.

Role-Playing Techniques

There is a potential downside to diversity, much as we found with dissent. Morale and job satisfaction can be lowered and identification with the group can be weakened (Flynn & Chatman, 2001; Milliken & Martins, 1996). The question, of course, is whether diversity and dissent necessarily fragment the group and lower morale and job satisfaction. In an attempt to raise diversity of views while ameliorating conflict and potential lowered morale, some researchers have advocated forms of structured debate. Techniques such as devil's advocate, for example, were recommended by Janis (1982) in his analysis of Cabinet-level fiascoes. Leonard and Swap (1999) suggest that devil's advocate is a good way to invite dissent and thus creativity, as have numerous other studies and reviews (Cosier, 1978; De Dreu & West, 2001; Katzenstein, 1996).

The origins of such a technique lie in a practice of the Roman Catholic Church in the early 16th century. When a person was proposed for beatification or canonization to sainthood, someone was assigned the role of critically examining the life and miracles attributed to that individual, his duty was to especially bring forward facts that were unfavorable to the candidate. Research that has attempted to investigate the efficacy of this technique has tended to use one or another operational definition of devil's advocate.

In many studies of devil's advocate, especially in the organizational behavior literature, researchers compare a situation where an expert makes a proposal with one where this expert's proposal is critiqued by a devil's advocate. A variant on this procedure is a comparison between groups who are in consensus versus groups where one person criticizes the favored proposal. Most research shows the devil's advocate technique to provide some benefit to decision making compared to the expert or consensus conditions (Cosier, 1978; Mason, 1969; Schweiger & Finger, 1984). The literature appears to be mixed as to whether devil's advocate is superior to some form of dialectical inquiry. The latter offers an alternative for consideration, whereas the former simply criticizes elements of the preferred position (Katzenstein, 1996).

A recent study, however, raises questions about the efficacy of role-playing techniques such as devil's advocate. In fact, it offers evidence that there may be negative unintended consequences of such a technique. In one study (Nemeth, Connell, et al., 2001), individuals in groups of four deliberated a personal injury case in an attempt to reach consensus. In one condition, one of the four consistently maintained a deviant position (favoring high compensation) and argued her position from a scripted set of arguments. In a second condition, an individual behaved exactly the same way; the only difference was that she was assigned the role of devil's advocate: she was asked to take a position that differed from the others. In both cases, the person was a confederate. In both cases, the arguments were identical.

The thinking that was stimulated by these two conditions of dissent, however, was quite different. Those faced with the authentic minority generated a greater proportion of internal thoughts, generated by the individual herself rather than thoughts that paraphrased others' views. Perhaps of more importance is the fact that, whereas the authentic minority stimulated thoughts on both sides of the issue, the devil's advocate stimulated thoughts that supported the person's initial views. There was evidence of cognitive bolstering. In other words, the devil's advocate stimulated thinking that confirmed initial views rather than stimulating divergent thinking about the issue or even much consideration of the opposing view.

The Value of Authentic Dissent

Throughout this chapter, we have argued that consensus, where no dissenting or deviant viewpoints are expressed, has potential downsides. People may readily assume that the majority view is correct and adopt it without reflection or serious consideration of alternatives. One might assume that such dissent is valuable to the extent that it presents an alternative, which may be correct. In fact, minority views that are superior do enhance the quality of group choice (McLeod, Baron, Marti, & Yoon, 1997; Stewart & Stasser, 1998). However, their value is more extensive than this. Dissent liberates people to voice their own authentic views. Perhaps more important, it stimulates individuals to think about the issue from more perspectives, to take more facts into account, and to think in original ways that permit the detection of new solutions (Nemeth, 1995, 1997).

The expression of dissent, however, is not without costs. Often, there is increased conflict and reduced morale and harmony (Jackson et al., 1995; Williams & O'Reilly, 1998). Thus, it is reasonable to speculate whether such stimulation can occur without the reduction in morale; to some extent, this motivated research on techniques such as devil's advocate. Yet, as we have seen, such techniques are not nearly as effective as authentic dissent. More important, they may be accompanied by enhanced confidence in one's original belief, a smugness that may occur because one assumes one has considered alternatives though, in fact, there has been little serious reflection on other possibilities.

At this stage of our understanding of the potential for role-playing techniques such as devil's advocate, it would be premature to suggest that one cannot mimic dissent in such a way that stimulation of creative thought ensues but without lowered morale. A recent study tried to mimic authentic dissent quite precisely but, again, pointed to the likely advantages of authentic dissent over any kind of role playing (Nemeth, Rogers, et al., 2001). This study, in which individuals in groups of four discussed a vacation scheduling problem in a firm, had several conditions, two of particular importance here. In one condition, an authentic minority took a position that differed from that of the other three and maintained it over time. In a second condition, an individual took the same minority position at the outset but was then asked to role-play the devil's advocate, arguing over time with exactly the same arguments as the authentic minority used. In other words, the conditions were identical except that one was asked to role-play a devil's advocate. In both the authentic and the consistent devil's advocate conditions, the person believed the same position and argued it the same way, yet the impact on others' thinking and problem solving differed.

In this study, individuals were asked to generate as many good solutions as possible to the general problem of vacation scheduling. The findings indicated that the authentic minority stimulated more solutions, and more creative solutions, than did the consistent devil's advocate. Given that, in both conditions, the person argued what she believed and used the same arguments, many found the results to be surprising. If you think a person is arguing what he or she believes, even when asked to role-play a differing position, why would this not have the same impact as someone arguing what he or she believes without being asked to role-play?

One reason is central to the entire issue of role-playing techniques. The dissenter is doing precisely that: playing a role. Thus, there is ambiguity as to whether the behavior (or arguments) comes from conviction or from the demands of the role. Second, you can't really argue with people who are role-playing. Their role is a script, and thus, they cannot change their mind (even this would be scripted in advance). This brings us to the point of why authentic minority views are so effective in stimulating divergent and creative thought and why role-playing techniques may be far less effective.

When a person is willing to differ from a majority, we call it courage. People understand the difficulty of maintaining a minority view; they know that people often are not sure they are correct and may fear ridicule and rejection (Nemeth, Endicott, & Wachtler, 1977). Thus, when we see that they are consistent, that they evidence a belief in a position that differs from the majority, we accord them admiration and courage (Nemeth & Chiles, 1988). We also wonder why they do this. In general, people do not assume that the minority view is correct, but the minority's consistency raises doubt about the majority position and stimulates a reappraisal of the entire issue (or stimulus array). In the process, people consider more information, look at that information in more ways, and evidence more complexity of thought. As a result, they make better and more creative decisions (Gruenfeld, 1995; Nemeth & Rogers, 1996; Nemeth, Rogers, et al., 2001). Without authentic differences and the courage manifested in their expression, it may not be possible to simulate the kinds of differing views that stimulate divergent and creative thought.

Looking to Corporate Culture

If we assume that most techniques aimed at mimicking dissent will suffer from the fact that they require playing a role and that this, by definition, limits their ability to stimulate divergent thought, we can do one of two things. We can mislead or deceive people into thinking that the person is not role-playing, or we can concentrate on how to "welcome and not fear" (Fulbright, 1964) the voices of dissent. Our assumption is that morale is not necessarily lessened by dissent; in fact, such a voice may be both liberating and energizing.

If we look at accounts of "hot groups," we see teams that are characterized as "vital, absorbing, full of debate, laughter, and very hard work," that "pump out ideas and possibilities at an astonishing rate" (Leavitt & Lipman-Blumen, 1995, pp. 109, 111). In keeping with the premise of this chapter, these are groups not given to easy consensus. In fact, they are characterized as climates where "numerous noisy and seemingly disorganized discussions are more the rule than the exception" (p. 111).

Rather than argue for morale and harmony through some kind of fit or superordinate goals or cohesion (Collins & Porras, 1994), some corporate cultures appear to invite dissent. Motorola, for example, is described as having a contentious culture, where business units are pitted against each other (Cabana & Fiero, 1995). GE has workout groups where employees voice their gripes. One Marriott policy states that if managers can't explain why they are asking employees to do something, the employees don't have to do it (Collins & Porras,

1994). Hewlett-Packard awards a medal of defiance to continue work on an idea contrary to the views of management (B. O'Reilly, 1997; Summerfield, 1990). It is difficult to assess whether these practices are simply rhetoric rather than deeply held and widely shared norms, but they do recognize the potential value of dissent.

The fact that rules or rhetoric do not, in and of themselves, give value to freedom of expression or dissent in a company is apparent in comparisons between companies, such as IDEO, that have successfully used brainstorming principles (Hargadon & Sutton, 1997; Sutton & Hargadon, 1996), and research on brainstorming. The research studies have investigated the efficacy of brainstorming rules: (1) concentrate on quantity of ideas; (2) don't criticize others' ideas; and (3) elaborate and build on others' ideas (Osborn, 1957). Apparently, such rules offer some benefit to a group's ability to generate ideas over no such rules. However, they rarely achieve the level of the individuals generating ideas alone (Diehl & Stroebe, 1991).

At IDEO, a company that specializes in design (and a profitable one at that), these rules are printed on the walls of the company. However, the culture is more than written rules. In the expressed attitudes and behaviors of individuals, in the rewards provided (both symbolic and tangible), one can see the embodiment of these rules. The behaviors and norms give meaning to the words. In such a culture, people feel free to generate many ideas without criticism or much fear of it and continually elaborate on each other's ideas.

We have yet to fully understand how such a culture emerges and how it is maintained. Companies whose product is creativity—creative designs that work—may be especially likely to support a culture of diversity and dissent, one illustrative of hot groups. Perhaps the early days of a company, when the workforce is small and on a mission, are conducive to this sort of atmosphere. The early days of Apple Computer evidence such a climate where young people seem relatively unconcerned with status, dress code, size of office, and moving up the corporate ladder. When the mission is important and everyone's contribution is needed and valued—perhaps this is the setting for contentious, energetic, creative cultures.

In more established corporations, perhaps the research and development units might achieve such a culture. However, to the extent that every worker has knowledge and ideas to contribute, we suggest removing the reasons for fear of reprisal or ridicule that exists in most companies and instead motivate people to voice the problems they see and the solutions they recommend. This is likely to require much more than diversity, much more than rhetoric, and much more than techniques that simulate opposition. Perhaps we need to truly recognize the benefits of diversity and dissent (Morrison & Milliken, 2000; Nemeth, 1995, 1997).

Note

1. It should be pointed out that many view this as a Western notion of creativity, in contrast to the Eastern view, which may concentrate more on states of personal

fulfillment or an expression of an ultimate reality (Lubart, 1999) or even be an exercise to create meaning out of irrationality. Whether one views the concept from the East or West, creativity is not the same as logic, and maxims and rigid boundaries are detrimental to creative thought. It may be more solvent, almost spilling out of the mind in divergent ways. The ability to allow one's mind to do this spilling is what Zen Buddhists practice their whole lives. One way by which they prod creativity is to present themselves with a dilemma that logic cannot answer (Suzuki, 1964).

References

Allen, V. L., & Levine, J. M. (1969). Consensus and conformity. *Journal of Experimental Social Psychology, 5,* 389–399.

Amabile, T. (1983). *The social psychology of creativity.* New York: Springer-Verlag.

Asch, S. E. (1955). Opinions and social pressure. *Scientific American, 193,* 31–35.

Asch, S. E. (1956). Studies of independence and conformity: A minority of one against a unanimous majority. *Psychological Monographs, 70* (No. 9, Whole 416).

Bantel, K. A., & Jackson, S. E. (1989). Top management and innovations in banking: Does the composition of the top team make a difference? *Strategic Management Journal, 10,* 107–124.

Barron, F. (1968). *Creativity and personal freedom.* New York: Van Nostrand.

Brodbeck, F. C., Kerschreiter, R., Mojzisch, A., Frey, D., & Schulz-Hardt, S. (2002). The dissemination of critical, unshared information in decision making groups: The effects of pre-discussion dissent. *European Journal of Social Psychology, 32,* 35–56.

Cabana, S., & Fiero, J. (1995). Motorola, strategic planning and the search conference. *Journal for Quality and Participation, 18,* 22–31.

Camacho, L. M., & Paulus, P. B. (1995). The role of social anxiousness in group brainstorming. *Journal of Personality and Social Psychology, 68,* 1071–1080.

Collins, J. C., & Porras, J. I. (1994). *Built to last: Successful habits of visionary companies.* New York: Harper Collins.

Conway, E., & Siegelman, J. (1979). *Snapping: America's epidemic of sudden personality change.* New York: Delta Books.

Cosier, R. A. (1978). The effects of three potential aids for making strategic decisions on prediction accuracy. *Organizational Behavior and Human Performance, 22,* 295–306.

De Dreu, C. K. W., & De Vries, N. K. (1993). Numerical support, information processing and attitude change. *European Journal of Social Psychology, 23,* 647–662.

De Dreu, C. K. W., & West, M. A. (2001). Minority dissent and team innovation: The importance of participation in decision making. *Journal of Applied Psychology, 86,* 1191–1201.

Deutsch, M., & Gerard, H. B. (1955). A study of normative and informational social influence upon individual judgment. *Journal of Abnormal and Social Psychology, 195,* 629–636.

Diehl, M., & Stroebe, W. (1991). Productivity loss in idea-generating groups: Tracking down the blocking effect. *Journal of Personality and Social Psychology, 61,* 392–403.

Easterbrook, J. A. (1959). The effect of emotion on the utilization and the organization of behavior. *Psychological Review, 66,* 183–201.

Esser, J. K., & Llindoerfer, J. S. (1989). Groupthink and the space shuttle *Challenger* accident: Toward a quantitative case analysis. *Journal of Behavioral Decision Making 2,* 167–177.

Flynn, J., & Chatman, J. (2001). Strong cultures and innovation: Oxymoron or opportunity? In S. Cartwright, C. Cooper, C. Earley, J. Chatman, T. Cummings, N. Holden, P. Sparrow, and W. Starbuck (Eds.), *International Handbook of Organizational Culture and Climate* (pp. 263–287). Sussex: John Wiley & Sons.

Fraser, C. (1971). Group risk taking and group polarization. *European Journal of Social Psychology, 1,* 493–510.

Fulbright, J. W. (1964, March 27). Speech to the United States Senate.

Gruenfeld, D. (1995). Status, ideology and integrative complexity on the U.S. Supreme Court: Rethinking the politics of political decision making. *Journal of Personality and Social Psychology, 68,* 5–20.

Guilford, J. P. (1950). Creativity. *American Psychologist, 5,* 444–454.

Hackman, J. R. (Ed.). (1990). *Groups that work (and those that don't)*. San Francisco: Jossey-Bass.

Hackman, J. R., & Morris, C. G. (1975). Group tasks, group interaction processes and group performance effectiveness: A review and proposed integration. In L. Berkowitz (Ed.), *Advances in experimental social psychology* (Vol. 8, pp. 45–99). New York: Academic Press.

Hargadon, A., & Sutton, R. I. (1997). Technology brokering and innovation in a product development firm. *Administrative Science Quarterly, 42,* 716–749.

Hinsz, V. B. (1990). Cognitive and consensus processes in group recognition memory performance. *Journal of Personality and Social Psychology, 59,* 705–718.

Isenberg, D. I. (1986). Group polarization: A critical review and meta-analysis. *Journal of Personality and Social Psychology, 50,* 1141–1151.

Jackson, S. (1992). Team composition in organizations. In S. Worchel, W. Wood, & J. Simpson (Eds.), *Group process and productivity* (pp. 138–173). London: Sage.

Jackson, S. E., May, K. E., & Whitney, K. (1995). Understanding the dynamics of diversity in decision making teams. In R. A. Guzzo & E. Salas (Eds.), *Team effectiveness and decision making in organizations* (pp. 204–226). San Francisco: Jossey-Bass.

Janis, I. L. (1982). *Groupthink: Psychological studies of policy decisions and fiascoes* (2nd ed.). Boston: Houghton Mifflin.

Kalven, H., Jr., & Zeisel, H. (1966). *The American jury*. Boston: Little, Brown.

Katzenstein, G. (1996). The debate on structured debate: Toward a unified theory. *Organizational Behavior and Human Decision Processes, 66,* 316–332.

Keppel, G., & Postman, L. (1970). *Norms of word association*. New York: Academic Press.

Kiesler, C. A., & Kiesler, S. B. (1969). *Conformity*. Reading, MA: Addison-Wesley.

Larey, T. S., & Paulus, P. B. (1999). Group preference and convergent tendencies in small groups: A content analysis of brainstorming performance. *Creativity Research Journal, 12,* 175–184.

Lawler, E. E. (1992). *The ultimate advantage: Creating the high-involvement organization*. San Francisco: Jossey-Bass.

Leavitt, H. J., & Lipman-Blumen, J. (1995, July/August). Hot groups. *Harvard Business Review,* 109–115.

Leonard, D., & Swap, W. (1999). *When sparks fly: Igniting creativity in groups.* Boston: Harvard Business School Press.

Lubart, T. I. (1999). Creativity across cultures. In R. J. Sternberg (Ed.), *Handbook of creativity* (pp. 339–350). Cambridge, UK: Cambridge University Press.

Martin, R., & Noyes, C. (1996). Minority influence and argument generation. In C. J. Nemeth (Ed.), *British Journal of Social Psychology: Special Issue on Minority Influence, 35,* 91–103.

Mason, R. O. (1969). A dialectical approach to strategic planning. *Management Science, 15,* B403–B414.

McGrath, J. E. (1984). *Groups: Interaction and performance.* Englewood Cliffs, NJ: Prentice-Hall.

McLeod, P. L., Baron, R. S., Marti, M. W., & Yoon, K. (1997). The eyes have it: Minority influence in face-to-face and computer-mediated group discussion. *Journal of Applied Psychology, 82,* 706–718.

Mill, J. S. (1859/1979). *On liberty.* New York: Penguin.

Milliken, F. J., & Martins, L. (1996). Searching for common threads: Understanding the multiple effects of diversity in organizational groups. *Academy of Management Review, 21,* 402–433.

Moorhead, G., Ference, R., & Neck, C. P. (1991). Group decision fiascoes continue: Space shuttle *Challenger* and a revised groupthink framework. *Human Relations, 44,* 539–550.

Morrison, E. W., & Milliken, F. J. (2000). Organizational silence: A barrier to change and development in a pluralistic world. *Academy of Management Review, 25,* 706–725.

Moscovici, S., & Doise, W. (1974). Decision making in groups. In C. J. Nemeth (Ed.), *Social psychology: Classic and contemporary integrations* (pp. 250–288). Chicago: Rand McNally.

Moscovici, S., & Zavalloni, M. (1969). The group as a polarizer of attitudes. *Journal of Personality and Social Psychology, 12,* 124–135.

Myers, D. G., & Bishop, G. D. (1970). Discussion effects on racial attitudes. *Science, 169,* 778–779.

Myers, D. G., & Lamm, H. (1976). The group polarization phenomenon. *Psychology Bulletin, 83,* 602–627.

Nemeth, C. J. (1986). Differential contributions of majority and minority influence. *Psychological Review, 93,* 23–32.

Nemeth, C. J. (1995). Dissent as driving cognition, attitudes and judgments. *Social Cognition, 13,* 273–291.

Nemeth, C. J. (1997). Managing innovation: When less is more. *California Management Review, 40,* 59–74.

Nemeth, C., & Chiles, C. (1988). Modeling courage: The role of dissent in fostering independence. *European Journal of Social Psychology, 18,* 275–280.

Nemeth, C. J., Connell, J. B., Rogers, J. D., & Brown, K. S. (2001). Improving decision making by means of dissent. *Journal of Applied Social Psychology, 31,* 48–58.

Nemeth, C., Endicott, J., & Wachtler, J. (1977). Increasing the size of the minority: Some gains and some losses. *European Journal of Social Psychology, 1,* 11–23.

Nemeth, C., & Kwan, J. (1985). Originality of word associations as a function of majority vs. minority influence processes. *Social Psychology Quarterly, 48,* 277–282.

Nemeth, C., & Kwan, J. (1987). Minority influence, divergent thinking and the detection of correct solutions. *Journal of Applied Social Psychology, 9,* 788–799.

Nemeth, C., Mayseless, O., Sherman, J., & Brown, Y. (1990). Improving recall by exposure to consistent dissent. *Journal of Personality and Social Psychology, 58,* 429–437.

Nemeth, C., Mosier, K., & Chiles, C. (1992). When convergent thought improves performance: Majority vs. minority influence. *Personality and Social Psychology Bulletin, 81,* 139–144.

Nemeth, C. J., & Rogers, J. (1996). Dissent and the search for information. *British Journal of Social Psychology, 35,* 67–76.

Nemeth, C. J., Rogers, J. D., & Brown, K. S. (2001). Devil's advocate vs. authentic dissent: Stimulating quantity and quality. *European Journal of Social Psychology 31,* 707–729.

Nemeth, C., & Wachtler, J. (1983). Creative problem solving as a result of majority vs. minority influence. *European Journal of Social Psychology, 13,* 45–55.

O'Reilly, B. (1997). The secrets of America's most admired corporations: New ideas, new products. *Fortune, 35,* 60–64.

O'Reilly, C. (1989). Corporations, culture and commitment: Motivation and social control in organizations. *California Management Review, 31,* 9–25.

O'Reilly, C. A., & Chatman, J. A. (1996). Culture as social control: Corporations, cults and commitment. *Research in Organizational Behavior,* 157–200.

Ornstein, R. (1991). *The evaluation of consciousness: Of Darwin, Freud and cranial fire: The origins of the way we think.* New York: Prentice-Hall.

Osborn, A. F. (1957). *Applied imagination.* New York: Scribner.

Pfeffer, J. (1994). *Competitive advantage through people.* Boston: Harvard Business School Press.

Rhoads, K. vL., & Cialdini, R. B. (2002). The business of influence: Principles that lead to success in commercial settings. In J. P. Dillard & M. Pfau (Eds.), *The persuasion handbook theory and practice* (pp. 515–542). New York: Sage.

Ryan, K. D., & Oestreich, D. K. (1991). *Driving fear out of the workplace: How to overcome the invisible barriers to quality, productivity and innovation.* San Francisco: Jossey-Bass.

Schachter, S. (1951). Deviation, rejection and communication. *Journal of Abnormal and Social Psychology, 46,* 190–207.

Schlesinger, A. M., Jr. (1972). *A thousand days.* Boston: Houghton Mifflin.

Schweiger, D. M., & Finger, P. A. (1984). The comparative effectiveness of dialectical inquiry and devil's advocacy: The impact of task biases on previous research findings. *Strategic Management Journal, 5,* 335–355.

Shepperd, J. A. (1993). Productivity loss in performance groups: A motivation analysis. *Psychological Bulletin, 113,* 67–81.

Simons, T., Pelled, L. H., & Smith, K. A. (1999). Making use of difference: Diversity, debate, and decision comprehensiveness in top management teams. *Academy of Management Journal, 42,* 662–673.

Stewart, D. D., & Stasser, G. (1995). Expert role assignment and information sampling during collective recall and decision making. *Journal of Personality and Social Psychology, 69,* 619–628.

Stewart, D. D., & Stasser, G. (1998). The sampling of critical, unshared information in decision-making groups: The role of an informed minority. *European Journal of Social Psychology 28,* 95–113.

Stroop, R. J. (1935). Studies of interference in serial verbal reactions. *Journal of Experimental Psychology, 18,* 643–662.

Summerfield, F. (1990, May). Paying the troops to buck the system. *Business Month,* 77–79.

Sutton, R. I., & Hargadon, A. (1996). Brainstorming groups in context: Effectiveness in a product design firm. *Administrative Science Quarterly, 41,* 685–718.

Suzuki, D. T. (1964). *An introduction to Zen Buddhism.* New York: Grove Press.

Van Dyne, L., & Saavedra, R. (1996). A naturalistic minority influence experiment: Effects on divergent thinking, conflict and originality in work groups. *British Journal of Social Psychology, 35,* 151–168.

Volpato, C., Maass, A., Mucchi-Faina, A., & Vitti, E. (1990). Minority influence and social categorization. *European Journal of Social Psychology 20,* 119–132.

Williams, K., & O'Reilly, C. (1998). Demography and diversity in organizations: A review of 40 years of research. *Research in Organizational Behavior, 20,* 77–140.

5

■■■■■ *Garold Stasser and Zachary Birchmeier*

Group Creativity and Collective Choice

■■■■

Group decision making is inherently a convergent process. The primary goal is for members to agree on one of several decision options. Examples of decision-making groups include a jury deciding the fate of a defendant in a criminal trial, a personnel committee deciding which of several candidates to hire or promote, and a family choosing a vacation spot. In each of these cases, the task is to narrow the options down to one that is collectively endorsed by the group. In this sense, group decision making seems to be the antithesis of group creativity, which connotes divergent processes and typically aims to introduce new and numerous options and ideas for consideration. Nonetheless, taking a broader perspective, there are divergent processes that may accompany and contribute to collective choice. On the one hand, decision-making groups often discuss the merits of the decision options before picking one. From an information processing view (Hinsz, Tindale, & Vollrath, 1997; Larson & Christensen, 1993), the more informed a decision, the better the decision. The more fully the group explores the merits of the options, the more likely that they will eliminate bad choices and pick good ones. Filling out the ledger of supporting and opposing arguments for alternatives is a divergent process. On the other hand, identifying decision options can also be a divergent activity. Whereas some decision environments provide the options to the group (e.g., the court or legal policy typically provides a jury with a set or range of possible verdicts), others permit or even require that the group generate the options. For example, a family's selection of a vacation spot must be preceded by generating a slate of options.

Indeed, the family can add options or create new ones from old ones in the process of identifying a mutually acceptable vacation.

In this chapter, we review the social psychological literature that has addressed the role of discussion and information exchange in group decision making. As we noted, generating, revising, and melding decision options are also critical processes for some decision-making groups. Clearly, generation and revision of decision options can involve brainstorming; other chapters in this volume speak more directly to these activities (see Milliken, Bartel, & Kurtzberg, this volume; and Nemeth & Nemeth-Brown, this volume).

The foregoing discussion suggests that the generation of decision options and the choice among these options are distinct processes. This distinction helps clarify the focus of this chapter. Nonetheless, it is an overly simplistic distinction. In fact, divergent and convergent processes in collective choice are undoubtedly entwined in complex ways. Whereas the literature that we review in this chapter focuses on information exchange and discussion when deciding among fixed decision options, it is also likely that the communication processes we consider are relevant at other stages in collective decision making. A dominant theme of this chapter is that unique information is often useful for identifying good decision options, but groups often overlook unique information and focus on information that they hold in common. We discuss at length some of the obstacles to effective dissemination of unique information in face-to-face discussions and consider the implications for identifying good choices among a set of decision options. It seems likely, however, that effective dissemination of unique information may also impact other stages of group process. For example, as suggested by Nemeth and Nemeth-Brown (this volume), the expression of novel points of view can promote divergent thinking. Thus, exchange of unique information in group discussion may not only help groups select good options but may also help them generate good choices for consideration.

Why Group Decisions?

There are many reasons for delegating a decision to a group. The reasons differ from one context to another and frequently differ among stakeholders within a context. Citizens may support the use of a jury as a means of representing "community values" in the adjudication of a case. However, the defendant may opt for a jury trial because he thinks he is guilty but his lawyer believes she can discredit key witnesses in the eyes of the jury—a ploy that she doubts will work if a judge decides the case. A department chair may delegate promotion decisions to a committee because he wants to diffuse responsibility for potentially contentious decisions. However, a CEO may delegate a marketing decision to a task force because she believes that the decision is sufficiently complex to require the input of experts representing different but complementary domains of knowledge and abilities.

Although the reasons for delegating decisions to groups are varied, they often rest on one of two different views of what groups do. On the one hand, group decision making can be viewed as a vehicle for identifying what is commonly believed or preferred: the group as a representative body. This representation function makes sense if the goal is to engender acceptance, satisfaction, or commitment to decisions, particularly when there are not readily available ways of objectively evaluating the quality of decisions (Festinger, 1954; Goethals & Darley, 1987). On the other hand, group decision making can be viewed as a vehicle for combining disparate points of view, knowledge, and ideas with the hope of reaching better decisions: the group as an information-processing body (Hinsz et al, 1997; Larsen & Christensen, 1993). The information-processing function is important when making decisions that are complex and information-rich and can be evaluated by objective criteria. The view of group decision making (representative or information processing) that dominates is rarely stated in practice and frequently remains an implicit assumption. Whereas group decision making can serve both functions, they tend to be associated with different types of interaction.

When the goal is to discover popular beliefs and preferences, group interaction tends to be preference-driven, characterized by the communication of opinions and preferences (e.g., voting) and identification of the dominant or majority position. Members may change their minds, but opinion change often represents acquiescence or conformity on the part of dissenting members (normative influence: Deutsch & Gerard, 1955; Kaplan, 1987). When the goal is to inform members and identify options that are supported by the preponderance of evidence, group interaction tends to be information-driven, characterized by the communication and integration of relevant information. Opinion change flows from learning new information and reevaluation of options in light of what's learned (informational influence). Often, either the preference-driven or the information-driven style dominates discussion. For example, Hastie, Penrod and Pennington (1983) identified two styles of jury deliberation. About a third of the juries they studied exhibited verdict-driven style of deliberation; they conducted polls early and frequently. Roughly another third of the juries displayed an evidence-driven style; these juries concentrated on reviewing the information presented in the trial, constructing a plausible story based on the evidence, and selecting the decision option that corresponded most closely to this plausible story (Pennington & Hastie, 1992). The deliberations of the remaining juries were not strongly characterized by either style.

Preference-driven interaction affords little opportunity for the emergence of innovative decision making. Group decisions are largely a reflection of the dominant sentiments of members at the onset of discussion. In contrast, information-driven interaction is more conducive to the discovery and adoption of creative decisions. By combining their knowledge, members can discover options that few of them supported at the onset of discussion. Collins and Guetzkow (1964) refer to this potential as an assembly bonus. What members know collectively can, in principle, contradict what they know individually; by assembling their unique knowledge, they can change their views of the decision options. As we will show, however, the promise of an assembly bonus does not ensure its realization. Even information-driven discussion can fail to communicate and combine information effectively.

Unique Information and Hidden Profiles

The potential for an assembly bonus depends on members having different subsets of relevant information. For ease of presentation, we distinguish two classes of information: unique information is information held by one member before group discussion; common information is information known by all members prior to discussion. Consider a simple example. Andi, Bo, and Chris constitute a hiring committee whose task is to recommend one of two applicants for a middle-management position. Suppose that all members of the committee know that applicant X has an MBA from a prestigious business school and has 10 years of marketing experience in large corporations. Additionally, they all know that applicant Y has a BA in accounting from a liberal arts university and has been a successful organizational consultant for five years. This information about the applicants is common information. Furthermore, suppose that Andi knows that X has no experience working in Latin American countries, whereas Y has consulted with several companies in Mexico City. Bo and Chris do not know this and thus it is unique information, uniquely held by Andi. Similarly, Bo knows things that Andi and Chris do not and Chris knows things that Andi and Bo do not. If Andi, Bo, and Chris share their unique information before they make a recommendation, they will be better informed. Being better informed, their collective decision may not be the decision that any of them would have made without the additional information they learned from each other.

A hidden profile can exist when information supporting one decision alternative is mostly common and information supporting another decision alternative is mostly unique. Figure 5.1 illustrates schematically a hidden profile. In the illustrated case, decision X has four items of supporting information (denoted X_1, X_2, X_3, and X_4) and Y has three items of supporting information (denoted Y_1, Y_2, and Y_3). If the items of information are equally important and relevant to the decision, X is the better choice. However, the supporting information for Y is commonly known, whereas the supporting information about X is mostly unique. Thus, before discussion, each of the three members will tend to favor Y based on what they individually know because they do not see the bigger picture. If Andi, Bo, and Chris mention their unique information during discussion, they will see that X is the superior choice and collectively endorse X even though they all favored Y before discussion. That is, the group discussion can reveal the hidden profile of information that favors X.

The example depicted in Figure 5.1 contains fewer items of relevant information than is typical for most decisions of interest. However, it highlights

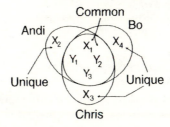

Figure 5.1. *Common and Unique
Information Distributed to Create a
Hidden Profile*

several features of hidden profiles. First, the possibility of hidden profiles is a compelling reason to delegate decision making to groups. Faced with a hidden profile, the group can discover a superior decision that none of the members supported individually. That is, hidden profiles are a class of decision problems that can result in emergent, innovative decisions by groups. Second, notwithstanding this potential advantage of group decision making, if the group decision is based primarily on members' prior preferences, they will miss the opportunity and choose the suboptimal decision Y. Third, if the hidden profile remains hidden, group members have no way of knowing that they failed; that is, if members do not communicate their unique information to others, they will not know that they have made a suboptimal decision. For example, Andi may recognize that X_2 favors X but, not knowing X_3 and X_4, will still think that Y is the better decision. Finding out that Bo and Chris also favor Y will serve to boost Andi's confidence that Y is the better choice. As a result, the group interaction may reinforce the ill-informed prior preferences rather than reveal the hidden profile. In this event, members may gain false confidence in the group's decision.

The key to revealing hidden profiles seems simple: communicate unique information. Nonetheless, groups often fail to do so (e.g., Hollingshead, 1996; McLeod, Baron, Marti, & Yoon, 1997; Stasser, Stewart, & Wittenbaum, 1995; Stasser & Titus, 1985, 1987). There are several hurdles that groups must jump to communicate effectively unique information and to discover hidden profiles. First, if members' preferences lead to a consensus or obvious compromise choice, the temptation to forgo extensive discussion may be great. As already noted, decisions based on prior preferences will reflect what members know in common more than what individuals know uniquely: the common knowledge effect (Gigone & Hastie, 1993, 1996). Second, even if groups rely on discussion of relevant information to inform their decision, their discussions may be dominated by common information. We consider several processes that contribute to this domination: collective information sampling (Larson, Christensen, Abbott, & Frantz, 1996; Stasser, Taylor, & Hanna, 1989; Stasser and Titus, 1987), advocacy discussion style (Stasser & Titus, 1985), social validation of information (Stewart & Stasser, 1995), and social credibility (Kameda, Ohtsubo, & Takezawa, 1997; Wittenbaum, Hubbell, & Zuckerman, 1999).

The First Hurdle: Consensus Implies Correctness

Consensus is often taken as evidence of correctness. Festinger (1954), in his seminal work on social influence, stated that people seek confirmation of their opinions from others in the absence of objective criteria for judging correctness. People may rely on consensus even when other forms of validation are available but not readily accessible. Chaiken and Stangor (1987; see also Kameda et al., 1997) advanced a similar idea, noting that people often use a consensus heuristic in evaluating attitudes: consensus implies correctness. As a result, initial majorities often determine a group's choice, particularly when deicisons cannot be readily evaluated using objective criteria (Davis, 1973; Laughlin & Ellis, 1986; Stasser, Kerr, & Davis, 1989).

If groups rely on degree of consensus as an indicator of correctness, they will fail to discover hidden profiles when they exist. Because of the nature of hidden profiles, members will tend to agree on an inferior decision and forgo the opportunity to exchange information. From the perspective of group members, this reliance on initial consensus probably does not seem like a risky strategy. Heuristics such as "consensus implies correctness" survive because they save effort and time. It is impossible to know how frequently hidden profiles arise in practice, and it is important to note that the presence of unique information does not imply that a hidden profile exists. For every instance of a hidden profile, there are probably several instances of unique and common information having similar implications: instances of unique information confirming, rather than contradicting, common information. In these instances, extensive exchange of unique information will only bolster the preferences that members bring to the group and reinforce the utility of the correctness heuristic. In other words, experience may suggest that consensus often does imply correctness. Unfortunately, unless group members exchange their unique information, they cannot know whether their unique and common information support the same decision. Thus, groups that rely heavily on the consensus heuristic will tend to make quick, and sometimes good, decisions. However, they will forgo the possibility of discovering innovative decisions when the opportunity exists.

How can groups jump the "consensus implies correctness" hurdle? On the one hand, members must expect that the exchange of information may lead to an emergent decision that is neither obvious nor appealing at the onset of discussion. The expectation may arise because of how they view the decision task and because of the social climate of the group. On the other hand, they must avoid the temptation of task and social factors that offer easy routes to consensus.

Laughlin (1980; Laughlin & Ellis, 1986) noted that decision tasks can be arrayed along a continuum of demonstrability. Demonstrability depends on several factors, including the existence of objective criteria or ways of assessing the quality of a decision, members' acceptance of the criteria and understanding how to apply the criteria, and sufficient member motivation to do the cognitive work to apply the criteria. Judgmental tasks are low in demonstrability, often because there is no obvious or widely accepted way to assess the quality of the decision. Group decisions for judgmental tasks are typically determined by the most popular preferences in the group at the onset of discussion. Intellective tasks are high in demonstrability and include math and logic problems and brainteasers. For intellective tasks, groups often recognize and adopt a correct answer as long as one or two members support the correct answer initially (Laughlin & Ellis, 1986: Stasser & Dietz-Uhler, 2001). However, most group decision-making tasks hover somewhere in the middle of the demonstrability continuum. Moreover, tasks can be nudged along the continuum in one direction or the other by members' views of the task and their level of motivation.

For example, consider an elementary problem in probability. A drawer contains six socks, three blue and three black. If two socks are drawn at random from the drawer, what is the probability that they will match? There is a demonstrably correct answer to this problem (0.4) following the rules of elementary probability theory. However, a group of math phobics may not know the appropriate rules or how to apply them. Even if one member happens to get the right answer, he or she may be unable to convince the others (who may be convinced that the wrong, but intuitively compelling, answer of 0.5 is right). Or, the members may know how to solve the problem but lack the motivation to apply the necessary reasoning and simply go with the most popular, intuitive answer. Given insufficient procedural knowledge or motivation in the group, this seemingly intellective problem becomes judgmental (Laughlin & Ellis, 1986).

Stasser and Stewart (1992) manipulated participants' perceptions of a murder mystery task. They suggested to some that considering all of the available clues would identify the guilty suspect (*solve* set: appearance of an intellective task) and to others that the clues may not be sufficient to identify unambiguously the guilty suspect (*judge* set: appearance of a judgmental task). In the judge set, groups were asked to judge the likelihood that each suspect committed the crime and, in dong so, select the most likely culprit. In the critical conditions of this experiment, the clues were distributed among the members of a group to create a hidden profile. That is, commonly shared clues tended to implicate the wrong suspect, whereas uniquely held clues exonerated the innocent suspects and implicated the guilty one. Under both solve and judge task sets, fewer than a third of the individuals chose the correct suspect before discussion. However, after discussion, about 70% of groups with a solve set chose the correct suspect. In contrast, only about 33% of groups with a judge set chose the correct suspect. Moreover, solve groups devoted more of their discussions to critical clues than judge groups did.

The framing of the task as a problem to be solved, as opposed to a judgment to be rendered, may have triggered a problem-solving climate within the group. This problem-solving climate likely discouraged reliance on members' prior opinions and encouraged the communication and consideration of information. Postmes, Spears, and Cihangir (2001) made a similar point. They created either a consensus or a critical thought norm in decision-making groups by having them complete "team-building" exercises that selectively reinforced one norm over the other. Groups then worked on an ostensibly unrelated decision-making task of selecting one of three candidates for a teaching position. Individuals read incomplete candidate descriptions that were constructed to create a hidden profile, made an initial private choice, and then met as a group to discuss and decide which candidate was best. Regardless of norm, only about 11% of individuals chose the best candidate prior to discussion. Interestingly, Postmes et al. essentially removed the hidden profile right after individuals made their private choice and before they met as a group. At this point, they gave everyone complete profiles and highlighted the information that they did not have earlier. Nonetheless, groups with the consensus norm performed little better than the individuals did prior to discussion; only 22% of consensus groups chose the best candidate. In contrast, critical thought groups benefited substantially from discussion, and 67% of these groups chose the best candidate after discussion. Thus, even when they had complete information handed to them at the onset of discussion, groups primed with a consensus norm seemingly ignored or discounted the information and let their prior preferences guide the group decision. However, groups primed to think critically used the information to revise their assessments of the decision alternatives.

In addition to task framing and group norms, external pressures, such as heavy workload and time pressures, may induce members to forgo the possible benefits of information search and exchange in favor of easier or quicker routes to consensus. For example, Gigone and Hastie (1993) asked groups to predict grades (on a grade scale from A to F with pluses and minuses) in a college course for 32 students based on six cues (e.g., attendance, ACT or SAT scores, high school GPA). For each target, the cue information was distributed so that some cues were given to all members before discussion and others were given to only one or two members. Thus, there was the opportunity for members to inform one another about relevant information before they rendered their group judgment. Nonetheless, Gigone and Hastie noted that group predictions were typically an average of the members' individual predictions, and the cues that they talked about en route to a group judgment had little effect on the group judgment. That is, the group judgment was based primarily on the individuals' prior judgments and the content of their discussions contributed little. Two characteristics of the grade-judging task seem relevant here. First, the group had to make many judgments, creating a fairly heavy workload. Second, the response scale provided a simple way of resolving any differences in their initial judgments, namely, averaging individual judgments.

In summary, groups frequently base their decisions on members' initial preferences. This preference-driven process is appealing when members initially agree on a decision or when a salient compromise position exists. Moreover, group norms, the perceived nature of the task, low member motivation, time pressures, and heavy workloads likely encourage groups to combine members' preferences as a way of reaching a decision. However, when a hidden profile exists, use of prior preferences in lieu of thoroughly discussing information prevents groups from discovering the superior option that is supported by their collective knowledge.

The Second Hurdle: Collective Information Sampling Favors Common Information

Even if groups adopt an information-driven decision process, they often fail to pool their information effectively. In many contexts, there is a tendency for members to bias their contributions to discussion to support their initial preferences (Schulz-Hardt, Frey, Luethgens, & Moscovici, 2000; Stasser, 1988; Stasser & Titus, 1985;). This bias may arise for several reasons. First, information that is consistent with one's preference may be more salient when searching for items to contribute to discussion. Second, members may be prone to defend their initial choices. This tendency may be particularly strong if members are required to report an initial choice (Houlett, Muzzy, & Sawyer, 2000). Because common information has more influence on initial individual preferences than unique information (the aforementioned common knowledge effect; Gigone & Hastie, 1993, 1996), members' defense of their initial preferences will tend to promote the discussion of common information. This bias in favor of common information is particularly relevant when a hidden profile exists. Referring back to the simple example in Figure 5.1, members will tend to favor Y because the common information supports Y. If they argue for their initial preferences, their discussion will rehash the common information at the expense of exchanging unique information (which supports X). Therefore, to discover the superior option, they must avoid not only simply combining their prior preferences but also letting their prior preferences bias their contributions to discussion.

Less obvious than biased information processing are the structural effects of collective information sampling. Even if individuals do not bias their contributions to favor initial preferences, the group is still more likely to mention an item of common information than an equally salient item of unique information. This sampling advantage of common information arises because any group member can mention an item of common information but only one can mention an item of unique information. It is as though the opportunities for items of common information to enter discussion are multiplied by the number of group members (Larson et al., 1996). As Stasser, Taylor, et al. (1989) demonstrate, this advantage of common information can be quite substantial. For example, in one of their experimental conditions, they requested that groups spend at least 15 minutes discussing the information about three decision alternatives before expressing any preferences or trying to reach a decision. Six-person groups who followed this procedure mentioned 70% of the common information but only 21% of the unique information.

There are two ways to mitigate this sampling advantage: exhaustive discussions and assignment of expert roles. If discussions continue long enough, the pool of available but unmentioned common information will become sufficiently small that members will necessarily start sampling unique information. Larson et al. (1996) showed that the likelihood of a group's mentioning unique items increases as the discussion progresses. Although this seems to be a simple remedy, at least two factors limit its effectiveness in practice. First, there are real and functional limits to the time groups can devote to discussion. Fatigue, boredom, and external pressures limit the opportunity for groups to explore information exhaustively. Second, opinions are often formed and solidified early in discussion, and early discussion has a substantial impact on a group's final discussion. Even if discussions are prolonged, common information will dominate the early phases of discussion and unique information will tend to emerge later, often after the decision is functionally made (see Larson et al., 1996; Wittenbaum & Stasser, 1996, for further discussion of these issues).

The example depicted in the first panel of Figure 5.2 helps illustrate the dynamics of collective information sampling and the potentially corrective function of assigned expert roles. In Figure 5.2, three discussants (Lawyer, Market Analyst, and Physician) are considering the merits of marketing a new drug. Let the pluses represent reasons to put the new drug on the market and the minuses denote reasons to withhold it. Additionally, suppose that these reasons are distributed over three domains of knowledge corresponding to the respective expertise of the three discussants. That is, Lawyer knows things pertaining to relevant points of law, represented by the L items. The Market Analyst and the Physician also know some things about the law but the Lawyer knows more. Similarly, the M items and P items represent relevant market and medical considerations. In this case, six items of common information support the decision to market the drug and nine items of unique information oppose such action. Assuming that the discussants are equally likely to mention all of the items that they bring to discussion, there are 3 (discussants) × 6 (items of common information) = 18 opportunities to mention common information and only 9 opportunities to mention unique items. Thus, the first item mentioned is much more likely to be common than unique information, and, as discussion progresses, the pool of common items will be explored more rapidly than the pool of unique information. Because the collective sampling process will tend to deplete the common pool more rapidly than the unique pool, eventually the content of discussion will shift to unique items. If they discuss enough information, the chance of mentioning unique information will approach and eventually exceed the chance of mentioning any of the remaining items of common information. Of course, by the time the sampling advantage shifts to unique information, members may have already functionally made their decision and the influence of the unique items may be muted.

The second panel of Figure 5.2 illustrates how assigned expert roles can, in theory, eliminate the sampling advantage of common information. If the discussants recognize and accept their respective expert roles in the context of the

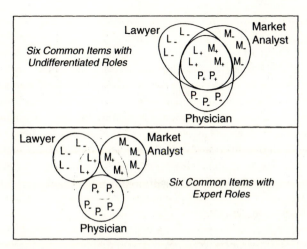

Figure 5.2. *Schematic of the Effect of Expert Roles on Responsibility for Communicating Common and Unique Information*

discussion, the sampling patterns should change. Suppose the Lawyer introduces only legal considerations and avoids bringing up market and medical considerations and the others likewise restrict their contributions to their domains of expertise. Under such a strict division of labor, the six common items lose their sampling advantage because only the relevant expert will mention each one.

Expert-driven information exchange seems an easy solution to the structural imbalance inherent in communicating common and unique information. However, the social and psychological impediments to this solution are real and the solution works better on paper than it does in practice. For example, Stasser, Vaughan, and Stewart (2000) distributed information in a three-alternative decision task so that each of three members had more information about one of the alternatives. Thus, in this case, expertise was operationalized as the amount of information that members had about the respective decision alternatives. Awareness of this expertise was manipulated in two ways. Some members were told before they reviewed the information about the decision alternatives that they would have access to more information about one of the alternatives than others would have (*forewarned*). In other groups, members' expertise was publicly announced at the onset of discussion (*role assigned*; e.g., "Member A received more information about Option A"). Forewarning had no detectable effect on the overrepresentation of common information in discussion. However, role assignment did increase the amount of unique information discussed without increasing the mentioning of common information.

Notwithstanding the documented benefits of assigned expert roles in this study and others (see also Stasser et al., 1995; Stewart & Stasser, 1995), the limits of this effect are notable. In Stasser et al. (2000) role assignment increased the percentage of unique items discussed from 29% to only 34%. By comparison, groups discussed 58% of common items. Additionally, a detailed analysis of discussion content revealed that group members did not adhere strongly to their expert roles. In spite of seemingly strong task and experimental demands to adopt expert roles (especially when they were publicly assigned), group members contributed many items that fell outside their designated domain of expertise. This failure was not due to their being unaware of their expertise. Both forewarning and public role assignment resulted in members reporting accurately their own and others' domains of expertise. Nonetheless, their contributions to discussion did not reflect this awareness. Other findings suggest that participants did accept responsibility for information in their designated domain of expertise but did not avoid mentioning common items that fell outside their expert domain. Thus, common items continued to benefit from having multiple potential sources of recall.

We suspect that, from the perspective of group members, expert roles signal primary responsibility for items associated with their expertise (in Figure 5.2, "the Lawyer should mention L items"). However, it is possible that such expert roles do not carry a normative injunction against mentioning things outside their expertise ("but the Lawyer can also mention M and P items if they come to mind"). Whereas going out of the bounds of one's expertise to bring up other information may seem reasonable, it can severely compromise the potential benefits of expert-driven discussion for pooling unique information. As long as common information has a sampling advantage, it will tend to displace the consideration of unique information.

In summary, information-driven process does not ensure that groups will effectively pool their unique information. When group members are inclined to contribute information that supports their prior preferences, discussion will tend to focus on common information, especially when a hidden profile exists. Even more pervasive, but less obvious, are the structural effects of collective information sampling as it unfolds during discussion. Even when members' contributions are unbiased by their preferences, common information will dominate discussion, especially during early phases of discussion. Lengthy discussions will diminish this domination and facilitate the mentioning of unique items. Moreover, when unique information is associated with recognized areas of expertise, having members concentrate their contributions on information within their expert domain may help shift the content of discussion toward unique knowledge. However, for expert roles to be effective, they must be strictly enacted. Such strict adherence to expert roles during discussion may not occur easily or naturally in many groups.

The Third Hurdle: Common Information Is Credible and Compelling

Getting unique information on the table does not ensure that groups will consider fully its implications. There is growing evidence that groups attend more to common information, perhaps because they find it more credible or compelling than unique information. This evidence comes from a variety of sources. First, groups are more likely to repeat common than unique information once it is mentioned in discussion (Larson et al., 1996; Stasser, Taylor, & Hanna, 1989). Second, after discussion, members are more likely to correctly remember common than unique information that was mentioned during discussion (Stewart & Stasser, 1995). Third, in written summaries of their discussions, groups are more likely to include the common than the unique items (Stewart & Stasser, 1995).

The clues to the processes that fuel the tendency to repeat common more than unique information are largely indirect. These clues are based primarily on the variables that eliminate or reduce the tendency to ignore unique information. High-status members (Larson et al., 1996), designated leaders (Larson, Foster-Fishman, & Franz, 1998) and members with task experience (Wittenbaum, 1998, 2000) are more likely than others to repeat unique information. Forewarning members (Stasser et al., 1995, 2000; Stewart & Stasser, 1995) that they have more information than others in a particular domain increases the repetition of unique information during discussion and the likelihood that it is retained on a written summary of discussion and correctly recalled after discussion. Parks and Cowlin (1996) found that the availability of written records facilitated an increased consideration of unique information. Additionally, they found that if information was given to two members prior to discussion, it was as likely to be repeated as was information given to all members. Thus, if one other member could attest to the veracity of information, it was seemingly granted as much consideration as information that all members had before discussion.

The implications of these findings are that social validation of information that emerges during discussion is important in gaining acceptance by the group. In the absence of social validation, other social cues signifying source credibility (status, experience, expertise) also establish the validity of unique information that arises during discussion. These social cues may act in two ways. One is that the cues convey source credibility: high-status, experienced, and expert sources know what they are talking about. The other is that members who enjoy high status or expert standing in the group may be more confident of their recall, convey this confidence in their conversation, and promote their unique information more actively (Hinsz, 1990). Finally, external memory aids, such as notes, may reduce the need for social validation and enhance the acceptance and consideration of unique information.

However, establishing the credibility of the unique information may not always ensure that it is granted equal consideration in shaping members' preferences and the group's decision. In the aforementioned study by Postmes et al. (2001), recall that they effectively removed any barriers associated with disseminating and validating unique information by giving members complete profiles immediately before the onset of discussion. Moreover, to ensure the salience of unique information, they highlighted it in the materials they distributed. Nonetheless, groups that were primed with a consensus norm seemingly did not use this unique information in their deliberations, and they rated unique information as less important than common information. In contrast, when groups were primed with a "critical thinking" norm, their decisions reflected the implications of the unique information and the importance of the unique information was not discounted. One interpretation of these findings is that unique information is not viewed as facilitating group consensus (Wittenbaum, Stasser, & Merry, 1996). Thus, if groups are primarily concerned with finding a mutually acceptable decision, they may avoid focusing on unique items and emphasize common information in their discussions.

Facilitating the Effective Pooling of Unique Information

To recap, groups are not very effective at pooling unique information. When unique and common information support different decision alternatives, groups typically opt for the decision that is supported by the common information. Several processes seem to promote the ascendancy of common information. First, discussions are often preference-driven. Groups are inclined to adopt positions that are popular among their members at the onset of discussion without systematically exploring information. Even if they do not agree initially, they frequently will adopt a salient compromise position if it exists. Second, when groups explore information, contributions to discussion are often biased to favor initial preferences. Because initial preferences tend to be shaped more by common than unique information, common information tends to dominate such biased discussions. Third, even if group members set aside or do not form initial preferences, the dynamics of collective information sampling favor the selection of common items, particularly in the early phases of discussion. Finally, when both common and unique items emerge in discussion, common items seem to have more staying power. The common items are repeated more often and are more likely to be retained in written summaries and remembered more accurately after discussion. Stated simply, group discussions are better vehicles for eliciting what members know in common than for pooling their unique knowledge. If the goal is to identify common knowledge and popular sentiment, this is a positive feature of group discussion. However, it does not promote the discovery of novel or innovative decisions. One cannot simply assume that groups will pool their collective knowledge in search of better decisions. If the goal is to promote consideration of novel or unpopular decision alternatives, one needs to consider carefully the conditions that promote effective information pooling.

We have approached the problem of creative group decision making from the perspective of the behavioral scientist. In the literature we have reviewed, the emphasis has been on isolating factors that facilitate or interfere with effective information pooling. From an applied perspective, the interest is not in demonstrating the causal impact of social and task variables but in designing a decision-making unit that works (Hackman, 1998). The remainder of this chapter summarizes what we know about information pooling in decision-making groups with the aim of identifying some general principles that will inform practice. Put simply, what can managers of or participants in decision-making groups do to increase the likelihood that unique information will be effectively pooled and innovative decisions will be discovered if they exist?

The SCOPE Model: Social Engineering

The practical principles can be organized with the mnemonic SCOPE: Social engineering, Climate, Opportunity, Procedures, and Expert roles. Social engineering is the overarching concept and underscores the idea that groups and their interaction need to be designed to promote effective information pooling. A successful athletic coach would not assemble a group of athletes and assume they will function effectively and efficiently as a team if she simply tells them to play the game. Even highly accomplished athletes need instruction, training, and experience to play successfully as a team. Similarly, one cannot assemble a group of knowledgeable people and assume that they will function effectively as a decision-making group. A social engineering approach involves several steps: defining the areas of expertise and experience that are relevant to the decision at hand; recruiting members that collectively cover the necessary areas of knowledge; and designing their interaction to promote effective information pooling. The rest of the SCOPE model addresses how to design effective interactions.

Climate

Viewing decision tasks as problems to be solved (Stasser & Stewart, 1992) and promoting norms of critical thinking (Postmes et al., 2001) are essential to clearing the hurdles that prevent information pooling. Groups that believe that information can lead to a demonstrably correct, or at least a defensible, solution are not inclined to let the "consensus implies correctness" heuristic guide their interaction. Belief that information leads to a solution discourages groups from adopting a position simply because it is popular. Moreover, when information search and integration are the central features of interaction, groups should be more receptive to new information and less inclined to ignore new information when it emerges. There are several ways to promote a climate that fosters reliance on information.

Stasser and Stewart (1992) simply told groups that consideration of all the clues in a murder mystery would identify the guilty suspect. Of course, in practice, one does not always know that information will lead to an unambiguous solution; often it does not. Nonetheless, one can underscore the general principle that active consideration of available information will often eliminate bad decisions and occasionally reveal an excellent decision. Additionally, group history can foster critical thinking. Recall that Postmes et al. (2001) promoted two distinct discussion styles by having groups perform either an evaluative or a cooperative task prior to discussion. The critical thinking engendered by the evaluative task apparently established a local norm that guided interaction in a later, and apparently unrelated, decision task. One implication is that decision-making groups, like athletic and work teams, can be trained to work together effectively (Moreland, Argote, & Krishnan, 1996). An important component of that training is to provide exercises that reinforce information exchange, constructive disagreement, and tolerance of deviant ideas and novel information. Moreover, members need to feel safe in promoting unique perspectives (see West's discussion of participative safety, this volume) and the expression of divergent points of view should be encouraged (see Nemeth & Nemeth-Brown's discussion of minority influence and divergent thinking, this volume).

Opportunity

Information pooling is a cognitively demanding process, and groups must be given the resources to make it feasible. Two resources are particularly relevant. First, group members must bring together complementary areas of knowledge. Much of our discussion has presumed that group members have unique information to contribute. Of course, this may not be the case in practice and is unlikely if groups are composed of members who share common experiences and interests. Groups of like-minded members will probably be highly cohesive and enjoy interacting, but each member will have little to contribute that others do not already know. As already noted, part of the social engineering task is to bring diverse sets of knowledge to the groups.

Second, time is a critical resource. Members must have, and feel that they have, the luxury of systematically exploring information. As collective information sampling theory suggests, initial contributions to discussion are most likely to be common information. The sampling advantage of common information will be continually reduced as discussion continues (Larson et al., 1996). Therefore, allowing groups sufficient time to complete their tasks also increases the likelihood that unique information will be brought to the group's attention.

Excessive workload can functionally limit time. If groups feel that they have to complete several tasks or are forced to divide their attention among several tasks, they will be less inclined to let information drive their decision making. Moreover, repetitive decision tasks encourage the adoption of simplified strategies such as combining prior preferences via some rule (e.g., majority wins or averaging). Unfortunately, groups cannot always control workload. However, they can prioritize tasks, accepting the risk of suboptimal choices for some decisions while freeing time to do the hard work of exploring information for important decisions. Such priorities should not be based on disagreement. The temptation is to reach quick decisions when members agree initially and prolong discussion when there is disagreement. As Figure 5.1 illustrates, however, groups can agree on decisions that are not supported by their collective knowledge. Thus, groups should give top priority to decisions that are regarded as important for realizing mutually valued goals.

Procedures

Gersick and Hackman (1990; Gersick, 1988) noted that groups quickly develop habitual routines for conducting their business. Unless critical events intrude (e.g., repeated failures or outside interventions), groups tend to continue using these routines without considering alternative ways of interacting and other strategies for completing their tasks. Nonetheless, how meetings are conducted can alter the flow of information in a group. Often, minor procedural variations can make a difference. For example, Hollingshead (1996) found that requiring groups to rank-order decision alternatives, as opposed to simply choosing the best option, increased the discussion of unique information and the likelihood that they would discover a hidden profile. She reasoned that ranking required discussing all alternatives and thus avoided the tendency to focus on one or two initially popular options. Houlette et al. (2000) found that, when members were not asked to indicate their preference before discussion, they were more likely to discover hidden profiles. Thus, if possible, one should discourage the formation of preferences before discussion. However, if members bring preferences to the table, they should postpone votes or informal expressions of these preferences. Once majority or popular positions are identified, discussions tend to center on these positions to the exclusion of options that have no initial support.

The nominal group technique (NGT) is a notable method for overcoming many of the hurdles to effective information pooling (Delbecq, Van de Ven, & Gustafson, 1975; Kerr, Aronoff, & Messé, 2000). Use of the NGT not only promotes information pooling but also discourages premature consensus seeking. NGT was originally designed for maximizing the use of ideas from brainstorming groups, but it can easily be applied to the pooling of information in a group decision-making context. In its original form, NGT uses a moderator to guide the group through four stages. First, the group's task is explained, and each member spends 10 to 20 minutes writing down any ideas that are pertinent to the task. In the second stage, members take turns reading aloud from their written lists in a round-robin fashion. The moderator transcribes each member's contribution on a whiteboard or flip chart. During the third stage, the group discusses each idea with the goals of clarifying, evaluating, and expanding on ideas. However, in this stage, they are asked to avoid stating preferences or attempting to reach a consensus. In the fourth stage, members privately rank their top five ideas or solutions. Average rankings for each idea are then computed to determine the most favored solution(s). The moderator may adopt the most highly ranked options or ask the group to repeat the third and fourth stages considering the reduced set of options.

With a few modifications and extensions, NGT can be implemented in the typical decision-making group. First, it seems that groups can be easily trained to enact these stages without the presence of a moderator. However, they would need to select a scribe to record the information on a public record (such as a flip chart) during the information-exchange stage. Second, the information-generation stage can be elaborated by asking members to consider each decision option separately and write down relevant information for each. This information-generation task could be further structured by asking participants to think of both supporting and opposing information for each option. The final stage can be modified so that members rank decision alternatives rather than ideas.

Most of the research evaluating the effectiveness of the NGT uses idea-generating tasks (Van de Ven, 1974). However, the procedure, with the foregoing suggested modifications, seems to offer several benefits to decision-making groups. First, individual knowledge is pooled in a systematic fashion. By having members first write down ideas and then contribute them in a round-robin discussion, the sampling advantage of common knowledge should be muted. In addition, condensing member contributions into a unified, external record may serve to increase attention to unique information that emerges during this information pooling. Knowledge that was once uniquely held may become less connected to its original source during the transfer to the written record (Durso, Hackworth, Barile, Dougherty, & Ohrt, 1998) and, as such, may gain equal footing with common information for later consideration.

Second, discussion is conducted without pressure to agree during the early phases of NGT. This frees members to evaluate ideas and synthesize information while obscuring the popularity of the decision alternatives. Third, the process of ranking various decision alternatives has also been shown to promote information pooling. As discussed earlier, Hollingshead (1996) found that asking members to rank-order decision alternatives was associated with more thorough consideration of all possible alternatives than if members were instructed to merely choose the best alternative. Ranking groups exchanged more information supporting initially unattractive alternatives and ultimately tended to make better decisions. This boost in decision quality was attributed to the more intense evaluation of supporting information for each alternative that was required for assigning numerical ranks to each option.

In addition to NGT, technological interventions have been demonstrated to improve group decision making. Termed Group Communication Support Systems (GCSS), these tools allow discussants to communicate via computer networks, often with relative anonymity. GCSS can remove logistical barriers to communication (e.g., competing for floor time) and provides an external record of all conversations. When GCSS uses text-only channels, simultaneous input from multiple anonymous parties is possible and promotes more equal participation and reduces concerns about evaluation. Whereas computer-mediated groups take longer to reach consensus, groups that are given ample time both to adjust to the medium and to discuss have been shown to make decisions that are comparable to face-to-face counterparts (Hollingshead, McGrath, & O'Connor, 1993; Sproull & Kiesler, 1992; Straus & McGrath, 1994).

Lam and Schaubroeck (2000), in particular, demonstrated that groups of midlevel managers faced with a hiring decision were more effective at uncovering hidden profiles in GCSS than in face-to-face interactions. Additionally, their GCSS groups discussed more unique information and made more critical arguments than comparable face-to-face groups. They attributed the success of computer-mediated groups to several factors: (1) reduced fear of evaluation; (2) increased willingness to abandon initially held positions; and (3) more equal participation by group members. They emphasized the role of anonymity in the GCSS environment as an important procedural factor.

These computer-supported discussion tools are often supplemented by voting mechanisms and displays of decision criteria. Combined with text-based chatroom capabilities, these tools are referred to as Group Decision Support Systems (GDSS). Several studies have extolled their ability to transform decision making, with benefits including deeper analysis of issues, more attempts at clarification and critical argumentation, and increased task focus (Nunamaker, Applegate, & Konsynski, 1988; Straus, 1997). The capabilities of these procedural tools and their potential as aids to divergent group decision making are discussed by other authors. Dennis, George, and Nunamaker (1988), Kraemer and Pinsonneault (1990), and McGrath and Hollingshead (1994) provide excellent reviews of the available tools, including summaries of the empirical studies of their benefits.

Expert Roles

Making explicit the locations of information and expertise within the group may be accomplished by assigning roles of expertise to particular members, a technique that has been shown to alter patterns of information exchange (Stasser et al., 1995, 2000; Stewart & Stasser, 1995; Wegner, 1986, 1995). Mutual recognition of expertise in a decision-making group offers at least two benefits. First, expert roles allow members to focus their contributions and increase the likelihood that uniquely held, expert knowledge will emerge during discussion. Thus, in the social engineering approach that we are suggesting, the group must not only be composed of members who bring complementary sets of knowledge but members also need to be aware of the expert roles they are expected to enact. As illustrated in Figure 5.2, these expert roles need to be sufficiently salient during interaction to focus members' contributions on their respective domains of expertise.

A second benefit is that information from recognized experts is credible. One indicant of credibility is the willingness of others to repeat it (Stasser et al. 1995, 2000; Stewart & Stasser, 1995). When the rest of the group knows that individuals are experts, these persons become recognized as credible sources of specific kinds of information (see discussions of transactive memory theory: Moreland et al., 1996; Wegner, 1986). Expectancies then emerge such that when an expert communicates something that is previously unknown to the group, there is no need to seek additional confirmation from others. Similar effects of repetition and acceptance of uniquely held information have been found for members recognized as being high in status (Larson et al., 1996) or experience (Wittenbaum, 1998).

Summary

The research on information pooling in decision groups has a consistent theme. Groups trying to reach consensus do not effectively pool information. The dynamics of unstructured discussion are conducive to eliciting widely shared knowledge and identifying popular decision alternatives but are not conducive to communicating unique information. Notwithstanding this theme, groups do occasionally make innovative decisions. In closing, we comment on three issues related to innovative decision making: the need for more research, the role of diversity in promoting innovative decision making, and the implications of Janis's (1972) work on groupthink.

Based on our understanding of the barriers to effective information pooling, we have proposed the SCOPE model as a way of identifying and implementing variables that will facilitate innovative process in decision-making groups. Some of the elements of the SCOPE model have strong empirical and theoretical support, whereas other elements are more speculative. Notably, NGT seems to offer many benefits. However, we know of no research that systematically documents these benefits in decision-making groups, particularly the suggested benefits regarding the pooling and use of unique information. Similarly, research on how computer-aided interactions affects information pooling is relatively new and sparse. In light of the increasing availability of technological support for group decision making, this area of research needs more attention. Thus, we offer the SCOPE model not only as a way of summarizing what we know but also as a heuristic device for identifying areas of potentially fruitful research.

Clearly, one way of promoting more innovative decisions is to compose groups with diverse perspectives and knowledge. In Steiner's (1972) terms, such diversity increases the potential productivity of the group. However, being diverse does not ensure that the group will benefit. This chapter illustrates some of important factors that may inhibit optimal group use of information resources. In another sense, these findings can be interpreted as an illustration of the limitations of member diversity. If groups tend to focus on what they know in common, the diversity that exists among a group's members will tend to be muted by their interaction. Nemeth and Nemeth-Brown (this volume) assert that diverse knowledge and perspectives must be not only voiced but also maintained throughout discussion to exert influence in the group. We have identified several hurdles that impede both the expression and maintenance of diversity in group discussion. If these hurdles are not cleared, innovation in group decision making will be compromised and the potential benefits of diversity will go unrealized.

It is also instructive to compare our analysis with Janis's (1972) concept of groupthink. He studied decisions of high-profile groups and concluded that such groups often exhibited groupthink: limited and defective information processing. In his case studies, contributing factors to groupthink included strong and opinionated leadership, group cohesiveness, feelings of invulnerability and morality, and external threat, often accompanied by a sense of urgency. Although members of these high-profile groups were undoubtedly knowledgeable and competent, they let their shared knowledge and perspectives discourage exploration of unique knowledge. Many of his observations are consistent with the conclusions that we have reached. However, we claim that limited and defective use of information in decision-making groups is much more pervasive than Janis's analysis suggests. He suggested that avoiding or counteracting the antecedents to groupthink will promote better information processing. For example, he recommended that leaders not express their preferences and that appointed devil's advocates actively contradict the dominant ideas or preferences in a group. These are useful recommendations (although note Nemeth & Nemeth-Brown's comments on the limits of devil's advocacy, this volume). However, the research we have reviewed suggests that incomplete information processing occurs even when the conditions favoring groupthink are not present. Thus, avoiding the antecedents to groupthink are not sufficient to ensure innovative decision making. If one wants to ensure innovative group decision making, one needs to compose the group and structure its interactions in ways that overcome the hurdles that inhibit effective information pooling: use of the "consensus implies correctness" heuristic, biased information exchange during discussion, and doubting the credibility of unique information.

Note

Preparation of this chapter was supported by National Science Foundation Grant BCS-0001910. We thank Paul Paulus, Bernard Nijstad, and Gwen Wittenbaum for their helpful comments and suggestions. Send correspondence to Garold Stasser, Department of Psychology, Miami University, Oxford, OH 45056. E-mail may be sent to stassegl@muohio.edu.

References

Chaiken, S., & Stangor, C. (1987). Attitudes and attitude change. *Annual Review of Psychology, 38*, 575–630.

Collins, B. E., & Guetzkow, H. (1964). *A social psychology of group processes for decision-making.* New York: Wiley.

Davis, J. H. (1973). Group decisions and social interaction: A theory of social decision schemes. *Psychological Review, 80*, 97–125.

Delbecq, A. L., Van de Ven, A. H., & Gustafson, D. H. (1975). *Group techniques for program planning.* Glenview, IL: Scott, Foresman.

Dennis, A. R., George, J. F., & Nunamaker, J. F., Jr. (1988). *Group decision support systems: The story thus far.* Tucson: MIS Department, College of Business and Public Administration, University of Arizona.

Deutsch, M., & Gerard, H. B. (1955). A study of normative and informational social influences upon individual judgment. *Journal of Abnormal and Social Psychology, 8,* 79–82.

Durso, F. T., Hackworth, C. A., Barile, A. L., Dougherty, M. R. P., & Ohrt, D. D. O. (1998). Source monitoring in face-to-face and computer-mediated environments. *Cognitive Technology, 3,* 32–38.

Festinger, L. (1954). A theory of social comparison. *Human Relations, 7,* 117–140.

Gersick, C. J. (1988). Time and transition in work teams: Toward a new model of group development. *Academy of Management Journal, 31,* 9–41.

Gersick, C. J., & Hackman, J. R. (1990). Habitual routines in task-performing groups. *Organizational Behavior & Human Decision Processes, 47,* 65–97.

Gigone, D., & Hastie, R. (1993). The common knowledge effect: Information sampling and group judgment. *Journal of Personality and Social Psychology, 65,* 959–974.

Gigone, D., & Hastie, R. (1996). The impact of information on small group choice. *Journal of Personality and Social Psychology, 72,* 132–140.

Goethals, G. R., & Darley, J. M. (1987). Social comparison theory: Self-evaluation and group life. In B. Mullen & G. R. Goethals (Eds.), *Theories of group behavior* (pp. 21–47). New York: Springer-Verlag.

Hackman, J. R. (1998). Why teams don't work. In R. S. Tindale, L. Heath, J. Edwards, E. J. Posavac, F. B. Bryant, Y. Suarez-Balcaza, E. Henderson-King, & J. Myers (Eds.), *Social psychological applications to social issues: Vol. 4. Theory and research on small groups* (pp. 245–267). New York: Plenum.

Hastie, R., Penrod, S. D., & Pennington, N. (1983). *Inside the jury.* Cambridge, MA: Harvard University Press.

Hinsz, V. B. (1990). Cognitive and consensus processes in group recognition memory performance. *Journal of Personality and Social Psychology, 59,* 705–718.

Hinsz, V. B., Tindale, R. S., & Vollrath, D. A. (1997). The emerging conceptualization of groups as information processors. *Psychological Bulletin, 121,* 43–64.

Hollingshead, A. B. (1996). The rank order effect in group decision making. *Organizational Behavior and Human Decision Processes, 68,* 181–193.

Hollingshead, A. B., McGrath, J. E., & O'Connor, K. M. (1993). Group task performance and communication technology: A longitudinal study of computer-mediated versus face-to-face work groups. *Small Group Research, 24,* 307–333.

Houlette, M., Muzzy, E. L. & Sawyer, J. E. (2000, August). Information sharing and integration in culturally diverse cross-functional groups. In J. E. Sawyer (Chair), *Decision-group composition, structure and processes: Applications of the hidden profile paradigm to group and organizational research.* Symposium presented at the annual meeting of the Academy of Management, OB and MOC Divisions, Toronto, Canada.

Janis, I. L. (1972). *Victims of groupthink.* Boston: Houghton Mifflin.

Kameda, T., Ohtsubo, Y., & Takezawa, M. (1997). Centrality in sociocognitive networks and social influence: An illustration in a group decision making context. *Journal of Personality and Social Psychology, 73,* 296–309.

Kaplan, M. F. (1987). The influencing process in group decision making. In C. Hendrick (Ed.), *Group processes* (pp. 189–212). Newbury Park, CA: Sage.

Kerr, N. L., Aronoff, J., & Messé, L. A. (2000). Methods of small group research. In H. T. Reis and C. M. Judd (Eds.), *Handbook of research methods in social and personality psychology* (pp. 160–189). Cambridge, UK: Cambridge University Press.

Kiesler, S., & Sproull, L. (1992). Group decision making and communication technology. *Organizational Behavior and Human Decision Making Processes, 52,* 96–123.

Kraemer, K. L., & Pinsonneault, A. (1990). Technology and groups: Assessment of the empirical research. In J. Galegher, R. E. Kraut, and C. Egido (Eds.), *Intellectual teamwork: Social and technological foundations of cooperative work* (pp. 375–405). Hillsdale, NJ: Erlbaum.

Lam, S. S. K., & Schaubroeck, J. (2000). Improving group decisions by better pooling information: A comparative advantage of group decision support systems. *Journal of Applied Psychology, 85,* 565–573.

Larson, J. R., Jr., & Christensen, C. (1993). Groups as problem-solving units: Toward a new meaning of social cognition. *British Journal of Social Psychology, 32,* 5–30.

Larson, J. R., Jr., Christensen, C., Abbott, A. S., & Franz, T. M. (1996). Diagnosing groups: Charting the flow of information in medical decision making teams. *Journal of Personality and Social Psychology, 71,* 315–330.

Larson, J. R., Jr., Foster-Fishman, P. G., & Franz, T. M. (1998). Leadership style and the discussion of shared and unshared information in decision-making groups. *Personality and Social Psychology Bulletin, 25,* 482–495.

Laughlin, P. R. (1980). Social combination processes of cooperative problem-solving groups on verbal intellective tasks. In M. Fishbein (Ed.), *Progress in social psychology* (Vol. 1, pp. 127–155). Hillsdale, NJ: Erlbaum.

Laughlin, P. R., & Ellis, A. L. (1986). Demonstrability and social combination processes on mathematical intellective tasks. *Journal of Experimental Social Psychology, 22,* 177–189.

McGrath, J. E., & Hollingshead, A. B. (1994). *Groups interacting with technology: Ideas, evidence, issues and an agenda.* Thousand Oaks, CA: Sage.

McLeod, P. L., Baron, R. S., Marti, M. W., & Yoon, K. (1997). The eyes have it: Minority influence in face-to-face and computer-mediated group discussion. *Journal of Applied Psychology, 82,* 706–718.

Moreland, R. L., Argote, L., & Krishnan, R. (1996). Socially shared cognition at work: Transactive memory and group performance. In J. L. Nye & A. M. Bower (Eds.), *What's new about social cognition? Research on socially shared cognition in small groups* (pp. 57–84). Thousand Oaks, CA: Sage.

Nunamaker, J. F., Applegate, L. M., & Konsynski, B. R. (1988). Computer-aided deliberation: Model management and group decision support. *Operations Research, 36,* 826–848.

Parks, C. D., & Cowlin, R. A. (1996). Acceptance of uncommon information into group discussion when that information is or is not demonstable. *Organizational Behavior and Human Decision Processes, 66,* 307–315.

Pennington, N., & Hastie, R. (1992). Explaining the evidence: Tests of the story model for juror decision making. *Journal of Personality and Social Psychology, 62,* 189–206.

Postmes, T., Spears, R., & Cihangir, S. (2001). Quality of decision making and group norms. *Journal of Personality and Social Psychology, 80,* 918–930.

Schulz-Hardt, S., Frey, D., Luethgens, C., & Moscovici, S. (2000). Biased information search in group decision making. *Journal of Personality and Social Psychology, 78*, 655–669.

Sproull, L., & Kiesler, S. (1992). Group decision making and communication technology. *Organizational Behavior and Human Decision Processes, 52*(1), 96–123.

Stasser, G. (1988). Computer simulation as a research tool: The DISCUSS model of
group decision making. *Journal of Experimental Social Psychology, 24*, 393–422.

Stasser, G., & Dietz-Uhler, B. (2001). Collective choice, judgment and problem
solving. In M. A. Hogg & S. Tindale (Eds.), *Blackwell handbook of social psychology: Group processes* (pp. 31–55). Oxford: Blackwell.

Stasser, G., Kerr, N. L., & Davis, J. H. (1989). Influence processes and consensus
models in decision-making groups. In P. Paulus (Ed.), *Psychology of group
influence* (2nd ed., pp. 279–326). Hillsdale, NJ: Erlbaum.

Stasser, G., & Stewart, D. (1992). Discovery of hidden profiles by decision-making
groups: Solving a problem versus making a judgment. *Journal of Personality and
Social Psychology, 63*, 426–434.

Stasser, G., Stewart, D. D., & Wittenbaum, G. M. (1995). Expert roles and information exchange during discussion: The importance of knowing who knows what.
Journal of Experimental Social Psychology, 31, 244–265.

Stasser, G., Taylor, L. A., & Hanna, C. (1989). Information sampling in structured
and unstructured discussions of three- and six-person groups. *Journal of Personality and Social Psychology, 57*, 67–78.

Stasser, G., & Titus, W. (1985). Pooling of unshared information in group decision
making: Biased information sampling during discussion. *Journal of Personality
and Social Psychology, 48*, 1467–1478.

Stasser, G., & Titus, W. (1987). Effects of information load and percentage of shared
information on the dissemination of unshared information during group discussion. *Journal of Personality and Social Psychology, 53*, 81–93.

Stasser, G., Vaughan, S. I., & Stewart, D. D. (2000). Pooling unshared information:
The benefits of knowing how access to information is distributed among members. *Organizational Behavior and Human Decision Processes, 82*, 102–116.

Steiner, I. D. (1972). *Group process and productivity.* New York: Academic Press.

Stewart, D. D., & Stasser, G. (1995). Expert role assignment and information sampling during collective recall and decision making. *Journal of Personality and
Social Psychology, 69*, 619–628.

Straus, S. G. (1997). Technology, group process and group outcomes: Testing the
connections in computer-mediated and face-to-face groups. *Human-Computer
Interaction, 12*(3), 227–266.

Straus, S. G., & McGrath, J. E. (1994). Does the medium matter? The interaction of
task type and technology on group performance and member reactions. *Journal
of Applied Psychology, 79*(1), 87–97.

Van de Ven, A. H. (1974). *Group decision-making and effectiveness: An experimental
study.* Kent, OH: Kent State University Press.

Wegner, D. M. (1986). Transactive memory: A contemporary analysis of the group
mind. In B. Mullen & G. Goethals (Eds.), *Theories of group behavior* (pp. 185–
208). New York: Springer-Verlag.

Wegner, D. M. (1995). A computer network model of human transactive memory.
Social Cognition, 13, 1–21.

Wittenbaum, G. M. (1998). Information sampling in decision-making groups: The impact of members' task-relevant status. *Small Group Research*, *29*, 57–84.

Wittenbaum, G. M. (2000). The bias toward discussing shared information: Why are high-status group members immune? *Communication Research, 27*, 379–400.

Wittenbaum, G. M., Hubbell, A., & Zuckerman, C. (1999). Mutual enhancement: Toward an understanding of the collective preference for shared information. *Journal of Personality and Social Psychology, 77*, 967–978.

Wittenbaum, G. M., & Stasser, G. (1996). Management of information in small groups. In J. L. Nye & A. M. Bower (Eds.), *What's new about social cognition? Research on socially shared cognition in small groups* (pp. 3–28). Thousand Oaks, CA: Sage.

Wittenbaum, G. M., Stasser, G., & Merry, C. J. (1996). Tacit coordination in anticipation of small group task completion. *Journal of Experimental Social Psychology, 32*, 129–152.

6

██████ *Paul B. Paulus and Vincent R. Brown*

Enhancing Ideational Creativity in Groups

Lessons from Research on Brainstorming

██████

Group creativity comes in many forms. It occurs whenever two or more individuals work together to create some new idea, product, or procedure. These individuals can be casual acquaintances or friends who get together to exchange ideas or solve a problem, or they can be members of an organized work group such as a scientific team, a product development team, or a committee. They can be short-term groups that meet for brief periods of time or long-term groups that work together for months or years on a series of projects. In all of these cases the presumption is that some type of collaboration, interaction, or exchange is important or necessary for creativity, innovation, or problem solving.

There are many accounts of the success of such collaborative adventures (Bennis & Biederman, 1997; John-Steiner, 2000). We do not doubt that such reported successes are real. However, there is an extensive literature on group processes relevant to creativity that suggests ways in which groups may often inhibit the creative process while at the same time giving the illusion to group members and even external observers that a high level of creativity is being attained (Paulus, 2000; Sutton & Hargadon, 1996). In fact, for some time, much of the groups literature suggested that groups were generally inimical to creativity and that collaboration should be avoided at all costs. More recently, we have discovered ways in which group interaction can in fact significantly enhance creativity. Some of our suggestions for improving creative idea generation in groups are supported by computer simulations of an associative memory model of individual and group brainstorming. The focus in this chapter is on the literature on group brainstorming or idea exchange using the specific rules suggested by Osborn (1957), the factors that limit its effectiveness, and ways to tap the creative potential of groups.

Productivity in Group Brainstorming

The Origins of Brainstorming

Brainstorming as a technique for idea generation has been used in a variety of group contexts. Hindu teachers in India have brainstormed with religious groups for over 400 years (Osborn, 1957), and Walt Disney encouraged artists to brainstorm in the 1920s. However, it was developed as a formal technique and popularized by Osborn, an advertising executive. Osborn's main concern was with increasing creativity in organizations. He felt that one of the main blocks to organizational creativity was premature evaluation of ideas. This would tend to inhibit the generation or presentation of ideas. Therefore, he proposed that individuals be trained to defer judgment of their own and others' ideas during the idea-generation process. He also emphasized that participants should focus on quantity, trying to generate as many ideas as possible. Brainstormers were encouraged to freewheel by stating all ideas that came to mind and to combine and improve on ideas presented in the group. He cited much informal evidence for the efficacy of following these brainstorming "rules," and his claim has been supported by controlled research. Brainstorming instructions do enhance the generation of ideas in comparison to conditions without such instructions (Parnes & Meadow, 1959).

The Process Loss Problem

Osborn's (1957) most controversial claim, that group brainstorming could be twice as productive as solitary brainstorming, has been repeated often (Prince, 1970; Rawlinson, 1981) and has stimulated much research demonstrating that, in fact, the opposite is true. Most controlled studies have found that solitary brainstorming is much more productive than group brainstorming (Diehl & Stroebe, 1987; Mullen, Johnson, & Salas, 1991). One problem with Osborn's data gathering approach was that he did not use a key control for the group interaction process: collections of individuals who did not generate ideas interactively. That is, to know whether group interaction is beneficial, one needs to compare the number of ideas generated by a group with the number of ideas generated by the same number of individuals brainstorming alone. The ideas generated by the individual brainstormers can then be combined to form a "nominal group" score that can be compared to the number of ideas generated by group brainstormers. For both the interactive group and the nominal group, only unique ideas are counted; that is, ideas that are essentially the same are not counted more than once. Contrary to Osborn's expectations, research using such nominal group comparisons found that interactive groups were actually much less productive than nominal groups (Diehl & Stroebe, 1987; Mullen et al., 1991). For example, Paulus and Dzindolet (1993) found that nominal groups of four produced an average of 77 ideas on the Thumbs Problem ("What would be the advantages and disadvantages of having an extra thumb on each hand?") in a 25-minute session, whereas interactive groups of four averaged only 45 ideas. This lower productivity of interactive groups in comparison to noninteractive controls has been termed "process loss" (Shepperd, 1993; Steiner, 1972) or "production loss" (Diehl & Stroebe, 1987).

Bases for Production Loss

The initially somewhat counterintuitive finding about process loss in brainstorming groups stimulated considerable research to determine causal factors (see Nijstad, Diehl, & Stroebe, this volume). Some research has documented that concern with evaluation from other group members (Camacho & Paulus, 1995), motivation loss due to lack of accountability for one's individual performance (Diehl & Stroebe, 1987), and the competition for speaking time in interactive groups (production blocking; Diehl & Stroebe, 1991) all may be contributing factors. It seems evident that a number of factors inherent in group interaction make it difficult for groups to reach their creative potential. This past research suggests that the obvious solution is to have individuals brainstorm alone. If group interaction is necessary or desired for other reasons, special efforts should be made to minimize evaluation apprehension, motivation losses, and production blocking (e.g., Pinsonneault, Barki, Gallupe, & Hoppen, 1999).

Osborn Revisited

The data clearly do not support an advantage of groups over solitary brainstormers, but it should be noted that Osborn's (1957) prediction of the efficacy of group brainstorming is usually taken out of context. He described effective group brainstorming in the context of a prior session of solitary writing. Subsequent group brainstorming is deemed more effective than individual brainstorming because

> in the same length of time, and under proper conditions, the average person can think up about twice as many ideas when working with a group than when working alone. Nevertheless, nearly all have agreed that an alternation between group ideation and individual ideation is desirable, since a combination of these two methods has produced maximum results in almost every case. (pp. 228–229)

Although Osborn does make the well-known twofold superiority of group brainstorming claim, this statement is strongly qualified. Such enhanced productivity requires proper conditions, and the most effective procedure is presumed to involve both individual and group brainstorming. In a later edition, this statement about the twofold superiority of group brainstorming is not repeated, but there is still an emphasis on the utility of combining solitary and group brainstorming: "To insure maximum creativity in teamwork, each collaborator should take time out for solitary meditations. By working together, and then alone, and then together, a pair is more likely to achieve the best in creative thinking" (Osborn, 1963, p. 146). Similarly, he stated, "Despite the many virtues of group brainstorming, individual ideation is usually more usable and can be just as productive" (p. 191). He also noted, "The fact is that group brainstorming is recommended solely as a supplement to individual ideation" (p. 142). Thus, in his 1963 edition, Osborn generally propounds the superiority of individual brainstorming, possibly in light of laboratory research indicating that brainstorming groups were not very productive (Taylor, Berry, & Block, 1958).

Osborn (1957, 1963) and other practitioners have suggested a considerable number of conditions as being necessary for optimal productivity in group brainstorming (Grossman, Rodgers, & Moore, 1989; Rawlinson, 1981). Groups should be trained for effective brainstorming and should employ facilitators or specially trained members that keep the group on task and highly motivated (Osborn, 1957, p. 235). Another important consideration is that groups should be heterogeneous. Groups in which individuals contribute a diversity of perspectives or knowledge bases allow for greater opportunities for creative combinations of ideas. Pairs of brainstormers who are intellectually compatible may be particularly effective (Osborn, 1963, p. 144). Both individual and group brainstorming are presumed to benefit from preliminary writing sessions, quotas or deadlines, brief breaks, and the use of specific, simple, and subdivided problems (Osborn, 1957, 1963). This chapter evaluates these prescriptions in light of recent data and theory.

Osborn (1957, 1963) also provided theoretical bases for the effectiveness of group brainstorming. Brainstorming in groups allows for "social facilitation" of activity levels. Highly productive members may stimulate others to high levels of productivity. This could involve a simple matching process (Brown & Paulus, 1996; Paulus & Dzindolet, 1993) or a degree of competitive rivalry to see who can generate the most ideas. Groups also allow for social reinforcement of idea generation. Group members may provide social rewards in the form of approval, agreement, or repetition of the same or similar ideas. This may increase motivation for idea generation. Finally, group members can cognitively stimulate mutually related ideas in each other. Thus, Osborn provided a compelling basis for future systematic research and practice on group ideation. We summarize this research, the theoretical perspectives, and implications for practice.

A Social Information Processing Model of Group Brainstorming and Creativity

In examining the group brainstorming process over the past 13 years, we have discovered that this process is influenced by a number of social and cognitive

processes (Paulus, Brown, & Ortega, 1999; Paulus, Larey, & Dzindolet, 2000).
We feel that an understanding of these interrelated processes can help explain
the occurrence of both production losses and gains in groups. When people are
involved in sharing ideas in groups, this sharing process provides information
that can affect both the *motivation* and the *ability* to generate ideas. The idea-
sharing process will inevitably vary in number and quality of ideas exchanged.
When group members are exposed to partners who share many ideas, they may
be motivated to perform at a similar high level, and the shared ideas may stimulate group members to think of additional ideas or categories of ideas. In contrast, unproductive partners may lower motivation to generate ideas and will
provide little stimulation for new ideas. Of course, there are limits in the ability
of individuals to process information as they are attempting to generate their
own ideas. Highly productive partners may limit others' opportunities to share
ideas, so there is likely to be an optimum pace of information sharing that provides both for high levels of motivation and cognitive stimulation without overwhelming the cognitive capacities of the group members.

Motivation and cognitive stimulation can also be affected by factors outside the group. Group motivation can be affected by intra- or intergroup competition, task structure, and facilitators or group leaders. Cognitive stimulation
can be influenced by task structure, the mode of idea sharing (e.g., oral vs. written), and ideas or category information presented by external sources such as
facilitators.

Our theoretical focus on the combined social, motivational, and cognitive
factors in group performance is also reflected in some prior theoretical models.
Baron (1986) has developed distraction-conflict theory of social facilitation to
account for the effects of social presence on task performance. In performing
tasks in the presence of others, individuals experience conflict between their
desire to devote cognitive resources to the task at hand and to attend to the social
cues provided by observers or coactors. This attentional conflict can hinder
performance on complex tasks. However, because the attentional conflict increases arousal levels, performance of simple or well-learned tasks may be facilitated. Furthermore, the degree of attention to others is affected by principles
of social comparison (Festinger, 1954). One is most likely to be concerned about
attending to individuals who have some implication for one's self-evaluation
(e.g., working on the same task; Sanders, Baron, & Moore, 1978). As we discuss
later in the chapter, where an individual focuses attention during a brainstorming task is extremely important; to the extent that attention is drawn away from
the idea-generation process itself or drawn away from the ideas being suggested
by other group members, the productivity of individual group members, and
thus ultimately of the group as a whole, will suffer. We also highlight the role of
social comparison processes in the idea-generation process.

Paulus (1983) developed the cognitive-motivational model of group task
performance to account for both social facilitation and social loafing effects in
task performance. Social factors such as group size and evaluation were assumed
to affect motivation, arousal, and task-irrelevant processes (e.g., distracting

thoughts/anxiety). As with other models of social facilitation, the specific outcomes were dependent on task complexity and characteristics of the social context such as positive or negative social consequences (Geen 1989; Zajonc, 1980). The models by Baron (1986) and Paulus have highlighted the importance of both motivational and cognitive factors in group productivity. We have continued to emphasize the importance of motivational and cognitive stimulation factors in group brainstorming (Brown, Tumeo, Larey, & Paulus, 1998; Paulus, Dugosh, Dzindolet, Coskun, & Putman, 2002).

Although in practice, the differential influence of cognitive and social/motivational factors may be difficult to disentangle, we discuss them separately because they involve unique underlying processes. Our categorization of social and cognitive factors may also be useful for practitioners as they attempt to develop procedures to optimize group creativity. We first discuss the role of social comparison and related motivational processes. Then we outline the cognitive processes that are involved in the group ideation process.

Motivational Factors

In discussing motivation, the distinction is often made between intrinsic and extrinsic motivation. Intrinsic motivation is "self-based" and is often seen as critical to creative achievements (Amabile, 1996; Hennessey, this volume). Extrinsic motivation is based on external and social pressures that motivate individuals to high levels of performance to attain rewards or approval. Although intrinsic motivation is a critical factor in the maintenance of creative efforts over a long period of time, in short-term settings like those involved in brainstorming sessions, extrinsic motivational factors may play an important role.

In short-term group brainstorming sessions, there are a number of sources of motivational cues. The experimenter's instructions may communicate the degree of importance of the task or provide other motivational cues. The experimenter or an assistant can serve as a facilitator to guide or motivate the brainstormers during a session. Brainstormers can be provided with high performance standards or comparison information about other successful individuals or groups. Task cues may provide brainstormers with information about what is expected of them. Indicators of the length of the session or breaking sessions into subsessions may affect the motivational level of brainstormers. The extent to which motivation is affected by information from others has been addressed by social comparison theory.

Social Comparison Processes

In his classic papers on social influence processes, Festinger (1954) proposed that we have a drive to compare our opinions and abilities to those of others. This presumes that we have some degree of uncertainty about our opinions and abilities and want to use the comparison process to reduce that uncertainty. Another presumption is that we would like to resolve that uncertainty in a positive manner. That is, we would like to discover that our opinions or beliefs are confirmed by others, so we tend to seek out for comparison those who are similar to us in other areas (e.g., Goethals & Darley, 1987). In regard to abilities, we might compare ourselves to those we believe might be slightly below us in ability (downward comparison) so that we can enhance our self-esteem (Gibbons & Gerrard, 1991; Turner, 1978). Alternatively, we might compare ourselves to those we perceive as slightly better than ourselves (Gibbons, Blanton, Gerrard, Buunk, & Eggleston, 2000); in that case, if we turn out to be better than they (e.g., in a game of tennis), we receive an extra boost in our self-esteem. It also gives us a reasonable goal for which to strive in terms of self-improvement. If we do not measure up at a specific time, that of course would be consistent with the fact that the other person is supposed to be slightly better and this would minimize the negative impact on our self-esteem.

In the idea-generation paradigm, social comparison processes can occur in a number of ways. First, group members can monitor the rate of idea generation and compare their own rate with that of other group members. Second, they can monitor and compare the quality of the ideas being shared. This monitoring process can have a number of consequences. It can affect the evaluations of self and group performance. For example, group members may develop an illusion that they are doing well because they are performing similarly to other group members (Paulus, Dzindolet, Poletes, & Camacho, 1993). The monitoring process can also have motivational consequences. Participants may become motivated to compete with each other in producing a high number of ideas or good ideas. Alternatively, they may free-ride on the efforts of the most productive group members by letting them do most of the talking. However, the initially more productive group members may decide that they are doing a disproportionate share of the work and adjust their performance in the direction of the low performers (downward matching). That is, they may decide not to play the "sucker" (Kerr & Bruun, 1983). Each of these types of processes has been observed in brainstorming groups.

Upward versus Downward Comparison

What determines whether upward or downward comparisons will predominate? We presume that if the setting emphasizes accountability and relative performance, social sharing may induce competition. For example, when group members are provided periodic comparison information during the course of a brainstorming session, they demonstrate enhanced performance (Paulus, Larey, Putman, Leggett, & Roland, 1996). In contrast, when group members feel that their contributions are anonymous or cannot be evaluated, there is a tendency of members to show reduced motivation or performance in groups (Diehl & Stroebe, 1987). We often find that under such conditions, individuals will also tend to make downward comparisons (Dugosh & Paulus, 2001; Paulus & Dzindolet, 1993).

So, social influence processes can affect brainstorming groups in a variety of ways. They can demonstrate process gains because of increased competitive motivation induced by the interaction process. This may involve mutual matching of high performance standards or levels. On the other hand, they can demonstrate process losses because of the opportunity to hide one's performance in the group or free-ride on the efforts of more productive members. Whether upward or downward processes predominate depends on a number of group characteristics.

For groups to function in an upward fashion it may be important for them to have a group culture that values high standards and performance (Gammage, Carron, & Estabrooks, 2001). This may not exist in short-term laboratory groups unless special procedures are used to induce such a culture. Work groups or teams that have appropriate leadership and strong commitment to shared goals may function quite differently than temporary ad hoc groups. Another factor that may be important is some level of intragroup trust. If group members trust each others' motives, they may compensate for group members who are not performing at a high level (Williams & Karau, 1991).

Social/Motivational Bases for Enhancing Brainstorming

The preceding discussion suggests that social comparison within and between groups can have a strong impact on task motivation. Under the right conditions groups can be disposed toward upward comparison and higher performance levels. However, there are many external factors that also can be influential in producing an upward comparison process or high levels of task motivation. Certainly, groups might be motivated by external rewards such as monetary incentives, grades, and public acclaim. We focus on four factors that have been examined for group brainstorming and performance: comparison information, facilitators, task rules, and leaders.

Comparison Information

When individuals are provided comparison information in a context in which goal achievement is valued, upward comparison information processes should be invoked. For example, when individual or group brainstormers are provided high comparison standards, they increase the number of ideas generated (Paulus & Dzindolet, 1993). In this study, participants were given performance expectations that were about twice as high as typical performance. As a result, performance of both nominal and interactive groups increased by about 40%. In a similar vein, when groups or individuals discover they have performed more poorly than other individuals or groups in a brainstorming session, they demonstrate increased performance in a subsequent brainstorming session (Coskun, 2000). In conditions where no feedback or positive feedback was provided, no such increase was observed. Several studies in which participants exchange ideas using computers have found that simple feedback about performance of other brainstormers increases brainstorming performance (Paulus et al., 1996; Roy, Gauvin, & Limayem, 1996; Shepherd, Briggs, Reinig, Yen, & Nunamaker, 1995–

1996). These findings are consistent with other research on the benefits of goals and competition on task performance (Stanne, Johnson, & Johnson, 1999). However, it should be noted that these types of manipulations do not reduce the performance gap between groups and individuals, as both appear to benefit similarly from such manipulations.

Facilitators

Although Osborn's (1957, 1963) rules are useful in increasing group productivity, they do not effectively address the variety of problems groups encounter. One often discussed problem is that some individuals dominate the interaction process and contribute most of the ideas (Bonito & Hollingshead, 1997), so it is important to encourage participation by all group members. Although there is an emphasis on quantity of ideas, group members often take time that could be used to generate new ideas to elaborate or explain their ideas. There are also often periods of inactivity when no one is presenting ideas. If these periods are long enough, they may be seen as a cue that the group has exhausted its idea store and that their task is finished (see Nijstad et al., this volume). Groups also have a tendency to generate ideas within specific categories of a problem and then go on to other categories; typically, they move on before they have exhausted the available ideas in a category. This could be a significant problem because some of the best ideas may be ones that are not immediately accessible (Brown et al., 1998).

When brainstorming occurs in organizations, groups typically are guided by a facilitator who ensures that groups avoid the above pitfalls (Grossman et al., 1989; Sutton & Hargadon, 1996). A number of recent studies have actually examined the potential benefits of using facilitators. A study by Offner, Kramer, and Winter (1996) used a condition in which trained facilitators helped groups adhere to Osborn's guidelines, prevented group members from engaging in irrelevant or disruptive discussions, and motivated continued performance. They found that groups with a facilitator performed as well as a nominal group. They replicated this effect in two additional experiments (Kramer, Fleming, & Mannis, 2001). The ratings of the participants and observation of effective facilitators suggested that the beneficial effects of facilitators were related either to their motivational effects or their ability to manage the interaction process effectively (e.g., limit interruptions and evaluation).

Oxley, Dzindolet, and Paulus (1996) conducted a similar study in which facilitators were provided with a specific set of guidelines based on a review of the facilitator literature. These included keeping group members focused on the task, not letting them tell stories, not letting them elaborate unnecessarily on expressed ideas, encouraging additional ideation when no one was talking, encouraging nonparticipants to contribute ideas, and reminding group members not to criticize. Group brainstormers in a condition with highly trained facilitators generated as many ideas as nominal groups and more ideas than nominal groups toward the end of the brainstorming session. Individuals in nominal groups were not provided with facilitators; thus, it remains to be determined whether facilitated interactive groups can outperform facilitated nominal groups. This question is partially addressed in the next section, where the effect of additional brainstorming guidelines is examined for both interactive and nominal groups. However, it is clear that group brainstormers will benefit from the help of trained facilitators.

Additional Brainstorming Guidelines or Rules

Osborn's (1957, 1963) brainstorming rules were designed to help creative groups function more effectively. Although these rules do seem to be helpful (Parnes & Meadows, 1959), it appears that facilitator guidance can have additional positive effects. One critical feature of facilitation is that groups are provided some additional guidelines. An interesting question is whether just providing groups with such additional guidelines will facilitate their performance. That is, if a few guidelines are helpful, maybe additional guidelines are even more helpful. This issue has been addressed in several studies (Putman, 1998, 2001). Putman provided some groups and individuals with regular brainstorming instructions and others with additional guidelines based on those used by Oxley et al. (1996). The additional instructions provided were as follows: (1) Do not tell stories or explain ideas; (2) when no one is saying ideas, restate the problem and encourage one another to generate more ideas; (3) encourage those who are not talking to make a contribution; (4) suggest that participants reconsider previous categories when they are not generating many more new ideas. To follow the instructions, each participant would have to take an active role in monitoring and guiding the group process. When conditions with the additional rules were compared to those that used only Osborn's rules, there was about a 40% increase in number of ideas generated. Somewhat unexpectedly, this increase occurred for both the group and individual brainstorming conditions, and the presence of an experimenter to remind group members to comply with the rules did not have any additional benefit. So it is evident that providing brainstormers with additional guidelines greatly increases their productivity. At this point, it is not clear why this is the case. The additional guidelines could be increasing the efficiency of the brainstorming process, or they could serve to provide participants additional motivation. Putman (2001) found some support for the efficiency hypothesis in that individuals and groups who received additional instructions used fewer words to express their ideas. We have probably just scratched the surface of discovering useful guidelines and the reasons for their efficacy.

Leadership

All of the key studies on group brainstorming have used leaderless groups. Informal leaders may emerge, but no formal leaders are appointed to motivate and guide the group process. In most real-world settings, groups or teams often have someone whose task is to lead the group toward its goals. These leaders may help set the agenda, guide the interaction process, and maintain a reward or compensation structure. Unlike facilitators, leaders are members of the group and may contribute to the group product. They may not have any special training in group dynamics, but it is hoped that they will have some skill in managing the group process.

A major concern of the leadership literature has been the impact of different styles of leadership. The effects of different leadership styles depend on such factors as the type of task, group type, and the relationship between the group and the leader (Bass, 1998; Chemers, 2001). Although directive leaders who are relatively authoritarian can be useful in motivating groups on simple tasks (Fiedler, 1967), for tasks that require creativity and self-motivation a leadership style that enhances intrinsic motivation and self-confidence may be optimal (Burpitt & Bigoness, 1997; Manz & Sims, 1987). Two styles may be useful in this latter type of setting. Transactional leadership is concerned with setting goals and providing feedback and reward for performance (Bass, 1985). This type of leadership may motivate group members to work hard to reach the implicit or explicit goals. Transformational leadership may be particularly helpful (Avolio & Bass, 1998; Bass & Avolio, 1994) for tasks that require a high level of intrinsic motivation. These types of leaders are sensitive to individual differences, focus on novel perspectives and approaches, and attempt to inspire group members to attain their collective goal in a cooperative manner. Such leaders can increase the confidence or motivation level of the group. This has been termed group potency (Guzzo, Yost, Campbell, & Shea, 1993) or collective efficacy (Bandura, 2000). Both transactional and transformational leadership have been shown to have positive effects on performance (Lowe, Kroeck, & Sivasubramaniam, 1996).

Leadership style has not been examined in conventional brainstorming groups. However, there are several studies of leadership in groups using a computer-based group decision support system. One study examined the effects of leadership style on various phases of the creative process using this paradigm (Sosik, Avolio, & Kahai, 1997). In the first phase that involved group brainstorming, transactional leadership was most effective in increasing ideational productivity. A second, writing phase involved writing a group report on the ideas generated. Transformational leadership had the most positive effect on the quality of the report produced in this phase. This positive effect of transformational leadership on electronic brainstorming was replicated in a second study (Sosik, Kahai, & Avolio, 1998), but in a third study both goal setting (transactional) and inspiration (transformational) were related to ideational creativity (Sosik, Avolio, & Kahai, 1998).

Thus, both transactional and transformational leadership may be useful in creative groups. Transactional leadership may be particularly useful for the production or generation of ideas, and transformational leadership may provide the motivation to persist in evaluating these ideas and possibly implementing them. The most effective leader may thus be one who combines both qualities (Avolio & Bass, 1988).

Cognitive Bases for Ideational Creativity

One of the reasons Osborn (1957, 1963) believed idea groups would be highly creative is that he assumed there would be much stimulation of mutual associations. Intuitively, the cognitive benefits of brainstorming in a group seem clear: people believe they come up with ideas in a group that they would not have thought of on their own. This is one reason for the popularity of group idea generation in business and industry. The intuition that groups might facilitate (or "prime") their members to think thoughts they might not have had in the context of solitary brainstorming is reminiscent of the notion from cognitive psychology that certain ideas or memories are more accessible than others (Tulving & Pearlstone, 1966). The concepts we have stored in long-term memory can be thought of as being connected in a lattice or network in such a way that related concepts are more strongly connected and thus more likely to activate each other (Collins & Loftus, 1975). Thus, concepts that are more closely connected to those that are currently active should be more accessible than those that are less strongly connected to current ideas. This way of representing the idea-generation processes also implies that it is situation- or context-dependent: which ideas are currently accessible depends on what is currently active in working memory.

Semantic Networks and an Associative Memory Model of Group Brainstorming

The notion that our knowledge is stored in some sort of semantic network is now standard and the evidence for it is quite strong.[1] Preceding a word with a conceptually related word facilitates the processing of the second word (semantic priming; Meyer & Schvaneveldt, 1971; Neely, 1991); lists of conceptually related items are recalled better than unrelated items, and related items tend to be grouped together during recall even if they were not presented together (clustering; Bousfield, 1953; Mandler, 1967); and often, giving people the category labels for items to be recalled facilitates recall (category cuing; Tulving & Pearlstone, 1966). Clearly, the retrieval of relevant information from one's long-term semantic memory is an important part of the process of group and individual brainstorming: you can't effectively brainstorm on a topic you know nothing about! However, it is recognized that creative idea generation that involves "novel combinations" of existing ideas may not be directly accounted for as the result of associative priming in a semantic network.

To use the semantic network representation as a basis for understanding group brainstorming, many details need to be specified so that quantitative predictions can be made. Because one goal of a model of group idea generation is to account for how groups of four, six, eight, or more interact, it would be unwieldy to explicitly represent four, six, eight, or more semantic networks and the interactions among them. Our approach is to represent a brainstormer's knowledge of a given task or problem as a matrix of categories. Each entry in this matrix represents the probability of generating one's next idea from the same category as the previous idea or from a different category. For example, for the University Problem commonly used in our laboratory, participants are instructed to come up with ideas about how to improve their university. For this task, an individual who is currently generating ideas on the topic of classes is more likely to continue on that topic, or a closely related topic such as exams, than to switch to a less related topic such as parking. The probability of staying with the category "classes" is thus higher than the probability of switching from "classes" to "exams," which would be higher than switching from "classes" to "parking." The matrix representation also includes a category called the "null category," which represents the probability of coming up with no idea during a given time interval. As a brainstorming session progresses and new ideas become harder to generate, the probabilities in the null category increase.[2] An example of a category matrix like those used in our simulations is shown in Figure 6.1.

A number of individual differences relevant to brainstorming are captured by the matrix framework. Fluency, or the amount of knowledge one has about the brainstorming problem and its categories, is represented as higher probabilities in the main body of the matrix relative to the null category (higher initial probabilities in the null category, which represents the likelihood of coming up with no relevant idea, imply that the brainstormer has less knowledge of a particular category). Convergent and divergent thinking styles also fit nicely into the framework. A convergent thinker is likely to stick with a category and explore it more deeply before moving on to generate ideas from other categories. Thus, a convergent thinker is represented by a matrix with relatively high within-category transition probabilities (the diagonal entries of the matrix). On the other hand, divergent thinkers are more likely to skip around among categories and so are represented by matrices with somewhat lower within-category transition probabilities (and correspondingly higher between-category transition probabilities, represented by the off-diagonal entries of the matrix).[3]

Accessibility

The property of the cognitive network that is perhaps most crucial to determining the effectiveness of group brainstorming is category accessibility. Relevant categories of ideas that have relatively weak connections to other categories will not generally be explored in isolation. These categories are the ones that require input from others to spark the generation of ideas. For example, a student who lives on campus in a dormitory may be less likely to generate ideas about parking when brainstorming on the University Problem. But if a student who commutes from off campus mentions parking, the dorm dweller may be able to come up with a few thoughts on the matter, perhaps recalling the parking difficulties his or her parents had when they visited campus. In the matrix framework, low-accessible categories are represented by low probabilities in the columns of the

	Classes	Campus	Buildings	Student life	Policies	Activities	Instruction	Parking	Dorms	Athletics	Food	Jobs	NULL
Classes	**0.74200**	0.07500	0.07500	0.07500	0.00750	0.00750	0.00750	0.00750	0.00075	0.00075	0.00075	0.00075	0.000
Campus	0.07140	**0.70638**	0.07140	0.07140	0.00714	0.00714	0.00714	0.00714	0.00071	0.00071	0.00071	0.00071	0.048
Buildings	0.06780	0.06780	**0.67077**	0.06780	0.00678	0.00678	0.00678	0.00678	0.00068	0.00068	0.00068	0.00068	0.096
Student life	0.06420	0.06420	0.06420	**0.63515**	0.00642	0.00642	0.00642	0.00642	0.00064	0.00064	0.00064	0.00064	0.144
Policies	0.04848	0.04848	0.04848	0.04848	**0.59760**	0.00485	0.00485	0.00485	0.00048	0.00048	0.00048	0.00048	0.192
Activities	0.04560	0.04560	0.04560	0.04560	0.00456	**0.56210**	0.00456	0.00456	0.00046	0.00046	0.00046	0.00046	0.240
Instruction	0.04272	0.04272	0.04272	0.04272	0.00427	0.00427	**0.52660**	0.00427	0.00043	0.00043	0.00043	0.00043	0.288
Parking	0.03984	0.03984	0.03984	0.03984	0.00398	0.00398	0.00398	**0.49109**	0.00040	0.00040	0.00040	0.00040	0.336
Dorms	0.03388	0.03388	0.03388	0.03388	0.00339	0.00339	0.00339	0.00339	**0.46591**	0.00034	0.00034	0.00034	0.384
Athletics	0.03124	0.03124	0.03124	0.03124	0.00312	0.00312	0.00312	0.00312	0.00031	**0.42961**	0.00031	0.00031	0.432
Food	0.02860	0.02860	0.02860	0.02860	0.00286	0.00286	0.00286	0.00286	0.00029	0.00029	**0.39330**	0.00029	0.480
Jobs	0.02596	0.02596	0.02596	0.02596	0.00260	0.00260	0.00260	0.00260	0.00026	0.00026	0.00026	**0.35700**	0.528

Figure 6.1. An example of the associative memory matrix representation for a hypothetical individual brainstorming on how to improve his or her university. Each entry represents the probability of generating an idea from the column category, given that the previous idea was generated from the row category. For example, if the brainstormer represented by this matrix generated an idea from the category "buildings," the probability that his or her next idea would also be from the "building" category is .67077. The null category (last column) represents the probability of generating no idea. Thus, higher numbers in the null category represent less knowledge (lower "fluency") for the row category. In this example, matrix fluency decreases from the first to last category: the hypothetical brainstormer has more ideas about classes and campus than about food or jobs. The diagonal of the matrix (numbers in boldface) represents the probability of staying within the same category. The brainstormer represented here is likely to generate many ideas from the same category before switching to a new category and so would be considered highly "convergent." The off-diagonal entries in the columns of the matrix represent the accessibility of the column category: the overall probability of generating an idea from the column category while currently thinking about one of the other categories for the task. The first four columns (campus to student life) represent high-accessible categories; the middle four columns (policies to parking) represent medium-accessible categories; and the next four columns (dorms to jobs) represent low-accessible categories. The off-diagonal column entries decrease by a factor of 10 from high to medium, and medium to low accessibility.

matrix, which determine the likelihood of entering a given category from the other categories relevant to the task. Simulations show that presenting a brainstormer with ideas from low-accessible categories not only increases the number of ideas generated from those categories, but increases the total number of ideas generated overall, thus making the individual a more productive brainstormer (Sherwood, 1998).

This prediction was supported in a study by Leggett (1997). She employed nominal brainstorming groups to evaluate cognitive stimulation in the absence of the negative social influences of others. Leggett played audiotapes containing ideas from either high- or low-frequency categories from the Thumbs Problem ("What would be the advantages and disadvantages of having an extra thumb on each hand?"). Category frequency was determined by examining protocols from participants in previous studies using the Thumbs Problem. A high-frequency category is considered to represent greater accessibility than a low-frequency category. Individuals who were primed in high-frequency categories obtained less benefit than those who were primed in low-frequency categories. In other words, priming categories that are already likely to be utilized did not enhance performance as much as priming categories unlikely to be utilized on one's own. This suggests that presenting primes from low-accessible categories of ideas can increase total idea generation by activating knowledge that would have gone untapped. Leggett also found that brainstormers given six primes from each category generated more ideas than those given only three primes per category, a result also predicted by our associative memory model.

In a related study, Dugosh, Paulus, Roland, and Yang (2000) primed individual brainstormers with ideas from an audiotape in a more ecologically valid way by also including "filler": comments often made by interactive brainstormers that are irrelevant to the task at hand (e.g., someone might remark "I hated typing class" if typing is mentioned during a brainstorming session on the Thumbs Problem). Providing individuals with external primes increased productivity as expected, again illustrating the potential benefits of cognitive stimulation; however, adding extraneous comments reduced the benefits of priming, illustrating one of the many ways in which group interactions work to subvert the potential benefits of working in a group. This result is predicted by our associative memory model because the irrelevant information causes fewer relevant categories to be active in short-term memory. Ultimately, the model also predicts that when the degree of extraneous information is high enough it will completely overcome the benefits of being primed by relevant ideas; that is, individuals who are primed with relevant ideas can still end up being less productive than an individual who is neither primed nor distracted.

Sequential Priming

Coskun, Paulus, Brown, and Sherwood (2000) showed that providing external primes also improves the performance of interactive brainstorming groups. However, because providing external primes improves the performance of individual brainstormers as well, this technique does not lead to a reduction in the productivity gap. Coskun et al. further demonstrated that the manner in which external primes are presented is crucial. Presenting all of the primes simultaneously is much less effective than presenting them sequentially, that is, one at a time every few minutes throughout the brainstorming session.

Although part of the explanation for the superiority of sequential presentation may be motivational (i.e., perhaps sequential presentation has a "pacing" effect), the associative memory model indicates that the limited capacity of short-term memory is an important factor. Short-term memory can be thought of as the subset of recently activated categories whose activation decays over time but that are still active enough to influence the idea-generation process (cf. Anderson, 1995; Cowan, 1995). In the model, a short-term memory parameter simply assigns a strength to categories from which ideas were most recently generated, and that strength decays fairly rapidly. Simulations demonstrate that the strength of short-term memory does not influence performance when a brainstormer is presented with regularly spaced sequential primes, but that high short-term memory strengths are required if simultaneous priming is to produce a significant benefit over a no-priming control condition. This implies that the effectiveness of sequential primes lies in the fact that they reduce the cognitive load of having to keep track of past ideas. The external primes act as a reminder of the relevant categories, possibly freeing the brainstormer to devote cognitive resources to other aspects of the interactive (and individual) idea-generation process.

Attention

At this point it should be noted how the associative memory model accounts for group performance, given that the matrix formalism itself is simply a representation of an individual brainstormer's knowledge and performance. It is the process of attention by which individual brainstormers are assumed to be linked into an interactive group. Individuals will be influenced by other group members to the extent that they are paying attention to each other's ideas. In the probabilistic framework of the model, attention is represented as the probability that an individual group member uses the current speaker's idea as the basis for generating his or her next idea (as opposed to simply continuing his or her own internal train of thought). This allows for possible differences in the degree to which individuals attend to their fellow group members.

Simulations predict that, in general, the more attention one pays to one's fellow group members, the better the performance of the group. Conversely, the more one's attention is distracted from the ideas of others by concern for the social aspects of group brainstorming, the more the performance of the group will decline. In particular, the more one attends to fellow brainstormers, the more one is likely to be primed to consider ideas from one's own low-accessible categories. In fact, the model predicts that, in general, if it were not for production blocking, the number of ideas generated by each group member would increase (at least up to a point) as group size increases (Brown et al., 1998). This reflects the results mentioned earlier from Leggett (1997; Dugosh et al., 2000), which indicate that providing brainstormers with external primes, especially primes from low-accessible categories, improves brainstorming productivity. Clearly, there are potential benefits to group idea generation.

One reasonable way to test the effects of attention on brainstorming performance is to instruct brainstormers that at the end of the brainstorming session they will be asked to recall the ideas they were primed with or the ideas generated by the group. There is some evidence that these memory instructions serve to improve brainstorming productivity (Dugosh et al., 2000). Interestingly, however, the effectiveness of memory instructions appears to be mixed. When participants listened to audiotapes or exchanged ideas by computer, instructions to memorize facilitated idea generation during the exposure session and afterwards. Apparently, the memorization instructions increased the extent to which participants attended to the ideas presented and in turn led to additional associations. Without memorization instructions, participants may be more likely to focus on the generation of their own ideas and, to some extent, ignore the ideas that are being presented simultaneously by others. However, when students were asked to exchange written ideas in a round-robin format (Paulus & Yang, 2000), memory instructions inhibited performance. In this paradigm, students were asked to read the ideas as they were passed from one person to the other. Because the instructions to read may have already ensured that participants attended to the ideas of others even while they were in the process of generating their own, instructions to memorize may simply have added an unnecessary extra demand that may have impeded the brainstorming effort (i.e., cognitive overload).

At this point, it is fair to say that although the group productivity gap is persistent in laboratory studies and a number of inhibitory factors have been well-documented, it is clear that under the proper conditions, group brainstorming should provide benefits that in general cannot be realized by solitary brainstormers. Because group interactions can lead to ideas that may not have been generated by solitary brainstormers (ideas from low-accessible categories), it is important to recognize that under the proper conditions, group brainstorming should prove beneficial regardless of whether the productivity gap between groups and individuals (which is measured in terms of quantity of ideas generated) can be overcome.

Cognitive Bases for Enhancing Group Brainstorming

When trying to create circumstances that optimize group performance, the goal is to maximize the benefits of cognitive facilitation (interactive priming) while at the same time minimizing the many inhibitory processes that serve to reduce group productivity. In a nutshell, this statement provides us with a formula for optimizing group performance. Our previous discussion suggests that factors that increase attention to novel ideas and enhance the processing of such ideas will increase the creativity output of groups. We now consider three additional methods that appear quite promising for theoretical reasons and that have garnered some empirical support: creating breaks in the brainstorming session, combining group and solitary brainstorming, and having group brainstormers interact by writing instead of speaking ("brainwriting"). Electronic brainstorming, or the use of networked computers on which individuals type their ideas and read the ideas of others, is another potential way to overcome many of the inhibitory factors associated with face-to-face brainstorming. This approach is discussed by Dennis and Williams (this volume).

Breaks

Mitchell (1998) and Horn (1993; see also Brown & Paulus, 1996) both demonstrated that having individuals take a short break (2–5 minutes) halfway through a 20-minute brainstorming session gives rise to an increase in productivity following the break compared to individuals brainstorming continuously without a break. Mitchell also varied the activities in which brainstormers were engaged during a break from orally brainstorming on the Thumbs Problem. Brainstormers who were asked to continue thinking about the task by writing down any ideas that came to mind during the break and brainstormers who had the brainstorming problem and instructions reread to them during the break both showed an increase in performance following the break relative to brainstormers who continued on without a break. Brainstormers who performed a verbal fluency task ("Think of an object that begins with each letter of the alphabet starting with the letter A") did not perform significantly better than the no-break controls in the period following the break. Brainstormers who took a break but who were not given any specific instructions or task during the break fell in between the two extremes.

Thus, the specific mental activity in which a brainstormer is engaged during a break is important: the above data clearly indicate that the contents of short-term memory during a break affect an individual's postbreak brainstorming performance. If the activity performed during the break does not allow the task-relevant ideas and concepts to remain active in short-term memory, then the relevant categories will have to be reactivated or "reloaded" following the break. (Low-accessible categories, which, by definition, are less likely to be reactivated, would be most strongly affected by short-term memory interference during a break.) This effect is demonstrated in model simulations: when the current contents of short-term memory are reduced or eliminated during a break, the postbreak performance suffers relative to the condition where the contents of short-term memory remain activated throughout the break.

Smith (1995, this volume) has discussed in detail the importance of brief breaks in overcoming mental blocks of previous experiences. That is, one may become fixated on a particular approach or category during some point in the idea-generation process. Brief breaks or changes to a novel context can provide a stimulus to take a different approach to the problem. In brainstorming settings, brief breaks may lead individuals to switch their ideation to a new domain or category from those previously considered. In this way, breaks can be seen as means of overcoming cognitive fixation on a limited range of categories.

Individual and Group Brainstorming

If we take the formula stated above at face value, we should look for some way to literally combine group and individual brainstorming. Of course, a person cannot be in two places at once and therefore cannot brainstorm alone while at the same time brainstorming in a group. But one can alternate group and solitary idea-generation sessions (as Osborn, 1957, 1963, suggested). Preliminary data from one of our laboratories (Leggett, Putman, Roland, & Paulus, 1996) make it clear that brainstorming in a group prior to brainstorming alone on the same topic produces more ideas over the course of the two sessions than does brainstorming alone in the first session and then brainstorming in a group in the following session.

Model simulations make clear the mechanisms that produce this advantage for the group-alone sequence. The cognitive facilitation that occurs in the group session carries over into the solitary session, where the brainstormer can continue without the hindrance of group inhibition. Whereas in most group sessions the potential cognitive advantages of the group interaction are overwhelmed by blocking and other inhibitory factors, an individual who follows a group session with a solitary session still has many of the ideas primed by the group active in short-term memory and is therefore able to use them to generate more ideas in a subsequent session. Furthermore, because a subsequent solitary session is not subject to blocking (and other inhibitory factors), the brainstormer can freely output those ideas. This facilitation shows up as a large "productivity spike" for solitary brainstormers in the second session in both the model simulations and the empirical data. This order effect is particularly strong when the initial group consists of heterogeneous members with differing knowledge of the task. The model simulations also predict that under ideal circumstances, a group session followed by a solitary session can even outproduce two back-to-back solitary sessions, although this advantage is expected to be small and has not yet been observed empirically. Simulations also indicate that a solitary brainstormer whose idea generation takes place after a group brainstorming session is likely to sample more categories from the task at hand than a similar brainstormer who works in two solitary sessions. This suggests an advantage of the group-alone sequence beyond any possible increases in overall productivity.

Brainwriting

Another way to take advantage of group priming effects while reducing blocking effects is to have group members interact by writing and reading rather than speaking and listening. Although this may seem a sensible way to implement the group brainstorming formula, it does not seem to be a technique that is often attempted. Perhaps such "brainwriting" is a good example of a low-accessible idea! We are so used to communicating orally when we are face to face that we just don't consider the alternatives. Paulus and Yang (2000) and Coskun (2000) tested interactive brainwriting as an alternative to interactive oral brainstorming. Instead of speaking their ideas as they occurred, group members wrote their ideas on a piece of paper and passed them on to the next group member, who read the idea on the slip of paper, added his or her own idea, and passed it on to the next group member. To prevent the slips of paper from becoming overcrowded and hard to read, brainwriters were asked to place slips that had accumulated four ideas in a pile in the center of the table. This assured that each brainwriter had the opportunity to look at each slip of paper at least once. This procedure resulted in interactive groups of brainwriters outproducing solitary brainstormers who wrote their ideas down on paper. These important results may be the first laboratory examples of face-to-face interactive groups outperforming an equal number of solitary brainstormers.

Although model simulations support the observation that interactive brainwriters can outperform an equal number of solitary brainwriters (Brown & Paulus, 2000), the simulation results are complex in some interesting ways. First, simulations predict that interactive brainwriting is not universally superior to individual brainwriting, but that it is most effective for heterogeneous groups (where members have differing knowledge of the brainstorming problem). More homogeneous groups actually show a productivity deficit in simulations. Second, performance of simulated brainwriting groups is an inverted U-shaped function of attention to the written ideas. Obviously, a brainwriter who does not read any of the ideas that are passed along will not benefit from the thoughts of his or her fellow brainwriters. A brainwriter who attends predominantly to the ideas of others will benefit from them to some extent, but not as greatly as someone who optimally balances the two goals of attending to the written ideas of others and following his or her own internal train of thought.

Applications

Our program of research has provided considerable support for our social information-processing model of group brainstorming. At the same time, many of our findings support recommendations made by Osborn (1957, 1963) many years ago. Osborn may have been a bit optimistic about the effectiveness of group brainstorming, but he was quite prescient about ways to optimize creativity in idea-sharing groups.

There are a number of pragmatic implications of our research findings and related theoretical framework. First of all, if groups are left to their own devices, are not trained, and interact in a nonstructured fashion, they will underperform in terms of creativity, innovation, and productivity. However, many tasks require group interaction or are most naturally done in face-to-face group situations. So it is important to develop some procedures to optimize the ability of groups to tap their creative potential. Our research suggests that we should pay particular attention to procedures that affect the social influence and cognitive information processes in groups. To optimize motivation, there should be some degree of accountability and possibly some competition among group members and/or among groups. The development of group norms emphasizing high standards, open exchange of ideas, and attention to contrary points of view is important for the group's eventual success. One of the most difficult tasks in groups is to attend to the ideas being shared and simultaneously carefully access one's own knowledge base for relevant ideas. The information-exchange process should involve an alternation between individual and group sessions. After group sessions, individuals should immediately take some time to reflect on the ideas exchanged and note additional ideas that come to mind at that point or in subsequent days. These can be shared in subsequent meetings. Information-sharing sessions should include brief breaks to allow the processing of ideas and information exchanged and to encourage groups to take a new direction when they recommence. It is best to tackle one aspect of a problem at a time rather than focusing on an entire range of issues at once. All of these proposals imply that groups should have some degree of training to increase their effectiveness in group creativity. And again, most of these recommendations were originally considered by Osborn but have now been placed on a somewhat firmer empirical and theoretical foundation.

We finish by providing a list of recommendations for improving the effectiveness of brainstorming groups:

- Hold individuals accountable for generating their share of ideas.
- Set high goals for the group's performance.
- Minimize blocking by using writing or computer-based interaction.
- Alternate group and individual brainstorming sessions. Whenever possible, individual sessions should take place with minimal delay following group sessions.
- If possible, compose groups with members with complementary or heterogeneous sets of task knowledge.
- Motivate participants to attend carefully to each other's ideas.
- Include brief breaks in brainstorming sessions.
- Focus as much as possible on one aspect of a problem at a time.
- Be trained with an explicit set of rules about effective group interaction.
- Use trained facilitators or leaders to guide and motivate brainstorming groups.

When guidelines are used, group idea generation can be very effective, perhaps even more effective than individual idea generation.

Notes

We would like to thank Bernard Nijstad and Wolfgang Stroebe for their insightful comments on an earlier version of this chapter. Thanks are also due to Scott Burris for helping to run many of the model simulations reported in this chapter while he was at the University of Richmond.

1. Nijstad, Diehl, and Stroebe (this volume) also present a model of cognitive processing in group brainstorming. The model SIAM (Search for Ideas in Associative Memory) is built on Raaijmakers and Shiffrin's (1981) SAM model (Search of Associative Memory) and therefore, like the model presented in this chapter, is also based on an associative memory framework. Thus, there are a number of similarities in the two models, with perhaps the major distinction being one of emphasis: our associative memory model emphasizes the structural properties of semantic networks, and SIAM emphasizes the active search process that takes place when a brainstormer (either alone or in a group) is seeking to generate novel ideas. The emphasis on an active search process in SIAM may make it a better candidate for exploring the process of constructing novel combinations of existing ideas.

2. This matrix representation of long-term semantic memory has some obvious similarities to existing mathematical memory models, such as Raaijmakers and Shiffrin's (1981) SAM model. SAM, in particular, represents individual ideas as "images" that are connected to each other with varying strengths; these strengths in turn determine the probability that a given image will activate another, related image. So, like the standard semantic network representation, SAM represents memory at the level of individual concepts. If a category is viewed as a collection of individual ideas, our matrix model can be thought of as a higher-level representation of SAM-like images: the entries in the matrix can presumably be derived from the association strengths among individual images in SAM (cf. Nosofsky's 1984 "mapping hypothesis").

3. Like SAM, which can capture the temporal nature of memory recall (e.g., serial position effects such as primacy and recency), our associative memory model captures some of the dynamic nature of individual and group brainstorming. The decrease in idea generation that takes place as a brainstorming session progresses is built into the model by decrementing the probability of generating another idea from a category each time a new idea is generated from that category. At the start of a session, the probability of staying in a category is higher than the probability of switching to any other category, so ideas from within the same category will tend to follow each other. Also, because a decrease in the probability of staying within a category is accompanied by an increase in the probabilities in the null category (which represent the likelihood of generating no new idea), switching to a new category will, on average, take longer than coming up with an idea from the same category. The result is that ideas tend to come in clumps, with more "blank time" between ideas from different categories than between ideas from the same categories. The SIAM model described in Nijstad et al. (this volume) accounts for these temporal patterns as well.

References

Amabile, T. M. (1996). *Creativity in context.* Boulder, CO: Westview Press.
Anderson, J. R. (1995). *Cognitive psychology and its implications* (4th ed.). New York: Worth.
Avolio, B. J., & Bass, B. M. (1988). Transformational leadership, charisma, and

beyond. In J. G. Hunt, B. R. Baliga, H. P. Dachler, C. A., Schriesheim (Eds.), *Emerging leadership vistas* (pp. 29–49). Lexington, MA: Lexington Books.

Avolio, B. J., & Bass, B. M. (1998). Individual consideration viewed at multiple levels of analysis: A multi-level framework for examining the diffusion of transformational leadership. In F. Danserau & F. Yammarino (Eds.), *Leadership: The multilevel approaches* (pp. 53–102). Stamford, CT: JAI Press.

Bandura, A. (2000). Exercise of human agency through collective efficacy. *Current Directions in Psychological Science, 9,* 75–78.

Baron, R. S. (1986). Distraction/conflict theory: Progress and problems. In L. Berkowitz (Ed.), *Advances in experimental social psychology* (Vol. 19, pp. 1–40). New York: Academic Press.

Bass, B. M. (1985). *Leadership and performance beyond expectations.* New York: Free Press.

Bass, B. M. (1998). *Transformational leadership: Industry, military, and educational impact.* Mahwah, NJ: Erlbaum.

Bass, B. M., & Avolio, B. J. (1994). *Improving organizational effectiveness through transformational leadership.* Thousand Oaks, CA: Sage.

Bennis, W., & Biederman, P. W. (1997). *Organizing genius: The secrets of creative collaboration.* Reading, MA: Addison Wesley.

Bonito, J. A., & Hollingshead, A. B. (1997). Participation in small groups. In B. R. Burleson & A. W. Kunkel (Eds.), *Communication yearbook 20* (pp. 227–261). Thousand Oaks, CA: Sage.

Bousfield, W.A. (1953). The occurrence of clustering in the recall of randomly arranged associates. *Journal of General Psychology, 49,* 229–240.

Brown, V., & Paulus, P. (1996). A simple dynamic model of social factors in group brainstorming. *Small Group Research, 27,* 91–114.

Brown, V. R., & Paulus, P. B. (2000, November). *Cognitive processes in group brainstorming.* Poster presented at the 41st annual meeting of the Psychonomic Society, New Orleans.

Brown, V., Tumeo, M., Larey, T. S., & Paulus, P. B. (1998). Modeling cognitive interactions during group brainstorming. *Small Group Research, 29,* 495–526.

Burpitt, W. J., & Bigoness, W. J. (1997). Leadership and innovation among teams: The impact of empowerment. *Small Group Research, 28*(3), 414–423.

Camacho, L. M., & Paulus, P. B. (1995). The role of social anxiousness in group brainstorming. *Journal of Personality and Social Psychology, 68,* 1071–1080.

Chemers, M. M. (2001). Leadership effectiveness: An integrative review. In M. A. Hogg & S. Tindale (Eds.), *Blackwell handbook of social psychology: Group processes* (pp. 376–399). Oxford: Blackwell.

Collins, A. M., & Loftus, E. F. (1975). A spreading-activation theory of semantic processing. *Psychological Review, 82,* 407–428.

Coskun, H. (2000). *The effects of outgroup comparison, social context, intrinsic motivation, and collective identity in brainstorming groups.* Unpublished doctoral dissertation, University of Texas, Arlington.

Coskun, H., Paulus, P. B., Brown, V., & Sherwood, J. J. (2000). Cognitive stimulation and problem presentation in idea generation groups. *Group Dynamics: Theory, Research, and Practice, 4,* 307–329.

Cowan, N. (1995). *Attention and memory: An integrated framework.* New York: Oxford University Press.

Diehl, M., & Stroebe, W. (1987). Productivity loss in brainstorming groups: Toward the solution of a riddle. *Journal of Personality and Social Psychology, 53*, 497–509.

Diehl, M., & Stroebe, W. (1991). Productivity loss in idea-generating groups: Tracking down the blocking effect. *Journal of Personality and Social Psychology, 61*, 392–403.

Dugosh, K. L., & Paulus, P. B. (2001). *Cognitive and social comparison processes in brainstorming.* Unpublished manuscript, University of Texas, Arlington.

Dugosh, K. L., Paulus, P. B., Roland, E. J., & Yang, H. C. (2000). Cognitive stimulation in brainstorming. *Journal of Personality and Social Psychology, 79*, 722–735.

Festinger, L. (1954). A theory of social comparison processes. *Human Relations, 7*, 117–140.

Fiedler, F. E. (1967). *An integrative theory of leadership.* Mahwah, NJ: Erlbaum.

Fiedler, F. E. (1978). Contingency and the leadership process. In L. Berkowitz (Ed.), *Advances in experimental social psychology* (Vol. 11, pp. 167–225). New York: Academic Press.

Gammage, K. L., Carron, A. V., & Estabrooks, P. A. (2001). Team cohesion and individual productivity: The influence of the norm for productivity and the identifiability of individual effort. *Small Group Research, 32*, 3–18.

Geen, R. G. (1989). Alternative conceptions of social facilitation. In P. B. Paulus (Ed.), *Psychology of group influence* (pp. 15–51). Hillsdale, NJ: Erlbaum.

Gibbons, F. X., Blanton, H., Gerrard, M., Buunk, B., & Eggelston, T. (2000). Does social comparison make a difference? Optimism as a moderator of the relation between comparison level and academic performance. *Personality and Social Psychology Bulletin, 26*, 637–648.

Gibbons, F. X., & Gerrard, M. (1991). Downward comparison and coping. In J. M. Suls & T. A. Wills (Eds.), *Social comparison: Theory and practice* (pp. 317–345). Hillsdale, NJ: Erlbaum.

Goethals, G. R., & Darley, J. M. (1987). Social comparison theory: Self-evaluation and group life. In B. Mullen & G. R. Goethals (Eds.), *Theories of group behavior* (pp. 27–47). New York: Springer-Verlag.

Grossman, S. R., Rodgers, B. E., & Moore, B. R. (1989, December). Turn group input into stellar output. *Working Woman*, 36–38.

Guzzo, R. A., Yost, P. R., Campbell, R. J., & Shea, G. P. (1993). Potency in groups: Articulating a construct. *British Journal of Social Psychology, 32*, 87–106.

Horn, E. M. (1993). *The influence of modality order and break period on a brainstorming task.* Unpublished honors thesis. University of Texas, Arlington.

John-Steiner, V. (2000). *Creative collaboration.* New York: Oxford University Press.

Kerr, N. L., & Bruun, S. E. (1983). Dispensability of member effort and group motivation losses: Free-rider effects. *Journal of Personality and Social Psychology, 44*, 78–94.

Kramer, T. J., Fleming, G. P., & Mannis, S. M. (2001). Improving face-to-face brainstorming through modeling and facilitation. *Small Group Research, 32*, 533–557.

Leggett, K. L. (1997). *The effectiveness of categorical priming in brainstorming.* Unpublished master's thesis, University of Texas, Arlington.

Leggett, K. L., Putman, V. L., Roland, E. J., & Paulus, P. B. (1996, April). *The effects of training on performance in group brainstorming.* Paper presented at the Southwestern Psychological Association, Houston.

Lowe, K. B., Kroeck, K. G., & Sivasubramaniam, N. (1996). Effectiveness correlates of transformation and transactional leadership: A meta-analytic review of the MLQ literature. *Leadership Quarterly, 7,* 385–425.

Mandler, G. (1967). Organization and memory. In. K. W. Spence & J. T. Spence (Eds.), *The psychology of learning and motivation* (Vol. 1, pp. 327–372). New York: Academic Press.

Manz, C. C., & Sims, H. P. (1987). Leading workers to lead themselves: The external leadership of self-managing work teams. *Administrative Science Quarterly, 32,* 106–129.

Meyer, D. E., & Schvaneveldt, R. W. (1971). Facilitation in recognizing pairs of words: Evidence of a dependence between retrieval operations. *Journal of Experimental Psychology, 90,* 227–234.

Mitchell, K. A. C. (1998). *The effect of break task on performance during a second session of brainstorming.* Unpublished master's thesis, University of Texas, Arlington.

Mullen, B., Johnson, C., & Salas, E. (1991). Productivity loss in brainstorming groups: A meta-analytic integration. *Basic and Applied Social Psychology, 12,* 3–23.

Neely, J. H. (1991). Semantic priming effects in visual word recognition: A selective review of current findings and theories. In D. Besner & G. W. Humphreys (Eds.), *Basic processes in reading: Visual word recognition* (pp. 264–350). Hillsdale, NJ: Erlbaum.

Nosofsky, R. (1984). Choice, similarity, and the context theory of classification. *Journal of Experimental Psychology: Learning, Memory, & Cognition, 10,* 104–114.

Offner, A. K., Kramer, T. J., & Winter, J. P. (1996). The effects of facilitation, recording, and pauses on group brainstorming. *Small Group Research, 27,* 283–298.

Osborn, A. F. (1957). *Applied imagination.* New York: Scribner.

Osborn, A. F. (1963). *Applied imagination* (2nd ed.). New York: Scribner.

Oxley, N. L., Dzindolet, M. T., & Paulus, P. B. (1996). The effects of facilitators on the performance of brainstorming groups. *Journal of Social Behavior and Personality, 11,* 633–646.

Parnes, S. J., & Meadow, A. (1959). Effect of "brainstorming" instructions on creative problem-solving by trained and untrained subjects. *Journal of Educational Psychology, 50,* 171–176.

Paulus, P. B. (1983). Group influence on individual task performance. In P. B. Paulus (Ed.), *Basic group processes* (pp. 97–120). New York: Springer-Verlag.

Paulus, P. B. (2000). Groups, teams and creativity: The creative potential of idea generating groups. *Applied Psychology: An International Review, 49,* 237–262.

Paulus, P. B., Brown, V., & Ortega, A. H. (1999). Group creativity. In R. E. Purser & A. Montuori (Eds.), *Social creativity in organizations* (pp. 151–176). Cresskill, NJ: Hampton.

Paulus, P. B., Dugosh, K. L., Dzindolet, M. T., Coskun, H, & Putman, V. L. (2002). Social and cognitive influences in group brainstorming: Predicting production gains and losses. In W. Stroebe & M. Hewstone (Eds.), *European review of social psychology* (Vol. 12, pp. 300–325). London: Wiley.

Paulus, P. B., & Dzindolet, M. T. (1993). Social influence processes in group brainstorming. *Journal of Personality and Social Psychology, 64,* 575–586.

Paulus, P. B., Dzindolet, M. T., Poletes, G., & Camacho, L. M. (1993). Perception of performance in group brainstorming: The illusion of group productivity. *Personality and Social Psychology Bulletin, 19,* 78–89.

Paulus, P. B., Larey, T. S., & Dzindolet, M. T. (2000). Creativity in groups and teams.

In M. Turner (Ed.), *Groups at work: Advances in theory and research* (pp. 319–338). Hillsdale, NJ: Erlbaum.

Paulus, P. B., Larey, T. S., Putman, V. L., Leggett, K. L., & Roland, E. J. (1996). Social influence process in computer brainstorming. *Basic and Applied Social Psychology, 18*, 3–14.

Paulus, P. B., & Yang, H. C. (2000). Idea generation in groups: A basis for creativity in organizations. *Organizational Behavior and Human Decision Processes, 82*, 76–87.

Pinsonneault, A., Barki, H., Gallupe, R. B., & Hoppen, N. (1999). Electronic brainstorming: The illusion of productivity. *Information Systems Research, 10*, 110–133.

Prince, G. M. (1970). *The practice of creativity.* New York: Harper and Row.

Putman, V. L. (1998). *Effects of facilitator training and extended rules on group brainstorming.* Unpublished master's thesis, University of Texas, Arlington.

Putman, V. L. (2001). *Effects of additional rules and dominance on brainstorming and decision making.* Unpublished doctoral dissertation, University of Texas, Arlington.

Raaijmakers, J., & Shiffrin, R. (1981). Search of associative memory. *Psychological Review, 85*, 59–108.

Rawlinson, J. G. (1981). *Creative thinking and brainstorming.* New York: Wiley.

Roy, M. C., Gauvin, S., & Limayem, M. (1996). Electronic group brainstorming: The role of feedback on productivity. *Small Group Research, 27*, 215–247.

Sanders, G. S., Baron, R. S., & Moore, D. L. (1978). Distraction and social comparison as mediators of social facilitation effects. *Journal of Experimental Social Psychology, 14*, 291–303.

Shepherd, M. M., Briggs, R. O., Reinig, B. A., Yen, J., & Nunamaker, J. F., Jr. (1995–1996). Invoking social comparison to improve electronic brainstorming: Beyond anonymity. *Journal of Management Information Systems, 12*, 155–170.

Shepperd, J. A. (1993). Productivity loss in performance groups: A motivation analysis. *Psychological Bulletin, 113*, 67–81.

Sherwood, J. J. (1998). *Modeling cognitive facilitation in brainstorming groups.* Unpublished master's thesis, University of Texas, Arlington.

Smith, S. M. (1995). Fixation, incubation, and insight in memory and creative thinking. In S. M. Smith, T. B. Ward, & R. A. Finke (Eds.), *The creative cognition approach* (pp. 135–156). Cambridge, MA: MIT Press.

Sosik, J. J., Avolio, B. J., & Kahai, S. S. (1997). Effects of leadership style and anonymity on group potency and effectiveness in a group decision support system environment. *Journal of Applied Psychology, 82*, 89–103.

Sosik, J. J., Avolio, B. J., & Kahai, S. S. (1998). Inspiring group creativity: Comparing anonymous and identified electronic brainstorming. *Small Group Research, 29*, 3–31.

Sosik, J. J., Kahai, S. S., & Avolio, B. J. (1998). Transformational leadership and dimensions of creativity: Motivating idea generation in computer-mediated groups. *Creativity Research Journal, 11*, 111–121.

Stanne, M. B., Johnson, D. W., & Johnson, R. T. (1999). Does competition enhance or inhibit motor performance: A meta-analysis. *Psychological Bulletin, 125*, 133–154.

Steiner, I. D. (1972). *Group process and productivity.* San Diego: Academic Press.

Sutton, R. I., & Hargadon, A. (1996). Brainstorming groups in context. *Administrative Science Quarterly, 41*, 685–718.

Taylor, D. W., Berry, P. C., & Block, C. H. (1958). Does group participation when using brainstorming facilitate or inhibit creative thinking? *Administrative Science Quarterly, 3*, 23–47.

Tulving, E., & Pearlstone, Z. (1966). Availability versus accessibility of information in memory for words. *Journal of Verbal Learning and Verbal Behavior, 5*, 381–391.

Turner, J. C. (1978). Social categorization and social discrimination in the minimal group paradigm. In H. Tajfel (Ed.), *Differentiation between social groups* (pp. 101–140). London: Academic Press.

Williams, K. D., & Karau, S. J. (1991). Social loafing and social compensation: The effects of expectations of coworker performance. *Journal of Personality and Social Psychology, 61*, 570–581.

Zajonc, R. B. (1980). Compresence. In P. B. Paulus (Ed.), *Psychology of group influence* (pp. 35–60). Hillsdale, NJ: Erlbaum.

7

■■■■■ *Bernard A. Nijstad, Michael Diehl, and Wolfgang Stroebe*

Cognitive Stimulation and Interference in Idea-Generating Groups

■■■■

Suppose you are the marketing director of a company that sells tailor-made software. You strongly believe that your company produces high-quality products and clients are usually quite satisfied with your service. However, over the past year sales have dropped. In fact, if the situation does not improve, the company will have financial problems by the end of next year. Your company evidently needs new ways to attract clients, and you feel that your coworkers in the marketing department may have some ideas. What would you do? Would you ask your coworkers to generate ideas on their own and present them to you at a later time? Or would you call a meeting and have a brainstorming session with your coworkers?

Most people would probably choose the latter option. One of the reasons is that they believe such a meeting would be highly effective. Research has shown that most people believe they can generate more creative ideas when working in a group compared to working alone (Paulus, Dzindolet, Poletes, & Camacho, 1993; Stroebe, Diehl, & Abakoumkin, 1992). Apparently, people believe that new associations and creative ideas can be sparked by the ideas of other group members and believe that interaction stimulates creative thinking. As a consequence, group brainstorming is one of the most popular ways to generate creative ideas.

In the 1950s, Alex Osborn (1957) suggested brainstorming as a method to improve the creativity of groups. When brainstorming, people are instructed (1) to generate as many ideas as possible, and (2) not to evaluate their ideas but defer judgment to a later stage of the problem-solving process. Osborn suggested that if these principles are applied, people can generate many good ideas and that creativity is enhanced, which in general seems to be true (see, e.g., Lamm & Trommsdorff, 1973; Stroebe & Diehl, 1994). Moreover, he suggested that brainstorming should be done in groups and that group members would generate more ideas than individuals working in isolation. As we have seen, most people tend to agree.

Over 40 years of controlled research in group brainstorming, however, has shown quite the contrary: a number of people working separately and whose nonredundant ideas are pooled (groups with no interaction, or nominal groups) produce more ideas and more good ideas than the same number of people who work in a group (e.g., Diehl & Stroebe, 1987; Lamm & Trommsdorff, 1973; Mullen, Johnson, & Salas, 1991; Taylor, Berry, & Block, 1958). This productivity loss of brainstorming groups as compared to individuals is substantial, increases with group size, and has consistently been found in groups with three members and more. Apparently, group interaction inhibits rather than stimulates creative idea generation.

This discrepancy between popular belief and experimental results raises at least three questions: How can the productivity loss of brainstorming groups be explained? How can productivity of these groups be improved? Why do people think that group brainstorming is more effective than individual brainstorming, whereas the opposite is true? The present chapter builds on some 15 years of research on group idea generation carried out at the University of Tübingen, Germany, and Utrecht University, The Netherlands. During these years, these three questions have been the primary focus of attention. However, our research program has increasingly shifted toward a cognitive approach. In this chapter, we present an overview of our studies. We do so in four sections. In the first section we describe some early research pertaining to the productivity loss of groups, possibilities for improving group performance, and the illusory belief that group brainstorming is more effective than individual brainstorming (also see Stroebe & Diehl, 1994). Next, we outline a cognitive approach to these issues and argue that many of our earlier findings can be interpreted as either cognitive interference or cognitive stimulation effects. In the third section we discuss more recent studies aimed at testing these ideas. In the final section we draw some conclusions and suggest practical implications and future directions for research.

Early Studies

Causes of the Productivity Loss

Why are people who work in groups less creative than people working separately? In our first paper (Diehl & Stroebe, 1987), three possible explanations of the productivity loss of brainstorming groups were examined. First, we argued that individual contributions are hard to isolate when working in a group and that group members cannot be held accountable for their contributions. This may lead group members to shirk effort and let others do the work (free-riding), whereas individuals who are accountable for their performance work harder. However, in that study, we found no support for this explanation. When group members were made individually accountable for their performance, the productivity loss was not substantially reduced. Because individual accountability should eliminate free-riding, this result rendered the free-riding explanation implausible.

A second possible explanation of the productivity loss of brainstorming groups is that, despite the instruction not to evaluate ideas, people may be concerned with a negative evaluation of their ideas by their fellow group members (evaluation apprehension). Because of this, group members may fail to mention low-quality or strange ideas, which would negatively affect their performance. People working individually cannot be evaluated by others and consequently would not suffer from evaluation apprehension. An experiment was designed in which we informed half of the participants that there were judges on the other side of a one-way screen and that these judges would rate the participants' ideas. In addition, some of the participants worked in interactive groups and others worked in nominal groups. It was predicted that the presence of judges would have more impact on individuals working in nominal groups because in interactive groups, high levels of evaluation apprehension are already present. However, this was not found. The presence of judges negatively affected the performance of groups as much as the performance of individuals. Moreover, despite the higher level of evaluation apprehension, nominal groups were still much more productive than interactive groups. These results did not confirm the evaluation apprehension interpretation of the productivity loss of real groups (but see Camacho & Paulus, 1995).

If free-riding and evaluation apprehension are ruled out, then what does cause the productivity loss of groups? In a review of the brainstorming literature, Lamm and Trommsdorff (1973) suggested that production blocking is one of the main factors causing the productivity loss of brainstorming groups. Production blocking arises from the implicit rule that in groups only one person speaks at a time. The consequence is that ideas cannot always be verbalized the moment they occur because group members must wait for their turn before they can express their ideas. This may cause forgetting or suppression of ideas or interference with a person's thought process.

The production blocking explanation had not been tested yet, so Diehl and Stroebe (1987) designed another experiment. Some participants brainstormed in interactive and some in nominal control groups. Further, there were three experimental conditions in which blocking was manipulated for participants working in separate rooms. Each room had a microphone and display with four lights, one green and the others red, which functioned like a traffic light. When someone talked, the green light was lit, and the displays of the other participants showed a red light. Participants in experimental conditions 1 and 2 were told to talk only when the red lights were off, and thus had to take turns to express their ideas. Moreover, in condition 1, participants could hear each other's contributions on headphones; in condition 2 this was not possible. Finally, participants in experimental condition 3 were informed about the lights but were told to disregard them and thus did not have to take turns. If blocking were a major cause of the productivity loss, productivity of participants in experimental conditions 1 and 2, with blocking, should be as low as in the interactive group control condition, whereas productivity of participants in experimental condition 3, without blocking, should be similar to the nominal group control condition. This is exactly what was found. Participants in conditions with blocking produced about half as many ideas as participants in conditions without blocking. These results clearly supported a production blocking explanation of the productivity loss.

Explaining the Blocking Effect

Although these results were an important step toward explaining productivity loss in brainstorming groups, it was not clear why blocking has such a large detrimental effect on productivity. A second series of experiments was designed to test the possible mechanisms underlying the effects of production blocking and possibilities to overcome the blocking effect (Diehl & Stroebe, 1991). A rather straightforward interpretation is that participants working in groups simply do not have enough time to express their ideas. Obviously, individuals brainstorming in isolation can express their ideas at any time, but in groups speaking time is shared among group members. However, it was found that when individuals were allowed to speak during only a part of the session (e.g., they were given 20 minutes to generate ideas but could use only 5 minutes for speaking), their performance was not affected. Moreover, individuals with limited speaking time still outperformed the interactive groups. This suggests that overall speaking time is not important, but that it matters *when* ideas can be expressed. The blocking effect occurs when ideas cannot be expressed soon after they are generated.

Next, we reasoned that speaking turns in groups are not very controllable or predictable because the first group member who speaks usually has the floor. Group members thus have to be attentive and monitor the discussion to find an opening to express their ideas, and this may distract them from generating ideas. By making the waiting time predictable (turn-taking with a fixed order) or controllable (group members could sign up on a speaking list, so they knew when their turn would come), we tried to overcome this problem. These manipulations, however, did not succeed in making group brainstorming more successful. Further, we reasoned that group members, once they generate an idea, constantly have to rehearse it in memory in order not to forget it before it can be expressed. This may prevent them from developing further ideas. To overcome this problem, participants in the next experiment were provided with a notepad. In addition, some of the participants could overhear each other's ideas and others could not, because it seemed possible that participants cannot use their notepads effectively when they are distracted by the ideas of others. Results were that note taking slightly improved performance, but only when communication was not available. Unfortunately, these results indicate that it is not easy to overcome the detrimental effects of production blocking in face-to-face brainstorming groups.

The conclusion of this series of studies was that group members are unable to effectively use the waiting times when other group members are talking (Diehl & Stroebe, 1991). Rather than limitations in speaking time, this seemed to be the major cause of the productivity loss of brainstorming groups. The mechanism, however, was not yet entirely clear. It seems plausible that limitations in cognitive capacity are important. Group members face the difficult tasks of listening to others, monitoring the discussion, and generating ideas at the same time, which may simply be too much for the cognitive system. The blocking effect may therefore be due to cognitive interference, although any direct evidence was missing. Another question is whether the blocking effect can be overcome and whether it is possible to improve the performance of groups. It is to this issue that we turn next.

Improving Group Performance

One way to enhance group performance is to carefully select the participants of brainstorming sessions. For example, one can try to maximize mutual cognitive stimulation by selecting a group of diverse people. If participants are very similar in background knowledge and expertise, no cognitive stimulation is to be expected because group members are likely to come up with very similar ideas. Using participants with divergent backgrounds may be more effective because they can develop more perspectives on the problem and generate more unique ideas (also see Milliken, Bartel, & Kurtzberg, this volume). Moreover, a new perspective suggested by one group member may subsequently trigger new ideas in others, ideas that they would otherwise not have thought of.

One study (Diehl, 1991; see Stroebe & Diehl, 1994) investigated this possibility. Participants first performed an association test on the topic of a later brainstorming session. Based on the amount of overlap among the dominant associations of the different participants, homogeneous groups (composed of participants who had very similar associations) and heterogeneous groups (composed of participants dissimilar in associations) were created. In addition, some participants were randomly assigned to a group. These groups either brainstormed together in one room (interactive groups) or they brainstormed individually in separate rooms (nominal groups). It was found that group heterogeneity did not make a difference for the performance of the nominal groups. However, the heterogeneous interactive groups outperformed the other interactive groups. Moreover, heterogeneous groups did not show the usual productivity loss, whereas the homogeneous groups and the random groups did. Further, the heterogeneous interactive groups generated semantically more diverse ideas than the other groups. It thus appears that selecting diverse group members can enhance the performance of brainstorming groups and bring it to the level of nominal groups.

It should be noted that even the members of heterogeneous groups had to take turns to express their ideas and thus suffered from the blocking effect. The fact that they were as productive as the nominal groups implies that there were productivity gains that counteracted the usual productivity loss due to blocking. If the blocking effect can be eliminated it may prove possible that interactive groups actually outperform nominal groups, and that the "whole" becomes more than "the sum of the parts." By using procedures that do not require turn-taking among group members, it is possible to eliminate production blocking. One of these procedures is "brainwriting," in which group members write down their ideas on a piece of paper and subsequently exchange their notes. Another procedure is "electronic brainstorming," in which group members enter their ideas in a computer system and can read the ideas of others on monitors. The advantages of these procedures are that production blocking is no longer a problem (i.e., group members do not have to take turns but can write or type simultaneously) and stimulation is possible because group members can read each other's ideas. Interestingly, several studies suggest that access to the ideas of others can have positive effects. Some studies of brainwriting (Paulus & Yang, 2000) and electronic brainstorming (e.g., Dennis & Valacich, 1993; Dugosh, Paulus, Roland, & Yang, 2000; Valacich, Dennis, & Connolly, 1994) have shown that groups who could share ideas outperformed the groups who could not share ideas. The most likely explanation is that it actually is stimulating to read the ideas of others, as long as production blocking is eliminated (also see Paulus & Brown, this volume; Dennis & Williams, this volume). What remains unclear, however, is how and why cognitive stimulation works.

What does seem clear is that people believe that it works, and that they experience facilitation as a consequence of idea sharing. This belief may be one of the reasons group brainstorming remains so popular despite the evidence of its ineffectiveness. We now discuss the reasons people believe that group idea generation is highly effective.

Enjoyment, Satisfaction, and the Illusion of Group Effectivity

As discussed above, face-to-face brainstorming groups are less productive than individuals. Yet, the experience of group brainstorming is usually very positive. Participants brainstorming in face-to-face groups report that they have enjoyed the brainstorming session, and group members enjoy the session more than individuals (e.g., Diehl & Stroebe, 1991; Paulus, Larey, & Ortega, 1995; Stroebe et al., 1992). People also report that they prefer working in groups above working individually, although this is less true for shy people (Camacho & Paulus, 1995). Most striking, however, is the finding that participants who have worked in a group report being more satisfied on average with their performance than participants who have worked individually, when in fact they have generated fewer ideas (e.g. Larey & Paulus, 1995; Paulus et al., 1993; Stroebe et al., 1992). In line with this finding, most people are convinced that group brainstorming is more effective than individual brainstorming. Researchers have found the optimism for group brainstorming performance so unrealistic that they have labeled it the "illusion of group effectivity" (Paulus et al., 1993; Stroebe et al., 1992).

These results raise the question of why people think that group brainstorming is so effective. Researchers have tested two possible explanations to account for the illusion of group effectivity. The first explanation (Stroebe et al., 1992) is that it will be hard for group members to differentiate between the ideas they have had themselves and the ideas suggested by other group members (memory confusion). As a result, members would claim to have had ideas that were really generated by another member. This would lead to an overestimation of their performance and would explain why people who brainstorm in groups are generally quite satisfied with their performance. Individuals, who cannot take credit for ideas not suggested by them, will be less satisfied. Stroebe et al. obtained support for this line of reasoning. Participants in their study worked in nominal or interactive groups. At a later time they were confronted with the list of ideas generated by their own (nominal or interactive) group. Participants who had worked in interactive groups often claimed that the ideas that were actually mentioned by another group member had also occurred to them. Participants who had worked in nominal groups and who had not heard the ideas of the other group members before made this claim much less often. Indeed, it appears that it is hard to differentiate between one's own ideas and the ideas of other group members, and memory confusion may contribute to the illusion of group effectivity.

Paulus et al. (1993) suggested a second explanation for the illusion of group effectivity. They assumed that people are motivated to compare their performance with that of others (social comparison). Group members, who have the opportunity to compare their performance with that of fellow group members, will usually find that their performance is quite similar (see Paulus & Dzindolet, 1993), which will result in high levels of satisfaction. Individuals, who do not have this opportunity, will be insecure and may presume that they have not done particularly well. Paulus et al. found that the opportunity for social comparison indeed caused higher levels of satisfaction, and social comparisons do seem to reduce uncertainty about one's own performance and lead to higher levels of satisfaction.

The studies of Stroebe et al. (1992) and Paulus et al. (1993) partly explain the illusion of group effectivity. In particular, memory confusion and social comparison processes can explain why group members are usually quite satisfied with their performance. However, some findings are not easily explained by either memory confusion or social comparisons. For example, it has been found that participants feel facilitated by the presence of other group members and think that the ideas of others are stimulating (Stroebe et al., 1992). It is not clear how memory confusion or social comparisons would result in this perception. Second, although both explanations can account for the high levels of satisfaction of group members, it is unclear why people in general think that group brainstorming is more effective than individual brainstorming. Indeed, why should the experience of a group member that he or she has done relatively well (as, for example, compared to the other group members) be attributed to group interaction and not to personal ability? Why should this lead to the belief that group brainstorming is more effective than individual brainstorming? It seems more plausible that communication in brainstorming groups is perceived to be stimulating and facilitating, which causes the impression that group brainstorming is highly effective.

Summary

The early studies described above offered much insight into group and individual idea generation. Production blocking, the fact that group members have to take turns to express their ideas, appears to be a major factor underlying the productivity loss of brainstorming groups. At the same time, idea sharing can have positive effects on performance, in particular in heterogeneous groups and when procedures are used that eliminate production blocking, such as brainwriting and electronic brainstorming. Further, memory confusion and social comparisons contribute to the high levels of satisfaction group members experience after a brainstorming session. However, the results also raised some interesting questions: Why exactly is blocking so detrimental to idea generation? Why and under what circumstances does idea sharing have positive effects on performance? Why is idea sharing perceived to be stimulating, and what is the relation between this perception of stimulation and the illusion of group effectivity?

In recent years, we have developed a cognitive theory of idea generation aimed at answering these questions (Nijstad, 2000; Nijstad, Stroebe, & Lodewijkx, 2002, in press; also see Diehl, 1991). This approach is outlined next. After that, we present some evidence for our theory and interpret the results of the early studies in terms of cognitive interference and stimulation.

A Cognitive Approach

The central assumption underlying our approach is that idea generation is essentially a cognitive or mental process that occurs within the individual group member's mind. However, this individual-level cognitive process is strongly affected by other group members, in particular by communication within the group. To derive hypotheses on how communication affects cognitive processes, it is necessary to have some insight into the relevant cognitive processes. To this end, we developed a model of idea generation called Search for Ideas in Associative Memory (SIAM). SIAM is based on Raaijmakers and Shiffrin's (1981) SAM (Search of Associative Memory) model of memory retrieval.

Following SAM, SIAM assumes two memory systems: a limited capacity short-term memory (STM) system, in which conscious operations are performed, and an unlimited long-term memory (LTM) system, in which previously acquired knowledge is stored. LTM is assumed to be partitioned into unitized images, localized sets of strongly connected and interrelated features (no visual or spatial representation is implied). These images are connected in a rich network, with many associations, levels, and categories. Semantically related images are presumed to have relatively strong mutual ties (cf. Brown, Tumeo, Larey, & Paulus, 1998; also see Paulus & Brown, this volume), and it is assumed that only one image may be active (in STM) at one time.

According to SIAM, brainstorming is a repeated search for ideas in associative memory. Ideas are generally new solutions to a problem and therefore cannot be directly retrieved from memory. However, neither is it possible to generate ideas ex nihilo, but previously acquired knowledge must be used. The generation of ideas is therefore a two-stage process, in which a stage of knowledge activation is followed by a stage of idea generation. Because knowledge must be relevant to the topic at hand, the initial activation of knowledge is a controlled process. Following Raaijmakers and Shiffrin (1981), we assume that a search cue is assembled in STM, which is used to probe LTM. The search cue contains (elements of) the brainstorming problem and/or some other elements, such as previously generated ideas. A cue-based search of LTM results in the activation of an image. Which image is activated is probabilistic and dependent on the strength of the association of the elements of the search cue to the features of the image.

When an image has been activated, it can be used to generate ideas by combining knowledge, forming new associations, or applying knowledge to a new domain (Mednick, 1962). This results in the generation of one or more ideas, which can subsequently be expressed. Further, ideas can be added to the search cue to activate new images in LTM, which in turn can be used to generate additional ideas. Because semantically related images are presumed to have strong mutual ties, successively activated images will often be semantically related. We propose that this leads to a "train of thought": a rapid accumulation of semantically related ideas. When a train of thought no longer leads to new ideas (i.e., searches are unsuccessful), a new search cue must be assembled, which is a process that takes some time. This new cue is used to probe memory, which results in the activation of new images and the generation of additional ideas. This process continues until the session is terminated. At the individual level, one implication is that some degree of semantic clustering of ideas should be found (i.e., successive ideas are often semantically related) and that within these clusters ideas can be generated relatively rapidly. Similar semantic and temporal clustering has been found in the free recall of categorized lists of words (Bousfield, 1953; Gruenewald & Lockhead, 1980).

An example may help to illustrate this process of idea generation. Suppose you work for a small theater and are asked to generate ideas on the topic of how to attract more visitors. Your first association to this topic is advertising, and you generate several ideas in this area, such as advertising in local newspapers and using direct mail to invite people who have previously visited your theater.

After a while, it gets more difficult to generate ideas in the area of advertising, and you realize that improving your facilities may also attract more visitors. Subsequently, you generate some ideas on that (e.g., building a fancy entrance, improving the interior of the theater). After that you brainstorm about what types of shows attract more people. This process continues until you finally run out of ideas or time. The point is that a brainstorming session can be seen as a series of successive trains of thought dealing with a particular semantic domain related to the problem (such as advertising, facilities, programming) and that before each new train of thought some thinking is required to activate knowledge in another semantic domain.

This process of idea generation is presumed to be applicable to both people who work individually and people who work in a group. However, working in a group differs from individual brainstorming. The most notable difference is that group members share their ideas. This implies that members can hear (or read) each other's ideas and that they have to take turns to express their ideas (in oral brainstorming). We propose that the exchange of ideas taking place in groups can both stimulate and interfere with the cognitive processes described above. In the next section, we describe some ways in which communication is stimulating or interfering and present recent evidence for our approach.

Cognitive Stimulation and Interference in Groups

Production Blocking and Cognitive Interference

Production blocking is an inevitable consequence of idea sharing in face-to-face groups. Blocking has been found to have a strong negative effect on performance, but it has been unclear why blocking is so detrimental to idea generation. We propose that blocking causes delays between the generation and the articulation of ideas because ideas cannot be expressed as long as another group member is talking, and that these delays interfere with the cognitive process of idea generation (cognitive interference). In particular, we propose that blocking interferes with idea generation in two qualitatively different ways, corresponding with SIAM's two stages of the idea-generation process. Thus, blocking may interfere with both the activation of images and the train of thought within a semantic domain.

Our first hypothesis is that a train of thought within a semantic domain may be prematurely aborted when ideas cannot be immediately expressed. The amount of information that can be active in STM at one point in time is limited. During a delay, activated images may become deactivated because images decay or are replaced by other items due to distraction (similar to looking up a phone number and forgetting it when it is not dialed immediately). When the image is no longer active, it cannot be used to generate further ideas, which makes a time-consuming new memory search necessary. Decay or replacement of images will be stronger with longer delays, and it is predicted that the interfering effects of production blocking increase with delay length. Thus, longer delays should lead to a lower level of productivity. This effect should be due to shorter trains of thoughts (shorter clusters of successive semantically related ideas) because a train of thought within a semantic domain is prematurely aborted. Further, shorter semantic clusters imply that fewer ideas are generated per semantic domain and that there will be more switching among different semantic domains.

Production blocking may also interfere with the activation of images. It is assumed that the activation of images is a controlled process that requires attention and cognitive capacity. With a load on STM because capacity is needed to remember ideas during a delay or because of distraction, this process will be negatively affected. One important source of distraction is the monitoring of delays. It often is unpredictable when one can express one's ideas, because usually there are no fixed speaking turns. In addition, the length of speaking turns may vary considerably, which introduces another source of unpredictability, even if speaking turns are fixed (cf. Diehl & Stroebe, 1991). Thus, both the onset and the end of delays often are unpredictable and need to be monitored, which takes cognitive capacity. It is predicted that this extra load on STM will interfere with the activation of new images and reduce the ability to start a new train of thought. Unpredictable delays should thus lead to a lower number of different semantic clusters, and therefore to a lower number of ideas. To summarize, the length of the delay is predicted to affect the cluster length (with longer delays resulting in shorter clusters of semantically related ideas), and delay unpredictability is expected to affect the number of clusters (with unpredictable delays leading to fewer semantic clusters).

We have tested these hypotheses in several studies (Nijstad, 2000; Nijstad et al., in press). To control the length and predictability of delays, we had individual participants brainstorm at a computer terminal. Some of these participants could enter their ideas whenever they wanted; others were confronted with delays during which they could not enter their ideas but had to wait for a short time in front of a blank screen. We systematically varied the length of the delays and made delays more or less predictable. The effects of delays were assessed on productivity (the number of ideas), and all ideas were content-coded in semantic categories. For each participant we established how many categories were surveyed (diversity), how many ideas per category were generated (within-category fluency), how many successive ideas on average fell in the same category (cluster length), and how many clusters were generated (number of clusters).

In the first study (Nijstad et al., in press), each time a participant wanted to enter an idea, he or she was blocked for a fixed length of time. Some were blocked with relatively short delays, others with longer delays. As predicted, it was found that longer delays led to shorter clusters of semantically related ideas and increased switching among semantic categories. As a result, productivity declined when delays were longer; in particular, the average number of ideas per category was lower. These results are in line with our prediction that relatively long delays (of, say, more than 5 seconds) interfere with a train of thought within a semantic category. Participants could not maintain their train of thought when they constantly had to wait before they could enter their ideas, and this led to shorter semantic clusters.

In a second study (Nijstad et al., in press), we made delays relatively unpredictable. Instead of being blocked each time a participant wanted to enter an idea, as in the previous study, participants were blocked at unpredictable times. They could be blocked several times before they could enter their ideas, but it was also sometimes possible to enter a few ideas before they were blocked. In addition, some participants were blocked with delays that were always of the same length, whereas for others delay length varied. It was found that the unpredictable delays, in particular when both the onset and the length of delays were unpredictable, led to fewer trains of thought (i.e., fewer clusters of successive semantically related ideas) instead of to shorter trains of thought. In this case, it appeared that the delays were distracting and interfered with the activation of new trains of thought. Once a train of thought was started, however, participants were able to maintain it, in particular when they could enter several ideas before they were blocked again. Taken together, these results suggest that the blocking effect indeed is due to cognitive interference in both stages of the idea-generating process.

However, although these findings are in line with our theorizing, they were obtained under rather artificial circumstances: people brainstorming individually at a computer terminal. The question, therefore, is whether the same effects can be obtained in real face-to-face groups. Does blocking in real groups also lead to more switching among semantic categories, shorter trains of thought, fewer trains of thought, and thought disruption? Some evidence indicates it does. For example, we have found that individuals working separately produce longer trains of thought than individuals working in an interactive group, and that group members more often switch categories than people working in isolation (Diehl, 1991). The lower level of semantic organization (or the higher level of switching) of group members indicates that their thinking was disrupted (cf. Basden, Basden, Bryner, & Thomas, 1997, for a similar finding in group remembering). Thus, results appear to generalize to real groups, and production blocking also interferes with the cognitive process of idea generation in real interactive groups.

Idea Sharing, Cognitive Stimulation, and Cognitive Interference

In the production-blocking studies, our participants had no access to the ideas of other group members. However, in real groups people do share ideas and can overhear or read each other's contributions. Based on SIAM, we propose that this can also strongly affect the individual group member's thought process. As you recall, SIAM proposes that idea generation is a two-stage process, in which a cue-based activation of knowledge is followed by the generation of ideas in a semantic domain. We propose that ideas generated by others serve as external stimuli and can be added to the search cue to probe LTM. We further suggest that these ideas are added to the search cue relatively automatically, provided that attention to these ideas is sufficiently high (also see Dugosh et al., 2000).

In general, ideas of others will stimulate idea generation (cognitive stimulation) because less time is needed to assemble search cues and search memory for problem-relevant knowledge. Depending on the semantic content of stimulus ideas, two types of positive effects are possible. First, ideas of others can activate knowledge that otherwise would not be accessible (cf. Brown et al., 1998; Higgins, 1996; Tulving & Pearlstone, 1966; also see Paulus & Brown, this volume). This is likely to happen when stimulus ideas are semantically diverse. Diverse stimuli activate a wide range of knowledge, including less accessible knowledge, which allows for the generation of semantically (more) diverse ideas and productivity gains. On the other hand, when stimulus ideas are semantically homogeneous they are unlikely to activate less accessible knowledge. However, within the range of accessible knowledge many ideas will be generated because the (limited) range of knowledge remains highly accessible throughout the session. This leads to productivity gains as long as the possibilities of generating additional ideas within this limited knowledge domain are not exhausted. To sum up, diverse stimulation will increase the breadth of idea production, whereas homogeneous stimulation will increase the depth of idea production.

On the other hand, stimulus ideas may also interfere with a train of thought (cognitive interference). When stimulus ideas activate an image that is at odds with a person's train of thought, it may be prematurely aborted. This may lead to shorter trains of thought, the loss of potential ideas, and increased switching among semantic domains. This will reduce the depth of idea production because it prevents rapid associations within a semantic domain. Cognitive interference is likely to occur when successive stimulus ideas activate semantically dissimilar images. When stimulus ideas are offered in clusters of successive semantically related ideas, cognitive interference may be less important because stimuli successively activate semantically related images and a train of thought can be maintained. Thus, productivity gains should be larger when stimuli are offered in clusters of semantically related ideas than when they are offered at random because stimulation is maintained and interference is prevented.

The most direct way to test these predictions is to expose participants to stimulus ideas that vary systematically in semantic content. Because this requires control over the content of stimuli, we again chose to use a computer paradigm (Nijstad, 2000; Nijstad et al., 2002). Participants were individually seated behind computers and were confronted with stimulus ideas that were previously generated by other participants. Some were shown ideas from a wide range of different semantic domains, others from only a few domains. In addition, for some the order in which the ideas were presented was random, with a high probability that successive stimuli were unrelated, whereas for others stimulus ideas were organized in small clusters of successive, semantically related ideas. Finally, participants in a control condition were not exposed to stimuli.

We found that participants who were exposed to stimulus ideas outperformed those who were not. In line with our predictions, these positive effects were due to two different processes. Participants exposed to a wide range of ideas generated more diverse ideas, and participants exposed to homogeneous ideas generated many ideas in fewer categories. In addition, when the sequence in which the ideas were presented was random, the level of switching among semantic categories was higher and semantic clusters were shorter, whereas ideas that were offered in short clusters did not lead to lower levels of semantic organization. The lower levels of semantic organization in the random sequence condition, however, did not lead to lower levels of performance, although we had predicted that this would happen. Apparently, the shorter trains of thought in the random sequence condition were not associated with lower productivity.

To explain these findings, we analyzed response latencies. For each idea we established how long it took to generate and enter it. Further, we made a distinction between category repetitions (i.e., an idea fell in the same category as the previous idea) and category changes (an idea fell in a different category from the previous idea). According to SIAM, category repetitions should be faster than category changes, because category repetitions are based on fast associations within a semantic domain. Indeed, in the control condition, with no stimulation, category repetitions were much faster than category changes. This finding confirms our hypothesis that within a train of thought ideas can be generated relatively rapidly, and that before a new train of thought is started (i.e., before a category change) some thinking is required that increases response latencies. However, in none of the experimental conditions (with idea exposure) was there a difference in response latencies between category repetitions and category changes. Instead, the response latencies of category changes were much shorter in the experimental conditions than in the control condition and were as fast as category repetitions.

In retrospect, these results are consistent with SIAM. SIAM assumes that when a train of thought within a category no longer leads to new ideas, a search cue needs to be assembled to probe memory for problem-relevant knowledge. This takes some time and generally will result in a new train of thought in another semantic category (i.e., a category change), which is why category changes in the control condition were slower. However, stimulus ideas are added to the search cue relatively automatically, which reduces the time needed to assemble search cues. Because a search cue needs to be assembled only when a train of thought within a category no longer leads to new ideas (i.e., before a category change), category changes should become faster when participants are exposed to stimuli, which is exactly what we found. In general, we believe that these findings show that stimulus ideas increase the accessibility of semantically related knowledge and reduce the time needed to search memory.

Again, we have used a computer paradigm to assess the effects of idea exposure on performance. In real groups, idea sharing is a more dynamic process. One group member who expresses an idea affects the others, which will subsequently affect what ideas they produce, and these ideas in turn affect the first person. This kind of mutual influence cannot be assessed using an idea exposure paradigm, such as the paradigm we have used. However, we have also run a study in which there was actual idea sharing among group members (Ziegler, Diehl, & Zijlstra, 2000). In this study, student participants worked in virtual groups. Group members entered their ideas into a computer and the system allowed for idea sharing among participants. Some participants could read each other's ideas on the monitors, whereas others worked in nominal groups and had no access to others' ideas. Idea sharing tended to lead to cognitive uniformity; that is, participants who could read the ideas of others generated ideas in fewer semantic categories than participants who could not. Thus, it appears that idea sharing does not always bring new insights and perspectives to group members but can also restrict the range of ideas to a lower number of semantic domains.

Besides cognitive stimulation resulting from increased accessibility of problem-relevant knowledge, uniformity may thus be a consequence of idea sharing in groups. When group members have access to each other's ideas, each idea constitutes a shared stimulus for all group members. Through a process of mutual influence, it may happen that groups become stuck in just a few semantic domains and have a hard time generating ideas in other domains (also see Larey & Paulus, 1999). However, this may be true only in relatively homogeneous groups, as in the studies of Ziegler et al. (2000) and Larey and Paulus, who have used relatively homogeneous groups of students. When groups are more diverse, cognitive uniformity is less likely because every participant can bring new insights and unique ideas to the task. Indeed, the previously discussed study on group heterogeneity shows that heterogeneous groups survey more semantic domains than do homogeneous groups (Diehl, 1991; see Stroebe & Diehl, 1994). Evidently, more research is needed to unravel the dynamic properties of idea sharing in groups.

Failures, Persistence, Satisfaction, and Enjoyment

The SIAM model also provides a useful means for understanding persistence and subjective experience of group members. SIAM assumes that idea generation is a search for ideas in associative memory. The search can be successful, in which case a new idea is generated. However, the search can also be unsuccessful: nothing is generated or an idea is generated that has already been mentioned. We propose that such a failure to generate new ideas will have important consequences for the process of idea generation. When the session proceeds, it becomes increasingly difficult to find new ideas. This rising number of failures experienced in the later stages of a session will lead to the impression that one is running out of ideas. This will lead to the expectation that continued brainstorming will not lead to many additional ideas (low expectancy). This will be a very powerful motive to terminate the brainstorming session. Thus, we argue that failures to come up with ideas are important determinants of brainstorming persistence. Persistence will be positively related to performance, and higher levels of persistence will generally lead to higher productivity (see, e.g., Diehl & Stroebe, 1991).

We hypothesize that group members experience fewer failures than individuals and that failures are much less salient in groups (Nijstad, 2000). Individuals have to fill the complete brainstorming session themselves; each time they cannot generate an idea, there will be a silence during which it is painfully clear that the individual is not productive. Group members, on the other hand, have a shared responsibility to fill the session. Times in which nobody is able to come up with ideas will be relatively rare, simply because in absolute numbers of ideas groups are more productive than individuals (although per person, they are less productive). Further, these periods of silence, which can be conceptualized as "collective failures," will be less prevalent in larger than in smaller groups because larger groups are more productive in absolute numbers of ideas. This leads to the hypothesis that expectancy of group members will remain higher than that of individuals and that groups will therefore be more persistent. Moreover, larger groups will be more persistent than smaller groups and persistence should increase with group size. Higher levels of persistence should lead to higher levels of productivity, which may allow groups to compensate for (part of) their productivity loss.

In one study, we examined persistence of individuals, dyads, and four- and six-person groups (Nijstad, Stroebe, & Lodewijkx, 1999). We instructed them to continue brainstorming until they felt it was a good time to stop. As expected, we found that persistence, as defined by self-chosen time to end the task, increased with group size. Further, because groups were more persistent than individuals, their productivity loss was much smaller than is usually found. For example, our four-person groups suffered a relatively small loss of about 10%, whereas a loss of 50% is not uncommon. Finally, when asked why they had stopped brainstorming, most people answered that they were running out of ideas. These results generally confirm that persistence is related to expectancy and failures.

In the postexperiment questionnaire of this study, we asked participants several questions regarding task enjoyment, satisfaction, and failures (see Nijstad, 2000; Nijstad et al., 1999). In line with previous research, we found that group members enjoyed the session more and were also more satisfied with their performance than were individuals. Interestingly, group size did not make a difference; members of dyads were as happy and satisfied as members of four- or six-person groups. Further, we also asked questions such as "How often were you unable to come up with ideas?" and "How often did you generate the same ideas more than once?" to measure failures. Much in line with our reasoning, we found that group members reported fewer failures than individuals and again that group size did not make a difference. Apparently, group interaction, regardless of group size, leads to a reduction in the perceived number of failures.

The experience of failures may have consequences for satisfaction and enjoyment. It seems plausible that a large number of failures leads to the impression that one is not performing well. If this were true, more failures should be associated with lower levels of satisfaction. Because group members experience fewer failures than individuals, this may explain in part why they are more satisfied with their performance. Our results indicate that this does seem to be the case: when we statistically controlled for failures (as measured in our questionnaire), the difference in satisfaction between group members and individuals disappeared (Nijstad, 2000). Thus, group members experience fewer failures, and when looking back at the session they feel that they have done well, whereas individuals experience more failures and think that they have performed poorly. Obviously, however, this does not reflect true performance, because fewer failures or fewer periods of silence in groups do not necessarily mean that a single group member is more productive.

The same line of reasoning applies to task enjoyment. It seems plausible that the session is not very enjoyable when participants experience many failures. Thus, the reduction of failures in groups may also be responsible for the higher levels of task enjoyment group members report as compared to individuals. Indeed, we have obtained evidence for this line of reasoning (Nijstad, 2000). When we statistically controlled for experienced failures, the difference in task enjoyment between individuals and group members disappeared. At least in part, failures are therefore related to subjective experience of brainstorming participants, both to satisfaction and enjoyment. The cognitive perspective we have introduced in this chapter, and the SIAM model of idea generation, can therefore account not only for effects of communication on performance, but also for subjective experience of group members.

Conclusions and Implications

Previous research has consistently shown that individuals are better idea generators than groups. To most people this is a surprise, because they think group brainstorming is more effective than individual brainstorming. In this chapter, we have summarized 15 years of research in the area of group idea generation. In these years, three interrelated questions have been addressed: Why do individuals outperform group members? How can the productivity of groups be improved? Why do people think that group brainstorming is more effective than individual brainstorming, although the opposite is true? We have argued that a cognitive approach may provide answers to these questions and that many of the previously obtained effects can be interpreted as either cognitive interference or cognitive stimulation effects.

According to our approach, idea sharing in groups affects the individual group member's cognitive processes. Our SIAM model conceptualizes idea generation as a two-stage search of associative memory. In the first stage, previously acquired knowledge is activated. In the second stage, this knowledge is used to generate ideas, leading to a train of thought within a semantic domain. Further, we argued that idea sharing affects this individual-level cognitive process in both stages and can be both stimulating and interfering. Stimulation occurs when the ideas suggested by others lead to the generation of ideas that would otherwise not be generated, and interference occurs when idea sharing disrupts the individual-level cognitive process of idea generation. Productivity losses (group members are outperformed by individuals) are found when interference is stronger than stimulation; productivity gains (group members outperform individuals) are possible when stimulation is stronger than interference.

In a number of studies (e.g., Diehl, 1991; Nijstad, 2000; Nijstad et al., 1999, 2002, in press; Ziegler et al., 2000) we have examined the effects of idea sharing on cognitive processes and performance. We have shown that production blocking, when group members have to take turns to express their ideas, interferes with the cognitive process of idea generation. We have further shown that access to other people's ideas in general has positive consequences, although it may also lead to idea uniformity in relatively homogeneous groups. In face-to-face brainstorming groups, interference seems to be much stronger than stimulation, and as a consequence, groups are less productive and creative than individuals. In situations where production blocking is eliminated, such as in brainwriting and electronic brainstorming paradigms, stimulation appears to be stronger than interference.

However, even in face-to-face groups people are usually convinced that group brainstorming is more effective than individual brainstorming. One of the factors underlying this phenomenon is that group interaction leads to a reduction in failures, instances that one is unable to come up with ideas, which leads to the impression that idea generation is facilitated in groups. As a consequence, people think that group brainstorming is very effective, a phenomenon that has been labeled the illusion of group effectivity.

Implications for Theory and Research

From a theoretical point of view, our cognitive approach fits well within the recently advanced conceptualization of groups as information processors (Hinsz, Tindale, & Vollrath, 1997). Information processing in groups takes place at both the individual and the group level. At the individual level, group members encode, store, retrieve, and generate information. At the group level, information processing involves the sharing of information during discussion. The perspective of groups as information processors suggests several interesting questions: Which information and ideas are shared, and which are not? How do groups combine information to come up with (creative) solutions and decisions? What is the effect of information and idea sharing on the individual-level cognitive processes? It is this last question we have addressed in the present chapter.

In line with the information-processing perspective, other researchers have addressed other questions. For example, studies in decision making have assessed what information is and is not shared during discussion and how groups combine information to come up with decisions and solutions (see Stasser & Birchmeier, this volume). However, most of this research has been done in situations where a fixed set of decision alternatives had to be evaluated. Research in the area of creative group decision making, in which decision alternatives are not given but have to be generated, is scarce. Although, as the present volume shows, there has been much work in the area of group idea generation, there is a lack of understanding of how groups choose among ideas that they have generated. As an idea-generation session is seldom the endpoint, but merely a first stage in the decision-making process, this is an unfortunate situation. It may well be, for example, that groups are not very effective when generating ideas, but that they are competent decision makers once ideas have been generated. This clearly represents an important area for future study.

In our cognitive perspective and SIAM model, task-related knowledge plays an important role. We maintain that, although ideas are generally new solutions to a problem, they cannot be generated without reference to previously acquired knowledge. An important distinction in this respect is between available and accessible knowledge (see Higgins, 1996; Tulving & Pearlstone, 1966). Knowledge may in principle be available to a person, but due to situational constraints may not be very accessible; the well-known tip-of-the-tongue phenomenon is an example of the inability to retrieve available information. As we argued, ideas of others may make certain knowledge more accessible. Whether idea sharing has positive consequences, such as cognitive stimulation, or negative consequences, such as cognitive uniformity, largely depends on the amount of overlap of accessible knowledge among group members. When the amount of overlap in dominant associations to a certain topic is relatively large, it is quite likely that the group becomes stuck in a few semantic domains and overlooks relevant other aspects of the task (i.e., it may lead to uniformity). When overlap is smaller, this may be less of a problem. Group diversity, in terms of accessible knowledge, may thus be an important determinant of group effectiveness. Clearly, more research is called for on the relation between group composition and group creativity, in particular related to the dynamic process of information and idea sharing in groups (also see Milliken et al., this volume).

Practical Applications

Our cognitive perspective suggests a relatively straightforward principle: Group performance can be maximized if cognitive interference is prevented and cognitive stimulation is maximized. As our work on production blocking shows, it may not be very feasible to overcome cognitive interference in face-to-face groups, in particular if the group is large and delays are long and unpredictable. It may thus be wise to use relatively small groups. Dyads appear to combine the advantages of limited cognitive interference and relatively high levels of productivity with high levels of satisfaction and task enjoyment. We therefore advise splitting larger groups into dyads. In addition, it may be beneficial to use rotating dyads, in which, periodically, new combinations of two individuals are made. It seems possible that input from another person may help idea generation later in the session, at the point where dyads are beginning to become "exhausted." It may be wiser to eliminate production blocking altogether by using procedures that do not require turn-taking among group members, such as brainwriting and electronic brainstorming (also see Dennis & Williams, this volume). These procedures combine the advantages of maintaining cognitive stimulation and preventing interference due to blocking.

To maximize cognitive stimulation, group composition seems to be of primary importance. In particular, group diversity in terms of dominant associations or accessible knowledge may be essential. However, although diversity may have positive effects, such as increased stimulation and idea diversity, it may also have negative effects, such as decreased levels of group identification and satisfaction (e.g., Williams & O'Reilly, 1998). It may even lead to misunderstandings, problems of communication among group members, and conflicts. Thus, although diversity may be an advantage, too much diversity may be a disadvantage, in particular if group members do not share a common understanding of the task and a common language to discuss it.

Further, one can try to maximize brainstorming persistence. Usually, performance of brainstorming groups declines in the course of a session (e.g., Diehl & Stroebe, 1991). According to our persistence studies, this decline leads to the impression of running out of ideas and the wish to terminate the session. To achieve high levels of persistence (and thereby of productivity), it is important to maintain a high level of productivity throughout the session. Our analysis suggests that one reason for the decline of performance is that old ideas (ideas that have already been mentioned) have a high level of activation and keep popping up, thereby preventing the generation of new ideas. There are a few ways this type of interference can be prevented or reduced. Introducing short breaks is likely to help, because during the break the level of activation of old ideas will decline, thereby opening up possibilities of generating new ideas. We have also found that exposure to another person's ideas moderates the decline of performance, in particular when these ideas are semantically diverse (Nijstad, 2000). The earlier mentioned concept of rotating dyads may be of help here, because input from a new partner may temporarily increase performance and lead to the impression that many more ideas are still possible. Further, it has been found that problem presentation is an important factor (Coskun, Paulus, Brown, & Sherwood, 2000; Dennis, Valacich, Connolly, & Wynne, 1996). It appears that breaking down a problem into several pieces stimulates the generation of large numbers of ideas for each of the pieces, perhaps because cognitive uniformity is prevented. A sequential presentation of the different aspects of the task is further likely to prevent the decline of performance across time because the introduction of each new aspect will be followed by a surge in activity. These interventions are likely to lead to large numbers of ideas and potentially also to increased levels of persistence.

Idea Generation and Group Creativity

Idea generation is a necessary and essential element of creativity. However, to be creative more is needed than large numbers of high-quality ideas. It is also essential to recognize a good idea and subsequently to overcome obstacles to implement it or to convince others of its quality. Indeed, creativity does not occur in a vacuum, and an idea will be called creative only if significant others agree that it is (see Hooker, Nakamura, & Csikszentmihalyi, this volume). All the different stages in the creative process, such as idea generation, idea evaluation and selection, and implementation, can be done either by groups or individuals. As most of the idea-generation literature shows, idea generation may be best left to individuals because effective procedures are required for groups to become good idea generators. However, instead of continuing to focus on the question of whether one should use groups in the creative process and how groups compare to individuals in idea generation, a better question might be when to use groups (also see Nijstad & De Dreu, 2002). As the present volume shows, there may be much to gain when groups are used in the right stages of the creative process.

Note

The authors wish to thank Paul Paulus and Vincent Brown for their helpful suggestions on an earlier draft of this chapter.

References

Basden, B. H., Basden, D. R., Bryner, S., & Thomas, R. L., III (1997). A comparison of group and individual remembering: Does collaboration disrupt retrieval strategies? *Journal of Experimental Psychology: Learning, Memory, and Cognition, 23,* 1176–1189.

Bousfield, W. A. (1953). The occurrence of clustering in the recall of randomly arranged associates. *Journal of General Psychology, 36,* 67–81.

Brown, V., Tumeo, M., Larey, T. S., & Paulus, P. B. (1998). Modeling cognitive interactions during group brainstorming. *Small Group Research, 29,* 495–526.

Camacho, L. M., & Paulus, P. B. (1995). The role of social anxiousness in group brainstorming. *Journal of Personality and Social Psychology, 68,* 1071–1080.

Coskun, H., Paulus, P. B., Brown, V., & Sherwood, J. J. (2000). Cognitive stimulation and problem presentation in idea-generating groups. *Group Dynamics, 4,* 307–329.

Dennis, A. R., & Valacich, J. S. (1993). Computer brainstorms: More heads are better than one. *Journal of Applied Psychology, 78,* 531–537.

Dennis, A. R., Valacich, J. S., Connolly, T., & Wynne, B. E. (1996). Process structuring in electronic brainstorming. *Information Systems Research, 7,* 268–277.

Diehl, M. (1991). *Kollektive Kreativität: Zur Quantität und Qualität der Ideenproduktion in Kleingruppen* [Collective creativity: On the quantity and quality of idea production in small groups]. Unpublished Habilitationschrift, University of Tübingen.

Diehl, M., & Stroebe, W. (1987). Productivity loss in brainstorming groups: Toward the solution of a riddle. *Journal of Personality and Social Psychology, 53,* 497–509.

Diehl, M., & Stroebe, W. (1991). Productivity loss in idea-generating groups: Tracking down the blocking effect. *Journal of Personality and Social Psychology, 61,* 392–403.

Dugosh, K. L., Paulus, P. B., Roland, E. J., & Yang, H. C. (2000). Cognitive stimulation in brainstorming. *Journal of Personality and Social Psychology, 79,* 722–735.

Gruenewald, P. J., & Lockhead, G. R. (1980). The free recall of category examples. *Journal of Experimental Psychology: Human Learning and Memory, 6,* 225–240.

Higgins, E. T. (1996). Knowledge activation: Accessibility, applicability, and salience. In E. T. Higgins & A. W. Kruglanski (Eds.), *Social psychology: A handbook of basic principles* (pp. 133–168). New York: Guilford.

Hinsz, V. B., Tindale, R. S., & Vollrath, D. A. (1997). The emerging conceptualization of groups as information processors. *Psychological Bulletin, 121,* 43–64.

Lamm, H., & Trommsdorff, G. (1973). Group versus individual performance on a task requiring ideational proficiency (brainstorming): A review. *European Journal of Social Psychology, 3,* 362–388.

Larey, T. S., & Paulus, P. B. (1995). Social comparison and goal setting in groups. *Journal of Applied Social Psychology, 25,* 1579–1596.

Larey, T. S., & Paulus, P. B. (1999). Group preference and convergent tendencies in small groups: A content analysis of group brainstorming performance. *Creativity Research Journal, 12,* 175–184.

Mednick, S. A. (1962). The associative basis of the creative process. *Psychological Review, 69,* 220–232.

Mullen, B., Johnson, C. & Salas, E. (1991). Productivity loss in brainstorming groups: A meta-analytic integration. *Basic and Applied Social Psychology, 12,* 3–24.

Nijstad, B. A. (2000). *How the group affects the mind: Effects of communication in idea generating groups.* Unpublished doctoral dissertation, Utrecht University, The Netherlands.

Nijstad, B. A., & De Dreu, C. K. W. (2002). Creativity and group innovation. *Applied Psychology: An International Review, 51,* 400–406.

Nijstad, B. A., Stroebe, W., & Lodewijkx, H. F. M. (1999). Persistence of brainstorming groups: How do people know when to stop? *Journal of Experimental Social Psychology, 35,* 165–185.

Nijstad, B. A., Stroebe, W., & Lodewijkx, H. F. M. (2002). Cognitive stimulation and interference in groups: Exposure effects in an idea generation task. *Journal of Experimental Social Psychology, 38,* 535–544.

Nijstad, B. A., Stroebe, W., & Lodewijkx, H. F. M. (in press). Production blocking and idea generation: Does blocking interfere with cognitive processes? *Journal of Experimental Social Psychology.*

Osborn, A. F. (1957). *Applied imagination* (2nd ed.). New York: Scribner.

Paulus, P. B., & Dzindolet, M. T. (1993). Social influence processes in group brainstorming. *Journal of Personality and Social Psychology, 64,* 575–586.

Paulus, P. B., Dzindolet, M. T., Poletes, G., & Camacho, L. M. (1993). Perceptions of performance in group brainstorming: The illusion of group productivity. *Personality and Social Psychology Bulletin, 19,* 78–89.

Paulus, P. B., Larey, T. S., & Ortega, A. H. (1995). Performance and perception of brainstormers in an organizational setting. *Basic and Applied Social Psychology, 17,* 249–265.

Paulus, P. B., & Yang, H. C. (2000). Idea generation in groups: A basis for creativity in organizations. *Organizational Behavior and Human Decision Processes, 82,* 76–87.

Raaijmakers, J. G. W., & Shiffrin, R. M. (1981). Search of associative memory. *Psychological Review, 88,* 93–134.

Stroebe, W., & Diehl, M. (1994). Why groups are less effective than their members: On productivity losses in idea-generating groups. In W. Stroebe & M. Hewstone (Eds.), *European review of social psychology* (Vol. 5, pp. 271–303). London: Wiley.

Stroebe, W., Diehl, M., & Abakoumkin, G. (1992). The illusion of group effectivity. *Personality and Social Psychology Bulletin, 18,* 643–650.

Taylor, D. W., Berry, P. C., & Block, C. H. (1958). Does group participation when brainstorming facilitate or inhibit creative thinking? *Administrative Science Quarterly, 3,* 23–47.

Tulving, E., & Pearlstone, Z. (1966). Availability versus accessibility of information in memory for words. *Journal of Verbal Learning and Verbal Behavior, 5,* 381–391.

Valacich, J. S., Dennis, A. R., & Connolly, T. (1994). Idea-generation in computer-based groups: A new ending to an old story. *Organizational Behavior and Human Decision Processes, 57,* 448–467.

Williams, K. Y., & O'Reilly, C. A., III. (1998). Demography and diversity in organizations: A review of 40 years of research. *Research in Organizational Behavior, 20,* 77–140.

Ziegler, R., Diehl, M., & Zijlstra, G. (2000). Idea production in nominal and virtual groups: Does computer-mediated communication improve group brainstorming? *Group Processes and Intergroup Relations, 3,* 141–158.

8

■■■■■ *Alan R. Dennis and Mike L. Williams*

Electronic Brainstorming
Theory, Research, and Future Directions

■■■■■

Communication is a fundamental element of group creativity. Researchers have long considered how to improve communication to improve group creativity, but unfortunately, the general conclusion of this research is that due to problems in the communication process, people generate fewer ideas when they work together in groups than when they work separately and later pool their ideas (i.e., in "nominal groups"; see Mullen, Johnson, & Salas, 1991; Paulus, Larey, & Ortega, 1995).

Over the past decade, a new form of computer technology called group support systems (GSS) has emerged. With GSS, group members communicate by exchanging typed messages instead of or in addition to speaking verbally. GSS have proven useful in improving group performance (Dennis, Wixom, & Vandenberg, 2001), particularly for creativity tasks such as idea generation.

What Are GSS?

GSS research began in the early 1980s at a variety of universities in the United States and Canada. One of the first systems to be available commercially was called GroupSystems, developed at the University of Arizona (Nunamaker, Dennis, Valacich, Vogel, & George, 1991). These early systems were designed to support system analysts and users in the construction of information systems.

They were designed as a series of networked microcomputers arranged in a U shape or in a tiered legislative style. At the front of the room were a meeting leader/facilitator and a large-screen video display.

GSS support a variety of tasks, but many groups using GroupSystems followed a similar sequence of events. A group leader would meet with a GroupSystems facilitator to develop an agenda for the meeting and to select GroupSystems tools to be used. Then, as the group meeting began, the participants typed their comments into their computer and the results were integrated and displayed on the large screen in the front of the room, as well as being available on each workstation. All participants saw the comments from the group but without knowing who contributed what because all comments were anonymous.

Although many systems were originally designed to be used with all participants meeting in the same room at the same time (e.g., GroupSystems), they have evolved to increasingly popular and ubiquitous Internet-enabled applications such as Groove, MSN Messenger, Yahoo Chat, ICQ, and Lotus Notes, enabling users to communicate with other group members over the Internet. Each different software package offers a slightly different set of features. Most enable the simple sharing of ideas and comments among team members. Some enable the comments to be rearranged and organized using headings. Some systems enable participants to vote or to use sophisticated multicriteria decision-making tools. Figure 8.1 shows a sample GSS meeting using Lotus Notes.

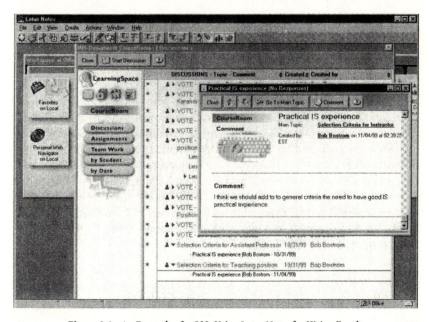

Figure 8.1. *An Example of a GSS: Using Lotus Notes for Hiring Faculty*

Electronic Brainstorming

Although GSS can be used to support many different tasks, much of the research has focused on creativity tasks such as idea generation or brainstorming. Virtually all GSS tools enable participants to exchange ideas and comments, and some provide special purpose tools to support what has come to be called electronic brainstorming (EBS).

The initial research on EBS suggested that EBS groups could generate more ideas than verbal brainstorming groups (Gallupe et al., 1992) and as many or more ideas as nominal groups who work in the presence of each other but do not exchange ideas (Dennis & Valacich, 1993). Recent research has challenged these early studies, suggesting that any productivity gains compared to nominal groups are an "illusion" (Pinsonneault, Barki, Gallupe, & Hoppen, 1999). This challenge has sparked a new debate over the illusion or pattern of EBS productivity compared to other approaches, a debate that has led different researchers to different conclusions (cf. Dennis & Valacich, 1999; Pinsonneault & Barki, 1999).

The goal of this chapter is to integrate the previous research on EBS and draw conclusions about the effects of EBS. We begin by examining the important theoretical underpinnings of EBS and then examine each of the important ways that EBS may change traditional approaches to creativity. We close with an examination of the effects of group size on performance, because group size is one of the dominant factors in the successful—and less successful—use of EBS.

Process Gains and Losses from GSS Use

Much of the prior GSS and EBS research has been guided by the process gains and losses framework (Hill, 1982; Steiner, 1972). Simply put, communication among group members introduces factors into the brainstorming process that act to improve performance (process gains) and factors that act to impair performance (process losses) relative to individuals who work separately without communicating but who later pool ideas (called nominal groups). Several dozen plausible sources of process losses and gains in verbal and electronic brainstorming have been proposed (see Camacho & Paulus, 1995; Mullen et al., 1991; Pinsonneault et al., 1999). Two process gains (synergy, social facilitation) and five process losses (production blocking, social loafing, evaluation apprehension, cognitive interference, and communication speed) have received the most research attention and are the ones that we believe are most important (Dennis & Valacich, 1999; Diehl & Stroebe, 1987; Pinsonneault & Barki, 1999; Pinsonneault et al., 1999). See Table 8.1.

Potential Process Gains

Synergy is the ability of an idea from one participant to trigger a new idea in another participant, an idea that would otherwise not have been produced

Table 8.1. Potential Process Gains and Losses

	Nominal Group Brainstorming	Verbal Brainstorming	Electronic Brainstorming
Process Gains			
Synergy	None	Increases as the size of the group increases	Increases as the size of the group increases
Social facilitation	Depends on group structure	Some effect	Some effect
Process Losses			
Production blocking	None	Increases as the size of the group increases	None
Evaluation apprehension	None	Increases as the size of the group increases	None
Social loafing	Depends on group structure	Increases as the size of the group increases	Increases as the size of the group increases
Cognitive interference	None	Increases as the size of the group increases	Some effect
Communication speed	Some effect	None	Some effect

(Dennis & Valacich, 1993; Lamm & Trommsdorff, 1973). Synergy, or the "assembly bonus" (Collins & Guetzkow, 1964), is perhaps the most fundamental potential source of process gains. Osborn's (1957) advice to "piggyback" on the ideas of others strives to increase the synergy that participants derive by doing so. Synergy can be expected to increase as the size of the group increases because there is likely to be a greater range of ideas with the potential to trigger new ideas (Dennis & Valacich, 1993; Gallupe et al., 1992; Valacich, Dennis, & Connolly, 1994). It should be noted that there is not a necessary, direct relationship between group size and synergy. Two important variables have been shown to affect the development of synergy in group creativity: diversity and attention. The diversity of team membership has been shown to be related to higher-quality team decision making (Gruenfeld, 1995; Jackson, 1992; Milliken, Bartel, & Kurtzberg, this volume) and group creativity (Bantel & Jackson, 1989; Jackson, May, & Whitney, 1995; K. Williams & O'Reilly, 1998). Diversity seems to have some effect on synergy, but the exact nature of the effect is still unclear. The second variable that affects synergy is attention to ideas. Recent research indicates that even small EBS groups can experience process gains from synergy when participants receive instructions to focus their attention and memory on the ideas presented by others (Dugosh, Paulus, Roland, & Yang, 2000; Paulus & Yang, 2000). Each of these studies serves to emphasize the value of synergy in EBS while simultaneously suggesting additional moderating variables on the effect of group size on synergy.

Social facilitation is the ability of the presence of others to affect one's performance (Allport, 1920; Levine, Resnick, & Higgins, 1993; Zajonc, 1965). If individuals are experienced in performing a task or expect that they can perform the task well, working in the presence of others improves performance (Robinson-Staveley & Cooper, 1990; Sanna, 1992). However, if individuals have low expectations about performance, working in the presence of others impairs performance (Robinson-Staveley & Cooper, 1990; Sanna, 1992). For relatively simple tasks such as those commonly used in brainstorming, social facilitation is typically seen as a potential process gain (Pinsonneault et al., 1999) but one with only a small effect (Bond & Titus, 1983). Social facilitation may also exist in nominal groups if participants work in the presence of each other even if they do not communicate, so it is best considered a process gain of group structure, not of group communication. Because it does not depend on whether or not participants can communicate (but rather on where they sit), we do not view social facilitation as a true process gain that can be attributed to group interaction, but one that potentially flows to even nominal groups that work in the same room but do not communicate.

Potential Process Losses

Production blocking refers to the need to take turns speaking in verbal brainstorming (Diehl & Stroebe, 1987). When participants are prevented from contributing an idea when they first think of it, they may forget it or suppress it because the idea later seems less relevant or original. If they try to retain the idea, they must focus on remembering it, which prevents them from generating new ideas or attending to the ideas of others (Diehl & Stroebe, 1991).

Production blocking is the single most important source of process loss in verbal brainstorming groups (Diehl & Stroebe, 1987; Gallupe, Cooper, Grise, & Bastianutti, 1994; Valacich et al., 1994). Production blocking in these groups increases as the size of the group increases because the probability of occurrence increases directly with the number of participants and because more participants are blocked as size increases (Dennis & Valacich, 1993; Gallupe et al., 1992; Valacich et al., 1994). Production blocking is nonexistent in nominal groups because group members do not communicate while generating ideas. Production blocking is essentially nonexistent in EBS groups because all participants can contribute ideas simultaneously (Dennis & Valacich, 1993; Pinsonneault et al., 1999; Valacich et al., 1994).

Evaluation apprehension may cause participants in verbal brainstorming to withhold ideas because they fear a negative reaction from other participants (Diehl & Stroebe, 1987; Lamm & Trommsdorff, 1973). Osborn's (1957) advice to withhold criticism tries to reduce evaluation apprehension. Evaluation apprehension should be minimal in nominal groups because participants do not share ideas, and when ideas are pooled, it is usually done anonymously. Evaluation apprehension in verbal brainstorming should increase as group size increases because there are more participants who might criticize an idea (Gallupe et al., 1992). EBS can be designed so that participants contribute ideas anonymously, which should reduce or eliminate evaluation apprehension (Cooper, Gallupe, Pollard, & Cadsby, 1998; Dennis & Valacich, 1993).

Anonymity has been shown to affect behavior in several studies (Diener, 1979; Diener, Fraser, Beaman, & Kelem, 1976; Saks & Ostrom, 1973; Siegel, Dubrovsky, Kiesler, & McGuire, 1986; Zimbardo, 1969). Frequently, anonymity is seen to produce a deindividuating cover for behavior that would not otherwise be produced (Diener, 1979). These deindividuating behaviors induce group participants to share ideas that might otherwise be withheld due to evaluative apprehension. There is some empirical evidence that participants in anonymous conditions contribute more controversial and nonredundant ideas than those in nonanonymous conditions (Cooper et al., 1998).

Prior research on anonymity in GSS is equivocal. Many laboratory experiments have examined the effects of anonymity on idea-generation performance, but virtually none has found any effects due to anonymity (Cooper et al., 1998; Dennis & Valacich, 1993). Prior studies on anonymity in EBS show no effects on inhibition (George, Easton, Nunamaker, & Northcraft, 1990; Hiltz, Turoff, & Johnson, 1989; Lea & Spears, 1991), group communication (Siegel et al., 1986), or group performance (George et al., 1990; Jessup, Connolly, & Galegher, 1990; Prentice-Dunn & Rogers, 1982). But anonymity does affect criticalness (Connolly, Jessup, & Valacich, 1990; Jessup et al., 1990; Lea & Spears, 1991; Postmes & Lea, 2000; Prentice-Dunn & Rogers, 1982) and produces more conservative decisions in a conservative organizational context (Hiltz et al., 1989).

One possible explanation for these equivocal findings is the operationalization of the anonymity construct itself. Pinsonneault and Heppel (1997) examined this problem in detail and argue that anonymity is a more complex concept than usually operationalized in the GSS literature. In existing GSS research, anonymity has been operationalized as the inability of group members to identify the origin of the messages they receive and the destination of the messages they send. However, Pinsonneault and Heppel suggest that anonymity should be reconceptualized as a subjective, continuous, multidimensional construct including the degree of liberation from social evaluation and the threats of punishment and retaliation. Future GSS research should attempt further empirical work on this important concept.

In contrast to the findings from laboratory experiments with undergraduate students, there is significant anecdotal evidence from field studies that anonymity can have significant effects (cf. Nunamaker et al., 1991). There are also strong theoretical arguments to suggest that anonymity can be important in some situations (Diener, 1979; Diener et al., 1976; Saks & Ostrom, 1973; Siegel et al., 1986; Zimbardo, 1969). We believe—but cannot prove—that anonymity is important in some organizational situations but has little effect on undergraduate students in laboratory settings who, by their nature, may be less inhibited than organizational employees in corporate settings.

Social loafing (or free-riding) is the tendency for individuals to expend less effort when working in a group than when working individually (Karau & Williams, 1993). Social loafing may arise because participants believe their contributions to be dispensable and not needed for group success and/or because responsibility for completing the task is diffused among many participants (Harkins & Petty, 1982; Karau & Williams, 1993; Latane, Williams, & Harkins, 1979). Social loafing is reduced when participants believe they are being evaluated as individuals rather than collectively as a group (Karau & Williams, 1993). Therefore, differences in social loafing become more noticeable when members of nominal groups believe themselves to be working as individuals, not as members of groups. As with production blocking, social loafing can be expected to increase as group size increases because perceived dispensability and diffusion of responsibility increase as the number of participants increases. Social loafing is also made stronger when anonymity is provided in EBS. In fact, anonymity is one of the basic manipulations of early social loafing studies (Bartis, Szymanski, & Harkins, 1988; Karau & Williams, 1993).

Cognitive interference is in many ways the inverse of synergy. Cognitive interference occurs when the ideas generated by other participants interfere with an individual's own idea-generation activities (Pinsonneault & Barki, 1999; Straus, 1996). Cognitive interference may be due to the need to attend to ideas presented by others as they appear (e.g., in verbal brainstorming, a spoken idea disappears as soon as it is uttered, so a missed idea is a lost idea). Cognitive interference may also be due to the content of the ideas contributed by others because ideas from others serve to stimulate cognitive activity in one area while limiting the flexibility of idea production (Nijstad, Diehl, & Stroebe, this volume; Ziegler, Diehl, & Zijlstra, 2000). That is, brainstorming may suffer from cognitive inertia by focusing idea generation on only one aspect of the overall task (Dennis & Valacich, 1993; Pinsonneault & Barki, 1999). The effect of cognitive inertia is strengthened by social influence processes and social convergence (Festinger, 1954; Larey & Paulus, 1999). As group members compare behavior across the group, they tend to converge at a similar level. When there is not a strong performance incentive, they tend to converge at the level of the least productive members (Camacho & Paulus, 1995; Larey & Paulus, 1995; Paulus & Dzindolet, 1993).

Process losses in verbal brainstorming groups due to cognitive interference should increase with group size because more people are contributing more ideas, which increases potential interference. EBS is less susceptible to cognitive interference because ideas are stored in the system as they are contributed, so participants need not attend to them as they arrive. Instead participants can generate ideas as they choose and interrupt their individual idea-generation process only when they desire the stimulation from others' ideas. Although EBS may still suffer from cognitive inertia, the ability to provide for, or to intentionally induce, multiple simultaneous dialogues or threads of conversation means that it is quite unusual for groups to focus on one narrow set of ideas (Dennis et al., 1997; Dennis, Valacich, Connolly, & Wynne, 1996). In other words, EBS allows group members to carry on multiple, potentially unrelated conversations concurrently. Group members are thus free to choose if and when they participate in each conversation stream. The ability of EBS to structure and direct participants' cognitive focus may be one of its most powerful contributions.

Some research also indicates a positive relationship between multiple simultaneous dialogues and performance in GSS groups (Valacich & Schwenk, 1985). However, this may induce cognitive interference as participants attempt to follow simultaneous dialogues that may increase as the size of the group increases (Pinsonneault & Barki, 1999; Pinsonneault et al., 1999). As the number and length of simultaneous dialogues increase, participants may experience information overload. In this condition, the amount of cognitive processing required exceeds the abilities of the individual participant to process the information (Nagasundarum & Dennis, 1993; Newell & Simon, 1972).

Several studies suggest that the ability of an EBS system to mitigate the effects of cognitive inertia and cognitive interference may be important. Two such studies are described here. In one study, cognitive inertia was mitigated by manipulating the number of dialogues in an idea-generation task (Dennis et al., 1997). A control group used an EBS module that allowed all 10 group participants to contribute to a single, common dialogue on screen. As each member saved an idea, it was automatically posted to the shared dialogue for all other group members to view. The treatment group participated in 11 simultaneous dialogues. Each subject began the experimental session with a different empty dialogue and started by typing an idea into it. This dialogue then was replaced by another dialogue (the most recently updated one), and the process was repeated. This is analogous to being at a party where every time you make a comment to one group, you are immediately whisked to another group to whom you listen, make another comment, and immediately move to another group. This manipulation mitigated cognitive inertia by allowing participants to be involved in multiple, simultaneous dialogues, thereby increasing the number of unique, high-quality, and novel ideas.

In a second study, cognitive inertia was manipulated by structuring the task (Dennis, Aronson, Heninger, & Walker, 1999). A control group worked for 30 minutes on a single unstructured task. A second group worked for three 10-minute periods on the same task divided into three subcategories. Groups in the partitioned task treatment generated 40% more ideas than groups in the nonstructured task treatment. This suggests that task structuring mitigated the effects of cognitive interference by refocusing members' attention more evenly across the entire solution space (see also Paulus & Brown, this volume).

Considering the findings of these studies, we believe the structure that EBS can impose on group discussion is an important reason for the improved performance of EBS groups. The primary advantage of structuring is the reduction of cognitive interference and inertia.

Communication speed is another potential process loss that is found in EBS and, to some extent, in nominal group brainstorming. Communication speed is influenced by the need to type or write rather than speak. For most people, speaking is faster than typing or writing (Williams & Karau, 1991), so the need to type may inhibit idea generation by slowing down communication

(Nunamaker et al., 1991). To date, no studies have examined this potential process loss of GSS in detail. It should be noted that, in prior studies, sometimes members of nominal groups have written their ideas, sometimes they have typed their ideas, and sometimes they have spoken their ideas. Members of EBS groups can either type or speak their ideas, although in practice, all research studies have required participants to type their ideas.

Summary of GSS Advantages

GSS have several advantages over traditional group communication processes. Whereas traditional group communication processes support serial communication, where each participant speaks in turn, GSS allows simultaneous entry into group communication. Any or all participants can enter the conversation simultaneously without queuing for their turn to speak.

Another unique feature of GSS is the support of groups that are not colo cated geographically or temporally. Although the original GSS were room-based, the rise of the Internet and Net-enabled organization has allowed the formation of groups that were not conceivable 30 years ago. GSS enable groups to form and operate without ever experiencing face-to-face communication. These so-called virtual teams (Lipnack & Stamps, 1997) have been the focus of extensive research (for a review of recent work, see Saunders, 2000).

Additionally, GSS avoid the communication problems associated with peer evaluation (Camacho & Paulus, 1995) by allowing anonymous involvement of participants. With anonymous participation, group members are able to evaluate communication without regard to the source. Another benefit is that GSS support parallelism or multiple simultaneous communication processes. This eliminates the competition for speaking time that burdens interactive groups (Diehl & Stroebe, 1991). Because GSS are enabled by networked computers they support the automatic storage of all communications for later review and analysis.

The Role of Group Size

One of the important factors in understanding the potential effects of GSS and EBS use is group size, because the balance of process gains and losses changes dramatically depending on the size of the group. Although previous research indicates that dyads perform about as well as nominal groups (Diehl & Stroebe, 1987; Mullen et al., 1991), size effects are clear in larger groups. Verbal brainstorming groups, for example, should experience synergy that increases as group size increases and some social facilitation effects, but also suffer from process losses that increase with the size of the group due to production blocking, social loafing, evaluation apprehension, and cognitive interference. Nominal group brainstorming (in which group members work in the same room by writing or typing ideas but do not exchange them) experiences gains from social facilitation but no gains from synergy. Likewise, if nominal groups anonymously sum the product of their work, they may experience some social loafing and communication speed problems but no production blocking, evaluation apprehension, or cognitive interference. EBS groups should also experience synergy that increases with the size of the group as well as some social facilitation effects. EBS groups are also likely to suffer from cognitive interference and problems due to communication speed and some social loafing that increases with group size.

Figure 8.2 offers a shorthand summary of these patterns. The figure does not attempt to display the detailed effects of individual process gains and losses on brainstorming methods, but merely indicates the overall trend effects for each method and the effects of group size. For example, overall process gains for both verbal and electronic brainstorming groups should increase with group size to some threshold level where the value of adding another participant will be only minimally positive. Process losses in verbal brainstorming groups should increase fairly quickly as the size of the group increases; previous research suggests that losses increase more quickly than gains, because nominal groups have outperformed verbal brainstorming groups. It should be noted, however, that some of the process losses incurred by verbal brainstorming groups will not follow a linear trend. For instance, although the effect of evaluative apprehension should increase with group size, social impact theory (Latane, 1981) suggests that this effect will level off when the group reaches a threshold size. Additionally, the effect of production blocking by a single participant in a small group (e.g., 3–5 members) will have a larger proportional effect than in a large group (e.g., 25+ members). That is not to suggest an eventual decrease in process losses, but a curvilinear relationship. In contrast, process losses for EBS groups start higher (because of communication speed problems and the inherent loss of typing versus speaking) but increase much more slowly with group size. The primary message of Figure 8.2 is the indication that at some point, process gains should exceed process losses, and EBS groups should outperform nominal groups.

Figure 8.2 suggests two conclusions. First, for verbal versus electronic groups, we would expect large EBS groups to generate more ideas than similar size verbal brainstorming groups. Our expectations for smaller groups are less clear. EBS introduces a fixed communication speed process loss due to the need to type, regardless of the size of the group. Conversely, small verbal groups suffer few production blocking losses, and, depending on the group, would also likely suffer few losses due to evaluation apprehension. We believe that for most small groups, the losses introduced in EBS due to the need to type would exceed the losses introduced in verbal brainstorming from production blocking and evaluation apprehension. Therefore, small verbal brainstorming groups should generate more ideas than similar size EBS groups.

Our second set of conclusions pertains to nominal versus electronic groups. Nominal groups experience gains only from social facilitation, the same gains we could logically expect for EBS groups. Electronic groups, however, experience synergy that increases with group size. Both nominal and electronic groups can be expected to experience similar losses due to social loafing (modest),

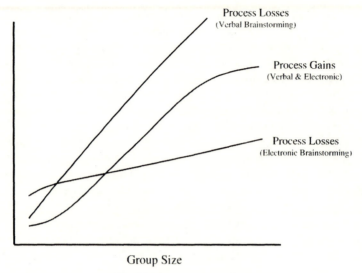

Figure 8.2. *Process Gains and Losses*

production blocking (none), and evaluation apprehension (none). Electronic groups may suffer from cognitive interference and may suffer more from communication speed effects because participants must type, whereas nominal groups can write, which may be faster. Once again, the use of EBS imposes an initial fixed cost, which may be overcome as group size increases. Thus, we expect that small nominal brainstorming groups should generate more ideas than small EBS groups. Conversely, large EBS groups should generate more ideas than large nominal brainstorming groups.

The natural question at this point is, what is a "small" group? We expect little difference for dyads using different modalities (nominal, verbal, EBS). With groups of three we find slight production losses in verbal groups and slight enhancement in writing groups (Coskun, 2000). With groups of four we get 50% production losses for verbal but for EBS (Dugosh et al., 2000) and writing (Paulus & Yang, 2000) we have found production gains. So the critical size of the group appears to be somewhere in the range of one to three members.

Testing Our Expectations

To test our expectations, we conducted a meta-analysis of prior research. We found 21 articles that compared EBS to verbal brainstorming or compared EBS to nominal group brainstorming. Because studies had different group sizes, we split the data by group size, so that the 21 studies produced 22 usable data points for the EBS versus verbal brainstorming comparison and 14 usable data points for the EBS versus nominal group brainstorming comparison.

It is beyond the scope of this chapter to describe in detail the statistical algorithm underlying a meta-analysis (see Hunter & Schmidt, 1990). In short, the mean number of ideas for the verbal brainstorming groups (or nominal brainstorming groups) is subtracted from the mean number of ideas for the EBS groups, and this difference is divided by the pooled standard deviation from both conditions to produce a weighted average effect size for each study. A positive effect size means that the EBS groups generated more ideas; a negative effect size means that the verbal or nominal groups generated more ideas. We then used linear regression to regress these effect sizes against group size to understand the effects of group size on idea-generation performance.[1]

Figure 8.3 shows a plot of the data points and the results of the regression for EBS versus verbal brainstorming. This plot demonstrates that the performance of EBS groups starts out below that of verbal groups but increases gradually as group size increases, so that by the time there are four members in a group, EBS groups produce noticeably more ideas than verbal brainstorming groups.[2]

Figure 8.4 shows a plot of the data points and the results of the regression for EBS versus nominal group brainstorming. This indicates that the performance of EBS groups starts out below that of nominal groups but increases gradually as group size increases, so that by the time there are nine members in a group, EBS groups produce noticeably more ideas than nominal groups.[3]

If we compare Figures 8.3 and 8.4, we see the same basic pattern: EBS groups underperform verbal and nominal brainstorming groups initially, with a gradual increase in performance as group size increases. For verbal brainstorming, the break-even point comes quickly, so that EBS groups produce more ideas in

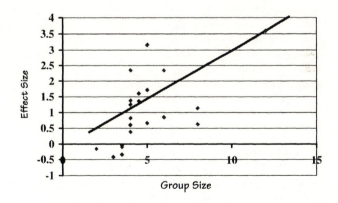

Figure 8.3. *Electronic Brainstorming versus Verbal Brainstorming*
Regression Results

Parameter	Estimate	t	p
Intercept	−.419	−0.84	0.410
Group size	0.305	3.29	0.004

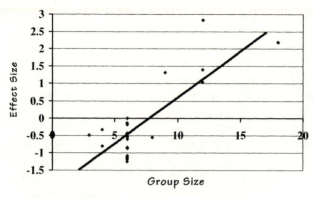

Figure 8.4. *Electronic Brainstorming versus Nominal Groups Regression Results*

Parameter	Estimate	t	p
Intercept	−2.043	−6.73	0.001
Group size	0.264	6.97	0.001

groups with just four members. For nominal group brainstorming, the break-even point comes later; it is not until group size hits eight or nine members that EBS groups begin to produce more ideas than nominal groups.

The results in Figures 8.3 and 8.4 generally support our arguments that EBS can be a useful technique. It can reduce important sources of process loss while still enabling synergy to occur. But although EBS appears to mitigate many of the process losses that increase with group size (e.g., production blocking, evaluation apprehension), it also appears to impose some initial fixed cost, which may be attributed to the need to type or merely to the need to interact with other group members. It is logical to assume that some fixed amount of cognitive interference is introduced simply by the need to monitor the work of other group members.

Implications and Conclusions

We believe that the use of EBS can play a key role in enhancing group creativity, particularly for larger groups that suffer from the process losses inherent in verbally interacting groups. Several conclusions can be drawn from EBS research. First, it is clear that EBS and GSS can improve group creativity in certain situations. The advantages of synergy and social facilitation as well as the ability to bridge time and space make GSS an invaluable tool for many groups. We recommend that large groups seeking to generate ideas choose first to work together using EBS, either in special-purpose meeting rooms equipped with computers or over the Internet using Web-based brainstorming tools or simply electronic mail. For smaller groups, the use of nominal groups, brainwriting (Paulus & Yang, 2000), or their organizational cousin, Nominal Group Technique (Delbecq, Van de Ven, & Gustafson, 1975; Van de Ven & Delbecq, 1971), still seems appropriate. However, given the ubiquitous use of computing technology in modern organizations, most nominal groups will most likely use computer-based tools to record ideas, thus making the sharing of ideas very simple using EBS tools or electronic mail.

Second, it appears that group size is the critical factor in determining the effectiveness of GSS to support productive group creativity. As group size increases, the benefits of synergy and reduced production blocking and cognitive interference are more noticeable. Smaller groups, however (especially those with two to three members), will receive fewer benefits from using GSS over verbal or nominal techniques.

Third, GSS seem to create group environments that have some fundamental differences from those of traditional verbally interacting groups. For instance, unlike verbal groups, GSS groups produce more ideas when participants are critical of the ideas generated by other members (Valacich & Schwenk, 1985). More research is required to explain why these changes occur, but their presence is well indicated by existing research. We speculate that the anonymity provided by GSS acts to separate ideas from their contributor so that criticism is more easily recognized as criticism of ideas, not of people. Anonymity may also shield participants from the faults of an idea as well as the negativity associated with criticism. Therefore, participants are more likely to share both ideas and criticisms.

Finally, with the rise of the Internet, GSS tools are increasingly ubiquitous. As tools like Lotus Notes, MSN Messenger, ICQ, and others are diffused throughout society, people become more accustomed to using the computer as a tool for communication. This familiarity should allow them to use GSS tools more effectively.

We believe our conclusions are reasonable and appropriate, yet future research is necessary. One area that we believe is most promising, both for theoretical and applied research, is the development of new tools. Most current EBS software tools simply automate existing techniques. However, computer technology enables participants to interact in ways that would not be possible without the computer. For example, Dennis et al. (1999) investigated the impact of a very simple dialogue structure: participants were simultaneously given three separate windows in which to enter ideas, each focusing on different aspects of the problem. This structure enabled participants to contribute ideas on different aspects of the problem simultaneously, something not possible in verbal brainstorming, in which every participant must listen to every other participant. This simple structure improved performance by about 50%.

The use of EBS enables the development and testing of a variety of far more complex structures, which may have greater or lesser impact on performance. Additional research is needed to develop and test new ways in which groups can work together to generate ideas.

The use of modified forms of EBS to test the effects of production block-ing, evaluation apprehension, and so on also creates opportunities to test other theoretical effects. Because new EBS tools can be created to simulate a variety of interaction patterns, it is possible to create tools that can act as a test bed for more fundamental theoretical concepts as well. For example, it is possible to create a simulator that acts in the same manner as a real EBS tool; participants believe themselves to be interacting with the other participants in the "group," but instead of receiving comments and ideas from the other participants, they receive prescribed comments and ideas from a database developed by the experimenter. In this way, we can create experimental conditions in which par-ticipants receive very stimulating ideas or nonstimulating ideas, receive support-ive comments or critical comments, receive ideas that induce cognitive inertia (one topic focus) or a diversity of topics. Likewise, such a simulator could be used to deliver identical thoughts and ideas to members of a decision-making group but to present the results of a prescripted group "vote" that purports to show that the participant is a member of a group majority or minority. Such a test bed could enable far more precise tests of theories of minority and majority decision making, among others.

This chapter has focused on group creativity, but the implications of GSS and EBS on creativity goes beyond simple idea generation. The essence of cre-ativity is the development and exchange of ideas that ultimately find their way into later stages of organization processes such as decision making and plan-ning. GSS can play important roles in improving performance in these stages as well (Dennis et al., 2001), by improving the sharing of information during group discussions (Dennis, 1996). Continued research into the use and usefulness of GSS will provide a richer understanding of how technology can enable more efficient and effective group processes and creativity.

Notes

1. For details of the meta-analysis procedures, contact the first author.
2. The regression was significant, $F(1,19) = 10.85$, $p = .004$, and explained 36% of the variation in results.
3. The regression was significant, $F(1,20) = 48.56$, $p = .001$, and explained 60% of the variation in results.

References

Allport, F. H. (1920). The influence of the group upon association and thought. *Journal of Experimental Psychology, 3*, 159–182.

Bantel, K. A., & Jackson, S. E. (1989). Top management and innovations in banking: Does the composition of the top team make a difference? *Strategic Management Journal, 10*, 107–124.

Bartis, S., Szymanski, K., & Harkins, S. (1988). Evaluation and performance: A 2-edged knife. *Personality and Social Psychology Bulletin, 14*, 242–251.

Bond, C. F., & Titus, L. J. (1983). Social facilitation: A meta-analysis of 241 studies. *Psychology Bulletin, 94*, 265–292.

Camacho, L. M., & Paulus, P. B. (1995). The role of social anxiousness in group brainstorming. *Journal of Personality and Social Psychology, 68*, 1071–1080.

Collins, B. E., & Guetzkow, H. (1964). *A social psychology of group processes for decision-making*. New York: Wiley.

Connolly, T., Jessup, L. M., & Valacich, J. S. (1990). Effects of anonymity and evaluative tone on idea generation in computer-mediated groups. *Management Science, 36*, 689–703.

Cooper, W. H., Gallupe, R. B., Pollard, S., & Cadsby, J. (1998). Some liberating effects of anonymous electronic brainstorming. *Small Group Research, 29*, 147–178.

Coskun, H. (2000). *The effects of out-group comparison, social context, intrinsic motivation, and collective identity in brainstorming groups*. Unpublished doctoral dissertation, University of Texas, Arlington.

Delbecq, A., Van de Ven, A. H., & Gustafson, D. H. (1975). *Group techniques for program planning*. Chicago: Scott Foresman.

Dennis, A. R. (1996). Information exchange and use in group decision making: You can lead a group to information but you can't make it think. *MIS Quarterly, 20*, 433–455.

Dennis, A. R., Aronson, J. E., Heninger, W. G., & Walker, E., II. (1999). Structuring time and task in electronic brainstorming. *MIS Quarterly, 23*, 95–108.

Dennis, A. R., & Valacich, J. S. (1993). Computer brainstorms: More heads are better than one. *Journal of Applied Psychology, 78*, 531–537.

Dennis, A. R., & Valacich, J. S. (1999). Electronic brainstorming: Illusions and patterns of productivity. *Information Systems Research, 10*, 375–377.

Dennis, A. R., Valacich, J. S., Carte, T. A., Garfield, M. J., Haley, B. J., & Aronson, J. E. (1997). The effectiveness of multiple dialogues in electronic brainstorming. *Information Systems Research, 8*, 203–211.

Dennis, A. R., Valacich, J. S., Connolly, T., & Wynne, B. (1996). Process structuring in group brainstorming. *Information Systems Research, 7*, 268–277.

Dennis, A. R., Wixom, B. H., & Vandenberg, R. J. (2001). Understanding fit and appropriation effects in Group Support Systems via meta-analysis. *MIS Quarterly, 25*, 167–194.

Diehl, M., & Stroebe, W. (1987). Productivity loss in brainstorming groups: Toward the solution of a riddle. *Journal of Personality and Social Psychology, 53*, 497–509.

Diehl, M., & Stroebe, W. (1991). Productivity loss in idea-generating groups: Tracking down the blocking effect. *Journal of Personality and Social Psychology, 61*, 392–403.

Diener, S. C. (1979). Deindividuation, self-awareness, and disinhibition. *Journal of Personality and Social Psychology, 37*, 1160–1171.

Diener, S. C., Fraser, E., Beaman, A. L., & Kelem, R. T. (1976). Effects of deindividuation variables on stealing among Halloween trick-or-treaters. *Journal of Personality and Social Psychology, 33*, 178–183.

Dugosh, K. L., Paulus, P. B., Roland, E. J., & Yang, H. C. (2000). Cognitive stimulation in brainstorming. *Journal of Personality and Social Psychology, 79*, 722–735.

Festinger, L. (1954). A theory of social comparison processes. *Human Relations, 7*, 117–140.

Gallupe, R. B., Cooper, W. H., Grise, M. L., & Bastianutti, L. (1994). Blocking electronic brainstorms. *Journal of Applied Psychology, 79,* 77–86.

Gallupe, R. B., Dennis, A. R., Cooper, W. H., Valacich, J. S., Bastianutti, L., & Nunamaker, J. F. (1992). Electronic brainstorming and group size. *Academy of Management Journal, 35,* 350–369.

George, J. F., Easton, G. K., Nunamaker, J. F., & Northcraft, G. B. (1990). A study of collaborative group work with and without computer based support. *Information Systems Research, 1,* 394–415.

Gruenfeld, D. (1995). Status, ideology and integrative complexity on the U.S. Supreme Court: Rethinking the politics of political decision making. *Journal of Personality and Social Psychology, 68,* 5–20.

Harkins, S., & Petty, R. E. (1982). Effects of task difficulty and task uniqueness on social loafing. *Journal of Personality and Social Psychology, 16,* 457–462.

Hill, G. W. (1982). Group versus individual performance: Are N + 1 heads better than one? *Psychology Bulletin, 91,* 517–539.

Hiltz, S. R., Turoff, M., & Johnson, K. (1989). Disinhibition, deindividuation, and group process: an approach to improving the effectiveness of groups. *Decision Support Systems, 5,* 217–232.

Hunter, J. E., & Schmidt, F. L. (1990). *Methods of meta-analysis.* Newbury Park, CA: Sage.

Jackson, S. E. (1992). Team composition in organizations. In S. Worchel, W. Wood, & J. Simpson (Eds.), *Group process and productivity* (pp. 138–173). London: Sage.

Jackson, S. E., May, K. E., & Whitney, K. (1995). Understanding the dynamics of diversity in decision making teams. In R. A. Guzzo & E. Salas (Eds.), *Team effectiveness and decision making in organizations* (pp. 204–226). San Francisco: Jossey-Bass.

Jessup, L. M., Connolly, T., & Galegher, J. (1990). The effects of anonymity on group process in automated group problem solving. *MIS Quarterly, 14,* 313–321.

Karau, S. J., & Williams, K. (1993). Social loafing: A meta-analytic review and theoretical integration. *Journal of Personality and Social Psychology, 65,* 681–706.

Lamm, H., & Trommsdorff, G. (1973). Group versus individual performance on tasks requiring identical proficiency (brainstorming): A review. *European Journal of Social Psychology, 3,* 361–388.

Larey, T. S., & Paulus, P. B. (1995). Individual and group goal setting in brainstorming groups. *Journal of Applied Psychology, 25,* 1579–1596.

Larey, T. S., & Paulus, P. B. (1999). Group preference and convergent tendencies in small groups: A content analysis of group brainstorming performance. *Creativity Research Journal, 12,* 175–185.

Latane, B. (1981). The psychology of social impact. *American Psychologist, 36,* 343–356.

Latane, B., Williams, K., & Harkins, S. (1979). Many hands make light the work: The causes and consequences of social loafing. *Journal of Personality and Social Psychology, 37,* 823–832.

Lea, M., & Spears, R. (1991). Computer-mediated communication, de-individuation and group decision-making. *International Journal of Man-Machine Studies, 34,* 283–301.

Levine, D., Resnick, L. B., & Higgins, E. T. (1993). Social foundations of cognition. *Annual Review of Psychology, 44,* 585–612.

Lipnack, J., & Stamps, J. (1997). *Virtual teams: Reaching across space, time, and organizations with technology.* New York: Wiley.

Mullen, B., Johnson, C., & Salas, E. (1991). Productivity loss in brainstorming groups: A meta-analytic integration. *Basic and Applied Social Psychology, 12,* 3–23.

Nagasundaram, M., & Dennis, A. R. (1993). When a group is not a group. *Small Group Research, 24,* 463–489.

Newell, A., & Simon, H. A. (1972). *Human problem solving.* Englewood Cliffs, NJ: Prentice-Hall.

Nunamaker, J. F., Dennis, A. R., Valacich, J. S., Vogel, D. R., & George, J. F. (1991). Electronic meeting systems to support group work. *Communications of the ACM, 34,* 41–61.

Osborn, A. F. (1957). *Applied imagination.* New York: Scribner.

Paulus, P. B., & Dzindolet, M. T. (1993). Social influence processes in group brainstorming. *Journal of Personality and Social Psychology, 64,* 575–586.

Paulus, P. B., Larey, T. S., & Ortega, A. H. (1995). Performance and perceptions of brainstormers in an organizational setting. *Basic and Applied Social Psychology, 17,* 249–265.

Paulus, P. B., & Yang, H. C. (2000). Idea generation in groups: A basis for creativity in organizations. *Organization Behavior and Human Decision Processes, 82,* 76–87.

Pinsonneault, A., & Barki, H. (1999). The illusion of electronic brainstorming productivity: Theoretical and empirical issues. *Information Systems Research, 10,* 378–382.

Pinsonneault, A., Barki, H., Gallupe, R. B., & Hoppen, N. (1999). Electronic brainstorming: The illusion of productivity. *Information Systems Research, 10,* 110–133.

Pinsonneault, A., & Heppel, N. (1997). Anonymity in group support systems research: A new conceptualization, measure, and framework. *Journal of Management Information Systems, 14,* 89–108.

Postmes, T., & Lea, M. (2000). Social processes and group decision making: Anonymity in group decision support systems. *Ergonomics, 43,* 1252–1274.

Prentice-Dunn, S., & Rogers, R. W. (1982). Effects of public and private self-awareness on deindividuation and aggression. *Journal of Personality and Social Psychology, 43,* 503–513.

Robinson-Staveley, K., & Cooper, J. (1990). Mere presence, gender, and reactions to computers: Studying human-computer interaction in the social context. *Journal of Experimental Social Psychology, 26,* 168–183.

Saks, M. J., & Ostrom, T. M. (1973). Anonymity in letters to the editor. *Public Opinion Quarterly, 37,* 417–422.

Sanna, L. J. (1992). Self-efficacy theory: Implications for social facilitation and social loafing. *Journal of Personality and Social Psychology, 62,* 774–786.

Saunders, C. S. (2000). Virtual teams: Piecing together the puzzle. In R. Zmud (Ed.), *Framing the domains of IT management* (pp. 29–50). Cincinnati, OH: Pinnaflex.

Siegel, J., Dubrovsky, V., Kiesler, S., & McGuire, T. (1986). Group processes in computer-mediated communication. *Organization Behavior and Human Decision Processes, 17,* 157–187.

Steiner, I. D. (1972). *Group process and productivity.* San Diego: Academic Press.

Straus, S. G. (1996). Getting a clue: The effects of communication media and information dispersion on participation and performance in computer-mediated and face-to-face groups. *Small Group Research, 57,* 448–467.

Valacich, J. S., Dennis, A. R., & Connolly, T. (1994). Idea generation in computer-based groups: A new ending to an old story. *Organization Behavior and Human Decision Processes, 57,* 448–467.

Valacich, J. S., & Schwenk, C. (1985). Devil's advocacy and dialectical inquiry effects on group decision making using computer-mediated versus verbal communication. *Organization Behavior and Human Decision Processes, 63,* 158–173.

Van de Ven, A. H., & Delbecq, A. (1971). Nominal and interacting group process for committee decision-making effectiveness. *Academy of Management Journal, 14,* 203–212.

Williams, K., & O'Reilly, C. (1998). Demography and diversity in organizations: A review of 40 years of research. *Research in Organizational Behavior, 20,* 77–140.

Williams, K. D., & Karau, S. J. (1991). Social loafing and social compensation: The effects of expectations of coworker performance. *Journal of Personality and Social Psychology, 61,* 570–581.

Zajonc, R. B. (1965). Social facilitation. *Science, 149,* 269–274.

Ziegler, R., Diehl, M., & Zijlstra, G. (2000). Idea production in nominal and virtual groups: Does computer-mediated communication improve group brainstorming? *Group Processes & Intergroup Relations, 3,* 141–159.

Zimbardo, P.G. (1969). The human choice: Individuation, reason and order versus deindividuation, impulse and chaos. In W. J. Arnold & D. Levine (Eds.), *Nebraska symposium on motivation* (pp. 237–307). Lincoln: University of Nebraska Press.

II

Group Creativity in Context

9

■■■■ *Beth A. Hennessey*

Is the Social Psychology of Creativity Really Social?
Moving Beyond a Focus on the Individual

■■■■

Creativity does not come about in a vacuum. Throughout history, there have been numerous instances of collaborative efforts that resulted in significant creative breakthroughs. As a young man, Albert Einstein and some friends formed a club they called the Olympia Academy. Each week, Academy members would take long walks through the mountains near Bern, discussing topics in physics and the philosophy of science and offering support and inspiration. In their race against Linus Pauling to uncover the mysteries of DNA, James Watson and Francis Crick also drew inspiration from one another, and it was a collaborative effort between Picasso and Braque that led to the initiation of the Cubist movement in art. Even when working alone, it is almost always the case that the individual creator is in some kind of influential relationship with others. Paul Gauguin and Vincent van Gogh shared a flat and painted side by side in Arles, and many of their Impressionist comrades drew their support from nightly meetings in the cafés of Paris.

The dedication of this volume to the phenomenon of group creativity speaks to our deep appreciation of the important role played by group interaction and group composition in the creative process. Yet curiously, with the exception of research that focuses specifically on small group creativity, the empirical study of creativity has often failed to include a consideration of anyone or anything beyond the individual doing the creating. Investigators interested in the psychology of creativity have typically chosen to decontextualize creativity. They have concentrated their efforts on the creative process, the creative person, or the creative product, but relatively little attention has been given to the creative milieu, to the environmental factors beyond the creator himself or herself, that contribute to creativity of performance.

The Social Psychology of Creativity

Drawing on our training in social psychology, my colleagues, most notably Teresa Amabile, and I have long argued that it is a mistake to stop at the individual level of analysis. In our work we emphasize the fact that a variety of environmental and person variables are necessary for creativity. More formally, our research is built on a three-part conceptualization of creative performance. For a creative solution to be found or a creative idea or product generated, an individual must approach a problem with the appropriate domain skills (background knowledge), creativity skills (willingness to take risks, experiment, etc.), and task motivation. Under ideal circumstances, a confluence of these three factors forms what Amabile (1997) has termed the "creative intersection."

It is certainly possible to teach (and learn) domain skills and perhaps even creativity skills; motivational orientation is much more ephemeral. In other words, although an individual's creativity skills (e.g., familiarity with brainstorming and related techniques or the ability to temporarily suspend judgment) or domain skills (e.g., knowledge of chemistry, physics, or engineering or facility with a paintbrush) may be fairly stable, our motivational state is highly variable and largely situation-dependent. Each of us finds some activities more interesting or enjoyable than we do others. None of us approaches every task with the same degree of excitement, and to some degree, our level of enthusiasm and task commitment is determined by the circumstances we find ourselves in. It is on this question of how our environment helps to shape our motivational orientation that we have focused our attention. The model on which our work is based tells us that there is a direct relation between the motivational orientation brought to a task and the creativity of performance on that task, and it is the environment that in large part determines that motivational orientation.

In our research and theorizing, we distinguish between two types of motivation. Intrinsic motivation is the motivation to do something for its own sake, for the sheer pleasure and enjoyment of the task itself. Extrinsic motivation, on the other hand, is the motivation to do something for some external goal. Researchers attempting to specify the key elements that set these two motivational orientations apart have often likened the intrinsic motivational state to an essentially carefree attitude of experimentation, and theorists tell us that a large number of features of task engagement contribute to intrinsic motivation. Often, the individual is curious about or in some other way stimulated by the presentation of an activity. With task participation come feelings of competence, mastery, or self-efficacy. And, perhaps most significant, while engaging in a task that they find intrinsically interesting, individuals feel that their involvement is free from strong external control: they get the sense that they are playing rather than working.

As described by Csikszentmihalyi (1990, 1996), the intrinsic motivational state is one of "optimal experience" or "flow." For most of us, flow is not an everyday occurrence, but when it does come, it is characterized by feelings of intense concentration and deep enjoyment, feelings that transport the individual into a new reality to "previously undreamed-of states of consciousness" (1990, p. 74).

Importantly, each of these hallmarks of intrinsic motivation focuses on the individual's inner phenomenological state. Whether prompted by just the right amount of novelty, feelings of competence, or a sense of control, the intrinsically motivated state comes about as the result of an internal, very individualized process—the complexities of which we are only beginning to appreciate.

Over 25 years of investigation into these motivational orientations have led us to the Intrinsic Motivation Principle of Creativity (IMPC): Intrinsic motivation is conducive to creativity, and extrinsic motivation is almost always detrimental. In its earlier incarnations, this proposed relation between motivational state and creativity of performance was advanced as a tentative research hypothesis. But investigators working in this tradition have now gathered so much unequivocal empirical evidence that this proposition has been elevated to the status of an undisputed principle.

In a basic research paradigm, study participants are randomly assigned to either constraint or no-constraint conditions. For instance, subjects are either led to expect a reward for their participation or no reward is mentioned, and then they are asked to produce some sort of observable product that can be assessed for level of creativity. Their motivational orientation (i.e., whether intrinsic or extrinsic) is also measured. Whether the targets of our investigation are preschoolers or 73-year-old seasoned research and development scientists, our findings are consistent. Over the years, we have identified five sure-fire killers of intrinsic motivation and creativity: expected reward, expected evaluation, surveillance, time limits, and competition (see Amabile, 1996; Hennessey, 1996). Often, when presenting this research evidence to students, I ask them to consider whether this list of killers might just as well be labeled as a recipe for the typical American classroom or, for that matter, the typical corporate setting. As unbelievable as it may seem, we have somehow managed to structure educational and research and development environments in such a way that intrinsic motivation and creativity are bound to suffer, if not be completely destroyed. The message is clear. The impact of environmental factors on motivation and creativity is substantial and must be attended to if the creativity of students in schools, artists in studios, and employees in the business world is to flourish.

Investigations of the type described earlier have recently been supplemented by the work of a small number of researchers who have moved beyond the confines of the individual experiment to offer comprehensive systems approaches to the social psychology of creativity. Amabile (1993), for example, has proposed a model outlining a variety of factors necessary to produce innovation in the workplace, and a similar so-called investment model has been offered by Sternberg and Lubart (1991). Gruber (1988) and Csiksentmihalyi (1988) have also taken a systems approach to their study of creativity; for my own part, I am currently working on an ecological approach to creativity in the schools (Hennessey, 2000). We are excited about these projects and believe that they hold substantial promise at both the theoretical and applied levels. Yet, for me at least, there remains one potentially important, even nagging, problem.

The overwhelming majority of these systems/ecological approaches, like most of the smaller-scale investigations on which they have been based, is entirely grounded in a focus on the individual's impersonal interaction with his or her environment. Although some theorists talk of supportive motivational milieus, corporate climate, or the complex social systems found in large organizations, the imposition of a deadline or the promise (and eventual receipt) of a reward or an evaluation is seen as primarily a mechanistic process. Only rarely has the social psychology of creativity been expanded to include a consideration of the interpersonal variables that may also serve to impact motivational orientation (and subsequently, creativity of performance). The interaction between experimenters and study participants, teachers and students, or supervisors and workers has been virtually ignored, as has the fact that experimental labs, classrooms, and places of business are populated with multiple individuals who perform not in isolation but in direct contact and communication with one another. Creativity researchers, and our culture as a whole, have tended to focus on individual geniuses and individual acts of creativity. Yet creativity is essentially a social phenomenon. Domain skills are most often taught and acquired in a group setting (see Hooker, Nakamura, & Csikszentmihalyi, this volume). Creativity skills are modeled for us by others, and the generation of creative ideas and the process of bringing those ideas to fruition frequently come as a result of group efforts.

Many years ago, social psychologists began to move beyond a narrow consideration of the individual doing the creating toward an appreciation of the profoundly negative impact that a variety of environmental factors can have on motivation and creativity of performance. Now we must ask whether those individuals who impose the environmental constraints or those persons with whom we socialize, study, or work might themselves be shaping our motivational orientation or contributing to the creativity of our performance. It is time to put the social back into the social psychology of creativity.

The empirical focus of the majority of contributors to this volume is, of course, on the phenomenology of creativity in a small group setting, and there has been a great deal of work done in this area. But the question of how an individual's intrinsic task motivation and task enjoyment might be influenced by interaction with others has been virtually ignored by both the "group creativity" as well as the "social psychology of creativity" camps. A review of papers published between 1984 and the present reveals only four or five investigations that have explicitly incorporated measures of motivational orientation into an analysis of creative performance in a group setting. And all but one of these publications focuses on the issue of teamwork and creativity in sports.

This omission is glaring. Nevertheless, a more detailed examination of the existing literature on the psychology of creativity reveals a number of contributions relevant to this question of how motivational orientation and creativity might be impacted by the actions and/or mere presence of others. In the pages that follow, I outline what I believe are many of the more promising and important areas of inquiry, some grounded in existing empirical work and others based on a more theoretical level of analysis.

Interpersonal Processes, Intrinsic Motivation, and Creativity

Historical Factors and Geographical/Regional Conditions

Research efforts to uncover the possible contributions of historical time and place to creative production have taken a variety of forms. Some investigators, most notably Dean Keith Simonton, have chosen to take a historiometry approach (see Simonton, this volume). Applying quantitative methods to the study of a wide range (sometimes 15,000 cases or more) of historically creative personalities and events, they seek to uncover general psychological laws or patterns, such as whether a particular political ideology or wartime circumstance breeds creative outcomes. Other researchers (e.g., Martindale, 2001) have turned to primarily qualitative methods of analysis and focus their attention on psychobiographical and psychohistorical studies of particular individuals. And a third group (e.g., Gardner, 1993, 1997, and Policastro & Gardner, 1999) has opted to conduct comparative research on a modest sample of creative individuals or events.

Although much of this work is focused on individual difference variables and issues of life span development, these investigative approaches have also revealed the importance of the sociocultural context for the shaping of motivation and subsequent creative production. Eminently creative persons have not randomly appeared across history, nor have they been found to be evenly distributed around the world in any one time period. Instead, genius has tended to surface during certain golden ages (e.g., turn-of-the-century Vienna), suggesting that political, economic, social, and cultural factors may play an integral role in the development of motivation (intrinsic or extrinsic) and realization of creative talent. Taken together, the research shows that the prevailing Zeitgeist or spirit of the times plays a significant role in determining both the number of creative persons and ideas that will emerge and the direction that those ideas will take.

Family Background

Early work linking creativity and family variables was concentrated almost exclusively on genetic explanations, but researchers have long shown at least a modest interest in the impact of family history (e.g., parental loss, illness, childhood trauma) on creative performance in adulthood. Most recently, attention has turned to more complex (and harder to study) family factors such as family climate, parenting style, and birth order effects that may play a role in shaping children's sense of self, self-esteem, and overall motivational orientation. One of the more consistent findings in these areas is that, if adult creativity is the goal, there must be a certain level of autonomy in parent-child relations. This optimal level of distance, especially between a mother and her son or daughter, allows the child to feel secure enough to explore and learn but at the same time helps to develop the self-confidence that will be so necessary for risk taking and creative exploration later in life (see Ainsworth & Marvin, 1995). Along these lines, researchers have consistently reported that in creative families, the parental relationship is especially egalitarian. Yet highly creative individuals often have been found to come from particularly difficult and stressful environments, almost as if disorder in the family serves to foster an independence of thought and a tendency toward creative thinking (see Kerr & Chopp, 1999; Olszewski, Kulieke, & Buescher, 1987).

Muddying the research waters, however, is a second substantial body of work revealing that many highly creative persons in the arts, science, and business domains came from especially nurturing and cohesive family backgrounds. Csikszentmihalyi (1996), for example, interviewed over 90 of the most creative persons in the world and found that in the majority of cases, it was the parents of these individuals who were credited with stimulating and supporting their children's interests. Taken together, these two streams of research seem to indicate that if creativity is to flourish in adulthood, childhood experiences must somehow combine the opportunity to think for oneself and the unfailing support and encouragement of a parent or some other adult mentor.

(Small) Group Creativity

Research focused on the generation, development, and assessment of creative ideas in group settings speaks directly to the fact that creativity is a social phenomenon. The exchange and evaluation of ideas, the modeling of creative processes, and the championing of new products or proposed solutions to problems all involve interaction with others. Investigations of brainstorming techniques and the employment of teams in organizations have underscored the impact of group composition on the motivational orientation of group members and the quality of ideas produced. We have learned a great deal about how to construct social situations and interactions that are most likely to facilitate creative performance, yet even studies in this area have tended to frame creativity as a largely individualistic process.

Researchers tell us that, when asked to be part of an idea-generating group, the majority of persons will not work to reap the potential benefits of working with colleagues who bring a diversity of expertise, backgrounds, and skills. Instead, group members tend to focus much of their attention and concern on how they themselves are being perceived by others. Intrinsic task motivation in other words, is often supplanted by the extrinsic need to appear competent. One especially thorny problem is that most individuals show a marked tendency toward conformity. Fearing criticism or rejection, group members have frequently been shown to avoid disagreement or self-censor thoughts they believe might be met with negative reactions (Nemeth & Nemeth-Brown, this volume; Paulus, 1999). Also prevalent is a tendency for individuals working in groups to compete with one another or to reduce their efforts, or loaf, if there is no expectation of individual accountability for the group's outcome. The group interaction process has also been shown to inhibit the individual's ability to generate novel ideas. When someone else is talking or going off on tangents, it is difficult to keep one's own ideas in mind, much less generate new ones (Nijstad, Diehl, & Stroebe, this volume; Paulus, 1999; Paulus & Brown, this volume).

In response to the difficulties presented by face-to-face sessions, many of the more recent research attempts to improve the efficacy of brainstorming techniques have focused on various forms of electronic idea-exchange processes (e.g., Dennis & Williams, this volume). In these approaches, individuals work simultaneously but alone and type their ideas on computers to be shared with others. At the end of such sessions, contributions are often summarized and evaluated by means of computer voting.

Whether they have studied conventional (often termed "interactive") or virtual ("nominal") brainstorming sessions, investigators tell us that the major benefits of interaction for creativity may come after the interaction process is complete and the individual is once again left to his or her own devices. When individuals have had time to let ideas incubate and reflect, new and creative insights are frequently the result (Paulus, 1999).

Classroom Climate

Cognitive Mechanisms

Researchers seeking an understanding of the mechanism by which extrinsic constraints come to undermine intrinsic task motivation and creative performance have traditionally assumed that the explanation lies within the individual doing the creating. For quite some time, investigators have understood that most of us are not all that in touch with our own motivations. We do not always know why we do the things we do. Almost as if we were outside observers of even our own actions, we seem to use essentially the same rubrics for explaining our own behaviors as we do for explaining others' behavior. In situations where both plausible internal and external (intrinsic and extrinsic) causes of behavior are present, we tend to discount the internal cause in favor of the external. A fourth-grade student participating in a prototypical investigation of the impact of expected reward who is asked to make a collage may think to herself, "I must be making this collage and telling this story not because they are fun and I want to but because this woman has told me that if I complete these tasks, she'll give me some stickers." A college student expecting that his haiku poem will be evaluated by a panel of experts may reason that he is putting effort into this writing task not because he finds it particularly interesting but because he wishes to avoid the embarrassment that would come with a negative assessment. In other words, when multiple explanations for our behavior are available, each of us will tend to discount our own intrinsic interest in favor of a purely external explanation for our task engagement.

In fact, some social psychologists have come to refer to this process as the discounting principle (e.g., Kelley, 1973). Other theorists turn to the overjustification hypothesis, a formulation derived from the attribution theories of Bem (1972), Kelley (1967, 1973), and deCharms (1968). According to this model, when a behavior is overjustified (when there exist both a possible internal and external cause for one's own or another's behavior), each of us will tend to overlook the internal cause (the presence of intrinsic task motivation) in favor of the external cause (a reward was at stake). In effect, we discount the excess justification for explaining why we did something.

Over the years, a number of these cognitively based explanations for the undermining of intrinsic motivation (and creativity of performance) have been offered (in addition to work on discounting or the overjustification effect, see also cognitive evaluation theory: Deci, Cascio, & Krussell, 1975; Deci & Ryan, 1980). All have proven useful for understanding the negative effects of extrinsic, environmental constraints on older children and adults, yet they fail to adequately explain why preschoolers and early elementary school students have also been observed to suffer decreases in intrinsic motivation and creativity. Simply stated, children under the age of 7 or 8 years have consistently been shown to lack the cognitive capabilities necessary for weighing multiple sufficient causes of behavior and employing discounting (e.g., Shultz, Butkowsky, Pearce, & Shanfield, 1975; Smith, 1975). How is it that when working under the expectation of reward or evaluation young children frequently demonstrate decreases in intrinsic motivation and creativity of performance yet seem cognitively incapable of engaging in the thought processes believed to underlie the overjustification paradigm?

An Affective Explanation

In some of my own recent work, I have attempted to move beyond the popular cognitive explanation of the undermining effects of extrinsic constraints toward a more holistic approach, which recognizes that rewards, evaluations, and other killers of motivation and creativity are most often promised and delivered in an interpersonal context. I hypothesize that the reduction of intrinsic interest in young children (and perhaps in all of us) is driven primarily by the learned expectation that rewards, deadlines, competition, and evaluations are usually paired with activities that need to be done—activities that often are not fun and sometimes are even aversive. The undermining of intrinsic interest and ultimately creativity of performance may result as much from negative emotion or affect as it does from cognitive analysis. Children may learn to view a task as "work" when they believe that their behavior is being coerced by another (e.g., a parent or a teacher), and they may react positively to that task as "play" when there are no constraints imposed. Negative affect engendered in the social interaction with a controlling other may be what leads to decrements in intrinsic interest (see Hennessey, 1999).

The Importance of Self-Determination

The important element here seems to be the preservation of a sense of self-determination. As Deci and Ryan (1985) explain, any extrinsic factors that support a sense of competence without undermining self-determination should positively contribute to intrinsic motivation. Thus, rewards or evaluations that are perceived as informational, useful, and informative as to the quality of one's performance rather than as controlling instruments of coercion can serve to increase involvement in the task at hand and should not be expected to have detrimental effects.

Deci and Ryan (1985) are representative of a small but growing number of theorists and investigators who have become dissatisfied with the comparatively narrow and disjointed approaches that have been applied to the study of human motivation. Tauer and Harackiewicz (1999) have also worked to bridge intrinsic motivation and performance-based approaches with a concentration on the individual's phenomenological experience while working under the expectation of evaluation. As these researchers explain, the effects of evaluative contingencies are not universal. The expectation that one's performance will be evaluated will be detrimental only if the interpersonal atmosphere of the evaluative setting causes the individual to feel intimidated or self-conscious. In situations in which individuals feel in control of their own destiny, motivation and creativity need not suffer.

As early as 1968, deCharms had advanced this notion of self-determination in his analysis of perceptions of control and motivation in the classroom. Terming students who perceived themselves to be in control of the learning process "origins" and those who perceived their achievement-related behaviors to be controlled by their teachers' highly controlling behaviors "pawns," this groundbreaking work set the stage for Deci et al.'s (1975) cognitive evaluation theory and Deci and Ryan's (2000; Ryan & Deci, 2000) self-determination theory (SDT) that were to follow.

At the core of SDT is the consideration of innate psychological needs and the degree to which people are able to satisfy these basic needs as they pursue and attain their valued goals. Individuals are seen to differ in their causality orientation, determined in part by past experiences of need satisfaction or thwarting. SDT does not view extrinsic motivation as the simple absence of intrinsic motivation. Rather, Deci and Ryan and colleagues differentiate among a variety of types of extrinsic motivation and contend that extrinsically motivated behaviors can vary in the degree to which they are self-determined versus controlled. Both the content and the *process* of motivational orientation are considered, as the focus of investigation shifts from an individual's inner experience to a consideration of the influence of interpersonal contexts on motivational outcomes.

Like deCharms, Deci and Ryan have frequently focused their research on the interpersonal arena of the classroom. In one series of field studies (Deci & Ryan, 1994), classroom climate was assessed either via teacher questionnaires or in terms of children's verbal descriptions of their educational environments, and motivational outcomes were evaluated. In a second set of laboratory investigations (Deci & Ryan, 1994), external events were presented in a variety of interpersonal contexts and motivation was again assessed. More specifically, Deci, Nezlek, and Sheinman (1981) looked at teachers' orientation toward promoting children's autonomy versus controlling their behavior. They reported that when children experienced the interpersonal context of the classroom as supporting of self-determination, they were more intrinsically motivated. Analyses revealed strong positive correlations between teachers' orientations and their students' motivational outcomes (motivation and perceived competence). Moreover, teachers' orientations were found to have impacted children's motivation within the first 6 to 8 weeks of school, and this influence remained strong throughout the year. Thus, Deci et al. conclude that it is the functional significance of one's environment (i.e., the individual's perception of the reward or evaluation contingency), rather than its objective properties, that affects motivational processes (see also deCharms, 1976; Ryan & Grolnick, 1986).

Corporate Settings

Climate

Like students in school, the motivation and creative performance of adults in the workplace have been found to be profoundly affected by the psychological climate of their surroundings. Scientists have found that the social climate of an organization—the behaviors and attitudes that characterize day-to-day life in a corporation, more institutionalized practices such as reward systems and promotion guidelines, and the coworkers themselves—is an important intervening variable at all levels of operation (see Isaksen, Winsemius, & Lauer, 1995).

Individuals employed in successfully creative organizations believe their jobs to be challenging and meaningful. They report that their own needs for stimulation are easily met in an environment characterized by lively debate. Employees feel free to search for information and to seek the support of others. There is an openness and trust among coworkers and a psychological sense of security prevails. When arguments and friction do occur, they are centered on ideas, not people. There is no room in creative organizations for personal antagonism (Ekvall, 1987, 1996; Turnipseed, 1994). All energies and attention are focused on the creative problems or challenges at hand and intrinsic motivation is allowed to flourish.

Empirical investigations supporting this view have generally taken one of two forms, with the primary unit of analysis being either an individual's motivational orientation and creative behavior or the creative achievements and motivation of an entire organization or group. One popular research design has involved the identification of especially innovative and noninnovative organizations and in-depth comparisons of their climates (see Burnside, Amabile, & Gryskiewicz, 1988). A second approach asks respondents to describe the climates surrounding both the most and the least innovative episodes of their career and searches for patterns in their responses (Amabile, 1983, 1996). Taken together, studies of organizational climate and creativity reveal that climate plays an important role in determining the motivational orientation and creativity of employees. One especially influential climate variable appears to be the leadership style adopted by managers.

Researchers report that the percent of variance (in creative outcome) accounted for by management style can range between 30% and 60% (Ekvall, 1999). Interestingly, persons who are highly creative themselves do not necessarily make the best leaders. In fact, an especially creative person in a leadership position can bring high levels of stress and frustration to the workplace situation. Leaders who are known for fostering intrinsic motivation and a creative climate are neither controlling nor rule-bound (Ekvall, 1999). They are strongly oriented toward people, pay a good deal of attention to relationships, and are always open to change. Successful managers of creative environments encourage the sharing of new ideas and recognize the value of debate. They work hard at not being too controlling, seek to establish the right balance between cooperation and competition, and see risk taking and failure as necessary components of the creative process.

Importantly, as is the case in the classroom, the provision of extrinsic rewards that offer useful information about one's competence can increase the likelihood that adult professionals in the workplace will be motivated to rise to unusual challenges and take the risks that are often necessary for creative accomplishment. Directive leaders who set high standards and provide significant rewards for creative accomplishments demonstrate what has been termed a transformational style of leadership (Goodwin, Wofford, & Whittington, 2001).

Culture

Although the constructs "corporate climate" and "corporate culture" are sometimes difficult to delineate in the literature, researchers and theorists tend to reserve the term *culture* to refer to deep-seated, perhaps even preconscious beliefs and assumptions, which are shared by most or all members of an organization and work to exert influence on the corporate climate through the establishment of values and norms (Ekvall, 1999). In other words, corporate culture is seen to lie behind climate. Climate is nearer the observable reality of the workplace than is culture, and unlike culture, climate tends to be local and group-specific and is very much influenced by a project leader's style.

Corporate culture is viewed more as an organizational-level factor than a product of interpersonal relations. Yet, at their very core, these powerful shared meanings that drive workers' and managers' thoughts, motivation, and behaviors are constructed and perpetuated in the interpersonal arena. Corporate leaders can and do play a major role in establishing central themes and the ways that "things are done around here." As Ford (1999) suggests, a shared healthy fear of rivals can add intensity and boost discomfort with the status quo, and a "we are all in this together" feeling can do much to thwart the killers of motivation threatening to invade from outside the organization.

Global Cultures

If a corporation's culture can be shown to impact the motivation and productivity of its employees, what kind of influence might the culture of an entire region or nation have on the creativity of its citizens? Csikszentmihalyi (1988, 1990) makes the convincing argument that creativity is never the result of individual actions alone. He points out that although psychologists have tended to view the creative act as an exclusively mental process, it is as much a cultural and social as it is a psychological event. Creativity presupposes a community of people who share ways of thinking and acting and who learn from each other and imitate each other's actions. The information that goes into a creative idea existed long before that individual with the idea came along. The necessary background information had been stored in the symbol system of the culture—the customary practices, the language, the specific notation of the domain—and a person without access to this information would not have been able to make a creative contribution.

At first glance, the investigation of the influence of culture on motivation and creativity may appear hopeless. How are we to define culture, much less quantify its effects? But if we can seek to study and understand something as nebulous as creativity, we can certainly do the same for culture. And, in fact, a number of researchers have begun to make great strides in this area.

Culture refers to a shared system of cognitions, behaviors, customs, values, rules, and symbols that are learned and socially transmitted (Lubart, 1999). Culture, in other words, concerns the manner in which a set of people interact with their social and physical environment. In 1976, Dawkins coined the term "meme" to refer to units of imitation, pieces of structured information or instructions for action that are worth remembering and that are passed from one generation to the next. Dawkins went on to propose that a second construct also be added to the cultural lexicon. He operationalized a "domain" as a system of related memes that change through time. In essence, memes are seen as the building blocks of culture. What changes these memes is creativity. Cultures differ in the way memes are stored. If they are recorded orally and can be transmitted only from the mind of one person to that of another, theorists argue that traditions must be strictly observed so as not to lose information, and creativity is not likely to be prized. In addition, in less complex cultures in which the separate domains are clearly related to each other, novelty in any one area is likely to be resisted because most innovations would involve a readjustment of the entire culture. In fact, according to Lubart, the level of creativity permitted on a topic is often inversely related to that topic's role in the maintenance of deep cultural patterns. In sum, creativity varies across cultures: to the extent that it is directed toward or away from certain domains of activity or social groups and to the extent that it is valued or nurtured.

Also largely culturally dependent are our conceptions of creativity and the creative process. Decisions about which ideas are creative, which are folly, and which are exciting and worthy of pursuit are relative and grounded in social agreement. According to the Western view, creativity must be defined and recognized in its relationship to an observable product. The Eastern view of creativity is far less focused on products or other tangible evidence of "work" produced. Instead, creativity is seen to involve personal fulfillment or the expression of an inner essence or ultimate reality (Lubart, 1999). Non-Western societies and religious traditions often conceptualize creativity as spiritual or religious expression rather than an innovative solution to a problem, an approach borrowed by the self-actualization movement advanced in the United States by humanistic psychologists during the 1950s and 1960s. In the East, the emphasis on originality is greatly reduced (Hallman, 1970). Creativity is seen to involve the reinterpretation of traditional ideas or the finding of a new point of view rather than a complete break with tradition.

As explained by Lubart (1999), in the Western view, creativity entails a linear progression to a new point. Cognition and problem solving are seen as key. On the other hand, according to Eastern conceptualizations, creativity involves circular movement in successive reconfigurations of an already existing initial totality. Clearly, the cultural perspective brought by researchers and theorists to the study of creativity greatly impacts how this phenomenon is defined, operationalized, and investigated. As Raina (1999) points out, the bulk of creativity research continues to be pursued within narrow, ethnocentric boundaries. Researchers are faced with the seemingly intractable problem of finding appropriate measures and of avoiding culture-bound definitions; as a result, very little truly cross-cultural work has been done.

Two Parallel Investigations: The U.S. and Saudi Studies

For my own part, I have begun to explore the issue of whether the intrinsic motivation principle of creativity can be applied cross-culturally. In other words, my colleagues and I have set out to discover whether environmental factors such as the promise of a reward or the threat of an evaluation, two powerful killers of intrinsic motivation and creativity of performance outlined earlier, can be expected to have the same deleterious effects in cultures very different from our own. Until recently, almost all the work on the social psychology of creativity has been entirely dominated by the Western view. We implicitly assumed that the principles we uncovered would hold true for persons of other nations, but we gathered no empirical research evidence to support or refute that claim. Recognizing this weakness in our research program, we thought that it was high time our theoretical models be explored from a cross-cultural perspective. Toward this end, my students and I undertook two complementary investigations, one in the United States and one in Saudi Arabia.

Researchers and theorists interested in cross-cultural comparisons have coined the terms *collectivist* and *individualistic* to help distinguish between two extremely different societal structures. According to Triandis (1996), the United States exemplifies an individualistic culture in that this society is driven by the core values of independence, self-reliance, and creativity. Collectivist cultures like Saudi Arabia's, on the other hand, emphasize obedience, cooperation, duty, and acceptance of in-group authority. Would these fundamental cultural differences translate into differential effects of expected reward on motivation and creativity of performance? In addition, previous research taught us that perseverance, tolerance of ambiguity, and risk taking are important for creativity, and we knew that the Saudi and U.S. cultures vary considerably on these dimensions. Finally, we hypothesized that one other unanticipated cultural difference might also drive our results. When it came time to translate our experimental instructions and measures, we found that there is no word for creativity in Arabic. With the help of some determined native speakers of Arabic we were able to circumvent this problem and successfully communicate to our Saudi colleagues what it was that we were interested in studying, but we were concerned about the impact of this linguistic difference on the young Saudi subjects taking part in our investigation.

In his recent book, Weiner (2000) observes that U.S. ideas of creativity are inextricably bound with traditional ideas of Western culture. As a society, we are driven by the widespread cultural and social premise that creativity is good. Clearly, there is a real danger that this bias may cause researchers to assume that wherever they go in the world, creativity will be viewed as a positive construct. But cultures clearly vary in the importance they give to creativity, and we questioned what it meant for the concept to be completely ignored in the language. As early as 1956, Whorf proposed that language plays a significant role in shaping thought. Whether the language we use structures our mental categories or simply reflects our culture's understanding of the world, we wondered whether it even made sense to study creativity in Saudi children.

Elementary school students in both nations took part in a prototypical study of the impact of reward on intrinsic task motivation and creativity of performance. Children ranging in age from 5 to 8 years were randomly assigned to one of two conditions. Participants in the Expected Reward condition were told that if they made a collage and told a story, they would be given a packet of stickers. Participants in the No Reward condition engaged in the same two activities without any expectation of reward. Both the storytelling and the collage activity have been used extensively in our U.S. research program.

All children met individually with a female experimenter (a native to their own country) for testing, and order of task presentation was counterbalanced throughout. Importantly, no mention of creativity was made to the children, who, on completing each of the two experimental activities, were asked to make self-reports of task difficulty and of their own level of task interest using 5-point Likert scales. Following the guidelines of the Consensual Assessment Technique (CAT; Amabile, 1982; Hennessey & Amabile, 1999), the children's stories and collages were rated for creativity and a variety of other dimensions by elementary school teachers familiar with the kinds of products children in this age group are likely to generate. Saudi teachers made ratings of products produced by Saudi children, and U.S. teachers served as judges for the collages and stories gathered in the United States. All ratings were based on our judges' own subjective judgments; they were not trained in any way, nor did they have the opportunity to confer with one another.

Interrater reliabilities were high for both the Saudi and U.S. samples, and a sum of the ratings made by the judges was computed for each product. In support of the IMPC, planned comparisons revealed that, in the United States, children in the No Reward condition found the storytelling and the collage-making tasks to be significantly more interesting than did children in the Expected Reward condition. Creativity ratings made on the products also confirmed our research hypotheses. Children in the No Reward condition produced collages and stories that were rated as significantly more creative than products made by children expecting a reward for their participation.

These findings were not unexpected. Quite some time ago, we moved beyond these relatively simple tests of the IMPC. Like any theoretical model, ours has become increasingly complex over the years. We now understand that not all rewards are created equal. Some are likely to be perceived as controlling; others that are seen by the recipient as sources of useful information about one's skills need not always undermine intrinsic motivation or creativity of performance. By the same token, we now realize that not all of us thrive under the same set of circumstances. Individual difference variables must also be considered. We have moved toward an examination of both state (situationally determined) and trait (more long-lasting/personality-based) levels of motivation. What we weren't at all sure of was what effect the expectation of reward would have on Saudi students. We have almost no data to support (or contradict) the notion that the IMPC holds in non-Western environments.

Planned comparisons revealed that, unlike their U.S. counterparts, Saudi children in the Expected Reward condition found the storytelling task to be just as interesting as did children in the No Reward condition. Also unexpected was the fact that there were no significant between-group (Reward vs. No Reward) differences in the creativity of stories or collages produced by Saudi students. Within the Saudi sample, however, there did emerge significant differences in the two groups' self-reports of interest in the collage-making task, with participants in the No Reward condition reporting significantly more intrinsic task motivation than their peers in the Reward group. Finally, because some previous research conducted by Mar'i and Karayanni (1983) in Arab cultures had indicated that males sometimes outperform females on creativity tests (perhaps due to females' submissive social roles, limited occupational choices, etc.), gender-based comparisons were conducted. No significant gender differences were found on either the creativity or intrinsic motivation measures.

In sum, the bulk of our findings from the Saudi Arabia sample stand in direct contradiction to the IMPC. An analysis of our data revealed that on the storytelling task, the expectation of reward failed to undermine either intrinsic task motivation or creativity of performance; on the collage task, expected reward again failed to undermine creativity, yet intrinsic task motivation was significantly negatively affected. How is it that, on the storytelling task, these children appeared relatively impervious to the offer of reward? And how were they able to maintain their creativity in the face of falling intrinsic motivation for the collage-making activity?

Are we to conclude that the IMPC is very much culture-specific? The issues are complex, and it is unrealistic to expect that any one study will illuminate the many cross-cultural factors that impact motivational orientation and creativity of performance. We do, however, have a few hunches.

Deci and Ryan (2000) postulate that, although the satisfaction of the innate psychological need for competence, autonomy, and relatedness is essential for the healthy development and well-being of all individuals, these needs may be satisfied while engaging in a wide variety of behaviors across cultures. Saudi society is described by some as being more collectivist in orientation than our own, and certainly our visits to the school where we collected data corroborated this view. According to SDT (Deci & Ryan, 2000; Ryan & Deci, 2000), the autonomy of our young Saudi students might be expected to be less adversely affected by the promise of a reward. In the collectivist culture of their classroom, Saudi students may not have been as quick as were their U.S. counterparts to experience the offer of a reward as a threat to their autonomy. In their view, they all share in the challenge of tasks presented to them and the individual threat is reduced.

Refining the Model

Must intrinsic motivation and creativity always suffer when task-contingent rewards are promised? These cross-cultural findings coupled with data collected by Deci, Ryan, and colleagues on the effects of informational versus controlling rewards tell us the answer is no. In addition, interviews with adults who rely on their creativity for their life's work lead us to conclude that for some persons under some circumstances, the imposition of extrinsic incentives can actually serve to augment intrinsic motivation and creativity of performance. When investigations into the social psychology of creativity were begun some 25 years ago, it was believed that the determinants of creativity were pretty much the same for everyone. In other words, high levels of extrinsic motivation were thought to preclude high levels of intrinsic motivation: as rewards were imposed, intrinsic motivation and creativity would necessarily be decreased. Now, a good many years and investigations later, most researchers taking a social psychological approach to the study of creativity have come to supplement their original conceptualizations with the recognition that under certain specific conditions, the expectation of a reward or an evaluation can sometimes increase levels of extrinsic motivation without having any negative impact on performance. In fact, some types of extrinsic motivation can actually enhance creativity of performance. Recent laboratory-based investigations have demonstrated, for example, that study participants given a choice about task engagement can come to perceive their receipt of a reward as a kind of bonus rather than a controlling extrinsic constraint (Amabile, Hennessey, & Grossman, 1986, Study 3). And researchers now understand that the powerful undermining effect of expected reward is most likely to occur when task-contingent rewards (rewards made conditional on simple task completion) have been promised. The impact of so-called performance-contingent rewards (rewards promised and delivered only if a certain level of competency or proficiency is reached) is far more complex. Under certain specific circumstances, the informational value implicit in performance-contingent rewards has been shown to augment feelings of self-efficacy, intrinsic task interest, and qualitative aspects of performance.

In the "real world" of work, the negative effects of extrinsic constraints have also not proven universal. For some people, certain extrinsic motivators have been shown to have either no effect or even a positive effect on task interest and creativity of performance. For example, in a study of commissioned and non-commissioned works by professional artists, the extrinsic incentive of a commission was seen by some artists as a highly controlling constraint and the creativity of their work plummeted. Yet, for those who looked at the commission as an opportunity to achieve recognition or a confirmation of their competence by respected others, creativity was enhanced (Amabile, Phillips, & Collins, 1996). Finally, interview studies in the corporate world have also revealed that, whereas the prospect of impending critical evaluation most often leads to low levels of intrinsic motivation and creativity, informative evaluation that conveys positive recognition of creative work can contribute to highly creative performance (Amabile & Gryskiewicz, 1987).

How can these differential effects be explained? Our data on these professionals parallel nicely the research carried out by Deci and colleagues, which explores the relevance of self-perception processes to the undermining of motivation and creativity of performance. Once again, it may not be the expectation of the reward or evaluation itself that undermines creativity; rather, it may be the interpersonal context in which that extrinsic constraint is imposed and the individual's subsequent interpretation of the imposed contingency and his or her own role in the reward or evaluation process that in large part determines whether performance will be undermined, enhanced, or remain unchanged. Based on these more recent findings, Amabile (1996) offers a revision of the IMPC, which says that, although extrinsic motivation is most often detrimental to creativity, informational or enabling extrinsic motivation can sometimes be conducive, especially if an individual's initial levels of intrinsic motivation are high.

Conclusions and Future Directions

Nearly three decades of research evidence have led researchers and theorists to stand firm in their support of the premise that intrinsic motivation is conducive to creativity. Whatever an individual's particular talents, domain skills, and creative thinking abilities, the conditions under which he or she works can significantly impact the level of creativity produced. Intrinsic motivation is still believed to be a primary driving force behind the creative process, and it is the social environment that, in large part, is credited with determining this motivational orientation.

Investigators interested in specifying this link between motivation and creativity initially focused on the performance of individuals in a variety of experimental settings. They directly manipulated aspects of the environment and looked for accompanying changes in the creativity of the ideas and products produced. More recent investigations have also incorporated nonexperimental methods such as surveys, interviews, and an examination of archival sources; now this list of research methodologies has been expanded to include cross-cultural investigations. This broadening of focus has convinced researchers that the original IMPC and related models had to be revised to reflect a more comprehensive systems approach. The impact of expected reward or expected evaluation is far too complex to be summarized in terms of absolutes. Individual difference variables, including cultural differences, are now being considered, and that is an important theoretical step forward. Researchers and theorists must now also turn their attention to the interpersonal context, the social situation, in which extrinsic constraints, such as reward and evaluation, are being promised and delivered.

Our theorizing about creativity has come a long way in the past half century. For many years, the long-held Western emphasis on individualism, with its concomitant celebration of long-suffering scientists, inventors, artists, writers, and composers, served to overshadow the roles played by those creators' collaborators or the families, corporations, and societies that nurtured them. This chapter began with the assertion that creativity does not happen in a vacuum. Perhaps if there were no learning effects, no past experience with rewards and evaluations, no individual differences in self-esteem, and only one universal culture, it might make sense to make sweeping statements claiming that evaluation and reward always (or never) have a negative impact on intrinsic motivation and creative aspects of performance. But people are highly complicated organisms, and rewards and evaluations are promised and awarded under a complexity of circumstances. As a field, social psychology has come to appreciate this fact. We are far from ready to entirely abandon the person-centered approach, but we now know that it is only with a consideration of the context, including the interpersonal context, in which people operate that we can ever hope to enrich our understanding of creative behavior.

References

Ainsworth, M., & Marvin, R. S. (1995). On the shaping of attachment theory and research: An interview with Mary D. S. Ainsworth (fall 1994). *Monographs of the Society for Research in Child Development, 60,* 3–21.

Amabile, T. M. (1982). Social psychology of creativity: A consensual assessment technique. *Journal of Personality and Social Psychology, 43,* 997–1013.

Amabile, T. M. (1993). Motivational synergy: Toward new conceptualizations of intrinsic and extrinsic motivation in the workplace. *Human Resource Management Review, 3,* 185–201.

Amabile, T. M. (1996). *Creativity in context.* Boulder, CO: Westview.

Amabile, T. M. (1997). Motivating creativity in organizations: On doing what you love and loving what you do. *California Management Review, 40,* 39–58.

Amabile, T. M., & Gryskiewicz, S. (1987). *Creativity in the R&D laboratory.* Technical Report no. 30. Greensboro, NC: Center for Creative Leadership.

Amabile, T. M., Hennessey, B. A., & Grossman, B. (1986). Social influences on creativity: The effects of contracted-for reward. *Journal of Personality and Social Psychology, 50,* 14–23.

Amabile, T. M., Phillips, E. D., & Collins, M. A. (1996). *Creativity by contract: Social influences on the creativity of professional artists.* Unpublished manuscript, Brandeis University, Waltham, MA.

Bem, D. (1972). Self-perception theory. In L. Berkowitz (Ed.), *Advances in experimental social psychology* (Vol. 6, pp. 2–62). New York: Academic Press.

Burnside, R. M., Amabile, T. M., & Gryskiewicz, S. S. (1988). Assessing organizational climates for creativity and innovation: Methodological review of large company audits. In Y. Ijiri & R. L. Kuhn (Eds.), *New directions in creative and innovative management: Bridging theory and practice.* Cambridge, MA: Ballinger.

Csikszentmihalyi, M. (1988). Society, culture and person: A systems view of creativity. In R. Sternberg & J. Davidson (Eds.), *The nature of creativity* (pp. 325–339). New York: Cambridge University Press.

Csikszentmihalyi, M. (1990). *Flow: The psychology of optimal experience.* New York: Harper Collins.

Csikszentmihalyi, M. (1996). *Creativity: Flow and the psychology of discovery and invention.* New York: Harper Collins.

Dawkins, R. (1976). *The selfish gene.* Oxford: Oxford University Press.

deCharms, R. (1968). *Personal causation.* New York: Academic Press.

deCharms, R. (1976). *Enhancing motivation: Change in the classroom.* New York: Irvington.

Deci, E. L., Cascio, W., & Krussell, J. (1975). Cognitive evaluation theory and some comments on the Calder and Staw critique. *Journal of Personality and Social Psychology, 31,* 81–85.

Deci, E. L., Nezlek, J., & Sheinman, L. (1981). Characteristics of the rewarder and intrinsic motivation of the rewardee. *Journal of Personality and Social Psychology, 40,* 1–10.

Deci, E. L., & Ryan, R. M. (1980). Self determination theory: When mind mediates behavior. *Journal of Mind and Behavior, 1,* 33–43.

Deci, E. L., & Ryan, R. M. (1985). *Intrinsic motivation and self-determination in human behavior.* New York: Plenum.

Deci, E. L., & Ryan, R. M. (1994). Promoting self-determined education. Scandinavian *Journal of Education Research, 38,* 3–14.

Deci, E. L., & Ryan, R. M. (2000). The "what" and "why" of goal pursuits: Human needs and the self-determination of behavior. *Psychological Inquiry, 11,* 227–268.

Ekvall, G. (1987). The climate metaphor in organization theory. In B. M. Bass & P. J. D. Drenth (Eds.), *Advances in organizational psychology* (pp. 177–190). London: Sage.

Ekvall, G. (1996). Organizational climate for creativity and innovation. *European Journal of Work and Organizational Psychology, 5,* 105–123.

Ekvall, G. (1999). Creative climate. In M. Runco & S. Pritzker (Eds.), *Encyclopedia of creativity* (pp. 403–412). New York: Academic Press.

Ford, C. (1999). Business strategy. In M. Runco & S. Pritzker (Eds.), *Encyclopedia of creativity* (235–243). New York: Academic Press.

Gardner, H. (1993). *Creating minds: An anatomy of creativity seen through the lives of Freud, Einstein, Picasso, Stravinsky, Eliot, Graham, and Gandhi.* New York: Basic.

Gardner, H. (1997). *Extraordinary minds: Portraits of exceptional individuals and an examination of our extraordinariness.* New York: Basic.

Goodwin, V. L., Wofford, J. C., & Whittington, J. L. (2001). A theoretical and empirical extension of the transformational leadership construct. *Journal of Organizational Behavior, 22,* 759–774.

Gruber, H. E. (1988). The evolving systems approach to creative work. *Creativity Research Journal, 1,* 27–59.

Hallman, R. J. (1970). Toward a Hindu theory of creativity. *Educational Theory, 20,* 368–376.

Hennessey, B. A. (1996). Teaching for creative development: A social-psychological approach. In N. Colangelo & G. Davis (Eds.), *Handbook of gifted education* (2nd ed., pp. 282–291). Needham Heights, MA: Allyn & Bacon.

Hennessey, B. A. (1999). Intrinsic motivation, affect and creativity. In S. Russ (Ed.), *Affect, creative experience and psychological adjustment* (pp. 77–90). Philadelphia: Taylor & Francis.

Hennessey, B. A., & Amabile, T. M. (1999). Consensual assessment. In M. Runco & S. Pritzker (Eds.), *Encyclopedia of creativity* (pp. 347–359). New York: Academic Press.

Isaksen, S. G, Winsemius, A., & Lauer, K. (1995). *A test of the validity of the climate for creativity questionnaire.* CPU report. Buffalo, NY: The Creative Problem Solving Group.

Kelley, H. (1967). Attribution theory in social psychology. In D. Levine (Ed.), *Nebraska symposium on motivation* (Vol. 15, pp. 192–238). Lincoln: University of Nebraska Press.

Kelley, H. (1973). The processes of causal attribution. *American Psychologist, 28,* 107–128.

Kerr, B., & Chopp, C. (1999). Families and creativity. In M. Runco & S. Pritzker (Eds.), *Encyclopedia of creativity* (pp. 709–715). New York: Academic Press.

Lubart, T. I. (1999). Creativity across cultures. In R. J. Sternberg (Ed.), *Handbook of creativity* (pp. 339–350). New York: Cambridge University Press.

Mar'i, S. K., & Karayanni, M. (1983). Creativity in Arab culture: Two decades of research. *Journal of Creative Behavior, 16,* 227–238.

Martindale, C. (2001). Oscillations and analogies: Thomas Young, MD, FRS, genius. *American Psychologist, 56*, 342–345.

Olszewski, P., Kulieke, M., & Buescher, T. (1987). The influence of the family environment on the development of talent: A literature review. *Journal for the Education of the Gifted, 11*, 6–28.

Paulus, P. B. (1999). Group creativity. In M. Runco & S. Pritzker (Eds.), *Encyclopedia of creativity* (pp. 779–784). New York: Academic Press.

Policastro, E., & Gardner, H. (1999). From case studies to robust generalizations: An approach to the study of creativity. In R. J. Sternberg (Ed.), *Handbook of creativity* (pp. 213–225). New York: Cambridge University Press.

Raina, M. (1999). Cross-cultural differences. In M. Runco & S. Pritzker (Eds.), *Encyclopedia of creativity* (pp. 453–464). New York: Academic Press.

Ryan, R. M., & Deci, E. L. (2000). Self-determination theory and the facilitation of intrinsic motivation, social development, and well-being. *American Psychologist, 55*, 68–78.

Ryan, R. M., & Grolnick, W. S. (1986). Origins and pawns in the classroom: Self-report and projective assessments of individual differences in children's perceptions. *Journal of Personality and Social Psychology, 50*, 550–558.

Shultz, T., Butkowsky, I., Pearce, J., & Shanfield, H. (1975). The development of schemes for the attribution of multiple psychological causes. *Developmental Psychology, 11*, 502–510.

Smith, M. C. (1975). Children's use of the multiple sufficient cause schema in social perception. *Journal of Personality and Social Psychology, 32*, 737–747.

Sternberg, R. J., & Lubart, T. I. (1991). An investment theory of creativity and its development. *Human Development, 34*, 1–32.

Tauer, J., & Harackiewicz, J. M. (1999). Winning isn't everything: Competition, achievement orientation, and intrinsic motivation. *Journal of Experimental Social Psychology, 35*, 209–238.

Triandis, H. C. (1996). The psychological measurement of cultural syndromes. *American Psychologist, 51*, 407–415.

Turnipseed, D. (1994). The relationship between the social environment of organizations and the climate for innovation and creativity. *Creativity and Innovation Management, 3*, 184–195.

Weiner, P. W. (2000). *Creatvity and beyond: Cultures, values and change.* Albany: State University of New York Press.

Whorf, B. L. (1956). *Language, thought and reality: Selected writings of Benjamin Lee Whorf.* Cambridge, MA: MIT Press.

10

John M. Levine, Hoon-Seok Choi, and Richard L. Moreland

Newcomer Innovation in Work Teams

Collaborative work is an increasingly important aspect of organizational life. Many organizations now assign their most critical tasks to small groups, particularly work teams (Hackman, 1990; Sundstrom, 1999). This is not surprising, because there are several reasons to believe that teams should be more effective than individual workers. Not only do most teams possess more task-relevant skills and knowledge than do individuals, but team members can also share these resources, redistribute responsibilities to meet new task demands, and motivate one another to work hard. Unfortunately, however, there is evidence that teams do not always provide the benefits they promise. Research in laboratory settings shows that teams often fail to realize their potential productivity because of coordination and motivation problems (Steiner, 1972). And research in organizational settings suggests that team effectiveness is often reduced by such managerial mistakes as using teams for tasks that are better done by individuals, assuming team members possess all the skills they need to work together, and failing to provide adequate organizational support for team activities (Hackman, 1998).

Personnel Turnover

One of the most daunting challenges for teams is personnel turnover, defined as the entry of new members and/or the exit of old members. Turnover represents a change in team composition that can have profound consequences for team performance because it alters both the distribution of knowledge within the team and the relations among team members.

Research on turnover has been done in both organizations and small groups. In reviewing the organizational literature, Argote (1993, 1999) concluded that the effects of turnover are mixed and depend on such factors as the organization's coordination requirements, the level of organizational structure, and the individual's skill level. Research on turnover in small groups indicates that turnover typically disrupts group performance but is more deleterious under some conditions than others. For example, group performance does not vary with the mean rate of turnover but declines when turnover is greater than usual (Trow, 1960). In addition, turnover causes fewer problems when group members work independently rather than interactively (Naylor & Briggs, 1965), and when the group has high rather than low structure (Devadas & Argote, 1995).

Although these and other studies (e.g., Hollenbeck et al., 1995) provide useful information about the impact of turnover, they only scratch the surface of a very complex phenomenon. In particular, they pay little attention to the possibility that turnover can have positive rather than negative consequences for group performance. Turnover can improve group performance through two mechanisms: the exit of oldtimers who lack the skills or motivation to help the group attain its goals, and the entry of newcomers who possess such skills or motivation. In this chapter, we focus on the latter mechanism.

Newcomers: Recipients or Sources of Influence?

Being a new member of a group or organization is stressful for several reasons, including reality shock due to unrealistic expectations about group life, information overload, uncertainty regarding role demands, and performance anxiety (Moreland & Levine, 1989). Therefore, it should not be surprising that newcomers are often highly susceptible to oldtimers' efforts to shape their attitudes and behaviors (Levine & Moreland, 1991, 1999). Newcomers, however, are not always passive recipients of influence.

Research in organizations indicates that newcomers often play an active role in their socialization and produce changes in the settings they enter (Bauer, Morrison, & Callister, 1998; Saks & Ashforth, 1997). Among the "proactive socialization" techniques that newcomers use are information seeking, general socializing, networking, and behavioral self-management (Ashford & Black, 1996; Morrison, 1993; Saks & Ashforth, 1996). Although these techniques are often used to help newcomers adapt to existing organizational practices, they also may lead to changes in these practices. For example, a newcomer's request to see sensitive information can prompt oldtimers to restrict access to such information via strengthened security clearances. Moreover, organizational newcomers who utilize proactive strategies are more likely than others to attempt job innovation (Feij, Whitely, Peiro, & Taris, 1995).

Focusing on small groups, Levine and Moreland (1985; Levine, Moreland, & Choi, 2001) analyzed a variety of unintentional and intentional mechanisms by which newcomers can produce innovation, defined as any significant change in the structure, dynamics, or performance of a group. In discussing unintentional innovation, Levine and Moreland noted that the need to impart group culture to newcomers can interfere with oldtimers' ability to perform other tasks, thereby harming group performance, and can stimulate oldtimers to think about group culture, thereby altering their views of the group's practices and norms. In addition, efforts to retain highly promising newcomers (and expel less promising ones) can absorb scarce group resources, thereby reducing the group's ability to achieve other goals. Finally, newcomers' presence can alter existing relationships among oldtimers, as when newcomers increase the size of a particular clique, and can change how the group relates to outgroups, as when competition for new members sours intergroup relations (Levine, Moreland, & Ryan, 1998).

The notion that newcomers can produce innovation is consistent with the large body of work on minority influence in groups (De Dreu & De Vries, 2001; Levine & Thompson, 1996; Moscovici, Mucchi-Faina, & Maass, 1994). In most situations, oldtimers outnumber newcomers, which means that newcomers are numerical minorities (Gruenfeld & Fan, 1999; Levine & Moreland, 1985; Levine et al., 2001). Minority status puts newcomers at a disadvantage, as indicated by the difficulty minorities have producing public agreement with their position (Wood, Lundgren, Ouellette, Busceme, & Blackstone, 1994) and by the hostility they elicit from majorities (Levine & Thompson, 1996). However, this does not mean that minorities are always weak. They often produce private agreement with their position (Wood et al., 1994), and, by using the right kinds of tactics, they may produce public agreement as well (Levine & Kaarbo, 2001). In addition, minority dissent can enhance group problem solving by stimulating divergent thinking on the part of the majority (Nemeth & Nemeth-Brown, this volume).

Determinants of Newcomer Innovation in Work Teams

The goal of this chapter is to analyze newcomer innovation in work teams. Although newcomers can produce innovation without intending to do so (Levine et al., 2001), our focus here is on intentional innovation. Therefore, we adopt West and Farr's (1990) definition of innovation as "the intentional introduction and application . . . of ideas, processes, products, or procedures, new to the relevant unit of adoption, designed to significantly benefit the individual, the group, organization, or wider society" (p. 9). According to West and Farr, innovation involves implementation as well as generation of ideas and does not require that ideas be novel in the absolute sense. In addition, innovation is a distinctly social phenomenon, in that it depends on social processes and produces social consequences.

The social nature of innovation is fundamental to our analysis, which views newcomer innovation as the outcome of an implicit or explicit negotiation between newcomers and oldtimers, both of whom play an active role in the socialization process (Levine & Moreland, 1994; Moreland & Levine, 1982). According to this perspective, innovation will not occur unless newcomers produce new ideas for improving team performance and oldtimers agree to implement these ideas. In the remainder of this chapter, we discuss characteristics and behaviors of newcomers and characteristics of teams that can affect this process. Because little explicit theoretical or empirical attention has been devoted to newcomer innovation in teams, many of our ideas regarding this phenomenon are based on extrapolations from work in related areas.

Characteristics and Behaviors of Newcomers

Newcomers' characteristics and behaviors influence innovation to the extent they affect (1) newcomers' motivation to introduce change into the team they are entering, (2) newcomers' ability to generate ideas that can enhance team performance, and (3) newcomers' ability to convince oldtimers to accept their ideas.

Newcomers' Motivation to Introduce Change

Three factors determine the extent to which newcomers are motivated to introduce change. These are their commitment to the team, their belief that they can develop good ideas for solving team problems, and their perception that their innovation efforts will be rewarded.

Newcomers' commitment to a team depends on its past, present, and anticipated future rewardingness. Thus, commitment is low when newcomers remember their past relationship with the team as less rewarding than previous alternative relationships, perceive their present relationship as less rewarding than current alternative relationships, and expect their future relationship to be less rewarding than future alternative relationships (Moreland & Levine, 1982). In general, newcomers are more motivated to change a team that elicits low commitment (because it is not rewarding) than a team that elicits high commitment (because it is rewarding). Such motivation, in turn, is likely to stimulate newcomers to identify problems in the team and suggest ways of solving them (cf. Moreland & Levine, 1992b). A possible exception to the negative relationship between commitment to a team and motivation to change it should be noted, however. When their commitment is extremely low, newcomers may be inclined to withdraw (either psychologically or physically) from the team rather than to try to change it.

A second determinant of newcomers' motivation to attempt innovation is their belief that they can develop good ideas for solving team problems. This assumption is consistent with work indicating that an individual's feeling of efficacy is important in producing change-oriented behavior (cf. Bandura, 1986; Farr & Ford, 1990). Several factors are likely to affect newcomers' feelings of self-efficacy. For example, newcomers who have produced good ideas in teams similar to the one they are joining will probably have higher self-efficacy for producing additional ideas. In addition, receiving prior training on the team task will probably lead to higher self-efficacy because such training provides mastery experiences (Bandura, 1995). Newcomers may also feel efficacious about producing good ideas as a result of observing similar others do so (Bandura, 1986). In addition to influencing newcomers' efforts to generate an initial idea, self-efficacy no doubt also affects their persistence in generating additional ideas if their initial idea is not accepted. Such persistence is important because successful innovations often demand considerable effort over a relatively long period of time (Bandura, 1995).

A third factor that can affect newcomers' motivation to attempt innovation is their perception that the innovation will produce positive consequences for themselves and the team as a whole. People who deviate from group norms are often disliked and punished (Levine & Thompson, 1996), and newcomers are typically expected to be anxious, passive, dependent, and conforming (Moreland & Levine, 1989). For these reasons, newcomers contemplating innovation are likely to worry about how oldtimers will react to their initiatives and to be hesitant in introducing innovations (Heiss & Nash, 1967) unless they believe their efforts will yield positive consequences. One factor that can affect this belief is the team's prior receptivity to innovations by others. The more similar the earlier innovations are to the one being proposed and the more similar the earlier innovators are to the newcomers, the more likely the newcomers are to believe that their innovation will be accepted, which in turn will increase their motivation to introduce the innovation. In addition, the more a team actively encourages innovation on the part of newcomers, the more likely they are to experience a sense of psychological safety (cf. Edmondson, 1999; West, 1990) and to believe that their innovation efforts will be rewarded (cf. Scott & Bruce, 1994), which should increase their motivation to suggest new ideas.

The size of the newcomers' faction may also affect their perception of the likely consequences of innovation (Levine & Kaarbo, 2001). As noted above, newcomers often avoid behaviors that appear assertive because they fear negative reactions from oldtimers. This tendency can be overcome, however, if two or more newcomers enter a team together and develop a sense of in-group solidarity (Becker, 1964; Van Maanen, 1984). Hence, newcomers in larger factions should be more assertive than those in smaller factions because the former are less likely to fear retribution and more likely to believe they can prevail (Zdaniuk & Levine, 1996). This is not to say, of course, that newcomers in smaller factions are always passive. When such newcomers identify strongly with their faction and feel they have nothing to lose by opposing oldtimers, they may be quite assertive (cf. Mullen, Brown, & Smith, 1992).

Newcomers' Ability to Generate Ideas

The traditional approach to understanding creativity involves identifying personality traits that predict an individual's level of creativity. These traits include attraction to complexity, preference for autonomy, self-confidence, social independence, tolerance of ambiguity, propensity for risk taking, and moderate anxiety (cf. Agrell & Gustafson, 1996; Barron & Harrington, 1981). It is likely that these traits will also predict newcomers' ability to generate innovative ideas in work teams.

An alternative approach focuses on individual differences in creativity style rather than level. According to Kirton (1976), there is a continuum of creativity style, ranging from adaptation to innovation. Adaptors suggest refinements of existing work practices, whereas innovators suggest radical changes in these practices. Thus, two individuals who have identical creativity levels may have very different creativity styles. Empirical findings from a variety of occupational settings support the independence of creativity level and style (Mudd, 1996). In regard to newcomers, Kirton's analysis suggests that both adaptors and innovators are capable of generating ideas for improving team performance, though the content of their ideas will differ.

Yet another approach to creativity focuses on cognitive skills rather than enduring personality dispositions. According to Barron and Harrington (1981), creativity is positively associated with a wide range of cognitive skills, including divergent thinking, forming multiple and unusual associations, visualizing potential solutions to problems, and effective problem finding. Similarly, Runco and Okuda (1988) argue that creativity requires such cognitive skills as problem finding, divergent thinking, and accurate evaluation of potential solutions to problems. Focusing on factors that influence individual role innovation, Farr and Ford (1990) suggest that the ability to innovate is positively related to the capacity to engage in a search process that explores multiple sources of new ideas.

In discussing the skills underlying creativity, Amabile (1983) distinguishes between skills related to creative thinking and skills related to specific task domains. The former include a cognitive style favorable to taking new perspectives and the ability to apply heuristics in exploring new ideas. The latter include knowledge of the task domain under consideration and the technical ability to perform tasks in this domain. We focus here on the role of task-related skills in newcomer innovation.

Newcomers' ability to generate useful ideas varies positively with their task-relevant knowledge and skills. One way to gain such knowledge and skills is to participate in individual training on the team task (e.g., attending flight school as a student pilot). Another, and often superior, way is to work as a member of another team doing the same or a similar task (e.g., piloting commercial aircraft for several years). Compared to newcomers with only individual training, those with prior team experience have a better sense of their coworkers' jobs and the response coordination requirements of the team task (Moreland, 1999). As a result, newcomers with team experience are in a better position to diagnose problems in their team's performance and develop solutions for these problems (Gruenfeld & Fan, 1999). In fact, such newcomers may even be superior to oldtimers at diagnosing team problems and generating ideas for improving team performance. Because they have had experience working on another team, they are not committed to the new team's routines and do not have strong personal ties to team members. As a result, they can view the team from a relatively detached perspective (Louis, 1980; Schuetz, 1944; Ziller, 1965) and may identity problems that oldtimers always ignored and suggest solutions that oldtimers never contemplated.

Finally, the number of newcomers entering a team may affect their ability to generate useful ideas. Newcomers in small factions, particularly solo newcomers, may experience high levels of arousal and self-focused attention (Kanter, 1977). They may also experience heightened concern about self-presentation, which can absorb their attentional resources (cf. Saenz, 1994). For these reasons, newcomers in small factions may have difficulty generating creative ideas.

Newcomers' Ability to Convince Oldtimers to Accept Their Ideas

Given that newcomers have the motivation and ability to introduce new ideas into a team, they must then convince oldtimers to accept their ideas. This final and critical step can be problematical for several reasons. Oldtimers may simply reject a new idea out of hand because they distrust newcomers' motives or skills, desire to maintain familiar task routines (Gersick & Hackman, 1990), or prefer shared to unshared information (Stasser, 1999). Alternatively, oldtimers may demand time to consider the implications of a new idea and may suggest revisions in it (cf. King & Anderson, 1990). And even after oldtimers accept a new idea in principle, they may be reluctant to implement it if doing so involves substantial costs (e.g., friction within the team, expenditure of time and money).

Several characteristics and behaviors of newcomers can affect their ability to persuade oldtimers to accept their ideas. One such characteristic is newcomers' external social status. Compared to low-status newcomers, high-status newcomers elicit more commitment from oldtimers (Moreland & Levine, 1989) because they bring valuable resources to the team (e.g., expertise, prestige) and are viewed as instrumental to achieving team goals (cf. Zander & Cohen, 1955). In the same vein, high-status newcomers are likely to elicit more favorable performance expectations than are low-status newcomers (cf. Milanovich, Driskell, Stout, & Salas, 1998). Finally, because they often have the option to leave the team for a more attractive alternative, high-status newcomers may be able to use the threat of departure to force oldtimers to accept their ideas for change (Ziller, 1965). High-status newcomers should thus find it easier to gain acceptance for new ideas (cf. Driskell & Mullen, 1990; Torrance, 1955) and should suffer less punishment for deviating from team norms (cf. Wahrman, 1970; Wiggins, Dill, & Schwartz, 1965). In fact, when they occupy leadership roles, high-status newcomers may be expected to produce innovation (cf. Coser, 1962; Homans, 1974) and may be rewarded for deviating from team norms (cf. Suchner & Jackson, 1976).

Another characteristic of newcomers that can affect their persuasive ability is the size of their faction. Extrapolating from work on minority influence, arguments can be made for two different relationships between newcomers' faction size and ability to exert influence (Levine & Kaarbo, 2001). On the one hand, larger factions may be more effective than smaller ones (Latané & Wolf, 1981; Tanford & Penrod, 1984) because larger factions are seen as more correct (Nemeth, Wachtler, & Endicott, 1977) and as more likely to retaliate if their views are rejected. In contrast, smaller factions may be more effective than larger ones because smaller factions seem more confident and courageous (Nemeth et al., 1977), more distinct and salient (Maass, West, & Cialdini, 1987), and less threatening.

Newcomers' persuasive ability can also be affected by their behavioral style, defined as the organization, timing, and intensity of their responses (Moscovici, 1985). One aspect of behavioral style, consistency, has received substantial attention from researchers interested in minority influence. According to Moscovici, consistency on the part of a numerical minority generates cognitive conflict in the majority, which stimulates careful examination and acceptance of the minority's position (see Nemeth, 1995, and Perez & Mugny, 1996, for alternative views). Although perceived consistency generally increases minority influence (Wood et al., 1994), one must be careful not to overgeneralize these findings. For example, certain kinds of inconsistent minorities (i.e., majority members who move to a minority position) can be more effective than consistent minorities (Levine, Sroka, & Snyder, 1977), and too much consistency can backfire if it is interpreted as rigidity (Mugny, 1982). Moreover, even if consistent newcomers are generally more influential than inconsistent newcomers, care must be taken to specify just what this influence entails. Extrapolating from the minority influence literature, one would predict that this influence typically will be private rather than public (Wood et al., 1994), which is obviously a problem for newcomers who want to produce behavioral (rather than just attitudinal) change in oldtimers.

A second important facet of behavioral style is the timing of the influence attempt. According to Hollander (1960), people gain "idiosyncrasy credits" by demonstrating competence on group tasks and conformity to group norms, which in turn give them the status necessary to introduce innovations into the group. Consistent with this reasoning, Hollander found that competent individuals who attempted to change a group's procedural norms were more successful if they conformed before initiating innovation than if they did not. The psychological processes underlying this effect are not well understood but probably involve increased trust in and liking for the conformer. In terms of newcomer innovation, Hollander's results suggest that newcomers who try to initiate changes immediately after entering an intact group may be less successful than those who initially conform to group norms. Moreover, like Levine et al. (1977), Hollander provides evidence that inconsistency can sometimes produce more influence than consistency (see Bray, Johnson, & Chilstrom, 1982).

Closely related to behavioral style is a set of impression management tactics designed to convince oldtimers that newcomers possess valid information about the team task and are motivated to enhance team performance (Levine & Kaarbo, 2001). For example, newcomers might seek to convey the impression that their suggestions are based on careful and objective analysis of team problems, that they possess special expertise as a function of prior experience on similar teams, that their views are shared by knowledgeable people outside the team, and that they are motivated by concern about team rather than personal welfare (cf. Ridgeway, 1982). To the extent newcomers can convince oldtimers that they possess these characteristics, they are more likely to gain acceptance for their ideas.

As all of this suggests, newcomers are typically assumed to lack the power to compel oldtimers to accept their ideas and hence must rely on informational tactics designed to demonstrate the validity of these ideas. In some cases, however, newcomers have other tactics at their disposal, including punishment/reward tactics, compositional tactics, and procedural tactics (Levine & Kaarbo, 2001). Punishment/reward tactics are available to newcomers who are viewed as valuable because they possess knowledge or skills that the team needs. Punishment tactics include threatening to (1) harm team performance either actively (e.g., via sabotage) or passively (e.g., via social loafing); (2) withdraw from the team; (3) discredit the team in the eyes of outsiders (e.g., via whistle-blowing); and (4) reduce the size of the team (e.g., via encouraging current members to leave and prospective members not to join). Reward tactics, which are the mirror image of punishment tactics, include promising to work hard to enhance team performance, remain on the team in spite of attractive options outside, and so on.

Compositional and procedural tactics are more subtle and hence less likely to be interpreted as motivated by desire to exert influence. Compositional tactics involve efforts to maximize the size of the newcomer faction, on the assumption that larger factions are more persuasive than smaller ones (cf. Hoyt, 1997; Stasser, Kerr, & Davis, 1989). Thus, newcomers might try to convince the team to recruit people who are sympathetic to their ideas and engineer the withdrawal of those who are unsympathetic. Procedural tactics involve efforts to control the team's procedures for processing information and reaching consensus. These procedures include the decision rule used to aggregate members' individual preferences (e.g., majority vs. unanimity), the manner in which alternatives are compared (e.g., sequentially vs. simultaneously), the timing of the decision (e.g., early vs. late in the discussion), and so on. For example, newcomers who convince a team to use the unanimity rule in deciding whether to accept a new idea are more likely to win acceptance of this idea than are newcomers who allow the team to use the majority rule (cf. Miller, 1989).

Finally, whether newcomers expect to remain on the team for a short or a long time, whether they belonged to similar teams in the past, and whether they are replacing former team members may affect their ability to convince oldtimers to accept their ideas. So far, we have focused on newcomers who expect to remain on the team for a long time, did not previously belong to similar teams, and are not replacing former members. However, other types of newcomers exist (Arrow & McGrath, 1995), and they may be more or less effective innovators than those we have emphasized. For example, *visitors*, who expect to remain on the team for a short time, typically are not perceived as instrumental to attaining long-term team goals. Therefore, they will probably elicit relatively low commitment from oldtimers, which should inhibit their ability to change the team (Gruenfeld & Fan, 1999; Gruenfeld, Martorana, & Fan, 2000). In contrast, *transfers*, who recently belonged to a similar team, have expertise on the team task. Hence, they will probably elicit relatively high commitment from oldtimers, which should enhance their ability to change the team. Oldtimers' commitment to *replacements*, who take the place of former members, is often influenced by the performance of the people they are following, as well as (or instead of) their own performance. Thus, newcomers replacing low-performing members may be overvalued and hence find it relatively easy to produce innovation, whereas those replacing high-performing members may be undervalued and hence find it relatively difficult to produce innovation. Finally, the impact of *consultants*, who join the team to observe its work practices and suggest improvements, may depend on how they gained entry into the team. Holding constant the quality of their suggestions, consultants who were selected by the team will probably find a more receptive audience for their ideas than will consultants who were "imposed" on the team by outsiders, such as managers.

Characteristics of the Team

As suggested earlier, newcomer innovation cannot be understood by focusing exclusively on the source of new ideas. Because innovation is the result of an implicit or explicit negotiation between newcomers and oldtimers, attention must also be devoted to the target of new ideas. We therefore turn now to an examination of team characteristics that affect receptivity to innovation efforts on the part of newcomers.

Team Openness

Groups vary in openness to membership change (Ziller, 1965). Open groups have unstable memberships with high rates of personnel turnover, whereas closed groups have stable memberships with low rates of turnover. Compared to closed groups, open groups have a shorter time perspective and hence implement decisions more quickly, work harder to minimize turnover-related problems, and are more receptive to new ideas (Ziller, Behringer, & Goodchilds, 1960). In light of this last characteristic, it is not surprising that newcomers find it easier to produce innovation in open than in closed groups (cf. Ziller, Behringer, & Jansen, 1961). In the case of open groups, the attractiveness of prospective members who might be recruited to join may affect newcomers' ability to produce innovation. If oldtimers believe they can replace current newcomers with others who will make stronger contributions to the attainment of group goals, they are unlikely to be receptive to current newcomers' ideas for change.

Team Composition

In recent years, discussions of group composition have focused on the impact of member diversity, defined as variability in demographic characteristics, personality traits, abilities, opinions, tenure in the group, and educational and functional background (Moreland, Levine, & Wingert, 1996; Neale, Mannix, & Gruenfeld, 1998; Williams & O'Reilly, 1998). Research on the effects of diversity suggests that it can be a double-edged sword (Milliken, Bartel, & Kurtzberg, this volume; Moreland et al., 1996). On the one hand, diversity can improve group performance because it increases the range of knowledge and skills available to the group and stimulates divergent thinking on the part of members. On the other hand, diversity can produce interpersonal conflicts and negative emotional reactions, which reduce members' motivation to work together and even their willingness to remain in the group (Amason & Schweiger, 1997; Jehn, 1997; O'Reilly, Williams, & Barsade, 1998). Paulus, Larey, and Dzindolet (2001) discussed the mixed effects of diversity in brainstorming groups, arguing that although diversity in members' knowledge can enhance a group's ability to generate creative ideas, it can also inhibit effective communication, decrease social interaction, and elicit a focus on shared rather than unshared knowledge.

Regarding the impact of diversity on newcomer innovation, several researchers have focused on how relational similarity between newcomers and oldtimers affects the process and outcome of socialization (Arrow, 1998; Jackson, Stone, & Alvarez, 1993). For example, Jackson et al. suggested that oldtimers are more attracted to similar than to dissimilar newcomers and more motivated to integrate similar newcomers into the group. For these reasons, oldtimers direct more deliberate communication to similar newcomers and consciously provide them with more evaluative information. These responses to newcomers may well enhance their ability to introduce innovation.

A major reason similar newcomers produce more innovation than do dissimilar newcomers is that they elicit more commitment from oldtimers (Levine & Moreland, 1985; Levine et al., 2001). But similarity is not a necessary condition for commitment, and in some cases, dissimilar newcomers elicit more commitment (and thereby exert more influence) than do similar newcomers. This occurs when newcomers' dissimilarity represents a form of superiority over oldtimers, for example, when newcomers possess unique skills or have access to scarce resources. Newcomer dissimilarity also may produce anxiety on the part of oldtimers, which may cause them to "bend over backwards" by evaluating newcomers positively and listening attentively to their suggestions (cf. Craig, 1996).

Team Size and Staffing Level

The relationship between team size and responsiveness to newcomer innovation is complex. On the one hand, larger teams may be more open than smaller teams to innovation because larger teams often have more diverse membership (and hence more experience dealing with new ideas) as well as more task-relevant resources that can be used to implement new ideas. On the other hand, larger teams have more directive leadership than do smaller teams (Mullen, Symons, Hu, & Salas, 1989), which, as suggested below, may discourage innovation. Larger teams also experience more conflict and have more difficulty reaching consensus than do smaller teams (Moreland & Levine, 1992a), which may reduce their likelihood of accepting and implementing innovations.

So, rather than focusing on the impact of team size, it may be more productive to consider the role of team staffing level, defined as the relationship between the number of people who belong to the team and the number of people needed to perform team tasks (Barker, 1968). An understaffed team has fewer members than it needs, an adequately staffed team has exactly as many members as it needs, and an overstaffed team has more members than it needs. Studies on the role of staffing level reveal that members of understaffed groups, compared to members of overstaffed groups, are more motivated to improve group performance and participate more actively in the group (e.g., Wicker, Kirmeyer, Hanson, & Alexander, 1976). More important for our purposes, group staffing level can influence newcomer innovation. Compared to adequately and overstaffed groups, understaffed groups are more eager to recruit and retain new members, which in turn makes them more receptive to newcomers' efforts to produce innovation (Cini, Moreland, & Levine, 1993; Petty & Wicker, 1974).

Team Development

Strangers with no history of group interaction typically behave differently than members of groups who have worked together for extended periods of time. Although the exact nature of the group development process is controversial (cf. Gersick, 1988; Moreland & Levine, 1988), there is widespread agreement that, over time, relationships among members stabilize and group structure and dynamics become more complex (e.g., Tuckman, 1965; Worchel, 1996). For these reasons, it is plausible to assume that newcomer innovations will be more readily accepted by teams in earlier rather than later stages of development (Moreland & Levine, 1988; but see Worchel, Grossman, & Coutant, 1994).

Team Cohesion and Climate

One consequence of team development is increased cohesion among members. Evidence indicates that members of cohesive teams are more likely to participate in and enjoy team activities, remain on the team and recruit others to join, and resist team disruptions than are members of noncohesive teams (Levine & Moreland, 1998). In addition, cohesion increases conformity to team norms (Festinger, Schachter, & Back, 1950) and punishment of those who deviate from these norms (Schachter, 1951). It would not be surprising, then, if members of cohesive teams tended to resist innovation efforts on the part of newcomers (cf. Brawley, Carron, & Widmeyer, 1988; Mills, 1957).

In addition to varying in cohesion, teams also vary in climate. According to West (1990), four aspects of climate influence work group innovation: the clarity of the team's objectives, the nature of the team's interpersonal processes, the team's level of commitment to excellence, and the team's norms regarding innovation. West argues that innovation is most likely in teams that have clear objectives, are nonjudgmental and supportive of individual suggestions, are committed to excellence, and have norms favoring innovation. The notion that climate plays an important role in work group innovation has received empirical support (Scott & Bruce, 1994), as has West's four-factor model of work group innovation (Anderson & West, 1998).

West's (1990) emphasis on the importance of norms is consistent with other work. Whereas some groups have norms discouraging dissent (Janis, 1982), others have norms permitting or even encouraging it (Coser, 1962). These norms affect the likelihood that people holding minority views will attempt to influence others and succeed in doing so (Moscovici & Lage, 1978). Moreover, group norms regarding innovation may affect how new members are socialized, with consequences for their later behavior. Jones (1986) argued that institutionalized socialization tactics (e.g., collective, formal procedures) produce custodianship, in which new members accept traditional role expectations. In contrast, individualized socialization tactics (e.g., individual, informal procedures) produce innovation, in which new members challenge traditional role expectations. Some support for these predictions has been obtained (e.g., Ashforth & Saks, 1996; Black & Ashford, 1995). Although little effort has been made to clarify why groups use particular socialization tactics, it may be that groups favoring custodianship adopt institutionalized tactics, whereas those favoring innovation adopt individualized tactics.

Team Leadership

Research on group problem solving has shown that leadership plays an important role in fostering creative solutions to problems. For example, Maier and Solem (1970) found that group solutions are improved if the leader protects minority views from social pressure and encourages the group to consider opposing perspectives. They found that disagreement in a group can serve as either a stimulus for innovation or a source of conflict, depending on the attitude of the leader.

Research on work group innovation also suggests that participative, or democratic, leadership has a positive impact on innovation (Nyström, 1979). Several mechanisms may underlie this relationship. First, creativity is often facilitated when individuals have high levels of discretion in how they perform their tasks (cf. Amabile, 1983). Second, individuals tend to be more committed to changes if they have participated in decisions regarding these changes (cf. West, 1990). Finally, democratic leaders stimulate a sense of empowerment among subordinates (Burpitt & Bigoness, 1997) and provide them with emotional support (West & Wallace, 1991), which are often critical for individuals to attempt innovation.

Extrapolating these findings to newcomer innovation, it is likely that newcomers will introduce more new ideas and will gain more acceptance for these ideas in groups with democratic as opposed to autocratic leaders. The importance of leaders in fostering/inhibiting newcomer innovation is consistent with work stimulated by Leader-Member Exchange Theory, which shows that leaders initiate more exchanges with highly competent than with less competent subordinates and establish close relationships with only a few key members of their groups (cf. Graen, 1976). There may be cases, however, in which democratic leadership reduces rather than increases the likelihood of newcomer innovation. For example, when it comes to implementing innovations, democratic leaders may be less effective than more controlling ones (cf. King & Anderson, 1995).

Team Performance

A final variable that can affect newcomer innovation is the team's performance level prior to the newcomer's entry. Just as a newcomer to an unsuccessful team may perceive that innovation is needed, so the team may believe that change is necessary. Such a belief should increase the team's receptivity to newcomer suggestions, compared to what might happen in a team with a history of success (Ziller & Behringer, 1960).

Team failure may not always increase the likelihood of newcomer innovation, however. Some unsuccessful teams are reluctant to change their existing work practices even though these practices are clearly maladaptive. As Gersick and Hackman (1990) argue, teams often react to failure by executing their existing routines with increased rather than decreased vigor. This presumably occurs because failure elicits increased commitment to current task strategies, perhaps because of cognitive dissonance. Such commitment, or entrapment, is particularly likely when teams have chosen (rather than been assigned) their initial strategy (Bazerman, Giuliano, & Appelman, 1984; Kameda & Sugimori, 1993). When entrapment occurs, newcomers may find it difficult, if not impossible, to produce innovation in failing teams.

The difficulty newcomers have producing innovation in failing teams may stem not only from team members' unwillingness to consider new ideas. Their inability to implement these ideas may also be important. Thus, even if a failing team finds a suggestion for change attractive, it may be unable to put this change into practice because of systemic problems (e.g., poor communication, lack of leadership, factional conflict) that contributed to its poor performance in the first place. It is also important to keep in mind that team members may attribute their performance to various causes, including effort, ability, and task strategy (cf. Hackman, 1990). It is plausible, then, that newcomer innovation will be more likely when members of failing teams attribute their performance to low effort or poor strategy (which are relatively easy to change) than to low ability (which is relatively difficult to change).

Conclusion

In this chapter, we emphasized the social nature of newcomer innovation in work teams, focusing on the reciprocal roles that newcomers and oldtimers play in producing innovation. Our analysis was based on the assumption that innovation cannot occur without implicit or explicit negotiation between newcomers, who suggest new ways of performing team tasks, and oldtimers, who accept these suggestions. We discussed a number of variables that are likely to influence this negotiation process, some associated with newcomers and others associated with the teams to which they belong.

With a few exceptions, we discussed newcomer and team variables separately, though they no doubt operate together in determining innovation. That is, team variables probably influence newcomer variables and vice versa. For example, team characteristics hypothesized to influence oldtimers' acceptance of newcomers' ideas may also influence newcomers' motivation to introduce change. In this context, we suggested that democratic team leadership may elicit more motivation to generate new ideas than does autocratic leadership. It is also likely that newcomers will be more motivated to suggest ideas when their team is understaffed (rather than adequately staffed or overstaffed), when it is in an early (rather than a late) stage of development, when it has a climate favoring (rather than inhibiting) innovation, and when it is performing poorly (rather than well). In all of these cases, newcomers are more likely to feel that their innovation efforts will produce positive consequences for themselves and/or the team as a whole.

In addition to cross-category influences, within-category influences are also likely. That is, newcomer variables probably influence one another, as do team variables. In the former case, for example, newcomers who are highly motivated to introduce change may work hard to acquire task-relevant skills, which in turn will increase their ability to generate ideas and convince oldtimers to accept these ideas. In the latter case, for example, the impact of team performance on receptivity to newcomers' suggestions may vary as a function of the team's level of development. Failing teams in early stages of development, which have a long time horizon, may be more motivated to improve their performance and hence more likely to accept newcomers' ideas for change than are failing teams in later stages of development, which have a short time horizon. Although space constraints preclude a detailed analysis of possible relationships between and among newcomer and team variables, these relationships clearly deserve systematic attention.

In discussing newcomer innovation, we have focused on the relations between newcomers and full members of their team who have attained all the rights and responsibilities of team membership (Moreland & Levine, 1982). Although full members are the primary targets of innovation efforts because they have more power and status than other team members, they are not the only targets. Newcomers sometimes seek to convince other categories of members to accept their ideas, with the hope that these people will provide assistance in convincing full members to accept the innovation. These presumptive allies include prospective members (who do not belong to the team but may do so in the future), other new members (who have recently joined the team), marginal members (who once had full member status but lost this status because of some transgression), and ex-members (who once belonged to the team but have left it). Thus, newcomers may form alliances with like-minded prospective members whom the group wants to recruit. In addition, newcomers may collaborate with other new members to ward off pressures to conform to team norms and to change these norms. Newcomers may also find allies among marginal members, who often have grievances against the team and are willing to fight for their views because they feel they have nothing to lose. Finally, newcomers may benefit from the support of ex-members who are motivated to change the team and have the resources or power to influence its activities. It is also worth noting that newcomers can sometimes make common cause with people outside the team (e.g., managers, clients) who have a vested interest in the team's success and are willing to pressure full members to accept newcomers' suggestions.

In closing, two caveats are in order. First, we are not arguing that team acceptance and implementation of newcomer suggestions necessarily improve team functioning. In some (perhaps many) cases, such receptivity has negative consequences, such as disrupting adaptive work patterns and creating conflict among team members, which could have been avoided by ignoring newcomers' ideas. Thus, a fundamental question for teams considering new ideas (proposed by newcomers or anyone else) is whether these ideas will improve team functioning, a question our analysis was not designed to answer. Second, we are not arguing that newcomers are the only, or even the best, source of innovation in work teams. Other methods for obtaining new ideas, such as observing teams performing similar tasks or reading descriptions of novel work practices, may be quite valuable. Thus, we are not recommending that teams constantly hire (and fire) workers to realize the benefits of newcomer-initiated innovation. Instead, we are arguing that teams should be sensitive to the potential contributions newcomers can make and should strive to develop a climate in which newcomers feel comfortable suggesting new ideas. We hope that our analysis of the social psychological processes underlying newcomer innovation provides a plausible foundation for this argument.

Note

Thanks are extended to Leslie Hausmann, Bernard Nijstad, and Paul Paulus for helpful comments on an earlier draft. Preparation of the chapter was supported by Army Research Institute Contract DASW01-00-K-0018. The views, opinions, and/or findings contained in this paper are those of the authors and should not be construed as an official Department of the Army position, policy, or decision. Correspondence should be addressed to John Levine, 516 LRDC Bldg., University of Pittsburgh, Pittsburgh, PA 15260. Email: jml@pitt.edu. FAX: 412-624-9149.

References

Agrell, A., & Gustafson, R. (1996). Innovation and creativity in work groups. In M. A. West (Ed.), *Handbook of work group psychology* (pp. 317–343). Chichester, UK: Wiley.

Amabile, T. M. (1983). *The social psychology of creativity*. New York: Springer-Verlag.

Amason, A. C., & Schweiger, D. M. (1997). The effects of conflict on strategic decision making. In C. K. W. De Dreu & E. Van de Vliert (Eds.), *Using conflict in organizations* (pp. 101–115). London: Sage.

Anderson, N. R., & West, M. A. (1998). Measuring climate for work group innovation: Development and validation of the team climate inventory. *Journal of Organizational Behavior, 19*, 235–258.

Argote, L. (1993). Group and organizational learning curves: Individual, system, and environmental components. *British Journal of Social Psychology, 32*, 31–51.

Argote, L. (1999). *Organizational learning: Creating, retaining, and transferring knowledge*. Norwell, MA: Kluwer.

Arrow, H. (1998). Standing out and fitting in: Composition effects on newcomer socialization. In M. A. Neale, E. Mannix, & D. H. Gruenfeld (Eds.), *Research on managing groups and teams* (Vol. 1, pp. 59–80). Greenwich, CT: JAI Press.

Arrow, H., & McGrath, J. E. (1995). Membership dynamics in groups at work: A theoretical framework. In B. M. Staw & L. L. Cummings (Eds.), *Research in organizational behavior* (Vol. 17, pp. 373–411). Greenwich, CT: JAI Press.

Ashford, S. J., & Black, J. S. (1996). Proactivity during organizational entry: The role of desire for control. *Journal of Applied Psychology, 81*, 199–214.

Ashforth, B. E., & Saks, A. M. (1996). Work-role transitions: A longitudinal examination of the Nicholson model. *Journal of Occupational and Organizational Psychology, 68*, 157–175.

Bandura, A. (1986). *Social foundations of thought and action*. Englewood Cliffs, NJ: Prentice-Hall.

Bandura, A. (1995). Exercise of personal and collective efficacy in changing societies. In A. Bandura (Ed.), *Self-efficacy in changing societies* (pp. 1–45). New York: Cambridge University Press.

Barker, R. G. (1968). *Ecological psychology*. Stanford, CA: Stanford University Press.

Barron, F., & Harrington, D. M. (1981). Creativity, intelligence and personality. *Annual Review of Psychology, 32*, 439–476.

Bauer, T. N., Morrison, E. W., & Callister, R. R. (1998). Organizational socialization: A review and directions for future research. In G. R. Ferris (Ed.), *Research in personnel and human resources management* (Vol. 16, pp. 149–214). Greenwich, CT: JAI Press.

Bazerman, M. H., Giuliano, T., & Appelman, A. (1984). Escalation of commitment in individual and group decision making. *Organizational Behavior and Human Decision Processes, 33*, 141–152.

Becker, H. S. (1964). Personal changes in adult life. *Sociometry, 27,* 40–53.

Black, J. S., & Ashford, S. J. (1995). Fitting in or making jobs fit: Factors affecting mode of adjustment for new hires. *Human Relations, 48,* 421–437.

Brawley, L. R., Carron, A. V., & Widmeyer, W. N. (1988). Exploring the relationship between cohesion and group resistance to disruption. *Journal of Sport and Exercise Psychology, 10,* 199–213.

Bray, R. M., Johnson, D., & Chilstrom, J. T. (1982). Social influence by group members with minority opinions: A comparison of Hollander and Moscovici. *Journal of Personality and Social Psychology, 43,* 78–88.

Burpitt, W. J., & Bigoness, W. J. (1997). Leadership and innovation among teams: The impact of empowerment. *Small Group Research, 28,* 414–423.

Cini, M., Moreland, R. L., & Levine, J. M. (1993). Group staffing levels and responses to prospective and new members. *Journal of Personality and Social Psychology, 65,* 723–734.

Coser, L. A. (1962). Some functions of deviant behavior and normative flexibility. *American Journal of Sociology, 68,* 172–181.

Craig, K. M. (1996). Are all newcomers judged similarly? Distinctiveness and time of entry in task-oriented groups. *Small Group Research, 27,* 383–397.

De Dreu, C. K. W., & De Vries, N. K. (Eds.). (2001). *Group consensus and minority influence: Implications for innovation.* Oxford: Blackwell.

Devadas, R., & Argote, L. (1995, May). *Collective learning and forgetting: The effects of turnover and group structure.* Paper presented at the meeting of the Midwestern Psychological Association, Chicago.

Driskell, J. E., & Mullen, B. (1990). Status, expectations, and behavior: A meta-analytic review and test of the theory. *Personality and Social Psychology Bulletin, 16,* 541–553.

Edmondson, A. (1999). Psychological safety and learning behavior in work teams. *Administrative Science Quarterly, 44,* 350–383.

Farr, J. L., & Ford, C. M. (1990). Individual innovation. In M. A. West & J. L. Farr (Eds.), *Innovation and creativity at work* (pp. 63–80). New York: Wiley.

Feij, J. A., Whitely, W. T., Peiro, J. M., & Taris, T. W. (1995). The development of career-enhancing strategies and content innovation: A longitudinal study of new workers. *Journal of Vocational Behavior, 46,* 231–256.

Festinger, L., Schachter, S., & Back, K. (1950). *Social pressures in informal groups.* New York: Harper.

Gersick, C. J. (1988). Time and transition in work teams: Toward a new model of group development. *Academy of Management Journal, 31,* 9–41.

Gersick, C. J., & Hackman, J. R. (1990). Habitual routines in task-performing groups. *Organizational Behavior and Human Decision Processes, 47,* 65–97.

Graen, G. (1976). Role making processes within complex organizations. In M. D. Dunnette (Ed.), *Handbook of industrial and organizational psychology* (pp. 1201–1245). Chicago: Rand McNally.

Gruenfeld, D., & Fan, E. T. (1999). What newcomers see and what oldtimers say: Discontinuities in knowledge exchange. In L. L. Thompson, J. M. Levine, & D. M. Messick (Eds.), *Shared cognition in organizations* (pp. 245–266). Mahwah, NJ: Erlbaum.

Gruenfeld, D. H., Martorana, P. V., & Fan, E. T. (2000). What do groups learn from their worldliest members? Direct and indirect influence in dynamic teams. *Organizational Behavior and Human Decision Processes, 82,* 45–59.

Hackman, J. R. (Ed.). (1990). *Groups that work (and those that don't)*. San Francisco: Jossey-Bass.

Hackman, J. R. (1998). Why teams don't work. In R. S. Tindale, L. Heath, J. Edwards, E. J. Posavac, F. B. Bryant, Y. Suarez-Balcazar, E. Henderson-King, & J. Myers (Eds.), *Theory and research on small groups* (pp. 245–267). New York: Plenum.

Heiss, J., & Nash, D. (1967). The stranger in laboratory culture revisited. *Human Organization, 26*, 47–51.

Hollander, E. P. (1960). Competence and conformity in the acceptance of influence. *Journal of Abnormal and Social Psychology, 61*, 365–359.

Hollenbeck, J. R., Ilgen, D. R., Sego, D. J., Hedlund, J., Major, D. A., & Phillips, J. (1995). Multilevel theory of team decision making: Decision performance in teams incorporating distributed expertise. *Journal of Applied Psychology, 80*, 292–316.

Homans, G. C. (1974). *Social behavior: Its elementary forms*. New York: Harcourt.

Hoyt, P. D. (1997). The political manipulation of group composition: Engineering the decision context. *Political Psychology, 18*, 771–790.

Jackson, S. E., Stone, V. K., & Alvarez, E. B. (1993). Socialization amidst diversity: Impact of demographics on work team oldtimers and newcomers. In L. L. Cummings & B. M. Staw (Eds.), *Research in organizational behavior* (Vol. 15, pp. 45–109). Greenwich, CT: JAI Press.

Janis, I. L. (1982). *Groupthink* (2nd ed.). Boston: Houghton Mifflin.

Jehn, K. (1997). Affective and cognitive conflict in work groups: Increasing performance through value-based intragroup conflict. In C. K. W. De Dreu & E. Van de Vliert (Eds.), *Using conflict in organizations* (pp. 87–100). London: Sage.

Jones, G. (1986). Socialization tactics, self-efficacy, and newcomers' adjustments to organizations. *Academy of Management Journal, 29*, 262–279.

Kameda, T., & Sugimori, S. (1993). Psychological entrapment in group decision making: An assigned decision rule and a groupthink phenomenon. *Journal of Personality and Social Psychology, 65*, 282–292.

Kanter, R. M. (1977). Some effects of proportions on group life: Skewed sex ratios and responses to token woman. *American Journal of Sociology, 82*, 465–490.

King, N., & Anderson, N. (1990). Innovation in working groups. In M. A. West & J. L. Farr (Eds.), *Innovation and creativity at work: Psychological and organizational strategies* (pp. 81–100). Chichester, UK: Wiley.

King, N. & Anderson, N. (1995). *Innovation and change in organizations*. London: Routledge.

Kirton, M. J. (1976). Adaptors and innovators: A description and measure. *Journal of Applied Psychology, 61*, 622–629.

Latané, B., & Wolf, S. (1981). The social impact of majorities and minorities. *Psychological Review, 88*, 438–453.

Levine, J. M., & Kaarbo, J. (2001). Minority influence in political decision-making groups. In C. K. W. De Dreu & N. K. De Vries (Eds.), *Group consensus and minority influence: Implications for innovation* (pp. 229–257). Oxford: Blackwell.

Levine, J. M., & Moreland, R. L. (1985). Innovation and socialization in small groups. In S. Moscovici, G. Mugny, & E. Van Avermaet (Eds.), *Perspectives on minority influence* (pp. 143–169). Cambridge, UK: Cambridge University Press.

Levine, J. M., & Moreland, R. L. (1991). Culture and socialization in work groups. In L. B. Resnick, J. M. Levine, & S. D. Teasley (Eds.), *Perspectives on socially shared cognition* (pp. 257–279). Washington, DC: American Psychological Association.

Levine, J. M., & Moreland, R. L. (1994). Group socialization: Theory and research. In W. Stroebe & M. Hewstone (Eds.), *European review of social psychology* (Vol. 5, pp. 305–336). Chichester, UK: Wiley.

Levine, J. M., & Moreland, R. L. (1998). Small groups. In D. T. Gilbert, S. T. Fiske, & G. Lindzey (Eds.), *The handbook of social psychology* (4th ed., pp. 415–469). Boston: McGraw-Hill.

Levine, J. M., & Moreland, R. L. (1999). Knowledge transmission in work groups: Helping newcomers to succeed. In L. L. Thompson, J. M. Levine, & D. M. Messick (Eds.), *Shared cognition in organizations: The management of knowledge* (pp. 267–296). Mahwah, NJ: Erlbaum.

Levine, J. M., Moreland, R. L., & Choi, H. S. (2001). Group socialization and newcomer innovation. In M. A. Hogg & R. S. Tindale (Eds.), *Blackwell handbook of social psychology: Group processes* (pp. 86–106). Oxford: Blackwell.

Levine, J. M., Moreland, R. L., & Ryan, C. S. (1998). Group socialization and intergroup relations. In C. Sedikides, J. Schopler, & C. A. Insko (Eds.), *Intergroup cognition and intergroup behavior* (pp. 283–308). Mahwah, NJ: Erlbaum.

Levine, J. M., Sroka, K. R., & Snyder, H. N. (1977). Group support and reaction to stable and shifting agreement/disagreement. *Sociometry, 40,* 214–224.

Levine, J. M., & Thompson, L. (1996). Conflict in groups. In E. T. Higgins & A. W. Kruglanski (Eds.), *Social psychology: Handbook of basic principles* (pp. 745–776). New York: Guilford.

Louis, M. R. (1980). Surprise and sense making: What newcomers experience in entering unfamiliar organizational settings. *Administrative Science Quarterly, 25,* 226–251.

Maass, A., West, S. G., & Cialdini, R. B. (1987). Minority influence and conversion. In C. Hendrick (Ed.), *Review of personality and social psychology* (Vol. 8, pp. 55–79). Newbury Park, CA: Sage.

Maier, N. R. F., & Solem, A. R. (1970). The contribution of a discussion leader to the quality of group thinking: The effective use of minority opinions. *Human Relations, 5,* 277–288.

Milanovich, D. M., Driskell, J. E., Stout, R. J., & Salas, E. (1998). Status and cockpit dynamics: A review and empirical study. *Group Dynamics: Theory, Research, and Practice, 2,* 155–167.

Miller, C. E. (1989). The social psychological effects of group decision rules. In P. B. Paulus (Ed.), *Psychology of group influence* (2nd ed., pp. 327–355). Hillsdale, NJ: Erlbaum.

Mills, T. (1957). *Group structure and the newcomer.* Oslo: Oslo University Press.

Moreland, R. L. (1999). Transactive memory: Learning who knows what in work groups and organizations. In L. L. Thompson, J. M. Levine, & D. M. Messick (Eds.), *Shared cognition in organizations: The management of knowledge* (pp. 3–31). Mahwah, NJ: Erlbaum.

Moreland, R. L., & Levine, J. M. (1982). Socialization in small groups: Temporal changes in individual-group relations. In L. Berkowitz (Ed.), *Advances in experimental social psychology* (Vol. 15, pp. 137–192). New York: Academic Press.

Moreland, R. L., & Levine, J. M. (1988). Group dynamics over time: Development and socialization in small groups. In J. E. McGrath (Ed.), *The social psychology of time: New perspectives* (pp. 151–181). Newbury Park, CA: Sage.

Moreland, R. L., & Levine, J. M. (1989). Newcomers and oldtimers in small groups. In P. Paulus (Ed.), *Psychology of group influence* (2nd ed., pp. 143–186). Hillsdale, NJ: Erlbaum.

Moreland, R. L., & Levine, J. M. (1992a). The composition of small groups. In E. J. Lawler, B. Markovsky, C. Ridgeway, & H. A. Walker (Eds.), *Advances in group processes* (Vol. 9, pp. 237–280). Greenwich, CT: JAI Press.

Moreland, R. L., & Levine, J. M. (1992b). Problem identification by groups. In S. Worchel, W. Wood, & J. A. Simpson (Eds.), *Group process and productivity* (pp. 17–47). Newbury Park, CA: Sage.

Moreland, R. L., Levine, J. M., & Wingert, M. L. (1996). Creating the ideal group: Composition effects at work. In E. H. Witte & J. H. Davis (Eds.), *Understanding group behavior: Small group processes and interpersonal relations* (Vol. 2, pp. 11–35). Mahwah, NJ: Erlbaum.

Morrison, E. W. (1993). Newcomer information seeking: Exploring types, modes, sources, and outcomes. *Academy of Management Journal, 36*, 557–589.

Moscovici, S. (1985). Social influence and conformity. In G. Lindzey & E. Aronson (Eds.), *Handbook of social psychology* (3rd ed., pp. 347–412). Reading, MA: Addison-Wesley.

Moscovici, S., & Lage, E. (1978). Studies in social influence IV: Minority influence in a context of original judgments. *European Journal of Social Psychology, 8*, 349–365.

Moscovici, S., Mucchi-Faina, A., & Maass, A. (Eds.). (1994). *Minority influence.* Chicago: Nelson-Hall.

Mudd, S. (1996). Kirton's A-I theory: Evidence bearing on the style/level and factor composition issues. *British Journal of Psychology, 87*, 241–254.

Mugny, G. (1982). *The power of minorities.* New York: Academic Press.

Mullen, B., Brown, R., & Smith, C. (1992). Ingroup bias as a function of salience, relevance, and status: An integration. *European Journal of Social Psychology, 22*, 103–122.

Mullen, B., Symons, C., Hu, L., & Salas, E. (1989). Group size, leadership behavior, and subordinate satisfaction. *Journal of General Psychology, 116*, 155–170.

Naylor, J. C., & Briggs, G. E. (1965). Team-training effectiveness under various conditions. *Journal of Applied Psychology, 49*, 223–229.

Neale, M. A., Mannix, E., & Gruenfeld, D. H. (Eds.). (1998). *Research on managing groups and teams* (Vol. 1). Greenwich, CT: JAI Press.

Nemeth, C. J. (1995). Dissent as driving cognition, attitudes, and judgments. *Social Cognition, 13*, 273–291.

Nemeth, C. J., Wachtler, J., & Endicott, J. (1977). Increasing the size of the minority: Some gains and some losses. *European Journal of Social Psychology, 7*, 15–27.

Nyström, H. (1979). *Creativity and innovation.* New York: Wiley.

O'Reilly, C. A., Williams, K. Y., & Barsade, S. (1998). Group demography and innovation: Does diversity help? In M. A. Neale, E. Mannix, & D. H. Gruenfeld (Eds.), *Research on managing groups and teams* (Vol. 1, pp. 183–207). Greenwich, CT: JAI Press.

Paulus, P. B., Larey, T. S., & Dzindolet, M. T. (2001). Creativity in groups and teams. In M. Turner (Ed.), *Groups at work: Theory and research* (pp. 319–338). Mahwah, NJ: Erlbaum.

Perez, J. A., & Mugny, G. (1996). The conflict elaboration theory of social influence. In E. H. Witte & J. H. Davis (Eds.), *Understanding group behavior: Small group processes and interpersonal relations* (Vol. 2, pp. 191–210). Mahwah, NJ: Erlbaum.

Petty, R. M., & Wicker, A. W. (1974). Degree of manning and degree of success of a group as determinants of members' subjective experiences and their accep-

tance of a new group member. *Catalog of Selected Documents in Psychology, 4,*
1–22.

Ridgeway, C. L. (1982). Status in groups: The importance of motivation. *American Sociological Review, 47,* 76–88.

Runco, M. A., & Okuda, S. M. (1988). Problem-discovery, divergent thinking, and the creative process. *Journal of Youth and Adolescence, 17,* 211–220.

Saenz, D. S. (1994). Token status and problem-solving deficits: Detrimental effects of distinctiveness and performance monitoring. *Social Cognition, 12,* 61–74.

Saks, A. M., & Ashforth, B. E. (1996). Proactive socialization and behavioral self-management. *Journal of Vocational Behavior, 48,* 301–323.

Saks, A. M., & Ashforth, B. E. (1997). Organizational socialization: Making sense of the past and present as a prologue for the future. *Journal of Vocational Behavior, 51,* 234–279.

Schachter, S. (1951). Deviation, rejection, and communication. *Journal of Abnormal and Social Psychology, 46,* 190–207.

Schuetz, A. (1944). The stranger: An essay in social psychology. *American Journal of Sociology, 49,* 499–507.

Scott, S. G., & Bruce, R. A. (1994). Determinants of innovative behaviors: A path model of individual innovation in the workplace. *Academy of Management Journal, 37,* 580–607.

Stasser, G. (1999). The uncertain role of unshared information in collective choice. In L. L. Thompson, J. M., Levine, & D. M. Messick (Eds.), *Shared cognition in organizations: The management of knowledge* (pp. 49–69). Mahwah, NJ: Erlbaum.

Stasser, G., Kerr, N. L., & Davis, J. H. (1989). Influence processes and consensus models in decision-making groups. In P. B. Paulus (Ed.), *Psychology of group influence* (2nd ed., pp. 279–326). Hillsdale, NJ: Erlbaum.

Steiner, I. D. (1972). *Group process and productivity.* New York: Academic Press.

Suchner, R. W., & Jackson, D. (1976). Responsibility and status: A causal or only a spurious relationship? *Sociometry, 39,* 243–256.

Sundstrom, E. D. (1999). *Supporting work team effectiveness: Best management practices for fostering high performance.* San Francisco: Jossey-Bass.

Tanford, S., & Penrod, S. (1984). Social influence model: A formal integration of research on majority and minority influence processes. *Psychological Bulletin, 95,* 189–225.

Torrance, E. P. (1955). Some consequences of power differences on decision making in permanent and temporary three-man groups. In A. P. Hare, E. F. Borgatta, & R. F. Bales (Eds.), *Small groups* (pp. 482–492). New York: Knopf.

Trow, D. B. (1960). Membership succession and team performance. *Human Relations, 13,* 259–269.

Tuckman, B. W. (1965). Developmental sequence in small groups. *Psychological Bulletin, 63,* 384–399.

Van Maanen, J. (1984). Doing new things in old ways: The chains of socialization. In J. L. Bess (Ed.), *College and university organizations* (pp. 211–246). New York: New York University Press.

Wahrman, R. (1970). Status, deviance, and sanctions. *Pacific Sociological Review, 13,* 229–240.

West, M. A. (1990). The social psychology of innovation in groups. In M. A. West & J. L. Farr (Eds.), *Innovation and creativity at work: Psychological and organizational strategies* (pp. 309–333). Chichester, UK: Wiley.

West, M. A., & Farr, J. L. (1990). Innovation at work. In M. A. West & J. L. Farr (Eds.), *Innovation and creativity at work: Psychological and organizational strategies* (pp. 3–13). Chichester, UK: Wiley.

West, M. A., & Wallace, M. (1991). Innovation in health care teams. *European Journal of Social Psychology, 21,* 303–315.

Wicker, A. W., Kirmeyer, S. L., Hanson, L., & Alexander, D. (1976). Effects of manning levels on subjective experiences, performance, and verbal interaction in groups. *Organizational Behavior and Human Performance, 17,* 251–274.

Wiggins, J. A., Dill, F., & Schwartz, R. D. (1965). On "status-liability." *Sociometry, 28,* 197–209.

Williams, K. Y., & O'Reilly, C. (1998). Demography and diversity in organizations: A review of 40 years of research. In B. Staw & R. Sutton (Eds.), *Research in organizational behavior* (Vol. 20, pp. 77–140). Greenwich, CT: JAI Press.

Wood, W., Lundgren, S., Ouellette, J. A., Busceme, S., & Blackstone, T. (1994). Processes of minority influence: Influence effectiveness and source perception. *Psychological Bulletin, 115,* 323–345.

Worchel, S. (1996). Emphasizing the social nature of groups in a developmental framework. In J. L. Nye & A. M. Brower (Eds.), *What's social about social cognition? Research on socially shared cognition in small groups* (pp. 261–282). Thousand Oaks, CA: Sage.

Worchel, S., Grossman, M., & Coutant, D. (1994). Minority influence in the group context: How group factors affect when the minority will be influential. In S. Moscovici, A. Mucchi-Faina, & A. Maass (Eds.), *Minority influence* (pp. 97–114). Chicago: Nelson-Hall.

Zander, A., & Cohen, A. R. (1955). Attributed social power and group acceptance: A classroom experimental demonstration. *Journal of Abnormal and Social Psychology, 51,* 490–492.

Zdaniuk, B., & Levine, J. M. (1996). Anticipated interaction and thought generation: The role of faction size. *British Journal of Social Psychology, 35,* 201–218.

Ziller, R. C. (1965). Toward a theory of open and closed groups. *Psychological Bulletin, 64,* 164–182.

Ziller, R. C., & Behringer, R. D. (1960). Assimilation of the knowledgeable newcomer under conditions of group success and failure. *Journal of Abnormal and Social Psychology, 60,* 288–292.

Ziller, R. C., Behringer, R. D., & Goodchilds, J. D. (1960). The minority newcomer in open and closed groups. *Journal of Psychology, 50,* 75–84.

Ziller, R. C., Behringer, R. D., & Jansen, M. J. (1961). The newcomer in open and closed groups. *Journal of Applied Psychology, 45,* 55–58.

11

████ *Charles Hooker, Jeanne Nakamura, and Mihaly Csikszentmihalyi*

The Group as Mentor
Social Capital and the Systems
Model of Creativity

████

In recent years, several significant studies of creativity have highlighted the importance of apprenticeship experiences in shaping the potential of young scientists, artists, thinkers, performers, and entrepreneurs. Walberg, Rasher, and Parkerson (1980) found that at least two-thirds of their sample of eminent personalities had been exposed to people of distinction in their field during early life experiences. Simonton (1984, 1988) showed that role models, whether impersonal paragons or personal mentors, played an irreplaceable role in the lives of most creative individuals. Feldman (1999) echoed the same point, and Gardner (1993), after reviewing the lives of Freud, Picasso, Einstein, Stravinsky, T. S. Eliot, Martha Graham, and Gandhi, found it inconceivable to envision any mature expert or creator devoid of competent mentoring.

Csikszentmihalyi's (1996) interviews with over 90 creative individuals in later life confirmed once again the crucial importance of master-apprentice relationships in fashioning careers of significant contribution and productivity. At the same time, however, some of the themes from these interviews raised questions that had been previously unaddressed: What are the practices of good mentors? How are knowledge and skills effectively transmitted from one generation to the next? How are guiding values attached to the instrumental knowledge bequeathed by mentors?

A particularly salient example from the creativity in later life sample (Csikszentmihalyi, 1996) will help illustrate the genesis of our present research. As part of the 1996 study, we interviewed three physicists about 80 years of age who had worked with Niels Bohr at some point in their career. Each of them had won some of the most prestigious awards in their field, short of the Nobel prize, and all three mentioned Bohr as a seminal influence in the development of their respective vocations—a mentor from whom they learned important insights about physics as well as how to lead a good life. During their interviews, all three emphasized Bohr's importance in terms of the broad discussions they had with him about important life issues (both concerning and beyond the scope of physics). They recounted times they shared with him eating meals, taking walks, and doing other everyday life activities, and they reflected on the general way he cared about them as persons as much as scientists. For each of them, Bohr had a "special way of teaching" that incorporated a holistic purview and a caring touch and that served to model not only scientific excellence but also civic integrity and humane responsibility. One of Bohr's students explained, "I lived as a member of his family . . . he had a great feel for people, their careers, and their problems." Another said, "He was always living with or among us . . . although he was much better than us, he was accessible. . . . He was interested to talk to us not only about physics, but also about philosophy, politics, and art. We went together to the movies." A third added, "As he walked around the table in his office talking about some of the great questions, you would have the feeling that you could understand how people such as Buddha or Confucius really existed. . . . He took his role as citizen and scientist very seriously . . . he had a great feeling of responsibility and citizenship."

From this example and others like it in the sample, we became intrigued with the notion that mentors such as Bohr, who embody such estimable ways of being in addition to excellence in their field, have an especially profound and lasting effect on their students, both as professionals and as people. From what we know of wider society, however, such mentoring unfortunately appears to be quite rare. The brilliance of teachers and mentors such as Bohr is not well understood and thus probably rarely practiced. Thus, we took the questions of good mentoring and the transmission of knowledge, skills, and values as our research agenda.

Surprisingly, many of our findings point to group dynamics and social networks as integral components of optimal mentoring practices. In this chapter, we first frame our research in the context of past research on mentoring. We then introduce the systems model of creativity and the concepts of social and cultural capital as helpful theoretical frameworks and vocabulary for our analysis of mentoring to follow. Next, we briefly recount our method and sample and provide a case study from our recent research illustrating, among other things, the importance of group dynamics in mentoring. We then further discuss group dynamics in mentoring and give broader perspective to the interaction we have observed between social capital and the systems model of creativity. Finally, we offer suggestions for extending our conventional conceptions of optimal mentoring.

Conceptions of Mentoring

Historically, social scientists have painted a picture of mentoring that looks very much like the image of Niels Bohr depicted by his intellectual offspring. Levinson (1978), for instance, described a mentor as someone who serves as advisor, sponsor, host, exemplar, and guide for a young person moving from dependence and naïveté into independence and sophistication in terms of vocational identity. The mentor's role, according to Levinson, is to welcome the initiate into a new work-related world; to acquaint him or her with its values, customs, resources, and key players; to provide a model that the protégé can admire and seek to emulate; and to offer counsel and moral support in times of stress. Most important, the "true mentor" will support and facilitate the realization of a dream of the young person, bestowing responsibility and trust on the burgeoning young novice.

Levinson (1978) also noted the complexity and variation inherent in mentoring relationships in general. They are not, as he said, "simple or an all-or-none matter" (p. 100). Rather, they may be only partially beneficial to a young person or seriously flawed and destructive, depending on the motives, capabilities, and disposition of the mentor (and of the apprentice). It is also possible for a mentoring relationship to be very limited and yet highly valuable to a young person's development. For example, some people have purely symbolic mentors whom they have never met, such as an inspiring figure from the past, but who nonetheless may have taught them a great deal about the nature and standards of a domain of interest. In all, theorists such as Levinson, Erikson (1959), and Vaillant (1977) have asserted that "good enough" mentoring relationships provide young people with sustained feelings of support, admiration, respect, appreciation, and gratitude that outweigh, but may not completely prevent, the opposite feelings of resentment, inferiority, and intimidation.

In addition to identifying mentors as basic sources of support and nurturance, the literature in both psychology and sociology has advanced the idea that a young person's prospects can be dramatically increased by apprenticing under a highly successful practitioner from a preceding generation, especially in the field of science (Crane, 1965; Kanigel, 1986; Simonton, 1988; Zuckerman, 1977). Zuckerman's study of Nobelists in science revealed this trend perhaps most interestingly. She found that apprentices who became successful scientists themselves reported scientific knowledge as the least important advantage bestowed on them by the laureates who trained them. Far more significant were other influences, such as professional connections and exemplary work standards. As students of the elite, Zuckerman's participants reported unparalleled access to resources (both physical and human), high visibility within their field, and the development of a self-image as one to whom the mantle of excellence and distinction was being passed. Because of these contributions, apprentices said they were able to develop exceptionally high levels of self-confidence. Concordantly, students attributed to the master scientists' example their own high standards of work, along with their ability to intuit important and feasible research problems and elegant solutions—forms of tacit knowledge crucial to creative scientific work and best learned through apprenticeship.

Thus, over the years, social science has documented the many positive (and negative) outcomes of apprenticeship. In so doing, it has also constructed, both implicitly and overtly, an ideal image of the mentor-apprentice relationship, which looks a great deal like the supportive, nurturing connection described by Bohr's students. It has also been shown, at least in the sciences, that training under eminence leads to eminence. Thus, the established ideal proffers elite practitioners supporting promising young novices with emotional, financial, and physical resources in addition to intangible assets such as high visibility, increased self-confidence, and domain-specific intuition. Although this is a helpful map to the process of mentoring and apprenticeship, it is nevertheless incomplete. What is left to be identified and articulated are the specific mechanisms involved in training those who become the best in their given field. We begin this process by examining the training structures and practices used by a highly successful lab in space science. We will see that there are other mechanisms that contribute to the overall effectiveness of training and mentorship. One such mechanism, which is explored in depth, is the role of a group of peers and colleagues in the apprenticeship process. However, before entering that discussion, it will be helpful to first introduce the systems model of creativity to provide a more precise vocabulary and a way of locating our investigation within the broader scope of research on creativity.

The Systems Model of Creativity

In contradistinction to other approaches to understanding creativity, Csikszentmihalyi (1988) introduced the systems model of creativity as an attempt to more fully acknowledge and explain the interaction between the individual and social and cultural factors involved in the creative process. Extended by Feldman, Csikszentmihalyi, and Gardner (1994; Csikszentmihalyi, 1996, 1999), the systems perspective (see Figure 11.1) views creativity not as the product of an isolated individual's aptitude or quirkiness, but as an interaction occurring among a talented individual, a domain of knowledge or practice, and a field of experts. Csikszentmihalyi (1988, 1996, 1999; Nakamura & Csikszentmihalyi, 2002) and Feldman et al. have fully articulated and defined the components of this model. Put briefly, the model begins with an individual who is dissatisfied with the existing state of affairs and wants to change a domain. To accomplish something creative, however, the newcomer must first apprehend an existing body of knowledge, develop a set of skills and abilities, and internalize key standards of quality, values, and beliefs. Having sufficiently mastered the rules, symbols, skills, values, and practices of a domain, the individual may then transform its content in a meaningful way (e.g., by developing a new process, proposing a

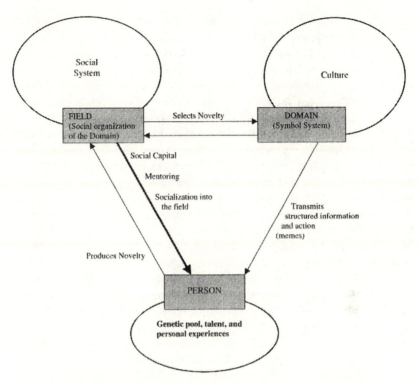

Figure 11.1. *The Systems Model of Creativity. For creativity to occur, a set of rules and practices must be transmitted from the domain to the individual. The individual must then produce a novel variation in the content of the domain. The new variation must then be selected by a field of experts for inclusion in the domain. In this chapter, we focus on the relationship between the field and the individual who aspires to add creatively to the domain. It is here that social capital is generated through mentoring and peer relationships.*

new theory, finding, or tool), which may then be labeled *creative* only if the associated field of experts deem it so. Gardner (1993) has pointed out that, averaged across domains, this process of acquisition, internalization, and incubation (preceding an initial creative contribution to a domain) generally takes a person about 10 years.

Let us briefly unpack this process and provide a brief example. The first step for an aspiring creator rests in adequately mastering what the systems model refers to as the *domain*: some already existing set of objects, rules, representations, or notations. It is simply the content the individual intends to work with or alter. The domain must be included as a component of the creative process because creativity does not exist in a vacuum (Csikszentmihalyi, 1999). It is impossible to introduce something "new" without reference to that which has preceded it: the "old," the already existing patterns or representations of knowledge.

Simply introducing novelty does not, of course, constitute an act of creativity. Many new ideas are generated every day and are quickly forgotten or ignored. To be creative, a variation must somehow be endorsed by the *field*: a group of experts entitled through their own accomplishments or position to decide what should or should not be included in the domain. The field is the social organization of the domain. It consists of gatekeepers—teachers, critics, editors, museum curators, agency directors, and foundation officers—whose role is to decide what should and should not be added to the existing set of knowledge and passed on to subsequent generations.

Let's take a brief example from the visual arts. An aspiring artist must first come to know the relevant domain. She must learn as much as possible about past works of art, historical movements, ideas, and leading figures in sculpture, painting, and drawing. She must develop abilities to expressively manipulate some medium—paint, pencil, paper, stone, metal, or clay. Perhaps most important, she must sufficiently internalize the standards and values of the field by paying attention to the things expressed by the teachers, experts, peers, and critics surrounding her, who ultimately will decide the merits of her work. In some cases, the field may not immediately open itself to a creator's ideas for change. In such cases, the successfully creative person must, for a time, create an entirely new field. This is what the Impressionist painters had to do in Paris in the late 19th century; when the field of academic art spurned their works, the Impressionists enlisted peers, collectors, critics, and galleries to generate enough energy to bring their cause to center stage. Having suitably mastered enough of the knowledge, symbols, and skills of the domain and having internalized the values and practices of the field, the budding artist may contribute to the content of the domain by developing new forms of representation or new techniques, by coming up with a new style, or perhaps by shifting aesthetic criteria in some meaningful way that is accepted and promulgated by the field.

Creativity involves social judgment. The systems model, therefore, seeks to move the concept of creativity from the plane of purely individual (subjective) recognition to a social (intersubjective) arena, wherein the full complexity of creativity can be recognized. Furthermore, it locates creativity within the larger process of cultural evolution, that is, creativity as analogous to the biological process of evolution. Evolution occurs when an individual organism produces a variation that is selected by the environment and transmitted to subsequent generations. So too, in cultural evolution, individuals create variation that is selected by the environment and passed on to future generations. What the systems model calls the field corresponds to the environment; the domain is analogous to the evolutionary genome. As such, creativity is the engine that drives cultural evolution.

Dawkins (1976) introduced the term "meme" to denote the building blocks of culture. Analogous to the role of genes in biological evolution, memes also carry instructions for action (e.g., the laws of physics, the principles of an artistic style, the recipe for baking a cake). However simple or complex, memes make up culture and provide blueprints for individuals, groups, and societal action. Memes make up domains. Domains in turn are subsets of culture.

Whereas genetic instructions are transmitted in sequences of nucleic acids, the instructions contained in memes are conveyed through learning. In this chapter, we are concerned with the process by which aspiring creators are taught the knowledge and skills of a domain and are socialized into the values and standards of the field. In other words, we are concerned with the transmission of memes. It is mainly in this capacity that the mentor-apprentice relationship impacts the development of a nascent individual creator; from our perspective this may be the crucial point at which guiding values and practices are instilled in individuals who will go on to control the field and domain and thereby direct a portion of our society and culture. From this perspective, a mentor is a gatekeeper to a domain who furthers a novice's access to a field, or, as we will come to discover, a mentor serves to increase a novitiate's social capital.

In what follows, we present and expand on a case study to demonstrate key mentoring mechanisms and techniques that, based on our observations, we believe to account for a significant amount of success and creative output in scientific lineages as well as in other fields. Central to all of the mechanisms we discuss is the idea of social capital. Indeed, we see the linking of social capital to mentorship and creativity as a key contribution of this chapter, and so let us turn now to introduce and discuss the concept.

Social Capital

A growing consensus among sociologists has come to define social capital as "the ability of actors to secure benefits by virtue of membership in social networks or other social structures" (Portes, 1998, p. 6). Pierre Bourdieu (1985), a French sociologist, first introduced the concept decades ago in his work with educational systems in Europe. He defined the term more specifically as "the aggregate of the actual or potential resources which are linked to possession of a durable network of more or less institutionalized relationships of mutual acquaintance or recognition" (p. 248). Bourdieu was interested in the way that social status and power interact with educational systems to directly affect children's educational outcomes and eventual social status as adults. In short, he documented ways in which the social status of a child affected his or her eventual level of educational attainment and position in society. By and large, Bourdieu and his colleagues argued that children from higher social classes retained their position in these ranks of society through relationships they formed, or were given access to, by virtue of their family's position in society (Bourdieu & Passeron, 1977). Bourdieu developed the concepts of social and cultural capital to provide a vocabulary for these processes. Social capital, for Bourdieu, is the relationships with other adults (parents, etc.) and peers that avail children access to resources (economic and human) and cultural information that help ensure the child's eventual success in schooling and in attaining status in society. Cultural capital, for Bourdieu, is embodied cultural information. This can be in the form of other people, such as teachers, experts, or peers who internalize areas of cultural information, or it can be found in materials such as books, computers, museums, or other cultural artifacts. For Bourdieu, social capital generally increases a person's access to cultural capital and thereby augments that person's own cultural capital (Portes, 1998). This boost in cultural knowledge, when coupled with the accompanying social networks and opportunities, helps pave the way for high achievement.

James Coleman (1990) popularized the idea of social capital in the United States. Borrowing from Loury (1987), he defined the term as "the set of resources that inhere in family relations and in community social organization and that are useful for the cognitive or social development of a child or young person" (Coleman, 1990, p. 302). Like Bourdieu, Coleman was interested in the intangible factors that contribute strongly to children's educational achievement and career success. Coleman's work was less of a critique and more practical in orientation than Bourdieu's, and so he broadened the definition of social capital somewhat, identifying it by its function of "making possible the achievement of certain ends that would not be attainable in its absence" (p. 304). In other words, we can use social capital to mean the social resources and relationships that assist an individual in the developing vocational and career opportunities that would otherwise not exist.

Having clarified relevant concepts, vocabulary, and perspective, let us now turn to our recent research in hopes that it will allow us to meaningfully relate social capital and the systems model and, in so doing, forge new ideas about apprenticeship and the importance of the group in mentoring and in creativity.

Sample and Method

The sample we used came from a larger ongoing study of apprenticeship across multiple professional domains, including medical genetics, journalism, business, modern dance, martial arts, and coaching. In both the case to follow and the overall project, the sampling strategy was "lab-" or "shop-focused." That is, through expert recommendations and our own research, leading figures were identified within a given field as individuals who led creative careers and who became known for training high-caliber successors who remained in the field and contributed significantly to the domain.

The case examined in this chapter came from a space science lab at a major Midwestern research university. We interviewed five scientists: the generation one (G1) lab head/mentor and four generation two (G2) students. All were White males (which was representative of this field), ranging in age from the G1, who was 81 years old, to the youngest G2, who was in his forties. The participants were dispersed across several regions of the United States, including the Midwest, the South, and the East and West Coasts.

The primary source of data was in-depth, semistructured interviews, which were designed to take approximately two and a half hours and covered broad as well as specific topics, including initial interest in the field; formative experiences; apprenticeship experiences; valued goals, practices, and beliefs; obstacles, pressures, and rewards; training the next generation; and larger vocational vision or purpose. The interviews were recorded and transcribed and then analyzed using a simple coding scheme.

Exploring Apprenticeship and Creativity in a Space Science Lab

With even a cursory review of his career, one must categorize G1 as a supremely successful scientist and mentor. "My theme is to get out of the classroom and into the world of discovery and exploration of new frontiers—and the earlier the better. That's my advice to students." As much as this was his pedagogy, it was also a direct reflection of the kind of life and career led by G1. A giant in the world of space science, G1 wasted no time delving into his own life's work. Immediately after completing his doctoral degree he was recruited to the Manhattan Project, where he joined the team that achieved the first self-sustaining nuclear reaction on the floor of a squash court turned makeshift laboratory. On the day after the United States dropped the atomic bomb on Hiroshima, G1 and a group of conscientious colleagues organized an aggressive campaign to bring nuclear power under civilian control to ensure its peaceful future use. The public concern and leadership evident in this effort proved indicative of G1's entire, lengthy career.

Soon after the Manhattan Project, G1 was appointed to the faculty of a major Midwestern university, where he remained for his entire career, continuing throughout to publicly promote his values in relation to science. During his tenure, G1 received numerous teaching awards and many of the most prestigious scientific awards, short of the Nobel. He supervised the construction and operation of some 35 space experiments and sponsored the work of 34 doctoral students, many of whom are among today's most eminent leaders in space science. One of G1's early apprentices explained, "He was a towering figure in 20th-century science. A large number of his students are research faculty members around the country. His impact has been extremely broad." In fact, G1's teaching and mentoring produced elite scientists who have headed major space science and space exploration laboratories around the country and who continue his concern for science and public policy.

Although one would have to characterize G1 as a supremely successful scientist, public figure, and mentor, his mentoring principles and practices ran surprisingly counter to the predominant conception of effective mentoring espoused by previous research and exemplified in the earlier example of Niels Bohr. First, we were struck by a consistent expression among G2 respondents of what we have come to call "benign neglect." Although G1 was decidedly not hostile and for the most part not inhibitive for his students, both he and his students described a remote, hands-off, management-style approach to teaching, mentoring, and running a lab. Second, despite the paucity of one-on-one contact with their mentor, G2s came away from their training with a shared set of core memes and approaches to research and managing creative groups. Third, as foreshadowed, we were surprised by the significance that G2 respondents assigned to peers, post-docs, and lab culture as components of their training that were equal to or more important than the one-on-one interactions they had with their mentor. Finally, throughout all the interviews, respondents emphasized the way in which trust and endowing apprentices with important responsibilities had a profound effect on motivation, performance (both individual and group projects), and the absorption of the memes being conveyed by the mentor.

Although none of the G2s used the term "benign neglect" to describe the remote mentoring style of G1, all of them discussed this aspect of their training experience in his lab. They described him as "distant," "not intimate," or "off on his own lily pad," and yet, at the same time, they discussed their training experience as "excellent," "high quality," and "highly supportive." Here is the way one G2 recounted his apprenticeship experience:

[G1's] style of doing research was all by sort of management. I would consider [G1] "science management." He wouldn't describe himself that way. He would be horrified. But basically he would meet with research people. . . . He'd be building several projects at a time. . . . And he'd have a meeting with the students every week. We'd get together for tea and cookies for an hour or two every week. And the students would give a report or something like that. In terms of one-on-one meetings, there were very few, especially with the students. My Ph.D. thesis, I think I spent a total of 15 minutes discussing it with him. He was basically just unavailable. And that was typical . . . because [G1] was just sort of infinitely busy and he would be on the phone or in meetings, and then he'd disappear, or he didn't want to be disturbed, or something like that. So that was the way he interacted.

When asked how much time he spent with G1, another G2 responded:

Directly, probably not a lot, maybe a few minutes every week or couple of weeks, something like that. There was an infrastructure that he had with various other staff who were working on the daily analysis and that's where I, from these guys, where I really learned most of the techniques.

Another described his interaction with G1 this way: "Well, it was less of a personal thing because he was hard to see, and a very busy person. . . . But he created the lab that had the kind of environment in terms of other people that helped students a lot."

From G1's perspective, there was a system to training creative space scientists who could go on to survive the vicissitudes of a competitive and rapidly changing field. Mainly, G1's approach seemed to incorporate two central principles: have multiple, overlapping projects running simultaneously, and bestow on his students high levels of trust and real responsibility. By having a whole sequence of research projects, or missions, running simultaneously, G1 was able to (1) expedite students' progress toward their Ph.D.; (2) provide students with valuable experience in various stages of different kinds of projects; and (3) increase the overall productivity of the lab and its constituent members. G1 was interested in his students' timely progression through graduate training mainly because he did not want them to become demoralized or discouraged by an overly prolonged period of arduous graduate research. "I'm a great believer in trying to keep the shortest possible time until they get their degree. . . . That's what alarms me about some of the other fields. I see students are up to six, seven, maybe eight years before they get a degree. This is devastating in my mind, in terms of doing creative work." After so many years of drudgery G1 believed students lost their zeal for science and research. So, to keep their time in apprenticeship to a minimum, G1 required his students to design a mission or write a grant that would become a future project and then use an existing mission as the basis for their thesis research. By this system, each student participated in every stage of research from conception to write-up, they were exposed to multiple projects, and they short-circuited the all too often hyperelongated process of attaining a Ph.D.

In case it appears G1 let his students off the hook too easily, let us point out the sizable responsibilities and expectations bestowed on those training in his lab. During his interview, G1 summed up the regimen:

> As I mentioned earlier, the student will help design with me a mission and if we get it . . . he will then have the opportunity to take data from a previous mission and find some new results and have that as a thesis. And I have a golden rule that the thesis has to be not only original, but it has to be in a refereed journal and I refuse to be a coauthor; that a student has to publish alone. It has to be a single authored student thesis. . . . Well, this is great because you see the reaction of some students when they suddenly get very fearful of . . . they're exposed to the world, no help, no support. You see, that's good. And then usually if we can . . . have them stay on [as a post-doc] . . . after they get their degree or as they're getting their degree they get their referee's reports and that can obviously be devastating . . . not necessarily right. But . . . in every field you get people who are trying to put others down, and so students who face that situation then, it's good to have them here. To be able to sort of hold their hand and say, "Look, don't worry. Let me show you one of the . . . referee reports I got."

This account shows clearly how G1 helped students very early to internalize the expectations of the field and thus avoid the rejection of their novel ideas and findings, or, if rejected, not to give up as a result. Of course, he himself held high expectations of his students and initiated them in a stepwise fashion into the full set of responsibilities of a tenured member of the field, at the same time maintaining a nurturing environment that would assuage the discouraging obstacles inevitably encountered by any fledgling professional.

It was not only through work on their own grant proposals and thesis publication that G1's students got a taste of real responsibility. It also came through the trust he showered on them in working on existing projects. Apprentices in G1's lab performed most, if not all, of the functions of conceptualizing research questions, writing research proposals, and designing, building, and launching exploratory instruments. Usually they did these things before they thought they were ready. One G2 recalls:

> I remember, my first hint that this was different than anything I'd ever done before was shortly after I was there. We came across a way of improving some of the detectors that we had. . . . This required making some calculations, and then these detectors would be constructed by cutting them out of crystals, and it would cost a lot of money to get it done. Okay. Fine. So, we were building an instrument, and so I did the calculations to find out how these detectors—what shape they should have to go on the instrument. And so I took my results to [G1], fully expecting him to pull out a pencil and paper and check my calculation. But he just ordered them. I thought, "Oh my God!" So I went back and checked them again. I was expecting a sort of tutorial. And that's just not the way things worked. I think that's fun. This was graduate school. But it was very interesting—I was horrified. It also showed he was trusting me. He was in essence saying, "Fine. We're going to go off and have these things built at the factory to your specs."

In this way G1 embodied the pedagogy he espoused of "getting out of the classroom and into the world of discovery and exploration of new frontiers—and the earlier the better." Quite consciously, it seems, he pushed his students into and beyond what Vygotsky (1978) calls "the zone of proximal development," and in so doing provided them with experiences that built tremendous self-confidence and an identity as a scientist capable of exceeding their own and others' expectations. Throughout the rest of this chapter, we emphasize the importance of other mechanisms in the training process (especially the roles of peers and networks of colleagues), but without this deep sense of trust, responsibility, and respect conferred by G1 on his students, none of these other mechanisms would have taken on sufficient vitality to forge such successful young scientists. It would be hard, in our estimation, to overstate the importance of this practice of trust and the willingness, on the part of G1, to delegate real responsibility to his apprentices. Without this, it seems unlikely that apprentices in his lab would have been able to safely internalize the high standards and tacit expectations of the field that have guided their contributions and creative successes since striking out on their own.

Although G1 endowed apprentices with ample physical resources and provided opportunities to take on new challenges and important responsibilities, it does not seem likely, from what has been described so far, that the apprentices from G1's lab would have received memes in any consistent or uniform fashion. That is, given the paucity of contact with G1 and the manner in which

G2s were left to learn on their own and from one another, one might expect a highly heterogeneous, haphazard transmission of memes. To a small extent this was true. There were differences in the sets of memes received by different G2s, which seemed to stem mainly from the timing of G2s' apprenticeships with G1. As G1's career and interests evolved, it appears that the emphasis of the work and of the students and staff in the lab shifted slightly, which in turn altered the kinds of memes afloat in the lab environment.

Overall, however, there was a common set of memes about how to do creative work shared by all of G1's apprentices, which more than likely set them apart from apprentices who trained under a different mentor. To begin with, all of the G2s we interviewed (as well as most of those we did not) were still conducting research in the basic scientific area they had pursued under G1's tutelage. It was also the case that all of the apprentices reported an especially hard-nosed commitment to "high quality" and "discovering truth." These are certainly universal scientific memes (as we have observed in our research in other domains, such as medical genetics), but G1's descendants appeared to hold these values especially dear. Finally, there was abundant evidence indicating that more specific practices and approaches to science, to public life, and to teaching were conveyed to and internalized by G1's apprentices.

All of the G2s indicated a serious commitment to fulfilling the public role of a scientist that they saw modeled by their mentor. One student said, "You could see that [G1] obviously took those kinds of responsibilities seriously. So, certainly . . . there has been a role model there to emulate." Another elaborated more fully:

> [G1] felt that he owed something more than just his own research, that he really often made an effort to make a wider contribution to science and society. And I think that the fact that he felt very strongly about that meant that he was not just a scientist. I don't want to make this sound negative, but there are some scientists who really focus totally on their science, and don't feel any wider responsibility. . . . [G1] was never that way. He was focused on his science, but at the same time he felt a broader responsibility. . . . So I think that was something which was an important style which I observed and which has continued even long since I've been a graduate student.

This G2 discussed at length his own continuing commitment to "communicate about science to the public" and to "engage the public in the scientific process." Others expressed these same commitments and also attributed them to the influence of their mentor as something that set their training in his lab apart from others.

Another distinguishing characteristic and meme of G1's lab appears to be the very methods he used to systematically manage his lab and its resources (human and otherwise). Although each of the G2s said they consciously attempted to spend more time with their own students because they would have liked to have received more individual attention from G1, they also reported learning important skills and strategies for managing a lab. One G2 discussed his internalization of this meme as follows:

> Space research is something that requires teams of people. It requires leading those teams, formulating direction for the teams. It requires writing proposals and dealing with people who will fund it, and gaining their interest in what you're doing. . . . So I think what I learned from [G1] was kind of research strategy in terms of how to . . . pick the problem, how to sort of have a bigger picture of where things were headed. Because each thing you do is usually a step. And he always had a larger view of the program. . . . [Similarly,] my style tends to be one where I encourage students I am supervising and post-docs working with me to learn and not just follow my direction.

This G2 went on to discuss how, in his first posting as director of his own lab, he attempted to set up a "miniature version" of his mentor's lab. Another G2 said he learned these group management and research strategy skills after he completed his Ph.D. but was still working with G1. Other G2s internalized these memes to greater or lesser degrees, and all acknowledged the strong presence of these memes in G1's lab.

It has been portended and discussed throughout our analysis thus far that perhaps the most striking trend in our data was the overwhelming importance of peers, post-docs, and lab culture in the apprenticeship experience. Resoundingly, apprentices described this as the primary way through which they learned the basic skills and abilities they needed to become successful in space science, and they highlighted it as one of the most important components of G1's lab that allowed them to become successful scientists. One G2 recounted:

> My advisor was a very busy person, but in his lab, there were people who were really my day-to-day mentors in a way. I learned a lot from them. . . . [G1] created a lab that had the kind of environment in terms of other people that helped students a lot. . . . I worked very closely with [a post-doc in the lab] as a graduate student, for my whole graduate career. He taught me really all the skills that you need to know—from the analysis of data and looking at problems, to the experiments themselves. He, as I said, was a great teacher in a sense by just having me work with him. . . . It was the kinds of hands-on stuff you don't learn in books.

Another G2 responded to the question "How did you learn things in the lab?" this way: "Well, very easy, because there were research associates working for [G1], there were other students, there were all these engineers. And that's how you worked. You were in this environment and you learned things." Another G2 added, "[G1] was managing a very good group of people, and he's a very good scientist. So the result is good stuff came out." Still another remarked, "The other graduate students were certainly—I learned a lot from them. . . . That was an important part of the opportunity too, was to have more senior graduate students that you could learn from. In fact, the first thing I worked on was another student's thesis experiment. That was a wonderful learning experience."

By both G1's and the apprentices' accounts, G1 understood his role as lab head as one who provided students with a rich learning environment in which they could "get excited about creativity and discovery in science." Other mentors, such as Bohr, have approached this basic task by nurturing students with large amounts of personal attention and acting as a constant source of support and guidance. As we have seen, the literature on mentoring has well documented this approach, and in many ways idealized it, but it has not accounted for other approaches such as the one we have described here. Our aim is not to discredit mentoring approaches that resemble Bohr's and that have been celebrated in the research literature; nor is it to draw comparisons. Instead, our goals are (1) to point out the plurality of effective mentoring methods; (2) to demonstrate the importance of the largely overlooked component of mentoring that involves the group of peers and colleagues surrounding a young apprentice; and (3) to enumerate additional ideal or optimal conditions for effective mentoring. It is to the latter two points that we now turn our attention.

The Group as Mentor

It has been emphasized throughout that peers and colleagues play an integral role in the training and mentoring process of young novices. The role of peer influence is not new to the literature on creativity. Feldman (1999) and Gardner (1993) both discussed the influence of small groups of peers on a creator, especially when working on a new style, theory, or paradigm. Often, creative forms of work and creative ideas are forged within a small group of colleagues (Feldman, 1999). Each of Gardner's seven exemplars benefited professionally from peer relationships. Similarly, Woodman Sawyer, and Griffin (1993) discussed the benefits of peer interaction in creative efforts. But none of these findings have been made in the context of apprenticeship or training processes. In fact, Feldman and Gardner mainly discuss the importance of these relationships after the process of formal training has already taken place. Although this is consistent with our findings, these relationships often begin and become significant during a person's apprenticeship to a particular mentor.

Recalling the concepts of social and cultural capital introduced earlier, we can more clearly articulate some of the mechanisms at play and the reasons we believe it's important to look at apprenticeship to gain a complete understanding of the role of peers and social capital in a person's career. To begin with, it appears that joining an elite lab is analogous to being born into a family of high social status. Just as Bourdieu (1985) showed that access to cultural information and important social networks are conferred on children of elite community members, apprentices of eminent mentors reap similar benefits. In this way, perhaps social capital explains Zuckerman's (1977) finding that scientists who studied under Nobelists tended to become highly successful also. But how does this occur? How does social capital bestowed on a young apprentice continue to have effects years later?

It appears this works in several ways. First, novices who train under reputable mentors are given their mentor's stamp of approval and association, which facilitates their way past subsequent "gatekeepers" in the field. Certainly this was the case with students from G1's lab, and we have found it to be true in most other professional fields as well. In some cases, a mentor may even use his or her eminence to prevail on behalf of the novice. In a recent journalism interview, for example, a now prominent editor of a major national newspaper recounted a story of his mentor's weighing in on his behalf when, as a sapling reporter, his press pass was revoked in Vietnam for publishing a story the military did not yet want released. Without his press badge his career could soon be over. Realizing this, and the tenuous case the military had against him, this reporter's mentor rallied journalists from around the country and mustered enough pressure to quickly have the press pass reissued. Needless to say, this now prominent editor could not have made it to the station in life he now occupies without his mentor's placing such a substantial social investment in him. This is but one dramatic case. Sometimes mentors actively go to bat for their apprentices in this way; more often, their association alone is sufficient to open necessary doors.

A second and similar way social capital serves to promote the careers of apprentices is by raising the novice's visibility within the field. That is to say, a mentor, along with the group of peers and colleagues from the mentor's lab, together help amplify the novice's presence within the field. Through collaborations with them, aspiring novices gain greater visibility beyond the lab, in the field, by having greater opportunities to publish, present, and make known their work. In our small sample alone, most of the G2s explicitly cited relationships they had formed while training under G1 as playing a significant role in attaining their first job. Such is the way it works in academic fields. Beyond academia, this type of social capital benefit occurs in much the same way. In the field of coaching, for example, training with a top coach and his or her staff affords a novice access to relationships with other excellent coaches and athletic staff. Several coaches we interviewed have stressed the importance of the visibility they were given as apprentices by being involved in conference meetings with other coaches, by being assistant coaches on successful teams that received mass media attention, and by developing a network of peers through their mentor. One can easily imagine how this same process works in other fields such as business management, journalism, law, and the arts.

Third, and perhaps most significant, the social capital of a mentor continues to positively affect the apprentice's career years later because apprentices often persist in working with colleagues and peers whom they have met through their mentor. In our case from the space science lab, almost all of the G2s continued collaborative relationships they had begun while under G1's tutelage, either with peers from within G1's lab or with colleagues they worked with beyond his lab. These same enduring collaborative bonds occur in other fields as well. Returning to coaching and journalism for further examples, in each of these fields, many, if not most, of our respondents reported continuing collegial relationships with peers forged during their time of training long after their apprenticeships were over. In fact, in both coaching and journalism, trust in one's colleagues appears to be so important that these relationships often continue to be primary throughout one's career. Journalists at times move en masse from one newspaper to another because these relationships are so crucial. Similarly, entire coaching staffs often change when a new head coach is appointed. People in these fields tend to hire people they have previously worked with or people recommended by colleagues they know they can trust.

There is another dimension to this last social capital benefit. The importance of the relationships with peers and colleagues formed during a person's training extends beyond trust. Put differently, there is a *creative* benefit that stems from this trust, namely, that it allows for a milieu to develop wherein creative ideas can incubate. It is said that Leonardo da Vinci learned as much from his fellow apprentices, such as Lorenzo di Credi, as he did from the workshop master Verrocchio, and Michelangelo learned from his fellow pupils in Ghirlandaio's atelier and from the other young men who assembled at the court of the Medici to discuss art and philosophy. In much the same way, many of our respondents said that their creativity was augmented as much by their peers and colleagues as by their mentor, and that the creative milieu did not cease when their time with the mentor ended. Instead, colleagues who share a deep sense of trust and safe feeling forged during their years of mutual apprenticeship often continue to draw on one another's insights, ideas, support, and reflection and, in so doing, find their creativity continuously enhanced.

Extending Our Conception of Optimal Mentoring

In light of our findings regarding the importance of social capital in apprenticeship, a new set of optimal mentoring conditions emerges. First, based on our observations, granting trust and real responsibility to the young apprentice appears crucial to the development of expertise and self-confidence. Through trust and real responsibility apprentices gain a palpable and contagiously exciting sense that their work really matters. It gives their training a new weight, without which their ideas would remain groundless, abstract, and casual. Only by experiencing real responsibility through the trust of the mentor do apprentices begin to gain a sense for what it must be like to be a practitioner in their selected domain. Only through this experience, and the awareness it brings, do they begin to value and internalize the standards and practices of the field.

Second, our research shows that a degree of psychological and social distance from the mentor is beneficial. Some might consider G1 from our case study an extreme example of this. His style of mentoring, which we at times termed benign neglect, was indeed especially hands-off. However, his heavy reliance on the milieu and networking of his lab both for day-to-day teaching of apprentices and for aiding them with career opportunities once they completed their time in training was in many ways exemplary. As such an extreme yet effective example, G1's lab points out mechanisms of mentorship that for the most part have been overlooked but, once discovered, can be seen at work in other lineages in other fields such as coaching and journalism. Mentors must provide support, nurturance, and guidance, but close one-on-one relationships are but one way of accomplishing this, and they alone may not be most effective.

This leads to and works hand in hand with our third and final suggested optimal mentoring condition: providing a systematized group of peers and professional colleagues within and beyond the lab or place of training. Within the lab, peers serve as sources of emotional support and expertise; they provide one another knowledge and intellectual inspiration; they model effective skills and behavior, and thereby supplement many of the roles traditionally thought to belong to mentors alone. Equally important, optimal mentors avail students a new network of colleagues in the larger field, beyond the mere confines of the place of training. From these colleagues, a novice gains not only new ideas and memes and different perspectives on the domain and the field; he or she also gains a new set of trusted collaborative partners. As we discussed earlier, all of the G2s in our sample reported other students and post-docs in G1's lab as being crucial to their training. But the importance of these relationships did not stop with the mastery of scientific principles or techniques, or even with the value of brainstorming and sharing ideas. All of the G2s extended the relationships they built in G1's lab to create important networks, which eventually made significant impacts on their career paths and professional affiliations. In most cases, a contact developed through their mentor played a direct role in securing their first job. Most G2s also continued to collaborate with colleagues from G1's lab, and in all cases they used one another as continuing sources of support and reflection for new ideas and projects. From this perspective, we can see that in addition to impacting students through modeling behavior and embodying values, an important function of mentors is to provide apprentices with state-of-the-art specialized information (cultural capital) and to help them navigate the social networks of the field (social capital).

In this way, understanding social capital enriches the definition of effective mentoring and helps to articulate more clearly a part of the systems model of creativity, namely, the role of the field (i.e., the mentor and an apprentice's peers and colleagues) in educating and socializing aspiring young people (see Figure 11.1). To be creative in any domain, a person must be able to build the appropriate cultural and social capital—to gain access to the knowledge and the institutions that will allow his or her novel ideas to be expressed. In this process, mentors, who act as gatekeepers to the domain, can either facilitate or terminate a novice's creative aspirations. Good mentors are those who can transmit enthusiasm and knowledge while also introducing the novice to the social realities of the relevant field. As we have seen, this process of building the cultural and social capital, which is requisite for creativity, does not necessarily involve one-on-one tutoring on the part of the mentor. It can take place instead in a studio or lab rich with peers and colleagues whom the mentor makes available and who act as incubators for new ideas.

If creativity is in short supply at a particular moment in time, this may not be due to the lack of young people with good ideas and serious motivation. It may be due instead to the lack of mentors who can provide the needed cultural and social capital and thus create the necessary conditions for the flowering of novel ideas.

Note

The Transmission of Excellence Study was generously supported by the Spencer Foundation.

References

Bourdieu, P. (1985). The forms of social capital. In J. G. Richardson (Ed.), *Handbook of theory and research for the sociology of education* (pp. 241–258). New York: Greenwood.

Bourdieu, P., & Passeron, J. C. (1977). *Reproduction in education, society and culture.* (R. Nice, Trans.). London: Sage.

Coleman, J. (1990). Social capital. In J. Coleman, *Foundations of social theory* (pp. 300–324). Cambridge, MA: Belknap Press of Harvard University Press.

Crane, D. (1965). Scientists at major and minor universities: A study of productivity and recognition. *American Sociological Review, 30,* 699–714.

Csikszentmihalyi, M. (1988). Society, culture, and person: A systems view of creativity. In R. J. Sternberg (Ed.), *The nature of creativity* (pp. 325–339). New York: Cambridge University Press.

Csikszentmihalyi, M. (1996). *Creativity.* New York: HarperCollins.

Csikszentmihalyi, M. (1999). Implications of a systems perspective for the study of creativity. In R. J. Sternberg (Ed.), *Handbook of creativity* (pp. 313–335). Cambridge, UK: Cambridge University Press.

Dawkins, R. (1976). *The selfish gene.* New York: Oxford University Press.

Erikson, E. (1959). *Identity and the life cycle.* New York: Norton.

Feldman, D. H. (1999). The development of creativity. In R. J. Sternberg (Ed.), *Handbook of creativity* (pp. 169–186). Cambridge, UK: Cambridge University Press.

Feldman, D. H., Csikszentmihalyi, M. & Gardner, H. (1994). A framework for the study of creativity. In D. H. Feldman, M. Csikszentmihalyi, & H. Gardner (Eds.), *Changing the world: A framework for the study of creativity* (pp. 1–45). Westport, CT: Praeger.

Gardner, H. (1993). *Creating minds.* New York: HarperCollins.

Kanigel, R. (1986). *Apprentice to genius.* New York: Macmillan.

Levinson, D. J. (1978). *The seasons of a man's life.* New York: Knopf.

Loury, G. (1987). Why should we care about group inequality? *Social Philosophy and Policy, 5,* 249–271.

Nakamura, J., & Csikszentmihalyi, M. (2002). The motivational sources of creativity as viewed from the paradigm of positive psychology. In L. G. Aspinwall & V. M. Staudinger (Eds.), *A Psychology of human strengths: Perspectives on an emerging field* (pp. 257–269). Washington: American Psychological Association Books.

Portes, A. (1998). Social capital: Its origins and applications in modern sociology. *Annual Review of Sociology, 24,* 1–24.

Simonton, D. K. (1984). Artistic creativity and interpersonal relationships across and within generations. *Journal of Personality and Social Psychology, 46,* 1273–1286.

Simonton, D. K. (1988). Developmental antecedents. In D. K. Simonton (Ed), *Scientific genius: A psychology of science* (pp. 107–134). Cambridge, MA: Cambridge University Press.

Vaillant, G. E. (1977). *Adaptation to life.* Boston: Little, Brown.

Vygotsky, L. S. (1978). *Mind in society.* Cambridge, MA: Harvard University Press.

Walberg, H. J., Rasher, S. P., & Parkerson, J. (1980). Childhood and eminence. *Journal of Creative Behavior, 13,* 225–231.

Woodman, R. W., Sawyer, J. E., & Griffin, R. W. (1993). Toward a theory of organizational creativity. *Academy of Management Review, 18*(2), 293–321.

Zuckerman, H. (1977). *Scientific elite.* New York: Free Press.

12

■■■■ *Michael A. West*

Innovation Implementation in Work Teams

■■■■

Ideas are ten a penny. Put a handful of bright engineers in a brainstorming session and they will come up with literally scores of clever ideas for new products or processes. Invention is the easy bit. Innovation, by contrast, is the genuinely difficult part . . . what it does depend on is the single-mindedness with which the business plan is executed, as countless obstacles on the road to commercialisation are surmounted, by-passed or hammered flat.—Economist (2001)

In this chapter I argue that understanding the factors that promote creativity in a team is less important in applied settings than understanding the factors that promote the implementation of ideas into practice and action. Generating creative ideas in a work group in organizational settings is relatively easy; implementing new products, processes, or procedures in work organizations is difficult and takes time because of resistance to change and structural and cultural barriers. Most work groups include people with domain-relevant skills and, often, creativity-relevant skills (see Hennessey, this volume) and who have worked together frequently generating ideas, so they have little difficulty generating creative ideas. This contrasts with student groups (which are often studied in group creativity research), who have little genuine context for their creative efforts and limited experience with one another. The work team, on the other hand, faces a huge task in moving from the stage of having an idea to implementing it effectively in an organization. They must overcome the suspicions and objections of myriad stakeholders who may be affected by the change. The health care team that wishes to introduce much greater nurse involvement in diagnostic and treatment processes for breast cancer patients may have to overcome the objections of doctors, professional associations, patients, and managers and is likely to experience considerable conflict on route.

Figure 12.1 offers a framework of the factors identified in research as likely to influence innovation implementation in work groups and uses an input-process-output structure. This structure artificially segments variables into

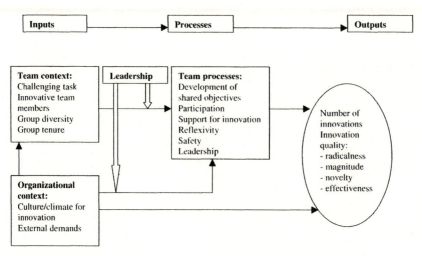

Figure 12.1. *An Input-Process-Output Model of Work Group Innovation*

inputs of teams, such as the task the team is required to perform (e.g., provide health care, make land mines, sell mobile phones), the composition of the group (such as functional, cultural, gender, and age diversity), and the organizational context (e.g., manufacturing, health service, large or small, organic, the demands it places on the team). Group processes mediate the relationships between inputs and outputs and include levels of participation, support for innovation, leadership, and the management of conflict. These processes create climates of, for example, safety and trust or threat and anxiety. The model proposes that leadership in teams plays a crucial role in moderating the effects of organizational and team context on team processes and thereby on innovation outputs. Outputs include the number of innovations, magnitude of innovation, radicalness (changes to the status quo), novelty, and effectiveness of innovation in achieving the desired end. I consider each of these elements of the framework below, but first, it is important to define what is meant by innovation.

Innovation is the introduction of new and improved ways of doing things. A fuller, more explicit definition of innovation is "the intentional introduction and application within a job, work team or organization of ideas, processes, products or procedures which are new to that job, work team or organization and which are designed to benefit the job, the work team or the organization" (West & Farr, 1990, p. 9). Innovation is restricted to *intentional* attempts to bring about benefits from new changes; these might include economic benefits, personal growth, increased satisfaction, improved group cohesiveness, better organizational communication, and productivity gains. Various processes and products may be regarded as innovations. These include technological changes such as new products, but may also include new production processes, the introduction of advanced manufacturing technology, or the introduction of new computer support services within an organization. Administrative changes are also regarded as innovations. New human resource management (HRM) strategies, organizational policies on health and safety, and the introduction of teamwork are all examples of administrative innovations in organizations. Innovation implies novelty, but not necessarily absolute novelty (West & Farr, 1990). Innovation encompasses both creative idea generation and idea implementation. What input, process, and output factors influence levels and qualities of innovation in work groups? I begin by considering the effects of two major categories of input factors: team context and organizational context.

Team Context

Inputs include, most importantly, the task that a team is required to perform, and it is the characteristics of team tasks and how these relate to innovation that I consider first. Then I consider the characteristics of the people who make up the team and their abilities and skills in working in teams, the diversity of attributes, perspectives, and skills they bring to the team's work, and finally, the length of time they have worked together.

Task Characteristics

The task a group performs is a fundamental influence on the work group, defining its structural, process, and functional requirements. Dimensions for classifying group task characteristics include task difficulty, solution multiplicity, intrinsic interest, cooperative requirements (Shaw, 1976), unitary versus divisible, conjunctive, disjunctive, and additive (Steiner, 1972), conflict versus cooperation, and conceptual versus behavioral (McGrath, 1984). These classification systems have been developed from within the experimental social psychology tradition and have not been adopted by researchers exploring group performance and innovation in organizational settings, probably because such goals as producing TV programs, battleground training, health care, product development, and providing financial services cannot be neatly categorized into discrete tasks and subtasks. Primary health care teams that maintain and promote the health of people in local communities have multiple stakeholders and a wide variety of tasks (Slater & West, 1999). Their team tasks are simple and difficult, unitary and divisible, involve conflict and cooperation, and demand both behavioral and conceptual responses. Such classifications therefore have limited utility in real-life settings.

A more useful alternative is action theory (Frese & Zapf, 1994; Hacker, 1986; Tschan & von Cranach, 1996; Volpert, 1984), which describes tasks in relation to their hierarchical, sequential, and cyclical process requirements. Tschan and von Cranach argue that tasks should be deconstructed into their hierarchical requirements (goals and subgoals); their sequential demands—the restrictions that are imposed on the order in which subtasks are carried out (we have to break the eggs before we can cook the omelette, but whether we plan a structure for our poem at the beginning or halfway through may vary depending on our approach); and the cyclical nature of information processing (orienting, planning, executing, evaluating). Tschan and von Cranach also point out that the nature of communication will vary considerably according to whether the group task element is low level (relatively automated elements require little or no communication or creativity, such as monitoring materials flow in an assembly line team) or high level, requiring considerable communication, creativity, and innovation (e.g., planning a new research program). However, action theory has not been used widely to inform studies of the effects of task characteristics on work group functioning. It could and should be. More hierarchical elements offer more opportunities for innovation. Low sequential demands suggest more opportunities for innovation. The more cyclical elements in a team's task, the more possibilities the task offers the team to innovate. Analyzing team tasks in the workplace using action theory would also offer a diagnostic procedure for determining whether it is a task that is best done by a team (which is inherently more innovative than an individual) or an individual (or group of individuals) working alone. Team tasks are likely to be more hierarchical, less sequential, and more cyclical. They are also more likely to offer opportunities for creativity and innovation than other tasks. To illustrate this, think of the difference between a soccer team's task and that of a baseball team. A soccer team's task is more hierarchical, less sequential, and less obviously cyclical than that of a baseball team. The opportunities for creativity and innovation in soccer are therefore much greater than those offered in baseball (although some U.S. colleagues may disagree, I think the case can be made convincingly!).

Sociotechnical systems theory (STST) provides another powerful framework for examining the effects of task design on work group innovation. Sociotechnical systems theorists (Cooper & Foster, 1971; Emery, 1959; Trist & Bamforth, 1951) argue that autonomous work groups provide a structure through which the demands of the social and technical subsystems of an organization can be jointly optimized. Thus, STST proposes that the technical subsystems of any work unit must be balanced and optimized concurrently with the social subsystem: technological and spatial working conditions must be designed to meet the human demands of the social system. The two subsystems are connected by team members' occupational roles and by cooperative and interdependent relationships. The key to effective performance is whether the work group can control variation in quality and quantity of task performance at source (Cordery, 1996). Such variance control implies innovation because the work group will introduce new and improved methods of working or technologies to achieve control of variance in task performance appropriately.

What characteristics of the work group and the group's task encourage innovation? The joint optimization of the two subsystems is more likely when work groups have the following characteristics:

- The team is a relatively independent organizational unit that is responsible for a whole task.

- The tasks of members are related in content so that awareness of a common task is evoked and maintained and members are required to work interdependently.
- There is a "unity of product and organization"; that is, the group has a complete task to perform and group members can identify with their own product (Ulich &Weber, 1996, p. 279).

Such conditions, according to theorists, will produce "task orientation," a state of interest and engagement produced by task characteristics (Emery, 1959). This is very similar to the concept of intrinsic motivation that Amabile (1983; Amabile & Conti, 1999) argues is so fundamental to creativity and innovation at work (see Hennessey, this volume). According to STST, therefore, the task is the central focus of a psychological view of activity (Hacker, 1994). Because it represents the intersection between the group and the organization, it is the most psychologically relevant element of the working conditions (Volpert, 1987). Blumberg (1988) makes the same point and proposes that the task is "the point of articulation between the social and technical systems, linking the job in the technical system with its correlated role behaviour in the social system" (p. 6). To the extent that the three characteristics of autonomous work groups described above are present, the more likely the group is to develop ideas for and implement new and improved products, processes, or procedures.

The task characteristics that evoke "task orientation" or intrinsic motivation (and therefore innovation), according to STST, are completeness (i.e., whole tasks), varied demands, opportunities for social interaction, autonomy, opportunities for learning, and development possibilities for the task.[1]

Gulowsen (1972) suggests that the degree of autonomy of the work group can be assessed in relation to group influence over (1) the formulation of goals: what and how much it is expected to produce; (2) where to work and number of hours (when to work overtime and when to leave); (3) choice about further activities beyond the given task; (4) selection of production methods; (5) distribution of task responsibilities within the group; (6) membership of the group (who and how many people will work in the group); (7) leadership: whether there will be a leader and who will be the leader; and (8) how to carry out individual tasks.

However, the case for the value of autonomy is not straightforward. Cohen and Bailey's (1997) review of work team effectiveness suggests that autonomy, contrary to a widely held view, is not necessarily a predictor of effectiveness or innovation in project teams. They cite Henderson and Lee's (1992) study of 41 information systems design teams which showed that the most effective teams are those in which managers assign tasks to team members and control how the jobs were done. Similarly, Kim and Leigh (1995) found that high team autonomy was associated with poor performance among 80 R&D teams in South Korea. Autonomy was helpful for a team's performance only when the organization supported innovation and pressure of work was high.

Recognizing that task requirements and the relationship between the technical and social subsystems have a major influence on levels of group innovation is an important prerequisite for considering the more dynamic influences on group innovation of other psychological, social psychological, and environmental factors. In summary, the extent of group autonomy (in an organizational context that supports innovation) and the task requirements of completeness, varied demands, opportunities for social interaction, opportunities for learning, and development opportunities will predict group creativity and innovation implementation. A central proposition of this examination of team innovation is that leadership processes in teams have a profound influence on moderating the relationship between task characteristics and team processes. Effective leadership can enhance the effects of autonomy (by encouraging risk taking and experimentation in task performance) or diminish their effects (when leadership inhibits the exploration of the limits of team members' autonomy). I explore these issues later in this chapter, but first consider another key input variable: team member characteristics.

Team Member Characteristics

Given a team task, the innovation process begins with the creativity of individuals. The generation of a new idea is a cognitive process, located within individuals, albeit fostered by interaction processes in teams (Mumford & Gustafson, 1988). Thus, first and foremost, innovative individuals are both creative and innovative (i.e., they don't just have creative ideas, they also try to implement them). They are people who have a preference for thinking in novel ways, who think globally instead of locally (distinguishing the forest from the trees). They have appropriate intellectual abilities, including synthetic abilities (to see problems in new ways and escape the bounds of conventional thinking), analytic abilities to recognize which ideas are worth pursuing, and the practical contextual abilities to persuade others of the value of their ideas (Sternberg & Lubart, 1996). Having a good idea about whether the Earth revolves around the sun or vice versa is not enough. Galileo, if he were alive today, might note that Richard Branson and Bill Gates did not succeed by simply being mavericks; they were also able to charm, persuade, and inspire people. To be innovative and creative we also require sufficient knowledge of the field to be able to move it forward, while not being so conceptually trapped in it that we are unable to conceive of alternative courses (Mumford & Gustafson, 1988). People who are confident of their abilities are more likely to innovate in the workplace. In a study of role innovation among more than 2,000 UK managers, Nicholson and West (1988) found that confidence and motivation to develop knowledge and skills predicted innovation following job change. Tolerance of ambiguity, widely associated with creativity, enables individuals to avoid the problems of following mental ruts and increases the chances of unusual responses and the discovery of novelty (Barron & Harrington, 1981).

Innovative people also tend to be self-disciplined, with a high degree of drive and motivation and a concern with achieving excellence (Mumford & Gustafson, 1988). This *perseverance* against social pressures presumably reduces the dangers of premature abandonment. Minority influence theory in social psychology suggests that perseverance acts to bring about change in the views of majorities and is a necessary behavioral style among innovators (for reviews, see Nemeth, 1986; Nemeth & Nemeth-Brown, this volume; Nemeth & Owens, 1996). An employee of 3M discovered Post-it notes because he sang in the church choir and needed some effective way of marking the place of hymns between services. Knowing of an adhesive with poor properties (it didn't stick well) being explored at 3M, he had the idea of using it on small strips of paper to mark the hymnal. But the real innovation came in his persistence in selling the idea to secretaries, chief executives, the marketing department, and the sales department in the organization. It became an annual $200 million business for 3M.

Innovative people tend to be self-directed, enjoying and requiring freedom in their work (Mumford & Gustafson, 1988). They have a high need for freedom, control, and discretion in the workplace and appear to find bureaucratic limitations or the exercise of control by managers frustrating (West, 1987; West & Rushton, 1989). Such people need clear work objectives along with high autonomy to perform well. Indeed, in a study of 13 oil company teams, Burningham and West (1995) found that the innovativeness of individuals in teams was superior as a predictor of team innovation to measures of group climate and process. In a more sophisticated longitudinal study of 27 top management teams in hospitals, West and Anderson (1996) found that the proportion of innovative individuals within the team did not predict the overall level of innovation but did predict the radicalness (changes to the status quo) of the innovations implemented by teams.

Another influence on team innovation is the extent to which team members have the relevant knowledge, skills, and abilities to work effectively in groups. Stevens and Campion (1994) believe that team members require appropriate team knowledge, skills, and abilities (KSAs), or "team integration skills" (see also Campion, Medsker, & Higgs, 1993). These are distinct from the technical KSAs that are relevant to task performance (such as medical skills for a physician on a breast cancer care team). They include conflict resolution skills, collaborative problem-solving skills, and communication skills such as the skill to utilize decentralized communication networks to enhance communication. Other key integration skills, they argue, include goal setting and performance management and the skill to coordinate and synchronize activities, information, and tasks among members. The more of these integration skills team members have, the more likely it is that the benefits of team working and team diversity will manifest, not just in terms of team performance, but also in innovation proposals and their successful implementation (Campion, Papper, & Medsker, 1996).

I propose that leadership processes in teams will moderate the relationship among team member characteristics, team processes, and innovation. Leadership processes will either encourage or block the expression of behaviors and skills supportive of team innovation. A dominant, directive leader may prevent attempts by team members to bring about change and steadily reduce their confidence and perseverance in initiating innovation implementation. More-over, such a leader might inhibit the expression of team KSAs by repeatedly dominating decision making or discussion. A more transformational leadership style (discussed later in the chapter) is likely to enhance the impact of individual characteristics such as confidence, innovativeness, and tolerance of ambiguity on group processes (such as support for innovation) and thereby innovation implementation.

Group Member Diversity

Are groups that are composed of very different people (e.g., in professional background, age, organizational tenure) more innovative than those whose members are similar? This question is prompted by the notion that if people who work together in groups have different backgrounds, personalities, training, skills, experiences, and orientations, they will bring usefully differing perspectives to the group. This divergence of views will create multiple perspectives, disagreement, and conflict. If this informational conflict is processed in the interests of effective decision making and task performance rather than on the basis of motivation to win or prevail, or conflicts of interest, this in turn will generate improved performance and more innovative actions will be the result (De Dreu, 1997; Hoffman & Maier, 1961; Pearce & Ravlin, 1987; Porac & Howard, 1990; Tjosvold, 1985, 1991, 1998).

Of the different classification systems for diversity (e.g., Jackson 1992, 1996; Maznevski, 1994), most differentiate between task-oriented diversity in at-tributes that are relevant to the person's role or task in the organization (e.g., organizational position and specialized knowledge) and those that are simply inherent in the person and "relations-oriented" (e.g., age, gender, ethnicity, social status, and personality; Maznevski, 1994). Jackson (1992) believes that the effects of diversity on team performance are complex: task-related and relations-oriented diversity have different effects that depend also on the team task. For tasks requiring creativity and a high quality of decision making, Jack-son (1996) says that "the available evidence supports the conclusion that team [task] diversity is associated with better quality team decision-making" (p. 67), citing evidence provided by Filley, House, and Kerr (1976), Hoffman (1979), McGrath (1984), and Shaw (1981).

The most significant study to date of innovation in teams is a UNESCO-sponsored international effort to determine the factors influencing the scientific performance of 1,222 research teams (Andrews, 1979; see also Payne, 1990). Diversity was assessed in six areas: projects, interdisciplinary orientations, specialties, funding resources R&D activities, and professional functions. Over-all, diversity accounted for 10% of the variance in scientific recognition, R&D effectiveness, and number of publications, suggesting that diversity does influence team innovation.

There is some evidence that heterogeneity in both relations-oriented and task-oriented domains is associated with group innovation, including heterogeneity in personality (Hoffman & Maier, 1961), training background (Pelz, 1956), leadership abilities (Ghiselli & Lodahl, 1958), attitudes (Hoffman, Harburg & Maier, 1962; Willems & Clark, 1971), gender (Wood, 1987), occupational background (Bantel & Jackson, 1989), and education (Smith et al., 1994).

Diversity in information, experience, and skills that leads to more comprehensive and effective decision making is the dominant explanation for the positive effects of diversity on team innovation. However, another explanation for the (still debated) effects of task-oriented diversity on team innovation is that functional diversity might influence work group performance as a result of the higher level of external communication that group members initiate precisely because of their functional diversity (Zenger & Lawrence, 1989). Mohrman, Cohen, and Mohrman (1995) point out that there are likely to be innovation benefits of good linkages between groups and teams and across departments within organizations. The cross-disciplinarity, cross-functionality, and cross-team perspectives that such interactions can produce are likely to generate the kinds of dividends related to innovation that heterogeneity within teams could offer.

In a study of 45 new product teams in five high-technology companies, Ancona and Caldwell (1992) found that when a work group recruited a new member from a functional area in the organization, communication between the team and that area went up dramatically. This would favor innovation through the incorporation of diverse ideas and models gleaned from these different functional areas. Consistent with this, the researchers discovered that the greater the group's functional diversity, the more team members communicated outside the work group's boundaries and the higher ratings of innovation they received from supervisors. The UNESCO research described above also showed that the extent of communication between research teams had strong relationships with scientific recognition of the teams, R&D effectiveness, number of publications, and the applied value of their work.

Although power and status in groups are likely to be associated with innovation in organizations (West, 1987; West & Anderson, 1996), status diversity, in contrast, is likely to threaten integration and safety in the group. The threat occasioned by disagreeing with high-status members is likely to restrict public speculation by lower-status group members. Such status differentials, as much social psychological research has shown, will retard integration because of the barriers to cohesiveness and shared orientation they create. For example, De Dreu (1995) has shown that power and status asymmetries in groups produce hostile interaction patterns, in contrast to groups in which there is power balance. Such hostility is clearly likely to inhibit creativity and innovation (West, 2002).

So, does diversity predict group innovation? The research evidence suggests that functional or knowledge diversity in the team is associated with innovation. However, when diversity begins to threaten the group's safety and integration (such as with status or age diversity), then creativity and innovation implementation will be likely to suffer (see Milliken, Bartel, & Kurtzberg, this volume). Where diversity reduces group members' clarity about and commitment to group objectives, levels of participation (interaction, information sharing, and shared influence over decision making), task orientation (commitment to quality of task performance), and support for new ideas, then it is likely that innovation attempts will be resisted. Diversity will also be affected by temporal factors because, over time, the experience of diversity in a group will be softened into familiarity. I therefore turn to consider how the tenure or age of a work team is likely to affect innovation.

However, the critical influence on how diversity affects group processes, I propose, is leadership within the team. Leaders who effectively integrate diverse perspectives and manage conflict effectively (e.g., by emphasizing shared objectives and vision) are likely to enhance the influence of diversity on innovation implementation in teams. Leadership processes that inhibit the integration of diverse perspectives (e.g., by exacerbating conflict between team members) will reduce or nullify the effect of diversity on group processes and, thereby, team innovation.

Group Tenure

To encourage innovation, should we try to keep work teams together over time or ensure a constant change of membership and therefore maintain its diversity? Katz (1982) suggested that project newcomers would increase creativity because they may challenge and thereby improve existing methods and knowledge (for an excellent and comprehensive discussion of newcomers and their effects on innovation in work teams, see Levine, Choi, & Moreland, this volume). He suggested too that the longer groups are together, the less they communicate with key information sources, scan the environment, and communicate internally within the group and externally. Members of such groups, he proposed, tend to ignore and become increasingly isolated from sources that provide the most critical kinds of feedback, evaluation, and information. This suggests that without changes in membership, groups may become less innovative as time goes by. Indeed, some research on diversity in teams (Bantel & Jackson, 1989; Jackson, 1996) suggests that longer tenure might be associated with increasing homogeneity and therefore low levels of innovation. The tenure of a group may result in lower requisite diversity for meeting the demands of the environment as a result of the increasing similarity of group members' attitudes, skills, and experiences through their close association (which symbolic interactionist approaches would suggest is likely).

However, tenure homogeneity has been positively related in some studies to frequency of communication, social integration within the group, and innovation (O'Reilly & Flatt, 1989). This may be because the longer people work together, the more they create a predictable and therefore safer social psychological environment. Such safety may enable the exploration and risk taking necessary for innovation (Edmondson, 1996).

The resolution of these positions may lie not in issues of tenure, diversity, and safety per se, but in the balance among these factors. It may be that tenure, diversity, and psychosocial safety interact in their influence on innovation. Where long tenure leads to high safety, this will lead to creativity and innovation, all other things being equal, because it will be safer to take risks and to continually introduce diverse perspectives (see, e.g., the discussion on minority influence below and Nemeth & Nemeth-Brown, this volume). Another possibility is that the longer teams work together, the more likely they are to develop and apply ways of working that enable them to achieve shared objectives and to implement appropriate participation strategies, effective communication, and decision-making processes, which in turn lead to innovation (West & Anderson, 1996). Leadership processes will play a crucial role in determining whether tenure translates into innovation.

The task a team is required to perform determines to a large extent the level of innovation a team can implement. High levels of autonomy ceded to the group over the performance of its work, interdependence in the work of the team members, and task identity (the team performs a whole task) together will influence the level of innovation. At the same time, the characteristics of group members (innovativeness; ability to work in teams; the diversity of skills, perspectives, and knowledge they bring to the task; and the length of time members have worked together) will influence the level of innovation. The reader can consider his or her own team and ponder on the extent to which the task demands innovation. Is the team composed of people who have a propensity to innovate (Bunce & West, 1995, 1996)? Do team members embody a diversity of knowledge, skills, and perspectives that, when combined, lead to ideas for new and improved ways of working? Are team members skilled at integrating their perspectives, activities, and knowledge, thus enabling interdependent teamwork? Have they worked together for a long enough time to be reasonably efficient at decision making and achieving a shared representation of their work and ways of working? Finally, are the leadership processes in the team such that these factors that favor innovation are enhanced? If so, I argue that the likelihood is that the team has the capacity to be highly innovative, but this capacity can be constrained or enabled by the organization within which the team works in powerful ways. It is to a consideration of the organizational context for team innovation that I turn next.

Organizational Context

How do organizations enable or inhibit team innovation? In this section, I suggest that the culture and the climate of the organization powerfully determine whether teams will attempt to introduce innovation. The demands an organization places on teams to perform will also affect innovation in a positive and powerful way because usually it is those demands in the environment that spur innovation. Necessity, I argue, is indeed the mother of invention.

Organizational Culture and Climate

Organizations create an ethos or atmosphere within which creativity is either nurtured and blooms in innovation or is starved of support. Supportive and challenging environments are likely to sustain high levels of creativity (Mumford & Gustafson, 1988; West, 1987), especially those that encourage risk taking and idea generation (Cummings, 1965; Delbecq & Mills, 1985; Ettlie, 1983; Hage & Dewar, 1973; Kanter, 1983; Kimberley & Evanisko, 1981). Employees frequently have ideas for improving their workplace, work functioning, processes, products, or services (Nicholson & West, 1988; West, 1987), but where climates are characterized by distrust, lack of communication, personal antipathies, limited individual autonomy, and unclear goals, implementation of these ideas is inhibited.

Creative, innovative organizations are those where employees perceive and share an appealing vision of what the organization is trying to achieve—one, therefore, that is consistent with their values (West & Richter, in press). Innovative organizations have vigorous and mostly enjoyable interactions and debates among employees at all levels about how best to achieve that vision. Conflicts are seen as opportunities to find creative solutions that meet the needs of all parties in the organization rather than as win-lose situations. And people in such organizations have a high level of autonomy, responsibility, accountability, and power: they are free to make decisions about what to do, when to do it, and whom to do it with. Trust, cooperativeness, warmth, and humor are likely to characterize interpersonal and intergroup interactions. There is strong practical support for people's ideas for new and improved products and ways of working or of managing the organization. Senior managers are more likely than not to encourage and support innovative ideas (within safe limits) even when they are unsure of their potential value. Such organizations will almost certainly find themselves in uncertain, dynamic, and demanding environments, whether this is due to competition, scarcity of resources, changing markets or legislation, or global and environmental pressures. After all, that is why innovation has always occurred: humans have adapted their organizations and ways of working to the changing environments they find themselves in.

The leaders of teams will play an important part in buffering team members from the negative effects on team innovation of organizational climate. A leader who fights for the autonomy of his or her team in an organization that is highly controlling will moderate the effects of organizational culture on team innovation. Equally, a leader who dominates the team, whether or not the organizational context is supportive of innovation and team autonomy, will likely dramatically reduce the positive influence of a supportive organizational culture on group processes (such as member participation in decision making) and thereby levels of team innovation.

Other indicators of culture are the size, age, and structure of the organization. The greater the complexity and more differentiated the organization's structure (in terms of departments, groupings, etc.), the easier it is to cross knowledge boundaries and the greater the number of sources from which innovation can spring. Collaborative idea development across an organization is often cited as a precondition for organizational innovation (Allen, Lee, & Tushman, 1980; Kanter, 1983; Monge, Cozzens, & Contractor, 1992; Zaltman, Duncan, & Holbeck, 1973). There is support for the notion that high centralization is a negative predictor of innovation (T. Burns & Stalker, 1961; Hage & Aiken, 1967; Shepard, 1967), and Lawrence and Lorsch's (1967) case studies showed that tightly coupled interdepartmental relationships fostered new product development in organizations. However, our research in manufacturing organizations (West, Patterson, Pillinger, & Nickell, 2000) also suggests that centralization may also be necessary to ensure innovation implementation. Zaltman et al. call this the innovation dilemma. Decentralization at the local level is necessary for creative ideas to be developed, but centralization may be required for the effective implementation of those ideas in the wider organization. The failure of many organizations to innovate may be a consequence of a failure to recognize this inherent tension.

The resolution of the dilemma may be team-based organizations (Mohrman et al., 1995). Teams (especially cross-functional teams) provide the sources for ideas, and the team-based organization also offers simultaneously centralized and distributed decision-making structures that enable successful innovation. Indeed, the extent of team-based working in organizations appears to be a good predictor of innovation (Agrell & Gustafson, 1996; Mohrman et al., 1995; West et al., 2000).

What of size and age as cultural indicators? Large organizations have difficulty changing their forms to fit changing environments. Yet organizational size has been a positive predictor of both technological and administrative innovations (Kimberly & Evanisko, 1981): innovative agility is more a characteristic of smaller organizations (Rogers, 1983; Utterback, 1974). Size may be a surrogate measure of several dimensions associated with innovation, such as resources and economies of scale. However, in large organizations, decentralization and specialization are not sufficient to ensure innovation. Integration across groups, departments, and specialities is also necessary for communication and sharing of disseminated knowledge, and this requires some centralization or the sophisticated development of team-based structures. More recent research, examining all 35 U.S. firms that produced microprocessors between 1971 and 1989, showed that smaller organizations were more likely to be the sources of innovation (Wade, 1996). Younger organizations appear to be more innovative, all other things being equal. The longer human social organizations endure, the more embedded become their norms and the more resilient to change become their traditions. Consequently, mature organizations will have difficulty innovating and adapting (Kimberly & Evanisko, 1981; Pierce & Delbecq, 1977). Our data from a 10-year study of 110 UK manufacturing organizations revealed that younger organizations (years since startup) were likely to innovate in products, production technology, production processes, work organization, and people management (West et al., 2000). Evidence from U.S. studies also suggests that younger organizations are the predominant sources of innovation (Wade, 1996).

Amabile's (1988, 1997) componential model of creativity and innovation provides a link among the work environment, individual and team creativity, and organizational innovation. The organizational work environment is conceptualized as having three key characteristics: (1) organizational motivation to innovate describes an organization's basic orientation toward innovation, as well as its support for creativity and innovation; (2) management practices include management at all levels of the organization but, most important, the level of individual departments and projects; supervisory encouragement and work group support are two examples of relevant managerial behavior or practices; and (3) resources are related to everything that an organization has available to support creativity at work. Amabile proposes that the higher the concurrent levels of these three aspects of the organizational environment, the more innovation. The central statement of the theory is that elements of the work environment impact individual and team creativity by influencing expertise, task motivation, and creativity skills. The influence of intrinsic task motivation on creativity is considered essential: even though the environment may have an influence on each of the three components, the impact on task motivation is thought to be the most immediate and direct. Furthermore, creativity is seen as a primary source of organizational innovation.

In a study examining whether and how the work environments of highly creative projects differed from the work environments of less creative projects, Amabile, Conti, Coon, Lazenby, and Herron (1996) found that five dimensions consistently differed between high-creativity and low-creativity projects: challenge, organizational encouragement, work group support, supervisory encouragement, and organizational impediments.

Challenge is regarded as a moderate degree of workload pressure that arises from the urgent, intellectually challenging problem itself (Amabile, 1988; Amabile et al., 1996; see also Hennessey, this volume). The authors carefully distinguish challenge from excessive workload pressure, which is supposed to be negatively related to creativity, and suggest that time pressure may add to the perception of challenge in the work if it is perceived as a concomitant of an important, urgent project. This challenge, in turn, may be positively related to intrinsic motivation and creativity.

Organizational encouragement refers to several aspects within the organization. The first is encouragement of risk taking and idea generation, a valuing of innovation from the highest to the lowest levels of management. The second refers to a fair and supportive evaluation of new ideas; the authors underline this by referring to studies that showed that whereas threatening and highly critical evaluation of new ideas was shown to undermine creativity in laboratory studies, in field research supportive, informative evaluation can enhance the intrinsically motivated state that is most conducive to creativity. The third aspect of organizational encouragement focuses on reward and recognition of creativity; in a series of studies, Amabile and colleagues (1996) showed that reward perceived as a bonus, a confirmation of one's competence, or a means of enabling one to do better, more interesting work in the future can stimulate creativity, whereas the mere engagement in an activity to obtain a reward can be detrimental. The final aspect refers to the important role of collaborative idea flow across the organization, participative management, and decision making in the stimulation of creativity.

Work group support indicates the encouragement of activity within the particular group. The four aspects thought to be relevant for this are team member diversity, mutual openness to ideas, constructive challenging of ideas, and shared commitment to the project. Whereas the first two may influence creativity through exposing individuals to a greater variety of unusual ideas, the last two are thought to increase intrinsic motivation.

Supervisory encouragement stresses the aspects of goal clarity, open supervisory interactions, and perceived supervisory or leader support. Whereas goal clarity might have an effect on creativity by providing a clearer problem definition, Amabile et al. (1996) argue that open supervisory interactions as well as perceived supervisory support may influence creativity through preventing people from experiencing fear of negative criticism that can undermine the intrinsic motivation necessary for creativity.

In reporting the last of the five factors, organizational impediments, Amabile et al. (1996) refer to a few studies indicating that internal strife, conservatism, and rigid, formal management structures represent obstacles to creativity. The authors suggest that because these factors may be perceived as controlling, their likely negative influence on creativity may evolve from an increase in individual extrinsic motivation (motivation through external factors but not the task itself) and a corresponding decrease in the intrinsic motivation necessary for creativity. However, research on impediments to creativity, in comparison to research on stimulants of creativity, is still comparatively limited.

External Demands

I argue that external demands on teams (e.g., competition with other organizations, time pressures, and challenging targets) are likely to stimulate innovation implementation in teams that have effective group processes. This contradicts the position taken by other authors in this volume (see, e.g., Hennessey). Research in manufacturing organizations (West et al., 2000) and in hospitals (West & Anderson, 1992) suggests that the lower the market share held by manufacturing organizations, the higher the level of product innovation. Moreover, the extent of environmental uncertainty reported by senior managers in these organizations (in relation to suppliers, customers, market demands, and government legislation) was a strong predictor of the degree of innovation in organizational systems (e.g., in people management practices). Taken together, these findings suggest that if the environment of organizations is demanding, these organizations (or the teams within them) are more likely to innovate to reduce the demand or uncertainty. This is likely also to influence the level of innovation of groups at work. The effort of initiating change in organizations, with all the attendant resistance, conflicts, and experiences of failure, is likely, in most instances, to elicit strong aversive reactions among group members. The impetus to maintain innovation attempts (in the absence of strong intrinsic motivation) must therefore be provided by an expectation of high rewards or by the perception of high demands, threat, or uncertainty (for an extension of this argument, see West, 2002).

The external context of the group's work, be it organizational climate, support systems, market environment, or environmental uncertainty, is likely to have a highly significant influence on both its creativity and its innovation implementation. People, groups, and organizations innovate at least partly in response to external demands. A number of studies have shown that high work demands are significant predictors of individual innovation (Bunce & West, 1995, 1996; West, 1989). Indeed, studies of work role transitions show that changing role objectives, strategies, or relationships is a common response to the demands of new work environments (West, 1987). Of course, excessive work demands can have detrimental effects also on stress levels, absenteeism, and turnover. But the point here is that individuals innovate at least partly in response to high levels of demand—and groups are composed of individuals. What is intuitively apparent is that the relationship between external demands and innovation implementation cannot be linear. Extreme demands or sustained high levels (as may be found in war time or in disaster situations) are likely to produce paralysis or learned helplessness. However, within the bounds of most work environments, which are not characterized by extreme demands (for further discussion, see Simonton, this volume), levels of external demands will positively predict levels of team innovation.

Therefore, I suggest that the organizational culture, climate, and level of demands provides a context that determines the level of group innovation both directly and via their impact on team inputs and team processes. Clearly, the culture will influence the group's task (the amount of autonomy they are given), the group's composition (cross-functional teams are more likely in organic organizations), and group processes (team members are more likely to be supportive of innovation in a culture that recognizes and rewards ideas for new and improved ways of doing things). We cannot treat work teams as isolated islands if we wish to understand creativity and innovation at work. The organizational context plays a powerful part in influencing both the level and type of innovation. But, I argue below, the most important factors are the interaction and socioemotional processes that occur within teams.

Team Processes

Task characteristics, group diversity, and organizational context all influence team processes, affecting the development and redevelopment of shared objectives, levels of participation, management of conflict, support for new ideas, and leadership (West, 1990, 1994). If sufficiently integrated (i.e., there are shared objectives, high levels of participation, constructive, cooperative conflict management, high support for innovation, and leadership that enables innovation), these processes will foster creativity and innovation implementation. Moreover, effective group processes will be both sustained by and increase the level of psychosocial safety in the group.

Developing Shared Objectives

In the context of group innovation, clarity of team objectives is likely to facilitate innovation by enabling focused development of new ideas, which can be filtered with greater precision than if team objectives are unclear. Theoretically, clear objectives will facilitate innovation only if team members are committed to the goals of the team. This is because strong goal commitment is necessary to maintain group member persistence for implementation in the face of resistance among other organizational members. Pinto and Prescott (1987), in a study of 418 project teams, found that a clearly stated mission was the only factor that predicted success at all stages of the innovation process (conception, planning, execution, and termination). Where group members do not share a commitment to a set of objectives (or a vision of the goals of their work), the forces of disintegration created by disagreements (and lack of safety), diversity, and the emotional demands of the innovation process are likely to inhibit innovation.

Participation in Decision Making

To the extent that information and influence over decision making are shared within teams and there is a high level of interaction among team members, the cross-fertilization of perspectives that can spawn creativity and innovation (Cowan, 1986; Mumford & Gustafson, 1988; Pearce & Ravlin, 1987; Porac & Howard, 1990) is more likely to occur. More generally, high participation in decision making means less resistance to change and therefore greater likelihood of innovations being implemented (Bowers & Seashore, 1966; Coch & French, 1948; Lawler & Hackman, 1969).

Conflict

Many scholars believe that the management of competing perspectives is fundamental to the generation of creativity and innovation (Mumford & Gustafson, 1988; Nemeth & Owens, 1996; Tjosvold, 1998). Such processes are characteristic of task-related conflict (as opposed to conflicts of relationship and processs conflict, see De Dreu, 1997). They can arise from a common concern with quality of task performance in relation to shared objectives. Task conflict includes the appraisal of and constructive challenges to the group's performance. In essence, team members are more committed to performing their work effectively and excellently than they are either to bland consensus or to personal victory in conflict with other team members over task performance strategies or decision options.

Dean Tjosvold and colleagues (Tjosvold, 1982, 1991, 1998; Tjosvold & Field, 1983; Tjosvold & Johnson, 1977; Tjosvold, Wedley, & Field, 1986) have presented cogent arguments and strong supportive evidence that such constructive (task-related) controversy in a cooperative group context improves the quality of decision making and creativity. Constructive controversy is characterized by full exploration of opposing opinions and frank analyses of task-related issues. It occurs when decision makers believe they are in a cooperative group context where mutually beneficial goals are emphasized, rather than in a competitive context; where decision makers feel their personal competence is confirmed rather than questioned; and where they perceive processes of mutual influence rather than attempted dominance.

For example, the most effective self-managing teams in a manufacturing plant that Alper and Tjosvold (1993) studied were those that had compatible goals and promoted constructive controversy. The 544 employees who made up the 59 teams completed a questionnaire that probed for information about cooperation, competition, and conflict within the teams. Teams were responsible for activities such as work scheduling, housekeeping, safety, purchasing, accident investigation, and quality. Members of teams that promoted interdependent conflict management (people cooperated to work through their differences), compared to teams with win-lose conflict (where team members tended to engage in a power struggle when they had different views and interests), felt confident that they could deal with differences. Such teams were rated more productive and innovative by their managers. Apparently, because of this success, members of these teams were committed to working as a team.

Another perspective on conflict and innovation comes from minority influence theory. A number of researchers have shown that minority consistency of arguments over time is likely to lead to change in majority views in groups (Maass & Clark, 1984; Nemeth, 1986; Nemeth & Chiles, 1988; Nemeth & Kwan, 1987; Nemeth & Owens, 1996; Nemeth & Wachtler, 1983). (For an account of this research and an assessment of how it relates to group creativity, see the excellent chapter by Nemeth & Nemeth-Brown, this volume).

De Dreu and De Vries (1993, 1997; see also Nemeth & Staw, 1989) suggest that a homogeneous workforce in which minority dissent is suppressed will reduce creativity, innovation, individuality, and independence. Disagreement about ideas within a group can be beneficial. Some researchers even argue that team task- or information-related conflict is valuable whether or not it occurs in a collaborative context because it can improve decision making and strategic planning (Cosier & Rose, 1977; Mitroff, Barabba, & Kilmann, 1977; Schweiger, Sandberg, & Rechner, 1989). This is because task-related conflict may lead team members to reevaluate the status quo and adapt their objectives, strategies, or processes more appropriately to their situation (Coser, 1970; Nemeth & Staw, 1989; Roloff, 1987; Thomas, 1979). However, De Dreu and Weingart (in press) suggest that high levels of conflict in teams, regardless of whether the conflict is focused on relationships or task, will inhibit team effectiveness and innovation.

In a study of newly formed postal work teams in the Netherlands, De Dreu and West (2001) found that minority dissent did indeed predict team innovation (as rated by the teams' supervisors), but only in teams with high levels of participation. It seems that the social processes in the team necessary for minority dissent to influence the innovation process are characterized by high levels of team member interaction, influence over decision making, and information sharing. This finding has significant implications for our understanding of minority dissent in groups operating in organizational contexts.

Overall, therefore, moderate task-related (as distinct from emotional or interpersonal) conflict and minority dissent in a participative climate will lead to innovation by encouraging debate (requisite diversity) and to consideration of alternative interpretations of information available, leading to integrated and creative solutions.

Support for Innovation

Innovation is more likely to occur in groups where there is support for innovation and innovative attempts are rewarded rather than punished (Amabile, 1983; Kanter, 1983). Support for innovation is the expectation, approval, and practical support of attempts to introduce new and improved ways of doing things in the work environment (West, 1990). Within groups, new ideas may be routinely rejected or ignored or attract verbal and practical support. Such group processes powerfully shape individual and group behavior (for reviews, see, e.g., Brown, 2000; Hackman, 1992), and those that support innovation will encourage team members to introduce innovations. In a longitudinal study of 27 hospital top management teams, Anderson and West (1998; West & Anderson, 1996) found that support for innovation was the most powerful predictor of team innovation of any of the group processes so far discussed.

Reflexivity

Team reflexivity is the extent to which team members collectively reflect on the team's objectives, strategies, and processes as well as their wider organizations and environments, and adapt them accordingly (West, 1996, p. 559). There are three central elements to the concept of reflexivity: reflection, planning, and action or adaptation. Reflection consists of attention, awareness, monitoring, and evaluation of the object of reflection (West, 2000). Planning is one of the potential consequences of the indeterminacy of reflection, because during this indeterminacy, courses of action can be contemplated, intentions formed, and plans developed (in more or less detail) and the potential for carrying them out is built up. High reflexivity exists when team planning is characterized by greater detail, inclusiveness of potential problems, hierarchical ordering of plans, and long- as well as short-range planning. More detailed implementation intentions or plans are more likely to lead to innovation implementation (Frese & Zapf,

1994; Gollwitzer, 1996). Indeed, the work of Gollwitzer and colleagues suggests that goal-directed behavior or innovation will be initiated when the team has articulated implementation intentions. This is because planning creates a conceptual readiness for, and guides team members' attention toward, relevant opportunities for action and means to accomplish the team's goal. Action refers to goal-directed behaviors relevant to achieving the desired changes in team objective, strategies, processes, organizations, or environments identified by the team during the stage of reflection.

Reflexivity can relate to team objectives, strategies, internal processes, development of group psychosocial characteristics, and external relations as well as the external environment. As a consequence of reflexivity, the team's reality is continually renegotiated during team interaction. Understandings negotiated in one exchange among team members may be drawn on in a variety of ways to inform subsequent discussions and offer the possibility of helpful and creative transformations and meanings (Bouwen & Fry, 1996). Research with BBC television program production teams, whose work fundamentally requires creativity and innovation, provides support for these propositions (Carter & West, 1998).

Group Psychosocial Safety

Group psychosocial safety refers to shared understandings, unconscious group processes, group cognitive style, and group emotional tone (Cohen & Bailey, 1997). Examples include norms, cohesiveness, team mental models (members share an understanding of the nature of the group's task, its task processes, how members are required to work together, and the organizational context), and group affect. In groups with high levels of psychosocial safety, it is suggested, there will be high creativity (see also Milliken et al.'s discussion of safety as a context for creativity, this volume). Creative ideas arise out of individual cognitive processes and, though group members may interact in ways that offer cognitive stimulation via diversity, creative ideas are produced as a result of individual cognitions. Evidence suggests that, in general, creative cognitions occur when individuals are free from pressure, feel safe, and experience relatively positive affect (Claxton, 1997, 1998). Moreover, psychological threats to reputation, dignity, "face," or identity are also associated with more rigid thinking (Cowen, 1952). Time pressure can also increase rigidity of thinking on work-related tasks such as selection decisions (Kruglansky & Freund, 1983). Another example of stress inhibiting the flexibility of responses is offered by Wright (1954), who asked people to respond to Rorschach inkblot tests. Half of the people were hospital patients awaiting an operation and half were controls. The former gave more stereotyped responses and were less fluent and creative in completing similes (e.g., "as interesting as . . ."), indicating the effects of stress or threat on their capacity to generate creative responses.

Jehn (1995) found that norms reflecting the acceptance of conflict within a group, promoting an open and constructive atmosphere for group discussion, enhanced the positive effect of task-based conflict on individual and team performance for 79 work groups and 75 management groups. Members of high-performing groups were not afraid to express their ideas and opinions. Such a finding further reinforces the notion that safety may be an important factor in idea generation or creativity.

Edmondson (1996) found major differences between newly formed intensive care nursing teams in their management of medication errors. In some groups, members openly acknowledged and discussed their errors (giving too much or too little of a drug or administering the wrong drug) and discussed ways to avoid their occurrence. In others, members kept information about errors to themselves. Learning about the causes of these errors as a team and devising innovations to prevent future errors were possible only in groups of the former type. Edmondson gives an example of how, in one learning-oriented team, discussion of a recent error led to innovation in equipment: an intravenous medication pump was identified as a source of consistent errors and so was replaced by a different type of pump. She also gives the example of how failure to discuss errors and generate innovations led to costly failure in the Hubble telescope development project. In particular, Edmondson (1996, 1999) argues that learning and innovation will take place only where group members trust other members' intentions. This manifests in a group-level belief that well-intentioned action will not lead to punishment or rejection by the team, which Edmondson (1999) calls "team safety": "The term is meant to suggest a realistic, learning oriented attitude about effort, error and change—not to imply a careless sense of permissiveness, nor an unrelentingly positive affect. Safety is not the same as comfort; in contrast, it is predicted to facilitate risk" (p. 14).

Leadership

Leaders of groups may seek ideas and support their implementation among members, promote only their own ideas, or resist change and innovation from any source. The leader, by definition, exerts powerful social influences on the group or team and therefore affects team performance (Beyerlein, Johnson, & Beyerlein, 1996; Brewer, Wilson, & Beck, 1994; Komaki, Desselles, & Bowman, 1989). For example, research in Canadian manufacturing organizations reveals that CEOs' age, flexibility, and perseverance are all positively related to the adoption of technological innovation in their organization (Kitchell, 1997). I propose that leadership processes moderate the effects of inputs (team and organizational contexts) on team processes and thereby affect the level and quality (magnitude, radicalness, and novelty) of the innovation (see Figure 12.1).

In any discussion of team leadership it is important to acknowledge that leadership processes are not necessarily invested in one person in a team. In most work teams there is a single and clearly defined team leader or manager, and his or her style and behavior have a considerable influence on moderating the relationships between inputs and processes. But leadership processes can be distributed such that more than one or all team members take on leadership roles at various points in the team's activities. Consider, for example, the breast cancer care team responsible for diagnosis, surgery, and postoperative treatment of patients. At various points, the oncologist, surgeon, and breast care nurse are likely to (and it is appropriate that they should) take leadership roles in the team (Haward et al., 2002).

Recent theories of leadership depict two dominant styles: transformational and transactional. Transactional leaders focus on transactions, exchanges, and contingent rewards and punishments to change team members' behavior (see Schriesheim & Kerr, 1977; Yammarino, 1996; Yukl, 1994). This style reflects an emphasis on the relationship between task-oriented leader behavior and effective group member performance. Transformational leaders influence group members by encouraging them to transform their views of themselves and their work. They rely on charisma and the ability to conjure inspiring visions of the future (e.g., Bass, 1990; J. M. Burns, 1978; House & Shamir, 1993). Such leaders use emotional or ideological appeals to change the behavior of the group, moving them from self-interest in work values to consideration of the whole group and organization. Although the reader may be tempted to conclude that only the transformational style will produce innovation, it is likely that both of these styles influence creativity and innovation by moderating the relationship between inputs and processes. Inspiration or reward can lead to the individual propensity to innovate being translated into innovation implementation. Rewards used by the leader will influence group creativity and innovation where these rewards are directed toward encouraging individual and group innovation, such as performance-related pay for new product development successes.

Knorr, Mittermeir, Aichholzer, and Waller (1979) found that the team leader's professional status and ability to plan and coordinate activities, integrate the team, and encourage career promotion predicted the climate for innovation in the team as well as its overall performance. McDonough and Barczak (1992) examined the relationships between a leader's cognitive problem-solving style and the team's cognitive problem-solving style in product development teams. Cognitive problem-solving style was characterized as either adaptive (conforms to commonly accepted procedures) or innovative (searches for novel solutions). When the technology they were required to use was familiar to the team, the leader's style was unimportant. However, when the technology was unfamiliar, teams whose leaders had an innovative cognitive style developed new products faster than other teams. For product innovation in familiar situations, it seems leaders can withdraw from the team, but when the situation is unfamiliar, a nonconforming leader enables the team to consider a variety of options.

No discussion of leadership in social or industrial/organizational psychology should neglect the impressive program of work carried out by Norman Maier and his colleagues in the 1960s and 1970s. Maier (1970) conducted a series of experiments with (mostly student) groups exploring the influence of different leadership styles on problem solving and creativity. The results suggested that the leader should encourage "problem-mindedness" in groups on the basis that exploring the problem fully is the best way of eventually generating a rich vein of solution options. The leader can delay a group's criticism of an idea by asking for alternative contributions and should use his or her power to protect individuals with minority views, so that their opinions can be heard (Maier & Solem, 1962; see also Osborn, 1957). Maier argued that leaders should delay offering their opinions as long as possible because propositions from leaders are often given undue weight and tend either to be too hastily accepted or rejected, rather than properly evaluated, a finding since replicated in a variety of applied studies. Maier concludes that leaders should function as "the group's central nervous system": receive information, facilitate communication, relay messages, and integrate responses—in short, integrate the group. The leader must be receptive to information but not impose solutions; be aware of group processes; listen to understand rather than to appraise or refute; assume responsibility for accurate communication; be sensitive to unexpressed feelings; protect minority views; keep the discussion moving; and develop skills in summarizing (Maier, 1970).

Leadership processes have a considerable influence on determining whether the inputs (such as team task, team member characteristics, organizational culture and climate, and demands on the team) are translated into group processes that support innovation implementation or smother both creativity and innovation. In this chapter, I have proposed that they play a major role in moderating the relationship between input variables and group processes and thereby innovation implementation. Generally, leadership is a topic that has been neglected in the study of group creativity and innovation since Maier's seminal work. As we move into an era when the imperatives for innovation in organizations are intense, it is important that social and industrial/organizational psychologists stretch their research to achieve a better understanding of how leaders influence creativity and innovation in teams.

Conclusions

I have argued that researchers eager to understand group creativity must focus more on the implementation of ideas than their generation in the workplace. It is the implementation of a good idea that advances our progress as a species, not merely the private creative idea-generation process. Too little research effort has been directed at implementation rather than idea generation. I have also suggested that the task a team performs is a key to understanding innovation implementation. It is motivating and challenging tasks that lead teams of innovative people with diverse backgrounds and perspectives to innovate. If we are to encourage team innovation in the workplace we must offer teams tasks that give them autonomy, challenge, and a sense of meaningfulness. But even with innovative people facing a challenging and motivating task, if the organization's culture is one of blame, suspicion, hostility, and control, team members' efforts are unlikely to translate into innovation. It is in organizations whose members share an appealing vision of what the organization is trying to achieve where vigorous debates on how best to achieve that vision are the norm; trust, cooperation, altruism, warmth, and humor characterize the climate. Innovation is encouraged in organizations in demanding environments; the IT revolution occurred in highly competitive, rapidly changing, and uncertain market environments.

I have proposed that, to understand innovation in work teams, we must also understand how leadership enables or inhibits the effects of inputs on team processes in innovation, and therefore leadership is an important topic for future study in this hugely important area. Team leaders play a crucial role in buffering the team from the pernicious effects, or enhancing in the team the nurturing effects, of organizational culture. Team leaders also can ensure that team member and task characteristics influence group processes in a way that leads to rather than inhibits innovation. But ultimately, I have suggested, it is the integrating and social interaction processes in teams that determine whether they will implement innovation.

Throughout this discussion, I have treated innovation as though it was a positive end in itself. There is a final reason to consider how we can best create the conditions for effective work team innovation implementation. Opportunities to develop and implement skills in the workplace and to innovate are central to the satisfaction of people at work (Nicholson & West, 1988), and innovation is vital to the effectiveness of organizations in highly demanding and competitive environments (Geroski, 1994). One of the most striking findings from our research on managerial job change (Nicholson & West, 1988) was how the mental health of those who moved to jobs that offered fewer opportunities to be innovative than had their previous job showed a bigger decline than among those who became unemployed. The Whitehall studies too have shown how important for mental health are variety of work and opportunity to use skills (Stansfield, Head, & Marmot, 1998). The creative challenge for psychologists is to help implement climates and cultures within their own organizations, and those they advise, so that team innovation and human well-being are enabled.

Notes

Thanks are extended to Bernard Nijstad and Paul Paulus for helpful comments on an earlier draft.

1. I would add another characteristic: task significance (Hackman & Oldham, 1975). This refers to the importance of the task in contributing to organizational goals or to the wider society. A lifeboat team in a rural coastal area with busy shipping lanes and a health and safety team in a high-risk industry are likely to be highly intrinsically motivated by the significance of their tasks. A debt collection agency for an accounting company is less likely to be intrinsically motivated.

References

Agrell, A., & Gustafson, R. (1996). Innovation and creativity in work groups. In M. A. West (Ed.), *The handbook of work group psychology* (pp. 317–344). Chichester, UK: Wiley.

Allen, T. J., Lee, D. M., & Tushman, M. L. (1980). R&D performance as a function of internal communication, project management, and the nature of work. *IEEE Transactions, 27*, 2–12.

Alper, S., & Tjosvold, D. (1993, June). *Cooperation theory and self-managing teams on the manufacturing floor.* Paper presented at the International Association for Conflict Management, Eugene, OR.

Amabile, T. M. (1983). The social psychology of creativity: A componential conceptualization. *Journal of Personality and Social Psychology, 45*, 357–376.

Amabile, T. M. (1988). A model of creativity and innovation in organizations. In B. M. Staw & L. L. Cummings (Eds.), *Research in organizational behavior* (Vol. 10, pp. 123–167). Greenwich, CT: JAI Press.

Amabile, T. M. (1997). Motivating creativity in organizations: On doing what you love and loving what you do. *California Management Review, 40*(1), 39–58.

Amabile, T. M., & Conti, R. (1999). Changes in the work environment for creativity during downsizing. *Academy of Management Journal, 42*, 630–640.

Amabile, T. M., Conti, R., Coon, H., Lazenby, J., & Herron, M. (1996). Assessing the work environment for creativity. *Academy of Management Journal, 39*, 1154–1184.

Ancona, D. F., & Caldwell, D. F. (1992). Bridging the boundary: External activity and performance in organisational teams. *Administrative Science Quarterly, 37*, 634–665.

Anderson, N., & West, M. A. (1998). Measuring climate for work group innovation: Development and validation of the Team Climate Inventory. *Journal of Organizational Behaviour, 19*, 235–258.

Andrews, F. M. (Ed). (1979). *Scientific productivity.* Cambridge, UK: Cambridge University Press.

Bantel, K. A., & Jackson, S. E. (1989). Top management and innovations in banking: Does the demography of the top team make a difference? *Strategic Management Journal, 10*, 107–124.

Barron, F. B., & Harrington, D. M. (1981). Creativity, intelligence and personality. In M. R. Rosenzweig & L. W. Porter (Eds.), *Annual review of psychology* (Vol. 32, pp. 439–476). Palo Alto, CA: Annual Reviews.

Bass, B. M. (1990). *Bass and Stogdill's handbook of leadership* (3rd ed.). New York: Free Press.

Beyerlein, M. M., Johnson, D. A., & Beyerlein, S. T. (Eds.). (1996). *Advances in the interdisciplinary study of work teams: Vol. 2 Knowledge work in teams.* London: JAI Press.

Blumberg, M. (1988). Towards a new theory of job design. In W. Karwowski, H. R. Parsaei, & M. R. Wilhelm (Eds.), *Ergonomics of hybrid automated systems* (Vol. 1, pp. 53–59). Amsterdam: Elsevier.

Bouwen, R., & Fry, R. (1996). Facilitating group development: Interventions for a relational and contextual construction. In M. A. West (Ed.), *The handbook of work group psychology* (pp. 531–552). Chichester, UK: Wiley.

Bowers, D. G., & Seashore, S. E. (1966). Predicting organizational effectiveness with a four-factor theory of leadership. *Administrative Science Quarterly, 11,* 238–263.

Brewer, N., Wilson, C., & Beck, K. (1994). Supervisory behaviour and team performance amongst police patrol sergeants. *Journal of Occupational and Organizational Psychology, 67,* 69–78.

Brown, R. J. (2000). *Group processes: Dynamics within and between groups.* London: Blackwell.

Bunce, D., & West, M.A. (1995). Changing work environments: Innovative coping responses to occupational stress. *Work and Stress, 8,* 319–331.

Bunce, D., & West, M. A. (1996). Stress management and innovation interventions at work. *Human Relations, 49,* 209–232.

Burningham, C., & West, M. A. (1995). Individual, climate and group interaction processes as predictors of work team innovation. *Small Group Research, 26,* 106–117.

Burns, J. M. (1978). *Leadership.* New York: Harper & Row.

Burns, T., & Stalker, G. M. (1961). *The management of innovation.* London: Tavistock.

Campion, M. A., Medsker, G. J., & Higgs, A. C. (1993). Relations between work group characteristics and effectiveness: Implications for designing effective work groups. *Personnel Psychology, 46,* 823–850.

Campion, M. A., Papper, E. M., & Medsker, G. J. (1996). Relations between work team characteristics and effectiveness: A replication and extension. *Personnel Psychology, 49,* 429–689.

Carter, S. M., & West, M. A. (1998). Reflexivity, effectiveness and mental health in BBC-TV production teams. *Small Group Research, 5,* 583–601.

Claxton, G. L. (1997). *Hare brain, tortoise mind: Why intelligence increases when you think less.* London: Fourth Estate.

Claxton, G. L. (1998). Knowing without knowing why: Investigating human intuition. *The Psychologist, 11,* 217–220.

Coch, L., & French, J. R. (1948). Overcoming resistance to change. *Human Relations, 1,* 512–532.

Cohen, S. G., & Bailey, D. E. (1997). What makes teams work: Group effectiveness research from the shop floor to the executive suite. *Journal of Management, 23,* 239–290.

Cooper, R., & Foster, M. (1971). Sociotechnical systems. *American Psychologist, 26,* 467–474.

Cordery, J. L. (1996). Autonomous work groups and quality circles. In M. A. West (Ed.), *Handbook of work group psychology* (pp. 225–246). Chichester, UK: Wiley.

Coser, L. A. (1970). *Continuities in the study of social conflict.* New York: Free Press.

Cosier, R., & Rose, G. (1977). Cognitive conflict and goal conflict effects on task performance. *Organizational Behaviour and Human Performance, 19,* 378–391.

Cowan, D. A. (1986). Developing a process model of problem recognition. *Academy of Management Review, 11,* 763–776.

Cowen, E. L. (1952). The influence of varying degrees of psychological stress on problem-solving rigidity. *Journal of Abnormal and Social Psychology, 47,* 420–424.

Cummings, L. L. (1965). Organizational climates for creativity. *Journal of the Academy of Management, 3,* 220–227.

De Dreu, C. K. W. (1995). Coercive power and concession making in bilateral negotiation. *Journal of Conflict Resolution, 39,* 646–670.

De Dreu, C. K. W. (1997). Productive conflict: The importance of conflict management and conflict issue. In C. K. W. De Dreu & E. Van de Vliert (Eds.), *Using conflict in organizations* (pp. 9–22). London: Sage.

De Dreu, C. K. W., & De Vries, N. K. (1993). Numerical support, information processing, and attitude change. *European Journal of Social Psychology, 23*, 647–662.

De Dreu, C. K. W., & De Vries, N. K. (1997). Minority dissent in organizations. In C. K. W. De Dreu & E. Van de Vliert (Eds.), *Using conflict in organizations* (pp. 72–86). London: Sage.

De Dreu, C. K. W., & Weingart, L. R. (in press). A contingency theory of task conflict and performance in groups and organizational teams. In M. A. West, D. Tjosvold, & K. Smith (Eds.), *Handbook of organizational teamwork and cooperation.* London: Wiley.

De Dreu, C. K. W., & West, M. A. (2001). Minority dissent and team innovation: The importance of participation in decision-making. *Journal of Applied Psychology, 68*, 1191–1201.

Delbecq, A. L., & Mills, P. K. (1985). Managerial practices that enhance innovation. *Organizational Dynamics, 14*, 24–34.

Economist (2001, June). *Technology Quarterly*, 3.

Edmondson, A. C. (1996). Learning from mistakes is easier said than done: Group and organizational influences on the detection and correction of human error. *Journal of Applied Behavioral Science, 32*, 5–28.

Edmondson, A. C. (1999). Psychological safety and learning behavior in work teams. *Administrative Science Quarterly, 44*, 350–383.

Emery, F. E. (1959). *Characteristics of sociotechnical systems.* London: Tavistock Insititute of Human Relations, Document No. 527.

Ettlie, J. E. (1983). Organizational policy and innovation among suppliers to the food-processing sector. *Academy of Management Journal, 26*, 27–44.

Filley, A. C., House, R. J., & Kerr, S. (1976). *Managerial process and organizational behaviour.* Glenview, IL: Scott Foresman.

Frese, M., & Zapf, D. (1994). Action as the core of work psychology: A German approach. In H. C. Triandis, M. D. Dunnette, & L. M. Hough (Eds.), *Handbook of industrial and organizational psychology* (2nd ed., Vol. 4, pp. 271–340). Palo Alto, CA: Consulting Psychologists Press.

Geroski, P. (1994). *Market structure, corporate performance, and innovative activity.* Oxford: Clarendon Press.

Ghiselli, E. E., & Lodahl, T. M. (1958). Patterns of managerial traits and group effectiveness. *Journal of Abnormal and Social Psychology, 57*, 61–66.

Gollwitzer, P. M. (1996). The volitional benefits of planning. In P. M. Gollwitzer & J. A. Bargh (Eds.), *The psychology of action: Linking cognition and motivation to behaviour* (pp. 287–312). New York: Guilford.

Gulowsen, J. A., (1972). A measure of work group autonomy. In L. E. Davis & J. C. Taylor (Eds.), *Design of jobs* (pp. 374–390). Harmondsworth, UK: Penguin.

Hacker, W. (1986). *Arbeitpsychologie.* Bern: Huber.

Hacker, W. (1994). Action regulation theory and occupational psychology: Review of German empirical research since 1987. *The German Journal of Psychology, 18*, 91–120.

Hackman, J. R. (1992). Group influences on individuals in organizations. In M. D. Dunnette and L. M. Hough (Eds.), *Handbook of industrial and organizational psychology*, 2nd ed. (pp. 199–267). Palo Alto, CA: Consulting Psychologists Press.

Hackman, J. R., & Oldham, G. (1975). Development of the job diagnostic survey. *Journal of Applied Psychology, 60,* 159–170.

Hage, J., & Aiken, M. (1967). *Social change in complex organizations.* New York: Random House.

Hage, J., & Dewar, R. (1973). Elite values versus organizational structure in predicting innovation. *Administrative Science, 18,* 279–290.

Haward, B., Amir, Z., Borrill, C. S., Dawson, J. F., Sainsbury, R., Scully, J., & West, M. A. (2002). *Breast cancer teams: The impact of constitution, new cancer workload, and methods of operation on their effectiveness.* Unpublished paper, Epidemiology and Health Services Research, University of Leeds, UK.

Henderson, J. C., & Lee, S. (1992). Managing I/S design teams: A control theories perspective. *Management Science, 38,* 757–777.

Hoffman, L. R. (1979). Applying experimental research on group problem solving to organizations. *Journal of Abnormal and Social Psychology, 58,* 27–32.

Hoffman, L. R., Harburg, E., & Maier, N. R. F. (1962). Differences and disagreement as factors in creative group problem solving. *Journal of Abnormal and Social Psychology, 64,* 206–214.

Hoffman, L. R., & Maier, N. R. F. (1961). Sex differences, sex composition, and group problem-solving. *Journal of Abnormal and Social Psychology, 63,* 453–456.

House, R. J., & Shamir, B. (1993). Toward the integration of transformational, charismatic, and visionary theories. In M. M. Chemers & R. Ayman (Eds.), *Leadership theory and research: Perspectives and directions* (pp. 81–107). San Diego, CA: Academic Press.

Jackson, S. E. (1992). Consequences of group composition for the interpersonal dynamics of strategic issue processing. *Advances in Strategic Management, 8,* 345–382.

Jackson, S. E. (1996). The consequences of diversity in multidisciplinary work teams. In M. A. West (Ed.), *Handbook of work group psychology* (pp. 53–75). Chichester, UK: Wiley.

Jehn, K. A. (1995). A multimethod examination of the benefits and detriments of intragroup conflict. *Administrative Science Quarterly, 40,* 256–282.

Kanter, R. M. (1983). *The change masters: Corporate entrepreneurs at work.* New York: Simon & Schuster.

Katz, R. (1982). The effects of group longevity on project communication and performance. *Administrative Science Quarterly, 27,* 81–104.

Kim, Y., & Leigh, B. (1995). R&D project team climate and team performance in Korea: A multidimensional approach. *R&D Management, 25,* 195–229.

Kimberley, J. R., & Evanisko, M. J. (1981). Organizational innovation: The influence of individual, organizational and contextual factors on hospital adoption of technological and administrative innovations. *Academy of Management Journal, 24,* 689–713.

Kitchell, S. (1997). CEO characteristics and technological innovativeness: A Canadian perspective. *Canadian Journal of Administrative Sciences, 14,* 111–125.

Knorr, K. D., Mittermeir, R., Aichholzer, G., & Waller, G. (1979). Leadership and group performance: A positive relationship in academic research units. In F. M. Andrews (Ed.), *Scientific productivity* (pp. 95–117). Cambridge, UK: Cambridge University Press.

Komaki, J. L., Desselles, M. L., & Bowman, E. D. (1989). Definitely not a breeze:

Extending an operant model of effective supervision to teams. *Journal of Applied Psychology, 74*, 522–529.

Kruglansky, A. W., & Freund, T. (1983). The freezing and unfreezing of lay influences: Effects on impressional primacy, ethnic stereotyping and numerical anchoring. *Journal of Experimental Social Psychology, 12*, 448–468.

Lawler, E. E., III, & Hackman, J. R. (1969). Impact of employee participation in the development of pay incentive plans: A field experiment. *Journal of Applied Psychology, 53*, 467–471.

Lawrence, P. R., & Lorsch, J. W. (1967). *Organization and environment: Managing differentiation and integration.* Boston: Harvard Business School.

Maass, A., & Clark, R. D. (1984). Hidden impacts of minorities: Fifty years of minority influence research. *Psychological Bulletin, 95*, 428–450.

Maier, N. R. (1970). *Problem solving and creativity: In individuals and groups.* Monterey, CA: Brooks Cole.

Maier, N. R., & Solem, A. R. (1962). Improving solutions by turning choice situations into problems. *Personnel Psychology, 15*, 151–157.

Maznevski, M. L. (1994). Understanding our differences: Performance in decision-making groups with diverse members. *Human Relations, 47*, 531–552.

McDonough, E. F., III, & Barczak, G. (1992). The effects of cognitive problem-solving orientation and technological familiarity on faster new product development. *Journal of Product Innovation Management, 9*, 44–52.

McGrath, J. E. (1984). *Groups: Interaction and performance.* Englewood Cliffs, NJ: Prentice-Hall.

Mitroff, J., Barabba, N., & Kilmann, R. (1977). The application of behaviour and philosophical technologies to strategic planning: A case study of a large federal agency. *Management Studies, 24*, 44–58.

Mohrman, S. A., Cohen, S. G., & Mohrman, A. M. (1995). *Designing team-based organizations: New forms for knowledge work.* San Francisco: Jossey-Bass.

Monge, P. R., Cozzens, M. D., & Contractor, N. S. (1992). Communication and motivational predictors of the dynamics of organizational innovation. *Organizational Science, 3*, 250–274.

Mumford, M. D., & Gustafson, S. B. (1988). Creativity syndrome: Integration, application and innovation. *Psychological Bulletin, 103*, 27–43.

Nemeth, C. (1986). Differential contributions of majority and minority influence. *Psychological Review, 93*, 23–32.

Nemeth, C., & Chiles, C. (1988). Modelling courage: The role of dissent in fostering independence. *European Journal of Social Psychology, 18*, 275–280.

Nemeth, C., & Kwan, J. (1987). Minority influence, divergent thinking and the detection of correct solutions. *Journal of Applied Social Psychology, 9*, 788–799.

Nemeth, C., & Owens, P. (1996). Making work groups more effective: The value of minority dissent. In M. A. West (Ed.), *Handbook of work group psychology* (pp. 125–142). Chichester, UK: Wiley.

Nemeth, C., & Staw, B. M. (1989). The trade-offs of social control and innovation within groups and organizations. In L. Berkowitz (Ed.), *Advances in experimental social psychology* (pp. 175–210). New York: Academic Press.

Nemeth, C., & Wachtler, J. (1983). Creative problem solving as a result of majority vs. minority influence. *European Journal of Social Psychology, 13*, 45–55.

Nicholson, N., & West, M. A. (1988). *Managerial job change: Men and women in transition.* Cambridge, UK: Cambridge University Press.

O'Reilly, C. A., & Flatt, S. F. (1989, August). *Executive team demography, organizational innovation, and firm performance.* Paper presented at the Academy of Management Conference, Washington, DC.

Osborn, A. F. (1957). *Applied imagination.* New York: Scribner.

Payne, R. L. (1990). The effectiveness of research teams: A review. In M. A. West and J. L. Farr (Eds.), *Innovation and creativity at work: Psychological and organizational strategies* (pp. 101–122). Chichester, UK: Wiley.

Pearce, J. A., & Ravlin, E. C. (1987). The design and activation of self-regulating work groups. *Human Relations, 40,* 751–782.

Pelz, D. C. (1956). Some social factors related to performance in a research organization. *Administrative Science Quarterly, 1,* 310–325.

Pierce, J. L., & Delbecq, A. L. (1977). Organizational structure, individual attitudes and innovation. *Academy of Management Review, 2,* 27–38.

Pinto, J. K., & Prescott, J. F. (1987). Changes in critical success factor importance over the life of a project. *Academy of management proceedings* (pp. 328–332).

Porac, J. F., & Howard, H. (1990). Taxonomic mental models in competitor definition. *Academy of Management Review, 2,* 224–240.

Rogers, E. M. (1983). *Diffusion of innovations* (3rd ed.). New York: Free Press.

Roloff, M. E. (1987). Communication and conflict. In C. R. Berger & S. H. Chaffee (Eds.), *Handbook of communication science* (pp. 484–534). Newbury Park, CA: Sage.

Schriesheim, C. A., & Kerr, S. (1977). Theories and measures of leadership: A critical appraisal of current and future directions. In J. G. Hunt & L. L. Larson (Eds.), *Leadership: The cutting edge* (pp. 9–45). Carbondale: Southern Illinois University Press.

Schweiger, D., Sandberg, W., & Rechner, P. (1989). Experimental effects of dialectical inquiry, devil's advocacy, and other consensus approaches to strategic decision making. *Academy of Management Journal, 32,* 745–772.

Shaw, M. E. (1976). *Group dynamics: The psychology of small group behaviour.* New York: McGraw-Hill.

Shaw, M. E. (1981). *Group dynamics: The psychology of small group behavior.* New York: McGraw-Hill.

Shepard, H. A. (1967). Innovation-resisting and innovation-producing organizations. *Journal of Business, 40,* 470–477.

Slater, J. A., & West, M. A. (1999). Primary health care teams: United Kingdom National Health System. In J. J. Phillips, S. D. Jones, & M. M. Beyerlein (Eds.), *Developing high performance work teams* (Vol. 2, pp. 199–214). Alexandria, VA: American Society for Training and Development.

Smith, K. G., Smith, K. A., Olian, J. D., Sims, H. P., Jr., O'Brannon, D. P., & Scully, J. A. (1994). Top management team demography and process: The role of social integration and communication. *Administrative Science Quarterly, 39,* 412–438.

Stansfield, S. A., Head, J., & Marmot, M. G. (1998). Explaining social class differences in depression and well-being. *Social Psychiatry and Psychiatric Epidemiology, 33,* 1–9.

Steiner, I. D. (1972). *Group process and productivity.* New York: Academic Press.

Sternberg, R. J., & Lubart, T. I. (1996). Investing in creativity. *American Psychologist, 51,* 677–688.

Stevens, M. J., & Campion, M. A. (1994, April). *Staffing teams: Development and validation of the Teamwork–KSA test.* Paper presented at the 9th annual meeting of the Society of Industrial and Organizational Psychology, Nashville, TN.

Thomas, K. W. (1979). Organizational conflict. In S. Kerr (Ed.), *Organizational behaviour* (pp. 151–84). Columbus, OH: Grid Publishing.

Tjosvold, D. (1982). Effects of approach to controversy on superiors' incorporation of subordinates' information in decision making. *Journal of Applied Psychology, 67,* 189–193.

Tjosvold, D. (1985). Implications of controversy research for management. *Journal of Management, 11,* 21–37.

Tjosvold, D. (1991). *Team organization: An enduring competitive advantage.* Chichester, UK: Wiley.

Tjosvold, D. (1998). Co-operative and competitive goal approaches to conflict: Accomplishments and challenges. *Applied Psychology: An International Review, 47,* 285–342.

Tjosvold, D., & Field, R. H. G. (1983). Effects of social context on consensus and majority vote decision making. *Academy of Management Journal, 26,* 500–506.

Tjosvold, D., & Johnson, D. W. (1977). The effects of controversy on cognitive perspective-taking. *Journal of Education Psychology, 69,* 679–685.

Tjosvold, D., Wedley, W. C., & Field, R. H. G. (1986). Constructive controversy, the Vroom-Yetton model, and managerial decision-making. *Journal of Occupational Behaviour, 7,* 125–138.

Trist, E. L., & Bamforth, K. W. (1951). Some social and psychological consequences of the longwall method of coal getting. *Human Relations, 4,* 3–38.

Tschan, F., & von Cranach, M. (1996). Group task structure, processes and outcome. In M. A. West (Ed.), *Handbook of work group psychology* (pp. 95–121). Chichester, UK: Wiley.

Ulich, E., & Weber, W. G. (1996). Dimensions, criteria and evaluation of work group autonomy. In M. A. West (Ed.), *The handbook of work group psychology* (pp. 247–282). Chichester, UK: Wiley.

Utterback, J. M. (1974). Innovation in industry and the diffusion of technology. *Science, 183,* 620–626.

Volpert, W. (1984). *Analysis of action structure: A contribution to research on job qualification.* Kön, Germany: Pahl Rugenstein.

Volpert, W. (1987). Psychological regulation of work activities/work action. In U. Kleinbeck & J. Rutenfranz (eds.). *Work Psychology: Encyclopedia of Psychology, Domain D. Series III, Volume 1* (pp. 1–42). Göttingen, Germany: Hogrefe.

Wade, J. (1996). A community level analysis of sources and rates of technological variation in the microprocessor market. *Academy of Management Journal, 39,* 1218–1244.

West, M. A. (1987). Role innovation in the world of work. *British Journal of Social Psychology, 26,* 305–315.

West, M. A. (1989). Innovation among health care professionals. *Social Behaviour, 4,* 173–184.

West, M. A. (1990). The social psychology of innovation in groups. In M. A. West & J. L. Farr (Eds.), *Innovation and creativity at work: Psychological and organizational strategies* (pp. 309–333). Chichester, UK: Wiley.

West, M. A. (1994). *Effective teamwork.* Leicester, UK: British Psychological Society.

West, M. A. (1996). Reflexivity and work group effectiveness: A conceptual integration. In M. A. West, (Ed.), *Handbook of work group psychology* (pp. 555–579). Chichester, UK: Wiley.

West, M. A. (2000). Reflexivity, revolution, and innovation in work teams. In M. M. Beyerlein, D. A. Johnson, & S. T. Beyerlein (Eds.), *Advances in interdisciplinary studies of work teams: Product development teams* (pp. 1–29). Stamford, CT: JAI Press.

West, M. A. (2002). Sparkling fountains or stagnant ponds: An integrative model of creativity and innovation implementation in work groups. *Applied Psychology: An International Review, 51,* 355–387.

West, M. A., & Anderson, N. (1992). Innovation, cultural values and the management of change in British hospitals. *Work and Stress, 6,* 293–310.

West, M. A., & Anderson, N. (1996). Innovation in top management teams. *Journal of Applied Psychology, 81,* 680–693.

West, M. A., & Farr, J. L. (1990). Innovation at work. In M. A. West & J. L. Farr (Eds.), *Innovation and creativity at work: Psychological and organizational strategies* (pp. 3–13). Chichester, UK: Wiley.

West, M. A., Patterson, M., Pillinger, T., & Nickell, S. (2000). *Innovation and change in manufacturing.* Birmingham, UK: Aston Business School, Aston University.

West, M. A., & Richter, A. (in press). Climates and cultures for innovation and creativity at work. In C. Ford (Ed.), *Handbook of organizational creativity.*

West, M. A., & Rushton, R. (1989). Mismatches in work role transitions. *Journal of Occupational Psychology, 62,* 271–286.

Willems, E. P., & Clark, R. D., III. (1971). Shift toward risk and heterogeneity of groups. *Journal of Experimental Social Psychology, 7,* 302–312.

Wood, W. (1987). Meta-analytic review of sex differences in group performance. *Psychological Bulletin, 102,* 53–71.

Wright, M. (1954). A study of anxiety in a general hospital setting. *Canadian Journal of Psychology, 8,* 195–203.

Yammarino, F. J. (1996). Group leadership: A levels of analysis perspective. In M. A. West (Ed.), *Handbook of work group psychology* (pp. 189–224). Chichester, UK: Wiley.

Yukl, G. A. (1994). *Leadership in organizations.* Englewood Cliffs, NJ: Prentice-Hall.

Zaltman, G., Duncan, R., & Holbeck, J. (1973). *Innovations and organizations.* London: Wiley.

Zenger, T. R., & Lawrence, B. S. (1989). Organizational demography: The differential effects of age and tenure distributions on technical communication. *Academy of Management Journal, 32,* 353–376.

13

■■■■■ *Linda Argote and Aimée A. Kane*

Learning from Direct and Indirect Experience in Organizations
The Effects of Experience Content, Timing, and Distribution

■■■

Large improvements in performance typically occur as groups and organizations gain experience. These "learning curves" have been found in both laboratory studies of small groups as they repeat a task (e.g., Argote, Insko, Yovetich, & Romero, 1995; Guetzkow & Simon, 1955; Leavitt, 1951) and field studies of organizational units as they gain experience in production (see Argote, 1999; Dutton & Thomas, 1984, for reviews).

Learning curves have been found in a variety of organizations. For example, the unit cost of producing aircraft (Alchian, 1963; Benkard, 2000; Wright, 1936), ships (Rapping, 1965), trucks (Epple, Argote, & Murphy 1996), and semiconductors (Hatch & Mowery, 1998) have been found to follow a learning curve. The cost of producing a unit of each of these products decreased at a decreasing rate as the organization gained experience in production.

Although early work on organizational learning curves focused on learning in manufacturing firms, recent work examines learning in service as well as manufacturing settings. For example, researchers have found that not only the time it takes to perform new surgical procedures (Pisano, Bohmer, & Edmondson, 2001) but also the complication rates associated with the procedures (Kelsey et al., 1984) follow the classic learning curve. Learning curves have also been found for a variety of performance indicators in organizations. These indicators include measures of costs (Yelle, 1979), quality (Argote 1993), plant operating reliability (Joskow & Rozanski, 1979), accidents (Greenburg, 1971), service timeliness (Argote & Darr, 2000), customer satisfaction (Lapré & Tsikriktsis, 2000), and organizational survival (Baum & Ingram, 1998).

Although learning curves have been found to characterize the performance of many groups and organizations, remarkable variation has been found in the rates at which these units learn. For example, in a longitudinal study of the performance of three truck plants that belonged to the same corporation and produced the same product, Argote and Epple (1990) found that (1) the performance of each plant followed a characteristic learning curve, and (2) the plants differed dramatically in the rates at which they learned.

Learning curves from these three plants are depicted in Figure 13.1. The cumulative number of trucks produced at each plant, a measure of the plant's experience, is plotted on the horizontal axis; the number of labor hours required to produce each truck is plotted on the vertical axis. As illustrated by the figure, the direct labor hours required to produce each truck decreased at a decreasing rate as the plants gained experience in production. Further, the rate of learning at each plant differed significantly from the other plants. Statistical tests resoundingly rejected the hypothesis that the learning curves at the plants came from the same underlying distribution (Argote & Epple, 1990).

This finding of dramatic differences in the rates at which organizational units learn from experience has also been documented in other organizational contexts (e.g., Adler & Clark, 1991; Chew, Bresnahan, & Clark, 1990; Dutton &

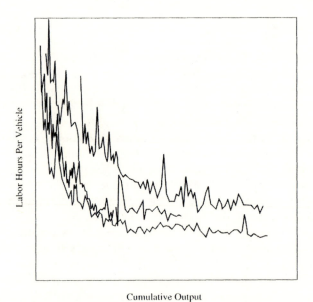

Cumulative Output

Figure 13.1. *The Relationship between Labor Hours per Vehicle and Cumulative Output for Three Plants. Reprinted with permission from L. Argote and D. Epple (1990, February), Learning curves in manufacturing, Science, 247 (4945). Copyright 1990, American Association for the Advancement of Science. Units omitted to protect confidentiality of data.*

Thomas, 1984). For example, Pisano et al., (2001) found that hospitals reduced significantly the time they took to perform new surgical procedures as the hospitals acquired experience with the procedure. Further, the 16 hospitals in the sample differed markedly in the rates at which their performance improved with experience. These field studies of organizational learning generally control for factors that might affect performance, such as differences in the scale of operation or differences in input characteristics (see Argote, 1999, for a discussion of factors that should be controlled for in assessing learning rates in organizations). Even after these differences are taken into account, however, the organizations differ in the rates at which they learn from experience.

The current chapter explores why some groups or organizations are better than others at learning from experience. We discuss factors found to facilitate or impede the rate at which groups and organizations learn. We pay particular attention to the role of experience and examine whether certain patterns of experience are more conducive to group or organizational learning than others. Thus, the chapter aims to address an important unanswered question about organizational learning identified in recent reviews of learning at the organizational (Schulz, 2002), intraorganizational (Argote & Ophir, 2002), and interorganizational (Ingram, 2002) levels of analysis: Which patterns of experience are most conducive to organizational learning?

Learning from experience is challenging in organizations because experience may not occur in a way that facilitates drawing appropriate inferences. In naturalistic settings, there may be only a small number of observations from which to learn (March, Sproull, & Tamuz, 1991). For example, an organization might launch only a few products over a period of many years. The small sample of products makes it hard to draw inferences about which product is most successful. The inference problem may be further complicated when the products differ from each other along more than one attribute. Thus, even if it is clear that one product is more successful than the others, it may be hard to identify the particular product attributes that led to success.

Learning from experience is also challenging in organizations because feedback may not be immediate or clearly associated with an organizational action. The poor quality feedback may lead organizations to draw inappropriate inferences about which actions produced positive outcomes—to engage in "superstitious learning" (Levitt & March, 1988). For example, many technology firms enjoyed enormous increases in their stock prices in the late 1990s. This feedback from the market led many firms to conclude that they had successful products and appropriate business models. However, the stock prices of many of these firms dropped dramatically in 2000 and a significant number of those firms were acquired or dissolved, suggesting that the inferences many of the firms had drawn from the extremely favorable feedback of the late 1990s were erroneous.

The focus of our chapter is on the group or organizational unit (e.g., work team, department, plant, organization). Thus, we examine learning at the level of the small groups, departments, and constituent parts of organizations as well as at the level of the overall organization. Learning also occurs at the individual level in groups. Indeed, learning curves were first discovered by psychologists analyzing the behavior of individuals as they gained experience with a task (Ebbinghaus, 1885/1964; Thorndike, 1898; Thurstone, 1919). Although we draw on findings about individual learning (e.g., Berry & Broadbent, 1984, 1987; Newell & Rosenbloom, 1981), reviewing the voluminous literature is beyond the scope of this chapter. Similarly, the literature on learning between organizations (see Ingram, 2002, for a review) and learning at the level of populations of firms (see Miner & Anderson, 1999; Miner & Haunschild, 1995, for reviews) is also beyond our scope.

Groups and organizational units learn both from their own direct experience and from the experience of other organizational units (Levitt & March, 1988). For example, an analysis of learning in pizza stores of a franchise found that each store learned from its own experience and from the experience of other stores in the franchise (Darr, Argote, & Epple, 1995). This type of learning is generally referred to as knowledge transfer because one organizational unit is affected by the experience of another (see Argote & Ingram, 2000, for an analysis of knowledge transfer).

Examples of learning from indirect as well as direct experience occurred in the context of introducing a new product, deep-dish pizza (Darr et al., 1995). When deep-dish pizza was introduced, the usual method of distributing toppings on a pizza was not effective. The usual method was to distribute toppings, such as pepperoni, evenly on a pizza before baking it. When this method was used on deep-dish pizza, however, the pepperoni cooked into an unappealing clump in the center of the pie. A method for arriving at a more satisfying distribution of pepperoni was created at one of the stores. It was discovered that if the pepperoni were distributed on the pizza before it was baked like spokes on a wheel, the melting and flow of the cheese during baking would result in an even distribution of pepperoni. This new method was very effective; it resulted in a more appealing product for customers and reduced food and labor costs at the stores. The method initially transferred to other stores in the same franchise. A consultant from the parent corporation subsequently transferred the method to other stores throughout the firm around the world. Thus, other stores benefited from the experience of the store that created the new procedure.

Evidence that organizations can benefit from the experience of other organizations has been found in other service and manufacturing settings. For example, a study of the introduction of new surgical procedures documented that when a hospital first began to perform an operation, the hospital benefited from the experience of other, more experienced hospitals (Kelsey et al., 1984). Similarly, an analysis of the introduction of a second shift at a manufacturing plant showed that the second shift benefited from experience acquired by the first shift (Epple et al., 1996). Also, Henderson and Cockburn (1996) found that knowledge transferred across related research programs within organizations in the pharmaceutical industry.

Because organizations learn not only from their own experience but also from the experience of others, we examine both types of experience in the current chapter. We identify the patterns of experience most conducive to organizational learning; more specifically, we analyze how the content, distribution, and timing of experience affect learning outcomes. We conclude with a discussion of what is best learned through direct experience and what is best learned through the experience of others.

Learning from Direct Experience

Content of Experience

What do organizations learn as they gain experience in production? What factors explain the learning curves shown in Figure 13.1? Many researchers have speculated about factors responsible for the performance gains associated with increased organizational experience. Hayes and Wheelwright (1984) hypothesized that organizational learning curves are due to individual learning, better selection and training of organizational members, improved methods, enhanced technology, more appropriate divisions of labor, improved product design, substitution of capital for labor, incentives, and leadership. Porter (1979) suggested that with experience, organizations learn to make methods and technology more productive, to design layout and work flow more efficiently, to develop specialized processes, to modify products to enhance manufacturing performance, and to institute better management control. Argote (1993) interviewed managers at manufacturing plants about which factors they thought were the most important contributors to learning curves. The factors the managers identified fell into four major categories: (1) increased proficiency of organizational members, including managers, direct production workers, and technical staff; (2) improvements in the organization's technology and layout; (3) improvements in the organization's structure, procedures, and methods of coordination; and (4) enhanced understanding of who in the organization was good at which tasks.

These lists of factors explaining the productivity gains associated with experience can be mapped onto a theoretical framework of the components of groups and organizations (see Arrow, McGrath, & Berdahl, 2000; McGrath & Argote, 2001). According to the framework, the three basic elements of organizations are *members*, *tools*, and *tasks*; members are the human component of organizations, tools are the technological component, and tasks are the intentional component. These basic elements of organizations combine to form subnetworks. The *member-member* network is the organization's social network. The *task-task* network is the sequence of tasks or routines employed in the organization. The *tool-tool* network is the sequence of technologies used by the organization. The *member-task* network (or the division of labor) assigns tasks to members. The *member-tool* network assigns tools to members. The *task-tool* network specifies which tasks are performed with which tools. Finally, the *member-task-tool* network specifies which members perform which tasks with which tools.

The list of factors discussed previously as responsible for organizational learning curves include improvements in the basic elements of organizations and their subnetworks. For example, researchers have suggested that organizational *members* become more proficient, *tools* become more effective, and *task* sequences become better developed as organizations gain experience. Similarly, organizational structures (the *member-member* network) become better articulated, and *tasks* and *tools* can be assigned to *members* on the basis of who is most qualified to perform (the *member-task* network) or use (the *member-tool* network) them. Further, as the organization gains experience, it determines which tasks are best performed by members and which are best performed by tools (the *member-task-tool* network). Thus, experience with members, tools, tasks, and their interactions enables organizations to fine-tune the basic elements and their subnetworks and thereby improve organizational performance.

We turn now to a review of empirical studies on the effect of various types of experience on organizational learning outcomes. In most of the naturalistic field studies and in many of the laboratory studies, members acquire experience working together on the same tasks with the same tools. From these studies, it is not possible to determine exactly which type of experience affected performance outcomes. Several studies, however, vary one type of experience while keeping other types constant. These studies permit stronger inferences about the content of experience most conducive to performance gains.

Experience with Members

On balance, the evidence suggests that experience with members improves organizational performance. For example, researchers have found that stable coal mine crews, where members were familiar with each other because there was little membership change, were more productive than crews with considerable membership change (Goodman & Leyden, 1991). Similarly, Pisano et al. (2001) suggested that hospitals with the best procedure times had surgical teams with stable membership. These naturalistic field studies of the relationship between group stability and performance suggest that providing members with experience working together has important benefits for organizational outcomes.

Laboratory studies that vary the experience members have working together complement the field studies. These laboratory studies provide insights into the mechanisms underlying the beneficial effects of member experience on performance. For example, Liang, Moreland, and Argote (1995) showed that groups whose members trained together rather than apart had better-developed transactive memory systems, where members knew who was good at which tasks. These transactive memory systems improved subsequent group performance.

In a second study, Moreland, Argote, and Krishnan (1996) created more permutations of experience. In one condition, group members gained experience practicing a task individually. In another condition, group members gained experience working together practicing a task different from the one they would perform in the subsequent testing session. In a third condition, group mem- bers gained experience practicing the same task they would perform in the test- ing session but with different group members. In the final condition, group members gained experience with the same members practicing the same task they would perform in the testing session. Both the transactive memory scores and the performance of groups in this last condition were superior to those in the other three conditions, which did not differ significantly from each other. Further, the superior performance of groups in the last condition was explained by their well-developed transactive memory systems. These results suggest that it is experience with the same members working on the same task that enables groups to develop knowledge of who is good at which aspects of the task. This knowledge in turn improves group performance.

Other benefits of experience working together have been documented. Group members become better at sharing information (Wittenbaum, 1996), generating ideas (Paulus & Dzindolet, 1993), and developing more sophisticated understand- ings of phenomena (Gruenfeld & Hollingshead, 1993) as they gain experience working together. Similarly, with experience, groups increase their ability to use members' informational resources and become less dependent on their most knowledgeable member (Watson, Michaelson, & Sharp, 1991). Further, as group members acquire experience, they become more familiar with one another and more comfortable expressing disagreement (Gruenfeld, Mannix, Williams, & Neale, 1996), which facilitates the sharing of uniquely held information. Group members also learn to recognize (Laughlin & Hollingshead, 1995) and trust (Liang et al., 1995) each other's expertise as they gain experience working together. With experience, members also become more cooperative (Chatman & Flynn, 2001) and better at negotiating (Neale & Northcraft, 1986).

The finding of a generally positive relationship between the extent of group member experience working together and group performance is qualified by evidence that too much experience working together can have deleterious ef- fects on performance. For example, Katz (1982) found a nonmonotonic inverted U-shaped relationship between group "longevity" (the average amount of time members worked together) and the performance of research and development teams. As group longevity increased, the performance of the laboratory groups initially increased and then decreased. Katz suggested that the performance decrement observed in groups after two to four years working together was due to those groups communicating less frequently with other groups and becom- ing isolated from external influences. Similarly, Kim (1997) found that too much experience hurt group performance. In particular, groups with both task and team experience performed more poorly than groups with only task experience, only team experience, or neither task nor team experience.

Research on the effects of member rotation and turnover on group perfor- mance is also relevant for evaluating the effect of member experience on per- formance outcomes. Several studies have examined the effects of moving new members into groups or organizations on learning and performance outcomes in those groups. These studies are reviewed in this section. Other studies of member rotation have focused on personnel movement as a mechanism for knowledge transfer across groups or organizations. These studies are reviewed in the section on learning from the experience of others.

Several studies have found that member rotation, especially moderate levels of rotation, facilitate creativity and performance. Ziller, Behringer, and Goodchilds (1962) found that the creative output of small groups with membership change was significantly greater than that of groups without membership change. Similarly, Arrow and McGrath (1993) found performance benefits from membership change. Student groups wrote better essays about their processes in weeks during which they experienced membership change than in weeks when membership was constant. The presence of new members appeared to make groups more aware of their own processes and structures and of how those processes and structures affected their performance.

In a study of the effect of temporarily moving members from one group to another, Gruenfeld, Martorena, and Fan (2000) found that although it did not result in knowledge being transferred from one group to another, it did result in the creation of new knowledge on the members' return to their group of origin. Thus, personnel movement appeared to stimulate the creation of new knowledge.

Similarly, Argote, Epple, Rao, and Murphy (1997) found that performance benefits were associated with moving new members into a manufacturing plant. The researchers found a nonmonotonic inverted U-shaped relationship between the number of direct production workers moving into the plant and plant productivity. As the number of new members moving into the plant increased, plant productivity initially increased and then decreased (Argote, 1999). Thus, moderate personnel movement improved plant performance.

Other studies have examined the effect of turnover of scientists and engineers or executives on group or organizational outcomes (Guest, 1962; Tushman & Rosenkopf, 1996; Virany, Tushman, & Romanelli, 1992; Wells & Pelz, 1966). Wells and Pelz found that turnover of scientists and engineers had a positive effect on the performance of their departments. Similarly, Virany et al. found that turnover of the chief executive officer and turnover in the executive team were positively associated with organizational performance for firms in the turbulent computer industry.

Although the addition of new members can stimulate the creation of new knowledge in groups and organizations, the departure of members can harm group and organizational performance. When members leave, the organization loses the ability to access their knowledge. Membership instability can also disrupt transactive memory systems or knowledge of who knows what in the organization. Along those lines, Hollenbeck et al. (1995) found that instability in group membership disrupted the leader's ability to effectively weight members' contributions.

Studies have identified conditions under which the loss of members is particularly costly. One factor on which the effect of turnover depends is the quality of departing members and their replacements. Argote et al. (1997) found that the departure of high-performing employees had a negative effect on a manufacturing plant's productivity. Based on results from a laboratory study, Trow (1960) concluded that turnover was less disruptive when the group had previous experience with the same rate of turnover and when replacements were at least as competent as departing members.

Organizational structures have also been found to mitigate the effects of turnover. Grusky (1961) found that managerial succession was less disruptive in large than in small firms. Grusky speculated that the greater use of procedures and hierarchies in the large firms buffered them from the disruptive effects of turnover. Devadas and Argote (1995) tested whether structure weakened the effect of turnover in a laboratory study of small groups. The researchers found an interaction between turnover and group structure: when turnover occurred, groups lacking procedures and a formal structure performed worse than groups with procedures and structures in place; when there was no turnover, the differently structured groups performed about the same. Similarly, Carley (1992) found in a simulation study that hierarchies were less affected by turnover than were teams.

The effect of turnover also depends on the complexity of the task. Argote et al. (1995) compared the effect of turnover on groups performing simple versus complex tasks in a laboratory study. The researchers found that although turnover hurt the performance of all groups, it had less impact on groups performing complex tasks. The departure of experienced group members was less costly for complex tasks because much of the knowledge of experienced members became obsolete due to the innovation that occurred on the complex task.

Taken together, findings about the effect of turnover on group and organizational performance suggest that there are conditions under which membership change is likely to have positive, negative, or little to no effect on performance. Membership change is most likely to have a negative effect on performance when (1) departing members are high performers and replacements are less skilled (Argote et al., 1997; Trow, 1960); (2) tasks are stable and do not involve innovation (Argote et al., 1995; Virany et al., 1992); and (3) few procedures or structures are in place to buffer the organization from the effects of turnover (Carley, 1992; Devadas & Argote, 1995; Grusky, 1961). Conversely, membership change is most likely to have beneficial effects on organizational outcomes when the organizations operate in changing or turbulent environments (e.g., Virany et al., 1992) and their tasks involve innovation (e.g., Wells & Pelz, 1966). In these environments, the knowledge of current members may become obsolete and new members may bring desired new knowledge into the organization.

Experience with Tasks

As noted previously, in many of the studies of the effects of membership stability, members acquired experience with the same tasks as well as with the same members. The results of those studies also suggest that experience with tasks improves group outcomes.

Kim (1997) separated the effect of experience with tasks and experience with members. In groups that had experienced a change in membership, experience with the task led to more sharing of uniquely held information, which in turn improved group performance. Similarly, Schilling, Ployhart, Vidal, and Marangoni (2003) found that experience with a similar and related task led to greater performance improvements than experience with the same task or with a completely different and unrelated task. Together, these laboratory studies suggest that experience with similar and related tasks improves group outcomes.

Experience with Tools

Experience with tools can facilitate group and organizational performance. An analysis of a narrowly averted aviation disaster described one of the contributors to the problem as the fact that the mechanics were "dealing with an unfamiliar engine" (Crossette, 2001) and apparently did not install a hydraulic pump properly. Experience with the same tool improves members' ability to work effectively with the tool. When a new tool is introduced, negative effects may occur.

As groups gain experience with the new tool, however, their performance typically improves. In several experiments, groups that used a new tool, a computer-mediated communication technology, were less effective initially than groups that used more familiar face-to-face communication tools. As groups gained experience using the new tool, however, their effectiveness increased to a level comparable to that observed with more familiar communication technologies. For example, Hollingshead, McGrath, and O'Connor (1993) found that group task performance and member satisfaction were initially lower for groups using computer-mediated communication but that this difference decreased as groups gained experience using the new communication tool. Similarly, Walther and Burgoon (1992) found that although computer-mediated groups were initially inferior to face-to-face groups in relational communication, communication of computer-mediated groups improved over time until it approximated the quality of communication in face-to-face groups. Along these lines, Wilson, Straus, and McEvily (2001) found that trust was initially lower in groups using new communication tools but that trust in those groups increased with experience to levels observed in groups using traditional communication technology.

Subnetworks

Subnetworks affect the extent to which organizational subunits are able to learn from their own experience. At a macro level, Ingram and Baum (1997) found that specialist organizations learned more from their own direct experience than generalist organizations. At the subunit level, dense member-member networks characterized by redundant ties among members have been linked to increases in information sharing and group performance (Reagans & Zuckerman, 2001).

Similarly, certain member-task networks are more likely than others to promote information sharing. Transactive memory systems or knowledge of who knows what (Wegner, 1986) have been found to promote the sharing of information in groups (Stasser, Vaughan, & Stewart, 2000; Stewart & Stasser, 1995). Groups in which members were aware of the specialized expertise each member possessed were more likely to surface unique information than groups whose members were not aware of each others' special expertise. Similarly, groups with a leader who possessed greater expertise were more likely to surface information uniquely held by one member than groups lacking a leader (Larson, Christensen, Abbott, & Franz, 1996). Although these studies begin to specify how characteristics of the subnetworks affect organizational learning outcomes, more research is needed on this important issue.

Distribution of Experience

Does the distribution of experience matter? Are groups composed of diverse members, for example, better at learning from experience than groups composed of similar members? Although the evidence on this issue is somewhat mixed, on balance, results suggest that groups composed of members with diverse backgrounds are more creative than groups composed of members with similar backgrounds. Evidence suggesting that heterogeneous groups innovate more than homogeneous groups has been found for top management teams (Bantel & Jackson, 1989; Lant, Milliken, & Batra, 1992), new product development teams (Eisenhardt & Tabrizi, 1995; Moorman & Miner, 1998), and groups with researchers from different scientific disciplines (Dunbar, 1995). Further, Eisenhardt and Tabrizi found that the benefits of heterogeneous new product teams were particularly pronounced in environments of rapid change.

Are certain dimensions of heterogeneous membership more beneficial for group creativity than others? Based on a comprehensive review of research on the effects of diversity on group performance, Williams and O'Reilly (1998) concluded that functional diversity, or diversity in members' backgrounds, was the dimension of diversity that consistently showed a positive effect on group creativity. They cautioned, however, that to realize the benefits of the larger pool of information and approaches that diverse members bring to the group, members must be able to deal effectively with the coordination and communication challenges that diverse membership poses.

Two studies focused on the effects of group diversity in a longitudinal context. Watson, Kumar, and Michaelson (1993) compared the performance over time of culturally homogeneous and culturally heterogeneous student groups. The researchers found that although the performance of homogeneous groups was initially superior to that of heterogeneous groups, the performance of heterogeneous groups improved at a faster rate than that of homogeneous groups until it equaled or surpassed the performance of homogeneous groups.

Analyzing the performance of organizations in a learning-curve framework, Ophir, Ingram, and Argote (1998) examined whether organizations composed of homogeneous members learned from their experience at a rate different from that of organizations composed of heterogeneous members. The context for their study was Israeli kibbutzim. Barkai and Levhari (1973) had previously determined that the performance of these kibbutzim followed a learning curve: the more experience the kibbutzim gained in farming, the more productive they were. Examining the interaction between experience and member heterogeneity, Ophir et al. found that homogeneous organizations learned or benefited more from their experience than heterogeneous organizations. The researchers suggested that the greater ability of homogeneous kibbutzim to learn from experience relative to their heterogeneous counterparts was due to the greater opportunities for and effectiveness of communication in homogeneous kibbutzim.

These results suggest that the relationship between group diversity and learning outcomes in social systems is complex. On the one hand, member diversity appears to enhance creativity in groups. This effect seems to occur because diverse members bring different perspectives to the group. For example, the diverse research groups in Dunbar's (1995) study brought the perspectives of different disciplines to the group. Dunbar found that the greater propensity of diverse laboratory groups to engage in analogical reasoning, where members identified similar approaches from other disciplines that were applicable to the current problem, contributed to the greater creativity of those groups. Thus, diverse members served as a conduit for transferring knowledge to the group.

In contrast to these results, there is some evidence that more homogeneous groups may be better than heterogeneous groups at learning from experience on an ongoing basis. Group homogeneity appears to facilitate the interpretation of experience in organizations and the translation of that experience into sustained performance improvements. It may not be homogeneity per se as much as its effect on communication that facilitates learning from experience. The results of the study by Reagans and Zuckerman (2001) are consistent with this conjecture: groups that achieved a high level of communication among heterogeneous members performed at high levels.

More research is needed on the effect of diversity on learning outcomes in groups and organizations. The effect of diversity is likely to depend on the dimension of diversity (Williams & O'Reilly, 1998), the particular performance outcome, the nature of the task, and the phase in the group's life cycle.

Although there has been more research on the effects of diversity of members than on the distribution of the other components of organizations, a few studies have examined the effect of diversity in tasks on group outcomes. In particular, these studies have examined the effect of related and unrelated task experience on group outcomes. Littlepage, Robison, and Reddington (1997) demonstrated that experience on related tasks increased group performance via improvements in individual group members' task ability, whereas experience on comparable but not related tasks increased group performance via improvements in members' ability to recognize the expertise of other group members. Schilling et al. (2003) found that related task experience was not only better than unrelated task experience at improving group outcomes but also better than the same identical experience. Some diversity of experience on similar tasks appears to facilitate group performance.

The benefits of diverse experience seem to be especially pronounced when organizations are specialists. Using data on U.S. commercial airline accidents and incidents reported from 1983 to 1997, Haunschild and Sullivan (2000) found that specialist firms learned more than generalists from heterogeneous accident experience.

Although the studies described above suggest that some task diversity is beneficial for learning outcomes, Pisano et al. (2001) argue that keeping a task the same, especially when it is first introduced, improves learning outcomes in organizations. More research is needed on the effects of task diversity on learning outcomes in organizations. It may be that task stability is beneficial at the start of production, but once members master that form of the task, introducing some diversity may provide members with a deeper understanding of the task and how to perform it most effectively.

Timing of Experience

The timing of experience can also have important consequences for group and organizational outcomes. Is it better to attempt to produce much output quickly as the organization scales up its production, or is it preferable to adopt a more measured pace of production? Is it more desirable to produce at an even or uneven rate of output?

Significant changes in the rate of output have generally been found to hinder group and organizational performance (Preston & Keachie, 1964). These "adjustment costs" associated with trying to dramatically increase the rate of output are illustrated in Lockheed's production of the L-1011 TriStar (see Argote, 1999, for an overview of the Lockheed case). Lockheed attempted to increase production of the L-1011 dramatically in the late 1970s. The company raised its rate of production from 8 aircraft in 1978 to 24 aircraft in 1979. To accomplish this rapid buildup, Lockheed increased the number of employees from 14,000 to 25,000 in two years. Many of the new employees hired during this period did not have a high school degree or previous experience in aircraft construction. These inexperienced workers were credited with negatively affecting Lockheed's learning curve ("TriStar's Trail," 1980): the labor hours required to build each aircraft increased dramatically during this period. Similarly, Boeing attempted in 1997 to double the rate of output of its aircraft very quickly (Holmes, 2001). Boeing was not successful at such rapid ramp-up: a shortage of employees and parts forced the firm to shut down temporarily two major assembly lines.

Not only are organizations hurt by adjustment costs associated with scaling up their labor forces so quickly, but they may also be hurt by knowledge depreciation or organizational "forgetting" (Argote, Beckman, & Epple, 1990; Benkard, 2000). Just as individual performance decays after an interruption such that it is typically inferior to that observed before the interruption, organizational performance may also decay or depreciate (Argote et al., 1990). The unit cost of producing each L-1011 aircraft rose rather than fell during the late 1970s, even though Lockheed's cumulative experience producing the L-1011 increased during this period. Benkard (2000) demonstrated that organizational forgetting or knowledge depreciation contributed to the upturn in costs observed in the Lockheed data. Having lost more than $15 million per year on the L-1011 program in the 1970s, Lockheed announced that it was phasing out production of the L-1011 in 1981 (Harris, 1981). It was the last commercial aircraft the firm produced.

These empirical findings on adjustment costs and organizational forgetting have important implications for the timing of experience in organizations. The results suggest that it is preferable to avoid large changes in the rate of output and to minimize stoppages or interruptions in production. Producing at more even rates of output is generally more effective than producing at highly variable rates.

The empirical results on the timing of production relate to simulation results on whether it is better to be a "fast" or a "slow" learner. March and his colleagues (e.g., see Herriott, Levinthal, & March, 1985; Levinthal & March, 1981; March, 1991) concluded that fast learning, where the organization scales up its production rapidly, can lead to premature specialization in a suboptimal strategy, which in turn can hurt long-term organizational performance. By contrast, slower learning enables the organization to explore a larger set of strategies and their effectiveness, which may in turn improve organizational performance over the long run.

Although it can be detrimental to attempt to scale up production too rapidly, there are benefits associated with beginning production. Going into production provides a firm with opportunities to learn by doing. This learning by doing is especially effective when the knowledge base underlying the organization's work is not well developed. For example, Pisano (1994) found that for chemical-based pharmaceuticals (where the underlying knowledge base was well understood), an emphasis on laboratory experimentation and learning *before* doing was associated with more rapid product development, whereas for biotechnology-based pharmaceuticals (where the underlying knowledge base was not well understood), laboratory experimentation did not speed product development. Under these conditions, when the effect of variables and their interactions was not well understood, it is through learning *by* doing that an organization acquires an understanding of how variables interact to affect performance. Similarly, Eisenhardt and Tabrizi (1995) concluded that learning *by* doing was more effective than planning or learning *before* doing for launching new products in the computer industry. Learning by doing is also key when knowledge is dependent on the context.

Being fast to start production at a slow rate may be the best strategy for organizations. Being fast to start production provides an organization with opportunities to learn how various factors and their interactions affect performance. Slowly ramping up production provides an organization the opportunity to explore different strategies and to identify the conditions under which they are effective as well as to correct problems while they apply to a few rather than to many units of output.

Learning from Indirect Experience

We use the same framework of members, tasks, tools, and their subnetworks to analyze the effect of those factors on the extent to which one organizational unit learns from the experience of another. Reviewed next is evidence on how characteristics of unit's members, tasks, tools, and their subnetworks (both within and between organizational units) and experience with members, tasks, and tools from other units affect the extent to which one organizational unit benefits from the experience of another.

Content of Experience

Experience with Members from Other Units

Moving members is a powerful mechanism for transferring knowledge to other organizational units (Allen, 1977; Almeida & Kogut, 1999; Galbraith, 1990; Rothwell, 1978). When members are moved from one organizational unit to another, they are able to transfer tacit as well as explicit knowledge (Berry & Broadbent, 1984, 1987) and to adapt knowledge to the new context (Allen, 1977).

The movement of both engineers and top executives has been associated with the transfer of knowledge between organizations. The movement of engineers from one firm to another in the semiconductor industry was associated with the transfer of knowledge about patents across those firms (Almeida & Kogut, 1999). Similarly, the movement of top managers in the semiconductor industry facilitated the transfer of product and market knowledge (Boeker, 1997). Firms were more likely to enter new product markets if they had recently hired a top manager from a firm that had been in that product market. Liberal arts colleges that were led by a president who had recently been hired from a school with a specific professional program (such as business, journalism, or nursing) were significantly more likely to introduce those professional programs (Kraatz & Moore, 2002).

Although members are generally effective knowledge conduits, social psychological processes affect members' willingness to both contribute knowledge and be influenced by knowledge (e.g., see Gruenfeld et al., 2000). More research is needed on the conditions under which moving members leads to knowledge being transferred from one organizational unit to another. Characteristics of rotating members, of the knowledge they bring, of the recipient organizational unit, and of the relationship between the rotating member and the recipient unit are likely to affect both the extent to which the rotating member shares ideas and the extent to which members in the recipient unit respond to those ideas.

In his field study in the semiconductor industry, Boeker (1997) found evidence that characteristics of the new member and the firm's top management team affected knowledge transfer. Teams were more likely to learn from new members when the member came from research and development and engineering versus marketing and sales, reported directly to the chief executive officer of the former firm, and had significant industry experience. Organizations where the top management team was low in tenure and small in size were more likely to learn from new members.

Experience with Tasks from Other Units

Characteristics of the task have also been found to affect the extent of knowledge transfer between units. Tasks that are well understood transfer more readily than tasks that are high in "casual ambiguity" (Szulanski, 1996). Relatedly, a task that is easy to observe and understand transfers more readily than a task that is difficult to observe (Meyer & Goes, 1988).

The task-task network also affects knowledge transfer. Knowledge that is embedded in routines transfers more readily than noncodified knowledge (Argote & Darr, 2000; Zander & Kogut, 1995). The earlier example of a new method for distributing toppings on pizza that transferred to other pizza stores illustrates properties of knowledge that transfers relatively easily to other organizations. The new method was observable and codified in a routine that could be easily taught to other employees.

Experience with Tools from Other Units

Knowledge acquired in one unit and embedded in its tools or tool-tool network has been found to transfer to other social units. Mansfield (1985) found that knowledge embedded in tools and technology by one organization transferred to other organizations in less time than it took for the original organization to develop the technology. Similarly, Epple et al. (1996) found that a new shift at a manufacturing plant reached a level of productivity in a couple of weeks that it had taken the first shift many months to achieve. The new shift used tools developed and refined by the first shift. Other studies have shown that knowledge embedded in tools transfers more readily to other organizations than knowledge embedded in human repositories (Argote & Darr, 2000; Zander & Kogut, 1995). Although moving tools from one organizational unit to another is a powerful way to effect knowledge transfer, moving tools is generally most effective when some members are moved along with those tools (e.g., see Galbraith, 1990). The strengths of members as a knowledge transfer mechanism complement the strengths of tools and routines as transfer mechanisms. Tools and routines provide consistency and facilitate transfer on a large scale. Members, on the other hand, provide subtle understanding and tacit knowledge not embedded in the tool or routine. Further, members are able to adapt the tool or routine to the new context.

Subnetworks Involving Members

Although the subnetworks involving members are generally not moved from one organizational unit to another, these subnetworks affect knowledge transfer across organizational units. Characteristics of the member-member or social network affect knowledge transfer. Social networks rich in "structural holes" (Burt, 1992), where units have nonredundant ties to other units, have been found to be an effective mechanism for importing knowledge from other organizational units (McEvily & Zaheer, 1999). In a related vein, Hansen (1999) found that "weak ties," characterized by infrequent and distant relationships between units, facilitated the search for knowledge in other units and reduced the time to complete new product development projects when knowledge was not complex and could be codified. By contrast, strong ties facilitated the acquisition and interpretation of knowledge that could not be codified. The repeated interactions inherent in strong ties were critical for understanding and interpreting noncodified, tacit knowledge.

The extent to which units are embedded in a superordinate relationship also affects the success of knowledge transfer. Knowledge transfers more readily across organizational units that are embedded in a superordinate relationship, such as a franchise or chain, than across independent units (Baum & Ingram, 1998; Darr et al., 1995; Ingram & Simons, 2002). For example, Darr et al. found that fast-food restaurants benefited from the experience of other restaurants in the same franchise but not from the experience of restaurants in different franchises. Similarly, Baum and Ingram found that hotels benefited from the experience of other hotels in their chain up to the time they joined the chain. After that, they benefited from the experience of other local hotels in their chain but not from the experience of nonlocal hotels. Routines imported from nonlocal markets after the hotel joined the chain may not have been relevant to local conditions and thus did not improve performance (see also Greve's, 1999, analysis of the branch system in radio markets).

Distribution of Indirect Experience

As suggested in the previous section, in order for the experience of other units to have a positive effect on the performance of a focal unit, the experience of the other units must be relevant for the focal unit and fit its context (Argote & Ingram, 2000). An important determinant of the relevancy of the knowledge is the similarity of the organizational contexts. Research has shown that knowledge is more likely to transfer across similar than dissimilar organizational contexts. For example, Darr and Kurtzberg (2000) found that organizational units were more likely to benefit from the experience of other units that followed a similar rather than a dissimilar strategy.

Much of the challenge in knowledge transfer is identifying knowledge for which the underlying structure is similar and relevant to the current problem. Superficial aspects of knowledge sometimes interfere with members' ability to recognize the relevance of certain knowledge for their context. For example, organizational members may see knowledge acquired in a different industry as irrelevant to their context when the underlying structure of the knowledge is the same. Encouraging members to identify the underlying structure of problems and abstract common principles facilitates knowledge transfer to new contexts (Thompson, Gentner, & Lowenstein, 2000).

Timing of Indirect Experience

Groups and organizations are particularly open to learning from the experience of others early in their life cycle. Several empirical studies have found that transfer of knowledge occurs when organizations start production but not after they have been producing for a while. In an analysis of success rates at angioplasty surgery, Kelsey et al. (1984) found that organizations were most likely to learn from the experience of others when they first began to perform a new surgical procedure. Similarly, Argote et al. (1990) found that shipyards that began production later were more productive than those with early start dates. Once shipyards began production, however, they did not benefit further from production experience at other yards. Along similar lines, Baum and Ingram (1998) found that Manhattan hotels benefited from the experience of hotels in different chains in the industry up to the time of the focal hotel's founding but not thereafter.

A couple of studies have found, however, that organizations learn on an ongoing basis from the experience of other organizations. In their study of imitation in choice of investment banker in corporate acquisitions, Haunschild and Miner (1997) found that firms learned from each other on a continuing basis. Similarly, Darr et al. (1995) found that pizza stores learned from other stores in the same franchise on an ongoing basis. The different results regarding whether learning is confined to the start of operation or occurs on a continuing basis may be due to the extent to which knowledge is embedded in technology at the organizations. For both the shipyards and the hotels, a significant amount of knowledge was embedded in the physical equipment, layout, and technology of the establishments. By contrast, less knowledge regarding the investment banker decision or pizza production was embedded in "hard" form. Thus, in the former organizations, the inertia may have been higher and their openness to the experience of others lower than in the latter organizations, where less knowledge was embedded in technology.

Learning from Direct versus Indirect Experience

The question then becomes: When is it better to learn from direct experience, and when is it better to learn from indirect experience or the experience of others? The answer to this question is a function of the extent to which the knowledge being learned is dependent on the context. General scientific principles are generally not dependent on the context (or are invariant over a wide range of contexts). By contrast, knowledge about individual members' skills and preferences is highly dependent on the context. It is better to learn this latter type of knowledge through direct experience, whereas scientific principles are an example of knowledge that can fruitfully be learned through the experience of others.

The framework of the basic components of organizations and their subnetworks, discussed previously, is useful in identifying which knowledge is highly dependent on the context and which is less dependent. As noted, according to the framework, the basic elements of organizations are members, tools, tasks, and their subnetworks. Knowledge about members and the subnetworks involving them is more dependent on the particular context than knowledge about tools or tasks. Tools are often provided by vendors and consultants who operate on a national or international level. Similarly, tasks are often prescribed by external sources such as governments, accrediting agencies, or consultants. One sees the same tasks performed and the same tools used across many organizational contexts.

Although tasks and tools may exhibit some variability across contexts, the variability is small relative to that of members. A tool, for example, may operate somewhat differently in humid than in nonhumid environments or in places where the power supply is stable than where it is not. This variability, however, is smaller and more predictable than the variability evidenced by members across organizational contexts. The number of ways members may differ across organizations is enormous and includes dimensions of skills, expertise, preferences, values, and attitudes that may all be relevant to organizational performance. Further, a member's behavior may be affected by the characteristics of other members with whom he or she is working. Therefore, the experience of one member or group working with another member is not always helpful in predicting what other groups or members would experience if they were to work with the same member.

This difference in the context-dependence of knowledge is a matter of degree. Certain dimensions of members with particular characteristics may not vary much across organizations. For example, it is assumed that all individuals who have received MBAs are able to do calculations such as computing net present value. However, the number of members in most organizations subject to the "homogenizing" influences of professional education and associations is small. Further, their professional training affects only a few dimensions of their performance. Thus, although we may be able to predict with a fair degree of confidence that an MBA can compute net present value, we do not know how sophisticated the MBA's analysis skills are or about a host of other characteristics of the MBA that are relevant to his or her performance in the organization. One can predict with much greater certainty what a tool (e.g., a computer) with a particular configuration will be able to do across organizational contexts than what a person with particular characteristics will be able to do or will choose to do across organizational contexts. The latter is best learned through direct experience with the person in the context. Further, because the subnetworks involving members also depend on knowledge about the member and his or her capabilities and preferences, knowledge about those subnetworks is also best acquired though direct experience.

Conversely, knowledge about tasks, tools, and the task-tool network is less dependent on context and more readily learned through indirect experience. Knowledge about tasks, tools, and task-tool sequences transfers more readily across organizations than knowledge about members and the subnetworks involving them (e.g., see Argote & Darr, 2000). The example of knowledge transfer across pizza stores is an example of a task sequence that transferred across organizations. The new routine for placing pepperoni on pizza was a task sequence that was not particularly dependent on context. It did not depend on special member skills and it did not affect the member-member networks of the organizations.

Conversely, knowledge embedded in the subnetworks involving members does not transfer as readily to other organizations. For example, Moreland et al. (1996) studied whether a "transactive memory system" (a network of member-task relations and member-tool relations) transferred from the group in which it was developed to a group composed of different members. Transactive memory systems that embodied knowledge about which group members were good at which task did not transfer to groups composed of different members. Similarly, Wegner, Erber, and Raymond (1991) found that imposing a division of labor (a member-task network) on an ongoing dyad that had already developed its own knowledge about who was good at what hurt the performance of the dyad.

Although direct experience is the better source of knowledge about members and the subnetworks involving them, one can learn about tools and tasks and their subnetworks through either direct or indirect experience. Learning about tools and tasks through the experience of others may in some cases be more efficient and effective than learning through one's own direct experience. For example, the second shift at a manufacturing plant learned in two weeks knowledge that it had taken the first shift many months to acquire (Epple et al., 1996). Similarly, technology has been found to spill over to competitors in less time than it took to develop the technology (Mansfield, 1985). Further, by learning through indirect experience, an organization accesses a much larger experience base and a deeper pool of expertise than the organization itself possesses. Thus, knowledge about tools, tasks, and their subnetworks may be more efficiently and effectively learned from indirect than direct experience.

Conclusion

Our goal in this chapter was to synthesize what is known about the patterns of experience that are most conducive to learning in groups and organizations. Thus, the chapter aimed to address an important unanswered question identified in several recent reviews of the organizational learning literature: What types of experience promote organizational learning? The chapter examined how the content, diversity, and timing of both direct and indirect experience affected learning outcomes.

Although evidence is emerging about the patterns of experience most conducive to organizational learning, more research is needed on this important question. A research agenda that we think is particularly promising is identifying how the subnetworks in groups and organizations affect learning and knowledge transfer outcomes. In addition, examining the interrelationships among experience content, timing, and diversity is likely to be a fruitful endeavor. For example, as we suggested previously, there may be an interaction between experience diversity and experience timing such that diversity of experience is beneficial in some but not other phases of the organization's life cycle.

Our chapter also addressed the question of what is best learned through direct experience and what is best learned through the experience of others. We have proposed that direct experience is the better source of knowledge about members and the subnetworks involving them. By contrast, learning about tools and tasks through the experience of others is often more effective and efficient than learning through direct experience. Research that identifies which knowledge is best learned through direct and which is best learned through indirect experience would make an important contribution.

Notes

Preparation of the chapter was supported by Army Research Institute Contract DASW01-00-K-0018. The views, opinions, and/or findings contained in this paper are those of the authors and should not be considered an official Department of the Army position, policy, or decision.

References

Adler, P. S., & Clark, K. B. (1991). Behind the learning curve: A sketch of the learning process. *Management Science, 37,* 267–281.

Alchian, A. (1963). Reliability of progress curves in airframe production. *Econometrica, 31,* 679–693.

Allen, T. J. (1977). *Managing the flow of technology: Technology transfer and the dissemination of technological information within the R&D organization.* Cambridge, MA: MIT Press.

Almeida, P., & Kogut, B. (1999). Localization of knowledge and the mobility of engineers in regional networks. *Management Science, 45,* 905–917.

Argote, L. (1993). Group and organizational learning curves: Individual, system and environmental components. *British Journal of Social Psychology, 32,* 31–51.

Argote, L. (1999). *Organizational learning: Creating, retaining and transferring knowledge.* Norwell, MA: Kluwer.

Argote, L., Beckman, S. L., & Epple, D. (1990). The persistence and transfer of learning in industrial settings. *Management Science, 36,* 140–154.

Argote, L., & Darr, E. D. (2000). Repositories of knowledge in franchise organizations: Individual, structural and technological. In G. Dosi, R. Nelson, & S. Winter (Eds.), *Nature and dynamics of organizational capabilities* (pp. 51–68). Oxford: Oxford University Press.

Argote, L., & Epple, D. (1990, February 23). Learning curves in manufacturing. *Science, 247,* 920–924.

Argote, L., Epple, D., Rao, R. D., & Murphy, K. (1997). *The acquisition and depreciation of knowledge in a manufacturing organization: Turnover and plant productivity.* Unpublished manuscript, Carnegie Mellon University, Pittsburgh.

Argote, L., & Ingram, P. (2000). Knowledge transfer in organizations: A basis for competitive advantage in firms. *Organizational Behavior and Human Decision Processes, 82,* 150–169.

Argote, L., Insko, C. A., Yovetich, N., & Romero, A. A. (1995). Group learning curves: The effects of turnover and task complexity on group performance. *Journal of Applied Social Psychology, 25,* 512–529.

Argote, L., & Ophir, R. (2002). Intraorganizational learning. In J. A. C. Baum (Ed.), *Blackwell companion to organizations* (pp. 181–200). Oxford: Blackwell.

Arrow, H., & McGrath, J. E. (1993). Membership matters: How member change and continuity affect small group structure, process, and performance. *Small Group Research, 24,* 334–361.

Arrow, H., McGrath, J. E., & Berdahl, J. L. (2000). *Small groups as complex systems: Formation, coordination, development, and adaption.* Thousand Oaks, CA: Sage.

Bantel, K. A., & Jackson, S. E. (1989). Top management and innovations in banking: Does the composition of the top team make a difference? *Strategic Management Journal, 10* (summer special issue), 107–124.

Barkai, H., & Levhari, D. (1973). The impact of experience on kibbutz farming. *Review of Economics and Statistics, 55,* 56–63.

Baum, J. A. C., & Ingram, P. (1998). Survival-enhancing learning in the Manhattan hotel industry, 1898–1980. *Management Science, 44,* 996–1016.

Benkard, C. L. (2000). Learning and forgetting: The dynamics of aircraft production. *American Economic Review, 90*(4), 1034–1054.

Berry, D. C., & Broadbent, D. E. (1984). On the relationship between task performance and associated verbalizable knowledge. *Quarterly Journal of Experimental Psychology, 36A,* 209–231.

Berry, D. C., & Broadbent, D. E. (1987). The combination of explicit and implicit learning processes in task control. *Psychological Research, 49,* 7–15.

Boeker, W. (1997). Executive migration and strategic change: The effect of top manager movement on product-market entry. *Administrative Science Quarterly, 42,* 213–236.

Burt, R. S. (1992). *Structural holes: The social structure of competition.* Cambridge, MA: Harvard University Press.

Carley, K. (1992). Organizational learning and personnel turnover. *Organization Science, 3*(1), 20–46.

Chatman, J. A., & Flynn, F. J. (2001). The influence of demographic heterogeneity on the emergence and consequences of cooperative norms in work teams. *Academy of Management Journal, 44,* 956–974.

Chew, W. B., Bresnahan, T. F., & Clark, K. B. (1990). Measurement, coordination and learning in a multi-plant network. In R. S. Kaplan (Ed.), *Measures for manufacturing excellence* (pp. 129–162). Boston: Harvard Business Press.

Crossette, B. (2001, September 10). Pilot who saved 304 people now finds heroism tainted. *New York Times,* pp. A1, A6.

Darr, E., Argote, L., & Epple, D. (1995). The acquisition, transfer and depreciation of knowledge in service organizations: Productivity in franchises. *Management Science, 41,* 1750–1762.

Darr, E. D., & Kurtzberg, T. R. (2000). An investigation of partner similarity dimensions on knowledge transfer. *Organizational Behavior and Human Decision Processes, 82*(1), 28–44.

Devadas, R., & Argote, L. (1995, May). *Collective learning and forgetting: The effects of turnover and group structure.* Paper presented at Midwestern Psychological Association Meetings, Chicago.

Dunbar, K. (1995). How scientists really reason: Scientific reasoning in real-world laboratories. In R. J. Sternberg and J. E. Davidson (Eds.), *The nature of insight* (pp. 365–395). Cambridge, MA: MIT Press.

Dutton, J. M., & Thomas, A. (1984). Treating progress functions as a managerial opportunity. *Academy of Management Review, 9,* 235–247.

Ebbinghaus, H. (1885/1964). *Memory: A contribution to experimental psychology.* (H. A. Ruger & C. E. Bussenius, Trans.). New York: Dover. (Original work published 1885).

Eisenhardt, K. M., & Tabrizi, B. N. (1995). Accelerating adaptive processes: Product innovation in the global computer industry. *Administrative Science Quarterly, 40,* 84–110.

Epple, D., Argote, L., & Murphy, K. (1996). An empirical investigation of the micro structure of knowledge acquisition and transfer through learning by doing. *Operations Research, 44,* 77–86.

Galbraith, C. S. (1990). Transferring core manufacturing technologies in high-technology firms. *California Management Review, 32,* 56–70.

Goodman, P. S., & Leyden, D. P. (1991). Familiarity and group productivity. *Journal of Applied Psychology, 76,* 578–586.

Greenberg, L. (1971). Why the mine injury picture is out of focus. *Mining Engineering, 23,* 51–53.

Greve, H. R. (1999). Branch systems and nonlocal learning in populations, *Advances in Strategic Management, 16,* 57–80.

Gruenfeld, D. H., & Hollingshead, A. B. (1993). Sociocognition in work groups: The evolution of group integrative complexity and its relation to task performance. *Small Group Research, 24,* 383–405.

Gruenfeld, D. H., Mannix, E., Williams, K., & Neale, M. (1996). Group composition and decision making: How member familiarity and information distribution affect process and performance. *Organizational Behavior and Human Decision Processes, 67,* 1–15.

Gruenfeld, D. H., Martorana, P. V., & Fan, E. T. (2000). What do groups learn from their worldliest members? Direct and indirect influence in dynamic teams. *Organizational Behavior and Human Decision Processes, 82,* 60–74.

Grusky, O. (1961). Corporate size, bureaucratization, and managerial succession. *American Journal of Sociology, 67,* 261–269.

Guest, R. H. (1962). Managerial succession in complex organizations. *American Journal of Sociology, 68,* 47–54.

Guetzkow, H., & Simon, H. A. (1955). The impact of certain communication nets upon organization and performance in task-oriented groups. *Management Science, 1,* 233–250.

Hansen, M. T. (1999). The search-transfer problem: The role of weak ties in sharing knowledge across organization subunits. *Administrative Science Quarterly, 44*(1), 82–111.

Harris, R. J., Jr. (1981, December 8). Lockheed plans to end output of L-1011 jet. *Wall Street Journal*, p. 3.

Hatch, N. W., & Mowery, D. C. (1998). Process innovation and learning by doing in semiconductor manufacturing. *Management Science, 11*, 1461–1477.

Haunschild, P. R., & Miner, A. S. (1997). Modes of interorganizational imitation: The effects of outcome salience and uncertainty. *Administrative Science Quarterly, 42*(3), 472–500.

Haunschild, P. R., & Sullivan, B. N. (2000). Learning from complexity: Effects of accident/incident heterogeneity on airline learning. *Best Paper Proceedings* Annual Meeting of the Academy of Management. Briarcliff, NY: Academy of Management.

Hayes, R. H., & Wheelwright, S. C. (1984). *Restoring our competitive edge: Competing through manufacturing.* New York: Wiley.

Henderson, R., & Cockburn, I. (1996). Scale, scope, and spillovers: The determinants of research productivity in drug discovery. *Rand Journal of Economics, 27*, 32–59.

Herriott, S. R., Levinthal, D., & March, J. G. (1985). Learning from experience in organizations. *American Economic Review, 75*, 298–302.

Hollenbeck, J. R., Ilgen, D. R., Sego, D. J., Hedlund, J., Major, D. A., & Philips, J. (1995). Mutlilevel theory of team decision making: Decision performance in teams incorporating distributed expertise. *Journal of Applied Psychology, 80*(2), 292–316.

Hollingshead, A. B., McGrath, J. E., & O'Connor, K. M. (1993). Group task-performance and communication technology: A longitudinal study of computer-mediated versus face-to-face work groups. *Small Group Research, 24*(3), 307–333.

Holmes, S. (2001, June 4). Boeing goes lean. *Business Week*, pp. 94B–94F.

Ingram, P. (2002). Interorganizational learning. In J. A. C. Baum (Ed.), *Blackwell companion to organizations* (pp. 642–663). Oxford: Blackwell.

Ingram, P., & Baum, J. A. C. (1997). Opportunity and constraint: Organizations' learning from the operating and competitive experience of industries. *Strategic Management Journal, 18*, 75–98.

Ingram, P., & Simons, T. (2002). The exchange of experience in a moral economy: Embedded ties and vicarious learning in kibbutz agriculture. *Management Science, 48*, 1517–1533.

Joskow, P. L., & Rozanski, G. A. (1979). The effects of learning by doing on nuclear plant operating reliability. *Review of Economics and Statistics, 61*, 161–168.

Katz, R. (1982). The effects of group longevity on communication and performance. *Administrative Science Quarterly, 27*, 81–104.

Kelsey, S. F., Mullin, S. M., Detre, K. M., Mitchell, H., Cowley, M. J., Gruentzig, A. R., & Kent, K. M. (1984). Effect of investigator experience on percutaneous transluminal coronary angioplasty. *American Journal of Cardiology, 53*, 56C–64C.

Kim, P. H. (1997). When what you know can hurt you: A study of experiential effects on group discussion and performance. *Organizational Behavior and Human Decision Processes, 69*, 165–177.

Kraatz, M. S., & Moore, J. H. (2002). Executive migration and institutional change. *Academy of Management Journal, 45*, 120–143.

Lant, T. K., Milliken, F. J., & Batra, B. (1992). The role of managerial learning and interpretation in strategic persistence and reorientation: An empirical exploration. *Strategic Management Journal, 13*, 585–608.

Lapré, M., & Tsikriktsis, N. (2000) *Knowledge acquisition and transfer in service settings: Customer outrage in airlines.* Unpublished manuscript, Boston University.

Larson, J. R., Christensen, C., Abbott, A. S., & Franz, T. M. (1996). Diagnosing groups: Charting the flow of information in medical decision-making teams. *Journal of Personality and Social Psychology, 71*(2), 315–330.

Laughlin, P. R., & Hollingshead, A. B. (1995). A theory of collective induction. *Organizational Behavior and Human Decision Processes, 61*, 94–107.

Leavitt, H. J. (1951). Some effects of certain communication patterns on group performance. *Journal of Abnormal and Social Psychology, 46*, 38–50.

Levinthal, D. A., & March, J. G. (1981). A model of adaptive organizational search. *Journal of Economic Behavior in Organizations, 2*, 307–333.

Levitt, B., & March, J. G. (1988). Organizational learning. *Annual Review of Sociology, 14*, 319–340.

Liang, D. W., Moreland, R., & Argote, L. (1995). Group versus individual training and group performance: The mediating role of transactive memory. *Personality and Social Psychology Bulletin, 21*, 384–393.

Littlepage, G., Robison, W., & Redington, K. (1997). Effects of task experience and group experience on group performance, member ability, and recognition of expertise. *Organizational Behavior and Human Decision Processes, 69*(2), 133–147.

Mansfield, E. (1985). How rapidly does industrial technology leak out? *Journal of Industrial Economics, 34*, 217–224.

March, J. G. (1991). Exploration and exploitation in organizational learning. *Organization Science, 2*, 71–87.

March, J. G., Sproull, L. S., & Tamuz, M. (1991). Learning from samples of one or fewer. *Organization Science, 2*, 1–13.

McEvily, B., & Zaheer, A. (1999). Bridging ties: A source of firm heterogeneity in competitive capabilities. *Strategic Management Journal, 20*, 1133–1156.

McGrath, J. E., & Argote, L. (2001). Group processes in organizational contexts. In M. A. Hogg & R. S. Tindale (Eds.), *Blackwell handbook of social psychology, Vol. 3: Group processes* (pp. 603–627). Oxford: Blackwell.

Meyer, A. D., & Goes, J. B. (1988). Organizational assimilation of innovations: A multilevel contextual analysis. *Academy of Management Journal, 31*, 897–923.

Miner, A. S., & Anderson, P. (1999). Industry and population-level learning: Organizational, interorganizational, and collective learning processes. *Advances in Strategic Management, 16*, 1–30.

Miner, A. S., & Haunschild, P. R. (1995). Population-level learning. *Research in Organizational Behavior, 17*, 115–166.

Moorman, C., & Miner, A. S. (1998). Organizational improvisation and organizational memory. *Academy of Management Review, 23*, 698–723.

Moreland, R. L., Argote, L., & Krishnan, R. (1996). Socially shared cognition at work: Transactive memory and group performance. In J. L. Nye & A. M. Brower (Eds.), *What's so social about social cognition? Social cognition research in small groups* (pp. 57–84). Thousand Oaks, CA: Sage.

Neale, M. A., & Northcraft, G. B. (1986). Experts, amateurs, and refrigerators: Comparing expert and amateur negotiators in a novel task. *Organizational Behavior and Human Decision Processes, 38*, 305–317.

Newell, A., & Rosenbloom, P. S. (1981). Mechanisms of skill acquisition and the law of practice. In J. R. Anderson (Ed.), *Cognitive skills and their acquisition* (pp. 1–55). Hillsdale, NJ: Erlbaum.

Ophir, R., Ingram, P., & Argote, L. (1998). *The impact of demographic composition on organizational learning: An empirical investigation of kibbutz agriculture, 1954–1965.* Paper presented at the meting of INFORMS College of Organizational Science National Conference, Seattle, WA.

Paulus, P. B., & Dzindolet, M. T. (1993). Social influence processes in group brainstorming. *Journal of Personality and Social Psychology, 64,* 575–586.

Pisano, G. P. (1994). Knowledge, integration, and the locus of learning: An empirical analysis of process development. *Strategic Management Journal, 15,* 85–100.

Pisano, G. P., Bohmer, R. M. J., & Edmondson, A. C. (2001). Organizational differences in rates of learning: Evidence from the adoption of minimally invasive cardiac surgery. *Management Science, 47*(6), 752–768.

Porter, M. E. (1979, October 22). Experience curve. *Wall Street Journal,* p. 30.

Preston, L. E., & Keachie, E. C. (1964). Cost functions and progress functions: An integration. *American Economic Review, 54,* 100–107.

Rapping, L. (1965). Learning and World War II production functions. *Review of Economics and Statistics, 47,* 81–86.

Reagans, R., & Zuckerman, E. (2001). Networks, diversity, and productivity: The social capital of corporate R&D teams. *Organization Science, 12*(4), 502–517.

Rothwell, R. (1978). Some problems of technology transfer into industry: Examples from the textile machinery sector. *IEEE Transactions on Engineering Management, EM-25,* 15–20.

Schilling, M. A., Ployhart, R. E., Vidal, P., & Marangoni, A. (2003). Learning by doing something else: Variation, relatedness, and organizational learning. *Management Science, 49,* 39–56.

Schulz, M. (2002). Organizational learning. In J. A. C. Baum (Ed.), *Blackwell Companion to organizations* (pp. 415–441). Oxford: Blackwell.

Stasser, G., Vaughan, S. I., & Stewart, D. D. (2000). Pooling unshared information: The benefits of knowing how access to information is distributed among group members. *Organizational Behavior and Human Decision Processes, 82,* 102–116.

Stewart, D. D., & Stasser, G. (1995). Expert role assignment and information sampling during collective recall and decision making. *Journal of Personality and Social Psychology, 69*(4), 619–628.

Szulanski, G. (1996). Exploring internal stickiness: Impediments to the transfer of best practice within the firm. *Strategic Management Journal, 17,* 27–43.

Thompson, L., Gentner, D., & Lowenstein, J. (2000). Avoiding missed opportunities in managerial life: Analogical training more powerful than individual case training. *Organizational Behavior and Human Decision Processes, 82,* 60–75.

Thorndike, E. L. (1898). Animal intelligence: An experimental study of the associative processes in animals. *Psychological Review: Series of Monograph Supplements, 2,* 1–109.

Thurstone, L. L. (1919). The learning curve equation. *Psychological Monographs, 26*(3), 1–51.

The TriStar's trail of red ink. (1980, July 28). *Business Week,* pp. 88, 90.

Trow, D. B. (1960). Membership succession and team performance. *Human Relations, 13,* 259–269.

Tushman, M. L., & Rosenkopf, L. (1996). Executive succession, strategic reorientation and performance growth: A longitudinal study in the U.S. cement industry. *Management Science, 42*, 939–953.

Virany, B., Tushman, M. L., & Romanelli, E. (1992). Executive succession and organization outcomes in turbulent environments: An organizational learning approach. *Organization Science, 3*, 72–91.

Walther, J. B., & Burgoon, J. K. (1992). Relational communication in computer-mediated interaction. *Human Communication Research, 19*(1), 50–88.

Watson, W. E., Kumar, K., & Michaelson, L. K. (1993). Cultural diversity's impact on interaction process and performance: Comparing homogeneous and diverse task groups. *Academy of Management Journal, 36*, 590–602.

Watson, W. E., Michaelson, L. K., & Sharp, W. (1991). Member competence, group interaction, and group decision making: A longitudinal study. *Journal of Applied Psychology, 76*, 803–809.

Wegner, D. M. (1986). Transactive memory: A contemporary analysis of the group mind. In B. Mullen and G. R. Goethals (Eds.), *Theories of group behavior* (pp. 185–205). New York: Springer-Verlag.

Wegner, D. M., Erber, R. & Raymond, P. (1991). Transactive memory in close relationships. *Journal of Personality and Social Psychology, 61*, 923–929.

Wells, W. P., & Pelz, D. C. (1966). *Scientists in organizations.* New York: Wiley.

Williams, K. Y., & O'Reilly, C. A. (1998). Demography and diversity in organizations: A review of 40 years of research. *Research in Organizational Behavior, 20*, 77–140.

Wilson, J. M., Straus, S. G., & McEvily, B. (2001). *All in due time: The development of trust in electronic and face-to-face groups.* Unpublished manuscript, Carnegie Mellon University, Pittsburgh.

Wittenbaum, G. M. (1996). *Information sampling in mixed-sex decision-making groups: The impact of diffuse status and task-relevant cues.* Unpublished doctoral dissertation, Miami University, Oxford, OH.

Wright, T. P. (1936). Factors affecting the costs of airplanes. *Journal of the Aeronautical Sciences, 3*, 122–128.

Yelle, L. E. (1979). The learning curve: Historical review and comprehensive survey. *Decision Sciences, 10*, 302–328.

Zander, U., & Kogut, B. (1995). Knowledge and the speed of the transfer and imitation of organizational capabilities: An empirical test. *Organization Science, 6*, 76–92.

Ziller, R. C., Behringer, R. D., & Goodchilds, J. D. (1962). Group creativity under conditions of success or failure and variations in group stability. *Journal of Applied Psychology, 46*, 43–49.

14

■■■■■■ *Dean Keith Simonton*

Creative Cultures, Nations, and Civilizations

Strategies and Results

■■■■■

Psychologists have tended to view creativity as an individual-level phenomenon. That is, they have tended to concentrate on the cognitive processes, personality traits, and developmental antecedents associated with individual creators. This focus follows naturally from the very nature of psychology as a scientific enterprise dedicated to understanding individual mind and behavior. Yet this tradition of "psychological reductionism" has also inspired an antithetical conception of creativity as an exclusively societal-level event. In the extreme form, that of a complete "sociocultural reductionism," the individual becomes a mere epiphenomenon without any causal significance whatsoever. Indeed, this alternative position would even seem to cast in doubt the dominant thesis of this book: that creativity might emerge through the interaction of individuals working within group settings. After all, the creative ideas that appear under such circumstances are still largely determined by psychological processes, however much they might be shaped by the effects of social exchange and evaluation.

In any case, this long-standing debate between individualistic and sociocultural conceptions of creativity has become closely linked with other critical issues in the social sciences, such as the relative impact of nature and nurture on individual behavior and the comparative influence of ethnocentrism and cultural relativism in cross-cultural observations. Therefore, to appreciate fully the respective roles of individual- and societal-level creativity, I must first briefly narrate the history of the controversy.

Historical Background

Francis Galton's 1869 *Hereditary Genius* may be considered the first scientific study specifically devoted to creative genius. By presenting extensive family pedigrees of eminent creators, leaders, and athletes, Galton hoped to show that genius was born, not made. Genius was merely the most extreme manifestation of substantial individual differences in what Galton called "natural ability." Those with exceptional natural ability would attain distinction in whatever they set their mind to, whereas those who lacked natural ability were doomed to obscurity. However, not all scientists were convinced, and the first criticism came from an unlikely source, the distinguished French botanist Alphonse de Candolle. If there was anyone who had firsthand experience with illustrious pedigrees, it was Candolle. His own father was a very eminent Swiss naturalist—so much so that Alphonse and his father were listed in Galton's chapter on "Men of Science." Moreover, Candolle's own son was already well on his way to becoming a notable botanist. This genetic background notwithstanding, Candolle believed that Galton had overlooked the significant role of the environment in determining the appearance of creative genius. To prove his point, he collected a massive amount of data documenting the impact of various environmental influences, with specific focus on outstanding creativity in the sciences. Candolle's results were published in his 1873 book *Histoire des Sciences et des Savants depuis Deux Siècles.*

Galton's response was immediate (Hilts, 1975). He quickly sent out questionnaires to Fellows of the Royal Society—the leading scientists of Great Britain—asking them to report various circumstances that might have contributed to their attainment of success. The resulting responses were then reported in Galton's 1874 *English Men of Science: Their Nature and Nurture.* As the subtitle suggests, Galton was then willing to admit that creative genius was not the exclusive product of genetic endowment.

Yet a close reading of this classic work reveals that Galton had really missed the main point of Candolle's inquiry. The environmental factors that Galton examined all focused on familial and educational variables; for example, Galton was the first behavioral scientist to draw attention to birth order. In contrast, Candolle's study had concentrated on factors of a much larger order of magnitude: those operating at the level of the whole nation or civilization. To be sure, Galton's methodology did not really permit him to delve very deeply into this subject. All of his survey respondents hailed from pretty much the same general cultural situation. That necessarily limited him to just a few minor observations about the national origins of various scientists (i.e., English, Scottish, Welsh, Irish, and immigrant) and the distribution of scientists across the British Isles.

Nonetheless, I believe that Galton also failed to appreciate the scope of Candolle's contribution because Galton had certain theoretical blinders on. In particular, though he might allow that individual differences in creativity within a nation might be partially ascribed to nurture, he was strongly inclined to view differences between nations and cultures as the repercussion of nature. Some peoples are genetically superior to others, and this is what accounts for any cross-cultural contrasts in the production of creative genius. This point is made clearest in *Hereditary Genius*, in which Galton devotes a whole chapter to "The Comparative Worth of Different Races." Moreover, in the chapter that follows, titled "Influences That Affect the Natural Ability of Nations," Galton confines discussion to practices that might cause the deterioration of the gene pool in a given population. It was by some dysgenic process that the superior race that defined the Athenians of antiquity supposedly resulted in the decline of the great civilization of Classical Greece. Moreover, unless Great Britain took care to introduce systematic and comprehensive eugenic programs, the British people would suffer the same fate.

It is the purpose of this chapter to show how very wrong Galton really was. The rise and fall of civilizations need not be ascribed to eugenic and dysgenic forces. On the contrary, the coming and going of great creative genius in various times and places can be better attributed to changes in the cultural, social, political, and economic circumstances that determine the extent to which the resulting milieu nurtures the development of creative potential and the expression of that developed potential. I make this case by reviewing the research literature that has accumulated on this subject since Candolle's (1873) pioneering study. This research has tended to adopt two rather contrasting yet complementary methodological approaches. On the one hand, cross-sectional research examines variation in the aggregate level of creative activity in groups of individuals, whether the groups are defined as civilizations, nations, societies, or cultures. The aim of this analytical strategy is to discern the *Ortgeist*, or "spirit of the place," that is most conducive to creative development and expression. On the other hand, time-series research scrutinizes the aggregate level of creativity displayed by a single group over historical time. The analytical unit then becomes a period of some specific duration, such as a year, decade, generation, or century. The goal of this methodological approach is to tease out the *Zeitgeist*, or "spirit of the times," that is most supportive of creativity at the group level.

■

Cross-Sectional Research on the Creative Ortgeist

One danger always threatens to undermine the scientific validity of any analysis of creativity in a cross-section of culturally distinct groups: ethnocentrism. The adverse effects of such cultural bias were well illustrated in Galton's (1869) *Hereditary Genius*. Having begun with the assumption that exceptional natural ability automatically manifests itself as overt genius, he had no problem making assertions about superior and inferior races based on the relative proportion of notables that various peoples had produced. Galton completely missed how extremely vulnerable were his inferences to the obvious complaint that an ethnocentric bias may permeate his data sources. That his lists of eminent creators and leaders contain more Europeans than non-Europeans is much more informative about the contents of British encyclopedias and biographical dictionaries than about the creativity of diverse world cultures (see also Simonton, 1998a).

In light of this pernicious problem, I focus on those studies that seem to have done the utmost possible to avoid ethnocentric bias. Qualifying investigations may be grouped into two categories according to the nature of the cross-sectional unit: cultures and nations.

Creative Cultures

One area where ethnocentric prejudices have often been allowed free rein is in diverse attempts to rank human cultures on an evolutionary scale. That is, cultures are placed on a dimension that runs from the "primitive" or "savage" to the "advanced" or "civilized." Of course, when such rankings are complete, the rater's own culture somehow ends up on top. The evaluator's criteria for assessing advancement are heavily biased by the cultural values and priorities that form part of his or her milieu. Nonetheless, it is possible to provide scaling of cultures according to more objective, even culture-free criteria. A good illustration may be found in the work of Carneiro (1970), who adopted an explicitly Spencerian conception of evolution in which "simplicity precedes complexity." The objective and quantitative manifestation of this increased complexity is the accumulation of certain economic, political, religious, social, military, legal, technological, and artistic traits. These traits will not appear randomly; rather, some traits will occur earlier in the evolution of a culture. There must be special religious practitioners, such as shamans, before there can evolve temples, and the latter in turn must emerge before there can be a temple that exacts tithes. Given this necessary ordering, Carneiro argued that a sound scientific test of the validity of evolutionary sequences would be to perform a statistical analysis to determine if the traits form an ordinal scale. So Carneiro applied this method to 100 world cultures that were assessed on 354 distinct traits. These traits pertained to subsistence, settlements, architecture, economics, social organization and stratification, political organization, law and judicial process, warfare, religion, ceramics and art, tools, utensils, textiles, metalworking, watercraft and navigation, and special knowledge and practices. The statistical analysis revealed that 90% of these traits formed a recurrent evolutionary scale. By letting a computer program rather than his subjective judgment do the trait scalings, Carneiro was less likely to make ratings that would exhibit some ethnocentric bias. This superior objectivity was apparent in the outcome. The 10 most complex societies on the basis of all 354 traits were: New Kingdom Egypt, Roman Empire, Assyrian Empire, Aztecs, China under the Han Dynasty, the Incas, the Kingdom of León, the Vikings, the Dahomey, and the Ashanti. Hence, all major racial groups are represented in this list of the top 10—quite an improvement over Galton's (1869) ratings of peoples.

Carneiro's (1970) scaling also sheds light on the cultural circumstances that are most likely to encourage creative activity, including the emergence of creative genius. Many of the scaled cultural traits have a direct connection with creativity, including craft specialization, craft production for exchange, full-time craft specialists, monumental stone architecture, full-time painters or sculptors, and full-time architects or engineers. Not only do these traits concern manifestations of cultural creativity, but in addition they form a temporal sequence (albeit the last two appear roughly simultaneously). The sequence essentially represents the emergence of professional artists from less dedicated artisans. In addition, these creativity traits exhibit an ordinal relationship with other culture traits. A society must attain a certain degree of political and economic complexity before there can appear full-time painters, sculptors, architects, and engineers. Having such full-time practitioners probably enhances the prospects for true genius to emerge, given the tremendous amount of effort that is required to develop technique and knowledge to the highest possible level (Ericsson, 1996). Outstanding creativity is not the business of amateurs. Therefore, the scaling of these traits tells us how far a culture must evolve before there can appear creative genius in these domains.

Yet a certain care must be taken to avoid an ethnocentric interpretation of these results. In particular, great caution must be exercised not to infer that the more complex groups are necessarily more creative than the less complex groups. In the first place, although a computer algorithm executed the scaling of the traits, the results remain only as good as the data input. It is possible that certain cultural traits were omitted from the analysis because they were not the kinds of attributes that tend to attract the attention of ethnographers immersed in their own culture. If these traits were included, it might happen that there are losses as well as gains as cultures increase in complexity. An example of this reversed trend is found in a cross-cultural investigation done by Martindale (1976). Martindale (1975, 1990) developed a computer content-analytical technique that scores textual materials for primary-process imagery. Although this method has been applied mostly to literary material, such as poetry and drama, Martindale (1976) also used it to assess primary-process imagery in the folktales of 45 preliterate cultures. He then scored these same cultures with respect to their level of societal complexity. The latter was based on technology, the number of craft specialties, subsistence level, economic institutionalization, social stratification, political complexity, demographic level, and religious level—not departing too substantially from what Carneiro (1970) employed as criteria. Significantly, the amount of primary process was then shown to be *negatively* correlated with the degree of societal complexity. Apparently, as a culture evolves, primary process declines.

Martindale's (1976) initial purpose for conducting this investigation was to test theories of the "primitive mentality" as proposed by Lévy-Bruhl (1978) and Cassirer (1925/1955). Primary process was thus taken as an index of "prelogical" or "dedifferentiated" thought. Yet it is possible to propose a rather different, and decidedly less ethnocentric, interpretation of this empirical finding. After all, there is abundant theoretical and empirical work that associates primary-process thinking with creativity (Ochse, 1989; Simonton, 1999b; Suler, 1980). That is, those who display exceptional levels of creativity are also highly likely to exhibit stronger tendencies toward fantasy, free association, playfulness, openness to experience, and so forth. This positive association then has an intriguing connection with Carneiro's (1970) demonstration that as a society evolves, creativity becomes concentrated in the hands of relatively few fulltime practitioners. These two trends together suggest that cultural evolution has costs as well as benefits. The average person is reduced to the status of the noncreative, and a select minority is elevated to the position of creative genius. This transformation is quite compatible with what many anthropologists are fond of pointing out, namely, that modern conceptions of the genius are not universal across humankind. In many "primitive" societies, creativity is an activity of an entire community rather than the specialty of an elite (Brenneis, 1990; Dissanayake, 1992). Almost everyone sings and dances, paints and carves, tells jokes and makes up stories.

Hence, perhaps a less ethnocentric conclusion is that as cultures grow in complexity, a transformation takes place in the nature of creative expression. Creativity evolves from a communal activity in which all group members participate to an individualistic specialization in which only relatively few display any talent. At one extreme, it is the genius of the whole people that is creative, whereas at the other extreme, it is the single genius who is creative. It is a moot question whether the total amount of creativity (on a per capita basis, of course) is more in one or another type of society. Probably that question could not be answered without exposing one's ethnocentric prejudices.

Creative Nations

Candolle (1873) was the first scientist to investigate how and why nations vary tremendously in their total creative activity. As noted earlier, he concentrated his efforts on just one form of creativity: the scientific. His specific goal was to determine the per capita representation of great scientists in various nations and then relate any cross-sectional differences to conspicuous characteristics of those nations. One advantage of focusing on exceptional scientists is that it facilitated the avoidance of ethnocentrism. Scientific contributions are judged by more universal standards than are, say, literary compositions. Furthermore, Candolle introduced an ingenious technique designed to remove any residual nationalistic biases that might contaminate his estimation of the scientific activity in various groups (cf. Lehman, 1947). Scientists were considered eminent only if they had attained a verifiable international reputation (i.e., one sufficient to earn them honors in a nation *other than* their own). Hence, a British scientist who was a Fellow of the Royal Society but who received no recognition by any foreign academy would not count in the assessment of Great Britain's level of scientific creativity. Under this scheme, Switzerland ended up supreme among the nations of the world, exceeding Candolle's native France in per capita output of great scientists by a ratio of about 5 to 1.

When these corrected cross-national measurements were compared with other attributes of the corresponding nations, Candolle (1873) was able to characterize the Ortgeist most favorable to scientific creativity. To begin with, the nation typically contains a substantial class of persons who do not have to spend most of their time earning a living through manual labor. In other words, the nation has a large proportion of persons who have both the leisure and the desire to devote themselves to intellectual and cultural activities. This attribute is also coupled with a long-standing cultural tradition that emphasizes the value of knowing the real world rather than focus on otherworldly matters. The general lay public, in particular, should demonstrate a substantial curiosity about the material world rather than be preoccupied with the imaginary or fictitious. More specifically, public opinion should be favorable to science and scientists rather than being antiscientific in tone. This favorable atmosphere will tend to take concrete form in an abundant provision of institutions and equipment supportive of scientific work, including large libraries, observatories, laboratories, and special collections. There will also be an abundance of families that have had a tradition of supporting their members' involvement in scientific or other intellectual activities.

The nation should allow sufficient freedom of intellectual inquiry so that its citizens feel free to express any opinion, at least with respect to scientific subjects, without fear of having to face severe consequences, such as criminal prosecution. Moreover, this freedom is accompanied by the liberty to engage in any lawful profession and to travel freely within and outside the nation's borders. The nation's tolerant policies also encourage the influx of foreign immigrants who are highly educated and who enjoy intellectual endeavors for their own sake rather than for the income that such activities might bring them. Furthermore, the nation usually boasts an educational system that is largely if not entirely independent of political or religious control. These institutions also have the resources and commitment to support intellectual inquiry on the part of both students and teachers. In line with these liberties, religious authority tends to play a relatively minor role. Whatever religious influence is present is benign, even supportive, rather than restrictive. In addition, the nation tends to be either a relatively small independent country or a country that entails the union of several independent states, rather than being subordinate to some large imperial system. The nation is typically located very close to other highly civilized nations rather than being isolated, and it is most likely to be situated where the climate is moderate rather than excessively cold or hot.

Last but not least, Candolle (1873) observed that certain languages tend to be most favorable to scientific activity, namely, English, French, and German. Because these may be considered the international languages of science, those nations that have one of these as their native tongue, or that widely encourage their citizens to acquire one of these as a second language, will have a definite edge. Interestingly, Candolle's complete lack of ethnocentric bias was revealed in his discussion of this factor. On the basis of his analysis of worldwide demographic trends, Candolle argued that English would eventually become the predominant language of scientific communication. He made this prophetic argument in a French book that, ironically, has never been translated into English. As a result, Candolle's brilliant contributions have been a bit neglected by scientists who now seldom bother to learn a language that has become much less important, just as Candolle himself predicted.

Admittedly, given that Candolle's (1873) work appeared a couple of decades prior to the introduction of correlational methods, the statistical part of his inquiry falls far short of contemporary standards. Even so, many of his somewhat qualitative generalizations have been replicated in more rigorous scientometric research (Szabo, 1985). Hence, there is ample reason for concluding that cross-national contrasts in aggregate scientific creativity reflect to no small degree a broad sociocultural milieu that is favorable to science. Moreover, many of the factors Candolle identified would probably be associated with creative activity of all kinds rather than being confined to just the scientific enterprise. This conclusion is reinforced by the research using time-series analysis.

Time-Series Research on the Creative Zeitgeist

Nearly a half-century after Candolle's (1873) work, Galton's (1869) genetic theory of creative genius was challenged from a totally different quarter. Alfred Kroeber, the distinguished cultural anthropologist, launched the attack. Kroeber had studied under Franz Boas, the German anthropologist whose opposition to race as a biological concept later provoked the Nazis to rescind his Ph.D. and burn his books. Like his mentor, Kroeber believed that contrasts among human groups were really the consequence of cultural differences, and thus ethnicity must replace race as the explanatory factor. From Kroeber's point of view, the causal primacy of culture applied with equal force to the phenomenon of creative genius. As a consequence, Kroeber launched a two-pronged attack on Galton's genetic thesis.

First, Kroeber (1917) argued that the individual creator is largely irrelevant to the creative products that highlight the annals of human civilization. The primary basis for this argument was the phenomenon in which two or more scientists or inventors independently originate the same discovery or invention. Kroeber mentioned such examples as the invention of calculus by Newton and Leibnitz, the formulation of the theory of evolution by natural selection by Darwin and Wallace, and the invention of the telephone by Bell and Gray. Kroeber was especially struck by the many occasions in which these multiple contributions were not only independent, but simultaneous besides. He believed that this phenomenon dramatically proves, beyond any doubt, that the works of so-called genius are actually the products of the sociocultural system. Galton's genetic determinism could thus be replaced with an environmental determinism, where the causal milieu was sociocultural in nature (for counterarguments, see Schmookler, 1966; Simonton, 1979, 1986b, 1986c, 1999b).

Second, Kroeber (1944) conducted a systematic empirical analysis that again established the inadequacy of Galton's genetic thesis. This analysis appeared in a classic volume titled *Configurations of Culture Growth*. Curiously, Kroeber turned away from ethnographic data for his demonstration, taking full advantage of the historical record instead. Furthermore, he adopted a methodological strategy superficially similar to that which Galton (1869) introduced in *Hereditary Genius*. That is, Kroeber compiled long lists of eminent creators in various domains of achievement, such as science, philosophy, literature, art, and music. Yet, besides being much more cross-cultural in scope—including the major creators of Chinese, Japanese, Hindu, and Islamic civilizations—these lists were chronological (to emphasize historical placement) rather than alphabetical (which stresses familial relationships). The lists proved that creative genius tends to cluster into cultural configurations, with golden and silver ages separated by dark ages (see also Sorokin & Merton, 1935; Spiller, 1929). Furthermore, the pace at which these clusters of genius come and go could not be explicated in genetic terms. It would require impossibly drastic and intrusive eugenic and dysgenic interventions to so quickly affect the gene pool in any large population.

Taken together, the phenomena of scientific and technological multiples and of cultural configurations imply that there exists some Zeitgeist that drives the appearance of major creators and their creations. At certain periods of history, the "times are ripe" for a golden age, whereas during other periods, the sociocultural system suffers from excessive stagnation or decadence, or what Kroeber (1944) styled the "exhaustion" of a given "cultural pattern." Unlike Candolle (1873), however, Kroeber made no attempt to collect data that might document the sociocultural conditions most favorable to a creative florescence. Fortunately, others since *Configurations of Culture Growth* have attempted to address this very question (e.g., Gray, 1958, 1961, 1966; cf. Kroeber, 1958). These follow-up inquiries have adopted a wide range of methodologies as well. Some have used large-duration units of analysis, such as generations or even centuries (Naroll et al., 1971), whereas others have used shorter time-series units, such as decades or years (Simonton, 1980a). Some inquiries tabulate the number of eminent creators per unit of time (Simonton, 1988), whereas others count single creative products, such as scientific discoveries or technological patents (Simonton, 1975b). Finally, some studies examine timewise fluctuations in creativity in individual nations (Simonton, 1976a), whereas others scrutinize those ups and downs in whole civilizations (Simonton, 1975c). Whatever the methodological details, ample evidence has accumulated to establish the Zeitgeist most supportive of creative activity at the group level. The pertinent factors can be roughly divided into two categories: short-term and long-term effects.

Short-Term Effects

Some sociocultural environments operate primarily on the adult creator. That is, they determine the realization of creative potential rather than the initial development of creative potential. These synchronous effects are of two kinds: the quantitative and the qualitative.

Quantitative Consequences

The most conspicuous example of short-term quantitative influence is international war. For example, annual fluctuations in the number of discoveries and inventions between 1500 and 1903 are negatively correlated with the frequency and intensity of balance-of-power wars (Simonton, 1980a). Although it has been sometimes argued that certain technological and medical advances have been stimulated by wartime circumstances (Norling, 1970), the net effect of war is negative even for technology and medicine (Simonton, 1976d, 1980a). This is not tantamount to saying that war never has a positive effect. Certainly, the development of the atomic bomb was the direct response to its relevance to an ongoing military problem. Nevertheless, because resources tend to be channeled only to those creative activities that are directly and immediately relevant, other forms of creativity usually suffer. A good example is literary creativity, which seldom is perceived to have the same military urgency as weapons of destruction. Thus, a study of 81 works by five major world dramatists found a negative correlation between a play's aesthetic success and the intensity of warfare during the time of its composition (Simonton, 1983a).

Qualitative Consequences

Warfare also influences the subtle characteristics of creative products, such as their form, style, and content (Simonton, 1977b, 1983a, 1986a). For instance, the thematic material featured in Shakespeare's plays have been found to correspond fairly closely to contemporary military affairs (Simonton, 1986d). Although it may seem a natural consequence to treat war when a nation is at war, other qualitative influences are not so obvious. For example, the popularity of the Don Juan theme in European literature, which is expressive of power motivation, is positively associated with territorial conquest (Winter, 1973). Even more subtle is what has been found in classical music: composers have been shown to alter the style of their melodies and harmonies when works are produced under wartime conditions (Cerulo, 1984; Simonton, 1986a, 1987b). In particular, the melodies become much more chaotic and unpredictable, in a sense reflecting the external circumstances in which the composition is conceived.

Yet war is not the only sociocultural context that can shape the very nature of creativity produced by a given nation or civilization. Research on the authoritarian personality suggests that authoritarians are individuals who feel threatened by external forces beyond their control (Adorno, Frenkel-Brunswik, Levinson, & Sanford, 1950). By the same token, when the people of a given nation feel themselves likewise threatened, they tend to display many of the symptoms of the authoritarian syndrome, such as superstition, anti-intraception, and an emphasis on rigid, conventional values. To illustrate, one investigation showed that economic hard times, such as high unemployment, enhances the rate at which individuals tend to join highly authoritarian churches, that is, churches that enforce conformity to religious dogma in word and deed (Sales, 1973). Not surprisingly, this connection between economic threat and authoritarianism also has implications for what kinds of creativity are most likely to be popular at the time (Doty, Peterson, & Winter, 1991). In particular, books advocating superstitious beliefs, such as astrology, tend to become more successful (Padgett & Jorgenson, 1982), whereas those that deal with "intraceptive" issues, such as psychoanalysis, tend to become less so (Sales, 1973). Another consequence along the same lines is a tendency for environmental threat to be positively associated with the relative prominence of parapsychological studies in the psychological literature (McCann & Stewin, 1984).

It is important to recognize that the foregoing effects, both quantitative and qualitative, tend to be relatively transient. Political systems seldom engage in all-out warfare for more than a few years at a time, so it is rare for creative individuals to spend their entire career under wartime conditions. Likewise, the booms and busts that characterize economic systems seldom endure an entire adult life. Long-term effects are not so volatile, but can be far more enduring.

Long-Term Effects

There are two main reasons a particular Zeitgeist may affect group-level creativity over the long haul. First, a given sociocultural condition may tend to change extremely slowly over historical time. If the causal features of the milieu display such inertia, then their repercussions may take generations, even centuries to unfold (see, e.g., Gray, 1958, 1961, 1966). Thus, war may come and go over a short time span, whereas the political systems that participate in those wars, such as the particular forms of monarchical or democratic governments, may exist over long periods of time. Likewise, whereas the economy may experience ups and downs, the fundamental basis of the economy—slave, feudal, capitalist, socialist, and so on—may require decades to transform.

The second cause of long-term effects is that a particular Zeitgeist may operate according to a specific time lag. The main causal basis for this lagged effect is that a given sociocultural milieu influences the initial development of creative potential rather than the final actualization of that potential. That is, these environmental forces and events provide the context in which creative talent must necessarily find nourishment. As a necessary repercussion, the full effect of a given milieu may not appear until a lag of a full generation, or somewhere between 20 and 25 years (Simonton, 1984b).

The first of these effects may be called inertial and the second developmental. They deserve to be examined separately.

Inertial Effects

Pitirim Sorokin (1937–1941), the eminent sociologist, offered a provocative theory of sociocultural change in his classic *Social and Cultural Dynamics*. Essentially, he argued that a predominant "mentality," or system of values, beliefs, and worldview, characterizes any civilization at a specified time. In a sense, the sociocultural mentality represents the "modal personality" of the civilization. Although Sorokin postulated the existence of several such mentalities, three assume primary importance in his theoretical model: the Sensate, the Ideational, and the Idealistic. The Sensate mentality is described as emphasizing the pleasures of the senses and the epistemological primacy of sensory experience, the importance of individualism and hedonistic ethics, the belief in determinism and in a materialistic and ever-changing reality, and the conception of abstract ideas as mere mental constructions or linguistic labels. The Ideational mentality, on the other hand, stresses the joys of the spiritual world, an epistemology based on reason or revelation, the primacy of the collective over the individual and of moral absolutes over personal needs, the belief in free will and in a world of unchanging mind or spirit, and the conception of abstract ideas as having a genuine real existence in that realm of pure being. The Idealistic mentality, finally, provides a balanced integration of Sensate and Ideational worldviews.

From our standpoint, two further aspects of Sorokin's theory are significant. First, civilizations will undergo gradual and cyclical shifts in the predominant mentality, often according to the sequence Ideational → Idealistic → Sensate. This transformation takes so long that any one civilization will have undergone only one or two complete cycles. In Western civilization, for example, there have been only two major Ideational periods (pre-Classical Greece and Medieval Europe), two Idealistic periods (Classical Greece and the High Renaissance), and two Sensate periods (Hellenistic/Roman and Modern Western). Second, the dominant mentality exerts a powerful influence over the forms of creativity that are most likely to be displayed. Thus, because science stresses materialism, determinism, nominalism, and empiricism, scientific discoveries and technological inventions are more likely to be associated with those periods in which a civilization is swayed by a Sensate mentality. In the case of art, in contrast, the prevailing mentality primarily affects the style and content favored by a given civilization at a particular point in its history. Hence, Ideational art treats spiritual and religious subjects, prefers highly abstract over extremely realistic representations, and avoids anything erotic, mundane, or pathological, whereas Sensate art relishes the highly realistic representation of the material world, including the depiction of erotic nudity, scenes from everyday life and landscapes, and the more ugly aspects of human existence. In short, according to Sorokin's theory, the quantity and quality of creativity is largely dictated by the Zeitgeist, as defined by the sociocultural mentality.

Although Sorokin (1937–1941) collected huge amounts of data purporting to confirm his theory, like Candolle (1873) he did not perform a very sophisticated statistical analysis. Nonetheless, subsequent investigations have lent support to some of his basic contentions (Ford, Richard, & Talbutt, 1996). For instance, the transhistorical changes in the philosophical components of the three main mentalities—such as the prevailing epistemological, ontological, and ethical systems—are indeed governed by large sweeping cycles rather than fickle fluctuations (Klingemann, Mohler, & Weber, 1982; Simonton, 1976b). A civilization cannot alter its core premises and precepts in just a generation or two.

Furthermore, there is ample evidence that various aspects descriptive of the sociocultural mentality are indeed associated with creative activity. For example, scientific discovery and technological invention are both more strongly linked to a Sensate than an Ideational philosophical system (Simonton, 1976b).

The foregoing investigations operated with Sorokin's own data but performed more advanced statistical analyses, sometimes adding additional measurements. Other researchers have confirmed the broad thrust of his theory using entirely different data sets and methodologies. Consider the following three examples.

First, using multidimensional scaling techniques, Hasenfus, Martindale, and Birnbaum (1983) have shown that stylistic labels such as Baroque, Classical, Romantic, and so forth do indeed describe similarities that transcend artistic genre, whether poetry, music, painting, or architecture. This suggests that underlying all forms of aesthetic expression is some modality-free stylistic Zeitgeist that merely manifests itself in the various media in which creators choose to express themselves. For example, when a "romantic mood" is "in the air," it permeates the style adopted by poets, composers, painters, and architects.

Second, the stylistic Zeitgeist itself may stand in accordance with extra-aesthetic aspects of the sociocultural system. For instance, one inquiry showed how the prevalent styles witnessed in the vase painting of ancient Greece bore a striking relation to the dominating social structure (Dressler & Robbins, 1975). Thus, when social stratification was very high, the paintings tended to reflect that fact, with highly complex, finely differentiated, and hierarchically arranged material.

Third, slow-changing political circumstances also have an impact on the creative activity displayed by a civilization. A clear case in point is political fragmentation, or the degree to which the civilization is divided into small sovereign units, such as the city-states of Classical Greece and Renaissance Italy. The occasional ambitions of an imperialist conqueror notwithstanding, the number of independent nations exhibits considerable transhistorical inertia from generation to generation. Hence, the effect of political fragmentation on group creativity can operate only at a glacial speed. Yet the impact of this variable is profound. This was first demonstrated by Naroll et al. (1971) in a secondary analysis of the data that Kroeber (1944) published in *Configurations of Culture Growth*. Across four major world civilizations—European, Islamic, Hindu, and Chinese—the aggregate level of cultural creativity was positively correlated with the number of independent states. This finding has been replicated by applying advanced time-series techniques to a sample of over 5,000 creators in Western civilization (Simonton, 1975c). Stated in inverse terms, the rise of great empires tends to sound the death knell of a civilization's creative achievements, just as has been speculated by various social scientists (e.g., Sorokin, 1947/1969; Toynbee, 1946).

The foregoing effects presumably would apply to male and female creators alike. Nonetheless, sometimes the Zeitgeist can have consequences that are gender-specific. One example is Confucianism, a philosophical system that argues for a social hierarchy in which women have the duty to occupy the inferior role vis-à-vis men. One generational analysis of Japanese civilization revealed that whenever Confucianism became the dominant ideology, the number of female creators declined (Simonton, 1992a). The creative activity of Japanese men, on the other hand, was left unscathed.

Developmental Effects

The acquisition of creative potential begins early in life and probably continues into early adulthood. Although a portion of this development may be under genetic control (Simonton, 1999c), there can be no doubt that environmental conditions play a role as well. Yet, as noted earlier, ever since Galton (1874), psychologists have tended to focus on those circumstances that are associated with home and school (Simonton, 1987a). The assumption is clearly that the familial and educational environments have a big impact on creative development. Even so, it should be apparent that beyond home and school is a pervasive and powerful world consisting of political, military, economic, cultural, and social events and contexts. One may easily leave home or drop out of school, but it is much more difficult to escape, say, civil war or economic depression. Moreover, considerable evidence has accrued that various aspects of the larger sociocultural milieu do indeed affect creative development (Simonton, 1984b). The bulk of this evidence is based on generational time-series analyses, which examine how the frequency of certain events in generation g influence the number of creative individuals who appear in generation $g + 1$, where the length of the generation is most typically a 20-year time interval (Simonton, 1984b). For example, using this approach, the following broad events and circumstances have been shown to influence the aggregate-level creativity after a generational lag.

First, political fragmentation provides a positive environment for the emergence of ideological diversity in a given civilization (Simonton, 1976c). That is, those periods that are characterized by a large number of independent states are most likely to nurture the emergence of thinkers who argue for a vast range of distinct philosophical positions. A classic example is the Warring States period of ancient China, in which most of the major schools of thought appeared, such as Confucianism, Taoism, and Legalism. Moreover, because ideological diversity is positively associated with creative activity in general (Simonton, 1976c), this means that political fragmentation exerts something of a lagged effect on creativity, via the intervening variable of ideological diversity. In line with what Mao Tse-Tung once preached (but never practiced), "Letting a hundred flowers blossom and a hundred schools of thought contend is the policy for promoting the progress of the arts and the sciences" (*Who Said What When*, 1991, p. 314).

Second, as noted earlier, political fragmentation tends to favor creativity. The opposite of political fragmentation is political integration, especially in the guise of large empires. Hence, what happens should come as no surprise when such empire states begin to display deep-rooted instability in the form of popular revolts, nationalistic uprisings, and other challenging movements of the masses: such events cause a resuscitation of creativity after a one-generation delay (Simonton, 1975c). Civil disturbances more generally conceived—riots, revolts, and rebellions, regardless of whether they occur under imperial systems—also shape the nature of philosophical thought. In particular, one generation after such events there is a distinct tendency for intellectual debate to polarize along various dimensions, such as being versus becoming, rationalism versus empiricism, determinism versus free will, individualism versus collectivism, and hedonistic versus principled ethics (Simonton, 1976f). It is as if the conflicts that plague the political world encourage young developing minds to consider more radical worldviews.

Third, sometimes political systems succumb to anarchy, to frequent coups d'etat, political assassinations, conspiracies, military revolts, and the like. In contrast to the event just discussed, these conflicts involve the "power elite" rather than the masses. In any case, such political instability created by those already in powerful positions has a devastating effect on the creative development of the youth who are exposed to these events (Simonton, 1975c). This negative effect is seen in the decline in creative activity in such fields as science, philosophy, literature, and music. Interestingly, only the visual arts are relatively immune from this unfortunate consequence. Hence, in the final days of great empires, when political instability becomes commonplace, great painters, sculptors, and architects can still appear, whereas the civilization sees a decline in great scientists, philosophers, writers, and composers.

Fourth, when civilizations open themselves up to the influx of alien ideas—via immigration, foreign travel, or study under foreign masters—they tend to experience a resurgence of creative activity (Simonton, 1997b). However, the lag in this case is two generations rather than one. The culture must first assimilate the novel ideas before they can leave an impression on the creativity displayed by the civilization. By the same token, when a nation closes the doors to external influences, it may take some time before the adverse consequences become apparent.

Fifth, creative activity in one domain can provide a favorable environment for creative activity in closely related domains (Simonton, 1975a). For instance, major advances in biology in one generation tend to be stimulated by the previous generation's level of activity in medicine, geology, and chemistry (Simonton, 1976d). Yet sometimes, these cross-generational effects are more qualitative than quantitative in nature. For example, the philosophical beliefs that constitute the Zeitgeist in one generation will exert an influence over related beliefs in the following generation (Simonton, 1978). Thus, if one generation features a large number of thinkers who advocate extreme skepticism (the epistemological stance that nothing can be known), the succeeding generation will contain more thinkers who espouse some form of fideism (the position that beliefs can be founded on faith alone, without regard to either the senses or reason). At times, even very mundane forms of creativity in one genre can have profound effects on creativity in a totally different domain. To illustrate, the magnitude of achievement motivation (i.e., *n* Ach imagery) in children's readers in the United States between 1800 and 1950 was shown to predict the per capita production of patents when the children exposed to those readers later became adults (deCharms & Moeller, 1962; see also Bradburn & Berlew, 1961; Cortés, 1960; for an overview, see McClelland, 1961).

The above enumeration lists only a small proportion of the total number of developmental effects that have been identified so far (Simonton, 1999a, 1999b). Yet the list should suffice to demonstrate that to a very large degree, the aggregate magnitude and type of creativity exhibited by a generation of adult individuals may reflect the events and conditions that shaped their childhood and adolescence.

Creative Genius in Sociocultural Context

This chapter began by discussing the debate between Francis Galton (1869) and Alphonse de Candolle (1873), a debate that Galton (1874) framed in terms of the classic nature-nurture issue. Although most psychologists have followed Galton in treating nurture in terms of family and school environments, a considerable literature has emerged that points to the significance of the larger sociocultural milieu. Some researchers have followed Candolle's example by examining cross-sectional units (nations or cultures) to discern the Ortgeist most conducive to creative activity at the aggregate level. Other investigators have pursued the approach pioneered by Kroeber (1944), Sorokin (1937–1941), and others by scrutinizing how time-series fluctuations in group-level creativity are associated with short- and long-term changes in the Zeitgeist. Taken together, the research demonstrates that a specific set of political, economic, social, and cultural circumstances are associated with a high level of creative activity at a particular time or place.

Although this inventory might seem to exclude psychology as being relevant to the scientific understanding of creativity, such a conclusion would be premature. There are at least five reasons why an exhaustive sociocultural reductionism is probably no more justified than its psychological counterpart:

1. Within any given cohort of human beings there exist substantial individual differences in creative behavior that cannot be explained in terms of either Ortgeist or Zeitgeist (Simonton, 1991, 1997a, 1998b). That is, not all creators born in the same generation are equally creative. Indeed, there is evidence that the larger the number of creators active in a given period, the greater is the variation in creativity displayed by those creators (Price, 1963; Simonton, 1999b).
2. The most illustrious creators of a given generation may actually conform less to the prevalent milieu than do their more obscure contemporaries (Simonton, 1976e, 1980b; cf. Simonton, 1992b). This independence of thought is coupled with a pronounced tendency to advocate extremist

positions and to conceive systems of ideas that combine beliefs in unusual combinations (Simonton, 1976e, 2000).

3. Variables that operate at the aggregate level may actually have very different causal effects at the individual level (Simonton, 1976e, 1977a, 1996). In particular, the factors that differentiate golden from dark ages are not necessarily identical to those that differentiate major from minor creators. Indeed, sometimes the correlation can change sign as we transfer from aggregate to individual levels of analysis.

4. Psychological processes frequently provide the mediating causal links between the sociocultural milieu and the individual creator (Simonton, 1984a, 1992b; see also Simonton, 1983b). Take, for example, the tendency for the influx of alien ideas and persons to stimulate creative activity within a civilization (Simonton, 1997b). This sociocultural effect is likely mediated by a developmental process, such as the positive consequences of bilingualism for individual creative development (Carringer, 1974; Lambert, Tucker, & d'Anglejan 1973; Lopez, Esquivel, & Houtz 1993).

5. Many sociocultural conditions are themselves the products of underlying psychological phenomena, such as motivational and cognitive processes. For instance, the likelihood that a nation will become involved in international war is a partial function of how its head of state scores on the power and affiliation motives (Winter, 1973, 1993) and on conceptual complexity (Suedfeld & Bluck, 1988; Suedfeld & Tetlock, 1977). Yet, as already noted, war has a conspicuous impact on the level and type of creativity exhibited by a nation at a particular point in time.

Thus, societal-level effects complement and expand rather than render utterly irrelevant a genuine psychological understanding of human creativity. Admittedly, psychology has a long way to go before these empirical findings are fully incorporated into the discipline. Although there have been many attempts to develop a "social psychology" or "ecology" of human creativity (e.g., Amabile, 1996; Csikszentmihalyi, 1990; Harrington, 1990; Martindale, 1994), these have not always made a substantial impression on the field. Many psychologists still insist on perceiving creativity as an entirely individual-level phenomenon. Nevertheless, when the research reviewed here is coupled with other findings discussed in other chapters of this book, it is apparent that this neglect cannot continue much longer. A comprehensive psychology of creativity must view it as a complex phenomenon that occurs at multiple levels, from individuals, interpersonal interactions, and problem-solving groups to cultures, nations, and civilizations.

References

Adorno, T. W., Frenkel-Brunswik, E., Levinson, D. J., & Sanford, R. N. (Eds.) (1950). *The authoritarian personality.* New York: Harper.

Amabile, T. M. (1996). *Creativity in context.* Boulder, CO: Westview.

Bradburn, N. M., & Berlew, D. E. (1961). Need for achievement and English economic growth. *Economic Development and Cultural Change, 10*, 8–20.

Brenneis, D. (1990). Musical imaginations: Comparative perspectives on musical creativity. In M. A. Runco & R. S. Albert (Eds.), *Theories of creativity* (pp. 170–189). Newbury Park, CA: Sage.

Candolle, A. de (1873). *Histoire des sciences et des savants depuis deux siècles.* Geneve: Georg.

Carneiro, R. L. (1970). Scale analysis, evolutionary sequences, and the rating of cultures. In R. Naroll & R. Cohn (Eds.), *A handbook of method in cultural anthropology* (pp. 834–871). New York: Natural History Press.

Carringer, D. C. (1974). Creative thinking abilities in Mexican youth. *Journal of Cross-Cultural Psychology, 5*, 492–504.

Cassirer, E. (1955). *The philosophy of symbolic forms* (Vol. 2). New Haven: Yale University Press. (Original work published 1925)

Cerulo, K. A. (1984). Social disruption and its effects on music: An empirical analysis. *Social Forces, 62*, 885–904.

Cortés, J. B. (1960). The achievement motive in the Spanish economy between the 13th and 18th centuries. *Economic Development and Cultural Change, 9*, 144–163.

Csikszentmihalyi, M. (1990). The domain of creativity. In M. A. Runco & R. S. Albert (Eds.), *Theories of creativity* (pp. 190–212). Newbury Park, CA: Sage.

deCharms, R., & Moeller, G. H. (1962). Values expressed in American children's readers: 1800–1950. *Journal of Abnormal and Social Psychology, 64*, 136–142.

Dissanayake, E. (1992). *Homo aestheticus: Where art comes from and why.* New York: Free Press.

Doty, R. M., Peterson, B. E., & Winter, D. G. (1991). Threat and authoritarianism in the United States, 1978–1987. *Journal of Personality and Social Psychology, 61*, 629–640.

Dressler, W. W., & Robbins, M. C. (1975). Art styles, social stratification, and cognition: An analysis of Greek vase painting. *American Ethnologist, 2*, 427–434.

Ericsson, K. A. (Ed.). (1996). *The road to expert performance: Empirical evidence from the arts and sciences, sports, and games.* Mahwah, NJ: Erlbaum.

Ford, J. B., Richard, M. P., & Talbutt, P. C. (Eds.). (1996). *Sorokin and civilization: A centennial assessment.* New Brunswick, NJ: Transaction.

Galton, F. (1869). *Hereditary genius: An inquiry into its laws and consequences.* London: Macmillan.

Galton, F. (1874). *English men of science: Their nature and nurture.* London: Macmillan.

Gray, C. E. (1958). An analysis of Graeco-Roman development: The epicyclical evolution of Graeco-Roman civilization. *American Anthropologist, 60*, 13–31.

Gray, C. E. (1961). An epicyclical model for Western civilization. *American Anthropologist, 63*, 1014–1037.

Gray, C. E. (1966). A measurement of creativity in Western civilization. *American Anthropologist, 68*, 1384–1417.

Harrington, D. M. (1990). The ecology of human creativity: A psychological perspective. In M. A. Runco & R. S. Albert (Eds.), *Theories of creativity* (pp. 143–169). Newbury Park, CA: Sage.

Hasenfus, N., Martindale, C., & Birnbaum, D. (1983). Psychological reality of cross-media artistic styles. *Journal of Experimental Psychology: Human Perception and Performance, 9*, 841–863.

Hilts, V. L. (1975). *A guide to Francis Galton's English Men of Science*. Philadelphia: American Philosophical Society.

Klingemann, H. D., Mohler, P. P., & Weber, R. P. (1982). Cultural indicators based on content analysis: A secondary analysis of Sorokin's data on fluctuations of systems of truth. *Quality and Quantity, 16*, 1–18.

Kroeber, A. L. (1917). The superorganic. *American Anthropologist, 19*, 163–214.

Kroeber, A. L. (1944). *Configurations of culture growth*. Berkeley: University of California Press.

Kroeber, A. L. (1958). Gray's epicyclical evolution. *American Anthropologist, 60*, 31–38.

Lambert, W. E., Tucker, G. R., & d'Anglejan, A. (1973). Cognitive and attitudinal consequences of bilingual schooling: The St. Lambert project through grade five. *Journal of Educational Psychology, 65*, 141–159.

Lehman, H. C. (1947). National differences in creativity. *American Journal of Sociology, 52*, 475–488.

Lévy-Bruhl, L. (1978). *Primitive mentality* (L. A. Clare, Trans.). New York: AMS Press.

Lopez, E. C., Esquivel, G. B., & Houtz, J. C. (1993). The creative skills of culturally and linguistically diverse gifted students. *Creativity Research Journal, 6*, 401–412.

Martindale, C. (1975). *Romantic progression: The psychology of literary history*. Washington, DC: Hemisphere.

Martindale, C. (1976). Primitive mentality and the relationship between art and society. *Scientific Aesthetics, 1*, 5–18.

Martindale, C. (1990). *The clockwork muse: The predictability of artistic styles*. New York: Basic Books.

Martindale, C. (1994). How can we measure a society's creativity? In M. A. Boden (Ed.), *Dimensions of creativity* (pp. 159–197). Cambridge, MA: MIT Press.

McCann, S. J. H., & Stewin, L. L. (1984). Environmental threat and parapsychological contributions to the psychological literature. *Journal of Social Psychology, 122*, 227–235.

McClelland, D. C. (1961). *The achieving society*. New York: Van Nostrand.

Naroll, R., Benjamin, E. C., Fohl, F. K., Fried, M. J., Hildreth, R. E., & Schaefer, J. M. (1971). Creativity: A cross-historical pilot survey. *Journal of Cross-Cultural Psychology, 2*, 181–188.

Norling, B. (1970). *Timeless problems in history*. Notre Dame, IN: University of Notre Dame Press.

Ochse, R. (1989). A new look at primary process thinking and its relation to inspiration. *New Ideas in Psychology, 7*, 315–330.

Padgett, V., & Jorgenson, D. O. (1982). Superstition and economic threat: Germany 1918–1940. *Personality and Social Psychology Bulletin, 8*, 736–741.

Price, D. (1963). *Little science, big science*. New York: Columbia University Press.

Sales, S. M. (1972). Economic threat as a determinant of conversion rates in authoritarian and non-authoritarian churches. *Journal of Personality and Social Psychology, 23*, 420–428.

Sales, S. M. (1973). Threat as a factor in authoritarianism: An analysis of archival data. *Journal of Personality and Social Psychology, 28*, 44–57.

Schmookler, J. (1966). *Invention and economic growth*. Cambridge, MA: Harvard University Press.

Simonton, D. K. (1975a). Interdisciplinary creativity over historical time: A correlational analysis of generational fluctuations. *Social Behavior and Personality*, *3*, 181–188.

Simonton, D. K. (1975b). Invention and discovery among the sciences: A p-technique factor analysis. *Journal of Vocational Behavior*, *7*, 275–281.

Simonton, D. K. (1975c). Sociocultural context of individual creativity: A transhistorical time-series analysis. *Journal of Personality and Social Psychology*, *32*, 1119–1133.

Simonton, D. K. (1976a). The causal relation between war and scientific discovery: An exploratory cross-national analysis. *Journal of Cross-Cultural Psychology*, *7*, 133–144.

Simonton, D. K. (1976b). Do Sorokin's data support his theory? A study of generational fluctuations in philosophical beliefs. *Journal for the Scientific Study of Religion*, *15*, 187–198.

Simonton, D. K. (1976c). Ideological diversity and creativity: A re-evaluation of a hypothesis. *Social Behavior and Personality*, *4*, 203–207.

Simonton, D. K. (1976d). Interdisciplinary and military determinants of scientific productivity: A cross-lagged correlation analysis. *Journal of Vocational Behavior*, *9*, 53–62.

Simonton, D. K. (1976e). Philosophical eminence, beliefs, and Zeitgeist: An individual-generational analysis. *Journal of Personality and Social Psychology*, *34*, 630–640.

Simonton, D. K. (1976f). The sociopolitical context of philosophical beliefs: A transhistorical causal analysis. *Social Forces*, *54*, 513–523.

Simonton, D. K. (1977a). Eminence, creativity, and geographic marginality: A recursive structural equation model. *Journal of Personality and Social Psychology*, *35*, 805–816.

Simonton, D. K. (1977b). Women's fashions and war: A quantitative comment. *Social Behavior and Personality*, *5*, 285–288.

Simonton, D. K. (1978). Intergenerational stimulation, reaction, and polarization: A causal analysis of intellectual history. *Social Behavior and Personality*, *6*, 247–251.

Simonton, D. K. (1979). Multiple discovery and invention: Zeitgeist, genius, or chance? *Journal of Personality and Social Psychology*, *37*, 1603–1616.

Simonton, D. K. (1980a). Techno-scientific activity and war: A yearly time-series analysis, 1500–1903 A.D. *Scientometrics*, *2*, 251–255.

Simonton, D. K. (1980b). Thematic fame, melodic originality, and musical Zeitgeist: A biographical and transhistorical content analysis. *Journal of Personality and Social Psychology*, *38*, 972–983.

Simonton, D. K. (1983a). Dramatic greatness and content: A quantitative study of eighty-one Athenian and Shakespearean plays. *Empirical Studies of the Arts*, *1*, 109–123.

Simonton, D. K. (1983b). Intergenerational transfer of individual differences in hereditary monarchs: Genes, role-modeling, cohort, or sociocultural effects? *Journal of Personality and Social Psychology*, *44*, 354–364.

Simonton, D. K. (1984a). Artistic creativity and interpersonal relationships across and within generations. *Journal of Personality and Social Psychology*, *46*, 1273–1286.

Simonton, D. K. (1984b). Generational time-series analysis: A paradigm for studying sociocultural influences. In K. Gergen & M. Gergen (Eds.), *Historical social psychology* (pp. 141–155). Hillsdale, NJ: Erlbaum.

Simonton, D. K. (1986a). Aesthetic success in classical music: A computer analysis of 1,935 compositions. *Empirical Studies of the Arts, 4,* 1–17.

Simonton, D. K. (1986b). Multiple discovery: Some Monte Carlo simulations and Gedanken experiments. *Scientometrics, 9,* 269–280.

Simonton, D. K. (1986c). Multiples, Poisson distributions, and chance: An analysis of the Brannigan-Wanner model. *Scientometrics, 9,* 127–137.

Simonton, D. K. (1986d). Popularity, content, and context in 37 Shakespeare plays. *Poetics, 15,* 493–510.

Simonton, D. K. (1987a). Developmental antecedents of achieved eminence. *Annals of Child Development, 5,* 131–169.

Simonton, D. K. (1987b). Musical aesthetics and creativity in Beethoven: A computer analysis of 105 compositions. *Empirical Studies of the Arts, 5,* 87–104.

Simonton, D. K. (1988). Galtonian genius, Kroeberian configurations, and emulation: A generational time-series analysis of Chinese civilization. *Journal of Personality and Social Psychology, 55,* 230–238.

Simonton, D. K. (1991). Latent-variable models of posthumous reputation: A quest for Galton's G. *Journal of Personality and Social Psychology, 60,* 607–619.

Simonton, D. K. (1992a). Gender and genius in Japan: Feminine eminence in masculine culture. *Sex Roles, 27,* 101–119.

Simonton, D. K. (1992b). Leaders of American psychology, 1879–1967: Career development, creative output, and professional achievement. *Journal of Personality and Social Psychology, 62,* 5–17.

Simonton, D. K. (1996). Individual genius and cultural configurations: The case of Japanese civilization. *Journal of Cross-Cultural Psychology, 27,* 354–375.

Simonton, D. K. (1997a). Creative productivity: A predictive and explanatory model of career trajectories and landmarks. *Psychological Review, 104,* 66–89.

Simonton, D. K. (1997b). Foreign influence and national achievement: The impact of open milieus on Japanese civilization. *Journal of Personality and Social Psychology, 72,* 86–94.

Simonton, D. K. (1998a). Achieved eminence in minority and majority cultures: Convergence versus divergence in the assessments of 294 African Americans. *Journal of Personality and Social Psychology, 74,* 804–817.

Simonton, D. K. (1998b). Fickle fashion versus immortal fame: Transhistorical assessments of creative products in the opera house. *Journal of Personality and Social Psychology, 75,* 198–210.

Simonton, D. K. (1999a). The creative society: Genius vis-à-vis Zeitgeist. In A. Montuori & R. Purser (Eds.), *Social creativity* (Vol. 1, pp. 265–286). Cresskill, NJ: Hampton Press.

Simonton, D. K. (1999b). *Origins of genius: Darwinian perspectives on creativity.* New York: Oxford University Press.

Simonton, D. K. (1999c). Talent and its development: An emergenic and epigenetic model. *Psychological Review, 106,* 435–457.

Simonton, D. K. (2000). Methodological and theoretical orientation and the long-term disciplinary impact of 54 eminent psychologists. *Review of General Psychology, 4,* 1–13.

Sorokin, P. A. (1937–1941). *Social and cultural dynamics* (Vols. 1–4). New York: American Book.

Sorokin, P. A. (1969). *Society, culture, and personality.* New York: Cooper Square. (Original work published 1947)

Sorokin, P. A., & Merton, R. K. (1935). The course of Arabian intellectual development, 700–1300 A.D. *Isis, 22,* 516–524.

Spiller, G. (1929). The dynamics of greatness. *Sociological Review, 21,* 218–232.

Suedfeld, P., & Bluck, S. (1988). Changes in integrative complexity prior to surprise attacks. *Journal of Conflict Resolution, 32,* 626–635.

Suedfeld, P., & Tetlock, P. (1977). Integrative complexity of communications in international crises. *Journal of Conflict Resolution, 21,* 169–184.

Suler, J. R. (1980). Primary process thinking and creativity. *Psychological Bulletin, 88,* 144–165.

Szabo, A. T. (1985). Alphonse de Candolle's early scientometrics (1883, 1885) with references to recent trends in the field (1978–1983). *Scientometrics, 8,* 13–33.

Toynbee, A. J. (1946). *A study of history* (abridged by D. C. Somervell, Vols. 1–2). New York: Oxford University Press.

Who said what when: A chronological dictionary of quotations. (1991). New York: Hippocrene Books.

Winter, D. G. (1973). *The power motive.* New York: Free Press.

Winter, D. G. (1993). Power, affiliation, and war: Three tests of a motivational model. *Journal of Personality and Social Psychology, 65,* 532–545.

15

Bernard A. Nijstad and Paul B. Paulus

Group Creativity
Common Themes
and Future Directions

The contributors to this volume have covered a wide range of issues related to group creativity, from individual-level processes to group interaction to the level of organizations, cultures, and societies. If the chapters demonstrate one thing, it is that creativity is not an individual-level phenomenon, but often (and perhaps always) involves some degree of social interaction. Others (such as "gatekeepers") may be involved in the evaluation of the creative contribution; ideas may need to be shared with others before they can be implemented or transfer to other groups or companies; or people may collaborate in the creative act. The main focus of the book is on the last: the effects of interaction in small groups on the creativity of group members or the group as a whole. Attention is also devoted to the context (i.e., organization, culture) in which groups work.

In this final chapter, we draw some conclusions from the contributed chapters. First, we discuss four common themes that we believe run through the various chapters. Next, we propose a framework for the study of group creativity. Using this framework, we then raise some questions that appear to provide interesting and worthwhile avenues for future research.

Common Themes

Theme 1: Group Diversity and Creative Potential

The basic resources of groups reside in their members. Group members bring knowledge, skills, and abilities to the group, without which the group task cannot be accomplished and group creativity would not be possible. In principle, the knowledge of a collection of individuals is larger than the knowledge of one individual, and the set of skills and abilities possessed by the group is larger than the set of skills and abilities possessed by an individual group member. One could therefore argue that groups have creative potential: because individual knowledge, skills, and abilities are combined, the group has the potential to be more creative than its separate members. Two heads should know more than one, but a group's creative potential first and foremost depends on the level of diversity in the group.

The chapter by Milliken, Bartel, and Kurzberg was completely devoted to this issue, and many of the other chapters recognized the importance of diversity for group creativity. Diverse groups do appear to offer the potential of stimulated creativity more than homogeneous groups do. In diverse groups, chances are that group members bring unique knowledge, skills, and expertise to the group. In more homogeneous groups, there will be more overlap among group members, and consequently, it is less likely that one member will come up with an idea, approach, or solution of which others could not have thought. Diverse groups seem to offer more creative potential, an idea that is reflected in the current popularity of cross-functional teams in organizations, teams that are composed of people with different professional backgrounds (see, e.g., Sundstrom, McIntyre, Halfhill, & Richards, 2000).

Even though the link between group diversity and creativity seems to make sense, the chapter by Milliken and colleagues shows that the link is by no means a simple one. First, there are different types of diversity with different effects. Milliken et al. distinguished between readily detectable diversity (e.g., sex, race, age) with immediate and mostly negative effects and diversity in underlying attributes (e.g., education, values, personality) with slower and potentially positive effects. Second, the effects of diversity may differ depending on which phase of the group's life is considered (i.e., the early formative or the later operations stage). A group member may be "that old man" in the early stages of the group's life, whereas later on, he may be a valued member of the team with unique contributions. Third, there are myriad factors that moderate the relation between diversity and creativity, such as the organizational context (also see below), the decision-making strategies used by the group, performance feedback, and leadership (also see West's chapter).

Several chapters deal directly with group diversity. Nemeth and Nemeth-Brown stress the importance of authentic dissent (or diversity of opinion). Dissent can be rooted in differences in backgrounds or knowledge. Authentic dissent stimulates creative thinking of group members. Stasser and Birchmeier's chapter deals with information diversity. It is plausible that in diverse groups (in terms of, say, age) information diversity is higher. One reason is that group members who differ from each other will have less overlap in their social contacts outside the group, which increases the group's social capital (also see below and the chapter by Hooker, Nakamura, & Csikszentmihalyi). Information diversity, as argued by Stasser and Birchmeier, may lead to innovative decisions, decisions that no individual might have made alone. Nijstad, Diehl, and Stroebe have found that group interaction often limits the range of ideas that are considered, leading to lower idea diversity (also see Smith's chapter). However, this is not true in heterogeneous groups. In particular, when group members have different dominant associations to a particular topic, the tendency to limit the range of ideas disappears. Again, different dominant associations will be related to differences in background and thus to group diversity. The brainstorming chapters show that reading or overhearing other group members' ideas can, under some conditions, lead to performance improvements.

If we take the evidence presented in this volume, it is possible to conclude that diversity is one of the most important factors in group creativity. In fact, if it were not for diversity, there would be no point in creative collaboration— why would we bring people together if they take the same approach to a problem, have the same opinion, the same ideas, or the same solutions? Indeed, evidence suggests that functional, informational, or cognitive diversity is associated with higher levels of group creativity and innovation (see the chapters by Milliken et al. and West). Even though diverse groups have creative potential, it often is not fully realized. It is to that issue we turn next.

Theme 2: Obstacles to the Realization of Creative Potential

Ivan Steiner (1972), in his seminal work on group productivity, introduced the following formula:

Actual Group Productivity = Potential Group Productivity − Process Loss.

According to Steiner, potential group productivity is determined by the group's resources (e.g., knowledge, skills, time) and the demands of the group task. If the resources possessed by group members are sufficient for adequate task performance, potential productivity is high. If the group does not possess the necessary resources, potential productivity is low and the group will be unable to perform well. However, even if the necessary resources are available to group members, performance may still fall below optimal. The reason is that many group processes do not foster high performance. Group members may be unmotivated to contribute to the group product (motivation loss), or coordination between group members may be suboptimal (coordination loss). In both cases, groups will fail to realize their full potential due to process loss.

Steiner's formula can easily be adapted to group creativity:

Actual Group Creativity = Potential Group Creativity − Process Loss.

This formula shows three things. First, under some circumstances, groups have creative potential and can achieve high levels of creativity, an issue discussed above. Second, this potential often will not be fully realized because of process loss. Third, adequate procedures are required to minimize process loss and come close to the group's optimal performance. In some cases, productivity gains may even be achieved (i.e., the group is more creative than its separate members; see, e.g., the chapters by Nemeth & Nemeth-Brown and Dennis & Williams).

Even though groups have potential for stimulated creativity, the promise of high performance often will not be fully realized. A dissenter who takes a different viewpoint may stimulate additional creative activity (see Nemeth & Nemeth-Brown). However, if his or her contribution is ignored or if the dissenter does not stick to his or her original point of view, the benefits will be modest at best. Similarly, if people do not share their unique information, or information is not taken into consideration, the emergence of creative group decisions is unlikely. Stasser and Birchmeier highlighted many reasons groups often do not profit from their complementary knowledge, including biased information sampling and the tendency to mention information that is consistent with one's opinion. Finally, much of the brainstorming research shows that groups often perform more poorly than individuals when it comes to idea generation due to various group processes, such as production blocking (see Nijstad et al.) and performance matching (see Paulus & Brown).

For groups to be creative, the group process must be structured in a way that prevents process loss. Several suggestions are provided in the various chapters. For example, groups should try to avoid premature consensus and conformity pressure. There are different ways to do this. Brainstorming procedures explicitly forbid premature evaluations of ideas and are directed at generating large quantities of ideas; this should prevent groups from settling on one particular idea or approach early in the session (also see the chapter by Smith). Stasser and Birchmeier's SCOPE model suggests that the group climate needs to foster criticism instead of compliance (also see West) and also stresses that groups need ample time to give members the opportunity to contribute their unique knowledge. As another example, the potential positive effect of cognitive stimulation in brainstorming groups often is not realized in face-to-face discussions. Reasons include production blocking and downward matching (see chapters by Nijstad et al. and Paulus & Brown). However, when different means of communication are used, such as brainwriting (sharing ideas on pieces of paper) and electronic brainstorming (sharing ideas through a computer interface), positive effects of communication are possible. As shown in Dennis and Williams's chapter on electronic communication, electronic groups hold some promise for stimulating higher levels of creativity, especially when groups are large. Further, there is some evidence that electronic groups do better than face-to-face groups when it is critical to share unique knowledge (Lam & Schaubroeck, 2000). In sum, there are potential benefits associated with collaboration in the creative act; however, efficient procedures are required to fully benefit from group interaction.

Theme 3: Group Climate

Another theme that runs through the volume is the importance of group climate. Some climates foster creativity, others inhibit creativity. Two types of group climate appear especially detrimental for high levels of creativity; interestingly, these climates are almost diametrically opposed. On the one hand, it is not very helpful when the group climate is restrictive, critical, and characterized by low levels of trust. This does not foster the sharing of unique or "wild" ideas or the expression of divergent viewpoints. On the other hand, a very harmonious climate characterized by high levels of cohesion does not lead to high levels of group creativity because such groups may be primarily directed at maintaining group harmony, may self-censor any differences of opinion, and may fall prey to the trap of premature consensus. Instead, a somewhat critical but open climate, in which new ideas are valued but in which there is no excessive consensus seeking, appears to be most beneficial for creative performance. Such a climate would allow for the expression of a different viewpoint or a "crazy" idea.

There is a link between group climate and the creative process. Creativity necessarily involves both divergent and convergent processes (also see the chapter by Milliken et al.). First, ideas have to be generated, a divergent process in which idea quantity and a broad approach are valuable. However, not all ideas will be equally good, and after the idea-generation process the ideas that are especially promising need to be selected and the consequences considered. This is a more convergent process. To perform well in the divergent process of idea generation, some openness of thought is necessary, and overly critical groups will not do well. However, during idea selection some criticism is essential, and a constructive debate among group members may lead to a better decision. In this case, premature consensus may lead a group astray to adopt a bad idea or approach (cf. groupthink; Paulus, 1998).

The theme of group climate was highlighted in several chapters. Hennessey stressed the importance of autonomy and openness and suggested that feelings of autonomy and self-mastery lead to intrinsic rather than extrinsic motivation. Intrinsic motivation, or doing a task for fun rather than because of external pressure, in turn leads to higher levels of creativity. Similarly, West argued that group innovation requires high levels of trust among team members and a group climate characterized by participative safety. On the other hand, Stasser and Birchmeier emphasized the importance of a critical group norm, preventing premature decisions that are directed only at group consensus (also see Nemeth & Nemeth-Brown). Hooker et al. observed that groups have an important role in the socialization of creative talents. In their case description of a space science lab, they show that high standards of excellence and a supportive climate in which group members help and train each other further the development of creative talents. Finally, an open climate will provide more opportunities for self-monitoring (see Milliken et al.) and team reflexivity (see West). A group that reflects on its own performance is likely to be more creative.

In sum, groups need to be open and safe and group members should feel free to offer "crazy" ideas; at the same time, there should be room for debate and constructive controversy. Perhaps it is best to deal with these issues by strictly separating idea generation from idea evaluation, as is suggested in Osborn's

(1957) brainstorming procedure: Do not critically evaluate ideas when they are being suggested, but stimulate debate and criticism when ideas need to be selected and implemented.

Theme 4: Group Environment

Individuals do not operate in isolation and neither do groups. Group members have contacts outside the group, new members replace oldtimers, the ideas and suggestions offered by a group may have consequences for other people, groups, and organizations, and group processes are affected by the group's environment. In short, the environment exerts an influence on groups, but groups also affect their environment. Part II of the book was therefore devoted to the issue of group creativity in context.

Levine, Choi, and Moreland discussed the role of newcomers in group innovation. Groups seldom are a closed system; usually, people enter and leave the group. This turnover has important implications because it alters the distribution of knowledge within the group and the relations among members. Newcomers can thus bring new knowledge and perspectives to the group. Further, they may take a minority position or strengthen existing minorities, which may lead to higher levels of creativity (also see Nemeth & Nemeth-Brown). However, unless oldtimers agree to implement ideas, a newcomer's ideas will not be very influential.

Groups are not a closed system in another regard: ideas as well as group members travel from one group to another or from one organization to the next. In fact, it can be argued that creativity is socially defined, and an idea can be called creative only to the extent that important others agree that it is a valuable contribution (e.g., Hooker et al.). Thus, ideas need to travel in order to reach the important others who can judge their merits. Only if important stakeholders (e.g., management) agree on its usefulness will an idea be implemented. Innovation implementation is extensively discussed in West's chapter. Innovation may also travel to other teams and other organizations. Knowledge transfer, or learning from indirect experience, is discussed in Argote and Kane's chapter. By innovation implementation and knowledge transfer groups will affect their environment: innovation means change not only for the group or the team but also for the external environment.

Further, group members have contacts outside the group. These outside contacts can be seen as the group's social capital (see Hooker et al.) and provide the group with information, support, or other resources. For example, management support is extremely valuable when it comes to innovation implementation (see West). Similar to newcomers who have to negotiate their ideas with oldtimers, groups need to negotiate the implementation of ideas with management. In a similar fashion, learning from indirect experience requires contacts outside the group. A group can benefit from creative ideas in other groups only when the groups are in contact. Although one can question whether learning from indirect experience can be called creative, certainly group functioning can be improved when groups learn from the experience and creativity of other groups.

Finally, the organizational or even national or cultural environment of the group can affect group creativity. In organizations in which creativity and innovation are not valued, group creativity will be severely constrained. Why should a group generate creative ideas when they are not valued or implemented in the organization? Similarly, if the group is not given some degree of autonomy over its own functioning, little creativity can be expected (see West; Hennessey). Simonton argues that nations, cultures, and civilizations differ in creativity. Interestingly, many of the variables that operate at the group level of analysis also appear to be applicable to nations, cultures, and civilizations. For example, the influx of foreigners is a predictor of creativity of a nation, which is very similar to the impact of newcomers in groups (see Levine et al). Further, a restrictive cultural climate, such as a conservative religious government, may have effects similar to those of a restrictive group climate.

It is clear that group context needs to be taken into account if we want to understand why some groups reach high levels of creativity and others do not. Groups are not closed systems but interact with their environment.

A Combination of Contributions Framework

We believe that the four common themes addressed above, as well as many other issues that have received attention in this book, can be organized in a "combination of contributions" framework. We think this framework has some potential to facilitate future research efforts, and it may also be a useful guide to stimulate creativity in "real life." We first describe this framework and then derive some questions from it for future research.

In our opinion, many group phenomena, including group creativity, can be understood with a combination of contributions framework of group functioning and performance (e.g., Hinsz, Tindale, & Vollrath, 1997; Stasser & Birchmeier, this volume). Within this framework, there is a distinction among three aspects of group functioning: group members, group processes, and group context. Group members bring resources to the group, and these resources determine the group's creative potential or what the group is able to accomplish. The contributions of group members need to be combined in some way to yield a group response. The ways in which individual members' contributions are combined constitute the relevant group processes. Finally, the context largely determines which group processes will occur and how individual contributions are combined. Eventually, this determines the quality and creativity of the group response. Thus, according to this framework, the resources of individual group members determine the potential creativity of the group (cf. theme 1, discussed above). However, group processes, or the way individual contributions are combined, determine whether the group in fact reaches its potential (cf. theme 2). Group processes, in turn, are influenced by the social climate (theme 3) and the environment (theme 4).

Figure 15.1 illustrates this framework. At the left-hand side of the figure (the shaded area) is a representation of an individual group member. Individuals have resources (knowledge, skills, abilities, etc.) available to them, but also have ways to obtain extra information and acquire new skills (arrow 1 in Figure 15.1). The individual member's resources are used to develop ideas, solutions, preferences, estimates, questions, and so on. The center of the figure can be conceptualized as the group information-processing space, in which the contributions of group members are combined (cf. Hinsz et al., 1997). Individuals contribute information to the group-processing space (arrow 2). These contributions may range from preferences, ideas, arguments, questions, and proposals, to goals and evaluative statements. Once contributed, information in principle is available to the other group members. Provided that members pay attention to the contributions of others, the information is added to the individual's knowledge base (arrow 3). The new information can subsequently be processed and can lead to a shift in preferences, new ideas, or a new argument. The information that is shared during group discussion (and was held in common prior to the discussion) and the way the different contributions are combined will affect the group response (arrow 4). The contributions of individuals need to be combined to produce a coherent, feasible, sensible, and creative group response. This response can then be implemented, transfer to other groups, and affect others outside the team (arrow 5).

Whether a group will achieve its creative potential mainly depends on the (social) context. The context, consisting of the task the group performs, the group climate, group norms, the larger organizational climate, and so on, drives group processes. It is therefore important to establish how the context affects the functioning of the group. Using Figure 15.1 as a guideline, we now turn to this issue and identify what we think are worthwhile questions to be addressed in future research. In general, these are questions of how the (social) context affects group functioning.

▬

Future Directions

Question 1: What Are the Relevant Inputs Group Members Bring to Their Task?

The knowledge, skills, and abilities of group members determine the creative potential of the group. These resources have been acquired through experience prior to the group task, but members can continue to learn while being a member of a group. Members also bring other inputs to the group, such as affective reactions, identification with other members, expectations, and motivation. All of these different inputs may be relevant for groups seeking to be creative on a particular task.

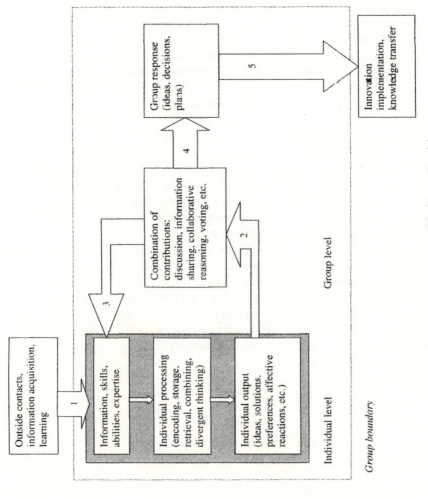

Figure 15.1. A Generic Model of Group Creativity

Several issues discussed in this book are relevant here. First, diversity implies that the group as a whole has more resources at its disposal and therefore has more creative potential. One important question for future research is to determine how group diversity relates to group creativity. There is some evidence that cognitive diversity can be helpful (see Milliken et al.; West), but there are many more issues that have not been resolved. One of these issues is the question of *how much* diversity is optimal for group creativity. Research by Dunbar (1997) has shown that groups with members who have slightly different (though related) areas of expertise are better problem solvers than groups in which members share the same expertise. However, one can easily imagine that too much diversity is not very helpful simply because group members will have difficulty following each other's reasoning. Future research should consider the question of exactly how different individual group members should be in order to be optimally creative.

Second, group members have outside contacts, and these can be used to acquire new information. For example, learning from indirect experience, as discussed in the chapter by Argote and Kane, implies the acquisition of knowledge or skills by a group member. In this respect, social capital will be important because it is defined as the number of contacts a group member has. Outside contacts can be valuable resources for individual group members (see Hooker et al.). An interesting question is whether groups with more outside contacts are more creative or innovative.

Question 2: Under What Conditions Are Individual Inputs Contributed in an Optimal Way?

A second issue that becomes evident when looking at Figure 15.1 is the question of what is and what is not shared during group interaction (arrow 2). Do group members discuss all the information available to them? Are certain ideas not mentioned because a member fears negative appraisal of his or her ideas? How can we optimize the exchange of relevant information among group members? In general, it can be argued that group members must be both *able* and *willing* to share the information (whether these are arguments, ideas, or other types of information) available to them.

Several issues are relevant here. Brainstorming research has shown that group members block each other's contributions. Because usually only one person speaks at a time, it is not always possible to contribute ideas to the group. Thus, blocking occurring in idea-generating groups affects the *ability* of members to contribute ideas. Further, if group members do not meet on a regular basis, there will be few opportunities to share ideas or solutions. West cited some evidence that minority dissent increases innovation only when group members participate in decision making and meet on a regular basis.

The issue of group climate is also relevant here. A restrictive group climate, characterized by low levels of interpersonal trust, will not foster exchange of information or ideas (e.g., West). When the group does not exchange relevant information or when members withhold ideas because of fear of critical evaluation, group creativity is bound to suffer. Further, the tendency of group members to advance arguments in favor of their own position or opinion will not be helpful when it comes to an unbiased assessment of creative contributions (cf. Stasser & Birchmeier). Also, if members feel that their contribution is not valued, they will lose their motivation to share information or ideas. In particular in the case of newcomers, this may severely constrain the potential positive effects of a "fresh look" at problems (see Levine et al.). Finally, some degree of autonomy of the group is likely to benefit information sharing (see Hennessey; West). Autonomy leads to higher levels of motivation to solve group problems. The conditions that foster and inhibit idea or information sharing thus present a second intriguing issue for future study.

Question 3: How Do the Contributions of Other Group Members Affect Individual-Level Cognition, Motivation, and Emotion?

To what extent are people affected by the information that becomes available during group interaction (arrow 3)? Do group members take new pieces of information into account? Do they pay attention to each other's ideas? Do some group members (e.g., high-status members or members who are similar) receive more attention than others? As argued by Paulus and Brown, attention is the factor that links group members to each other. When attention is paid to the contributions of other group members, will this have positive effects (such as cognitive stimulation) or negative effects (such as cognitive interference; see Nijstad et al., Dennis & Williams)? As argued by Hinsz et al. (1997), the utterances of others may stimulate or interfere with cognitive processes of group members, and this provides "a new area to address the relative impact of process gains (e.g., stimulated cognitive processes . . .) and process losses (e.g., interference. . .) in small group performance" (p. 49). In general, group creativity will be enhanced when stimulation is stronger than interference, whereas it will be constrained when interference is stronger than stimulation.

What others do or do not contribute to the group discussion may also impact group members' motivation or affective reactions. For example, Paulus and Brown showed that members tend to match each other's performance. Thus, if others contribute few ideas, group members tend to lose their motivation and contribute fewer ideas as well. An interesting topic for future studies may thus be differences in ability and motivation of group members to contribute to the group product. Further, more disagreement among group members can be beneficial because it stimulates divergent thinking (see Nemeth & Nemeth-Brown). However, if disagreement leads to emotional conflicts, group performance is likely to suffer (e.g., Jehn, 1995). Thus, if others respond in an emotional way to differences of opinion, the benefits of controversy for creativity will not materialize.

Question 4: How Are Individual Contributions Combined to Yield a Creative Group Response?

Another important question is the extent to which the group response (e.g., the report, plan, idea, innovation) reflects the information that has been presented during group interaction. How do groups combine their information, ideas, and preferences to come to a group response (arrow 4)? Of primary importance here is the group task. Different kinds of tasks require different combination strategies. West describes a number of task dimensions that are relevant. Using the classification of Steiner (1972), idea generation is a maximizing additive task, in which the group product is the sum of the different contributions (ideas) of group members and in which the goal is to come up with as many ideas as possible. However, choosing among these ideas is an optimizing disjunctive task, in which the group must choose the single best idea from the pool of ideas they have generated. The combination of individual contributions is thus quite different in an idea-generation task from that in a decision task.

Unfortunately, very little attention has been devoted to the effects of different kinds of tasks on group creativity. Further, groups often do not work on a single task but on multiple tasks. These tasks are both additive and disjunctive, involve both conflict and cooperation, and are both maximizing and optimizing (see West). However, to understand group processes, the type of task must be taken into account. Group processes will be quite different in, for example, a Eureka-type problem-solving task compared to a judgmental task involving personal preferences (see, e.g., Laughlin & Ellis, 1986). In a Eureka problem, the group will have the correct solution if one member can solve the problem and demonstrate the correctness of the answer to the others. However, in a judgmental task, there is no correct answer, and groups will generally go with the majority. Relevant in this respect is the distinction between preference-driven group processes and information-driven group processes (see Stasser & Birchmeier). Preference-driven processes generally lead to a win of the majority over the minority, whereas in information-driven group processes there is a chance that a minority with good arguments wins. It is important to establish which factors, apart from task type, determine whether groups use an information-driven or a preference-driven approach.

As argued above, group creativity involves both the generation of ideas and the selection of the best ideas to be implemented. An interesting question in this regard is when groups will feel that they have generated a sufficient number of ideas and start selecting among them to come to a group response. In other words, when should the group stop generating ideas or approaches (divergent thinking) and start limiting the range of options and elaborate on the best ideas (convergent thinking)? Although premature consensus may limit group creativity, eventually a time should come when the group starts to limit the options available to them and reaches consensus about the group response. In this respect, time limits may be important. Research (Gersick, 1988) has shown that groups tend to shift from one phase of the group's task to the next when they have used approximately half of the time available to them. Also, it is of interest whether the different stages of creative problem solving (e.g., idea generation, idea selection, idea implementation) are best performed by individuals or by groups, and whether the same people should be involved in all stages of the process. Research should consider these questions. For example, although much is known about idea generation in groups and about group decision making, very little is known about the combination of the two: How do groups perform when they have to select among the ideas they have previously generated? What determines group effectiveness in that case?

Question 5: Under What Conditions Does Group Creativity Affect the Environment of the Group?

Finally, the group's response needs to be implemented in some way: in one's own group, in the organization, or even in other organizations. The factors that influence effective implementation of creative responses represent a fifth set of questions of primary importance. These issues are extensively discussed in the chapters by West and Argote and Kane, so we will not repeat them here. One issue that was mentioned in West's chapter, however, deserves some attention. West identified what he called the "innovation paradox." This refers to the fact that power decentralization seems beneficial for creativity, but the implementation of creative ideas requires some degree of power centralization. West suggested that the solution to this paradox is team-based decision making: the team should have enough autonomy to be able to implement their ideas. The power paradox thus presents one of the more convincing arguments for group creativity.

The combination of contributions framework thus offers some powerful insights into group creativity. However, some cautions are in order. First, the model is by no means complete. For example, the issue of team development has not been addressed, although this would probably be possible using the processes identified by the model. More developed groups use different combinatory processes. Second, the model is a metamodel, mainly suited to organizing results and deriving questions for future research efforts. To derive specific predictions about when group creativity will be fostered and when it will be harmed, one needs additional theorizing. Many theories, hypotheses, and processes have been explored in this book.

▬

Conclusion

Some 10 years ago, it was generally believed that groups should not be used for creativity because of inherent process loss in the creative process (e.g., Stroebe & Diehl, 1994). By now we know that groups can achieve high levels of creativity and can sometimes outperform their separate members. Furthermore, it has become increasingly clear that group interaction often is required in some of the stages of the creative process. In the information age it has simply become impossible for single individuals to possess all the relevant information, knowledge, and expertise. Moreover, creativity is socially defined, and creative ideas should be implemented or evaluated by others even before they can be called creative. We propose that the study of group creativity offers many possibilities, particularly if scholars draw from a wide range of domains. By including chapters written by social psychologists, organizational psychologists, information systems scholars, and cognitive psychologists, we hope to have contributed to the developing field of the psychology of group creativity.

References

Dunbar, K. (1997). How scientists think: On-line creativity and conceptual change in science. In T. B. Ward, S. M. Smith, & J. Vaid (Eds.), *Creative thought: An investigation of conceptual structures and processes* (pp. 461–493). Washington, DC: American Psychological Association.

Gersick, C. J. P. (1988). Time and transition in work teams: Towards a new model of group development. *Academy of Management Journal, 31*, 9–41.

Hinsz, V. B., Tindale, R. S., & Vollrath, D. A. (1997). The emerging conceptualization of groups as information processors. *Psychological Bulletin, 121*, 43–64.

Jehn, K. (1995). A multimethod examination of the benefits and detriments of intragroup conflict. *Administrative Science Quarterly, 40*, 256–282.

Lam, S. S. K., & Schaubroeck, J. (2000). Improving group decisions by better pooling information: A comparative advantage of group decision support systems. *Journal of Applied Psychology, 84*, 565–573.

Laughlin, P. R., & Ellis, A. L. (1986). Demonstrability and social combination processes on mathematical, intellective tasks. *Journal of Experimental Social Psychology, 22*, 177–189.

Osborn, A. F. (1957). *Applied imagination.* New York: Scribner.

Paulus, P. B. (1998). Developing consensus about groupthink after all these years. *Organizational Behavior and Human Decision Processes, 73*, 362–374.

Steiner, I. D. (1972). *Group process and productivity.* New York: Academic Press.

Stroebe, W., & Diehl, M. (1994). Why groups are less effective than their members: On productivity losses in idea-generating groups. In W. Stroebe & M. Hewstone (Eds.), *European review of social psychology* (Vol. 5, pp. 271–303). London: Wiley.

Sundstrom, E., McIntyre, M., Halfhill, T., & Richards, H. (2000). Work groups: From the Hawthorne studies to work teams of the 1990s. *Group Dynamics: Theory, Research, and Practice, 4*, 44–67.

Index

Accountability, 4, 112, 116, 130, 139, 187, 256 (*see also* Free-riding; Social loafing)
Achievement motivation, 319
Action theory, 247–248
Amabile, Teresa, 182
Ambiguity, tolerance of, 250
Anagram task, 68–69, 73
Analogical reasoning, 288
Apple computer, 79
Assembly bonus effect, 87–88, 163 (*see also* Productivity gains)
Authoritarian personality, 313
Autonomy, 7, 186, 189–190, 196, 256, 330 (*see also* Self-determination)
in work groups, 248–250, 255–256

Baseball, 248
Bay of Pigs, 64, 66
Birth order effects, 186, 305
Bohr, Niels, 226–228, 233, 239
Bolstering, 76, 90

Brainstorming, 4–7, 35, 45, 79, 86, 101, 110–136, 137–159, 182, 186, 242, 245, 328–330 (*see also* Brainwriting; Electronic brainstorming)
alternating group and individual, 29, 112–113, 127–128, 130
associative memory model of, 110, 121–122
attention in, 114, 125–126, 130, 149
and breaks, 113, 127–128, 130, 156
cognitive failures in, 151–154
cognitive interference in, 7, 138, 141, 146–149, 153–156
cognitive overload in, 126
cognitive stimulation in, 6–7, 113–115, 121, 124, 126, 128–129, 138, 141, 146, 148–151, 153–156
cognitive uniformity in, 29, 151, 154–155
facilitators in, 113–115, 117–120, 130
fixation in, 7, 16, 21, 28–29, 127–128